South-East Asian Social Science Monographs

The Singapore Dilemma

# The Singapore Dilemma
## The Political and Educational Marginality of the Malay Community

Lily Zubaidah Rahim

**OXFORD**
UNIVERSITY PRESS

# OXFORD
UNIVERSITY PRESS

4 Jalan Pemaju U1/15, Seksyen U1, 40150 Shah Alam,
Selangor Darul Ehsan, Malaysia

Oxford University Press is a department of the University of Oxford.
It furthers the University's objective of excellence in research, scholarship,
and education by publishing worldwide in

Oxford New York

Athens Auckland Bangkok Bogotá Buenos Aires Calcutta
Cape Town Chennai Dar es Salaam Delhi Florence Hong Kong Istanbul
Karachi Kuala Lumpur Madrid Melbourne Mexico City Mumbai
Nairobi Paris São Paulo Singapore Taipei Tokyo Toronto Warsaw

with associated companies in Berlin Ibadan

Oxford is a registered trade mark of Oxford University Press
in the UK and in certain other countries

Published in the United States
by Oxford University Press, New York

© Oxford University Press 1998
First published 1998
Second impression 2001

All rights reserved. No part of this publication may be reproduced,
stored in a retrieval system, or transmitted, in any form or by any means,
without the prior permission in writing of Oxford University Press.
Within Malaysia, exceptions are allowed in respect of any fair dealing for the
purpose of research or private study, or criticism or review, as permitted
under the Copyright Act currently in force. Enquiries concerning
reproduction outside these terms and in other countries should be
sent to Oxford University Press at the address above

Library of Congress Cataloging-in-Publication Data
Rahim, Lily Zubaidah, 1960–
The Singapore dilemma: the political and educational marginality
of the Malay community/Lily Zubaidah Rahim.
p. cm.— (South East-Asian social science monographs)
Includes bibliographical references and index.
ISBN 983 56 0032 5 (b)
1. Malays (Asian people)—Singapore. 2. Singapore—Social
conditions. 3. Singapore—Economic conditions. 4. Singapore—
Politics and government. 5. Education—Singapore. I. Series.
DS610.25.M34R34 1998
959.57—dc21
CIP

Typeset by Indah Photosetting Centre Sdn. Bhd., Malaysia
Printed by Printmate Sdn. Bhd., Kuala Lumpur

*Terima kasih to my parents,
A. Rahim Ishak and Mawan Wajid Khan,
and to
Mark John Keevers*

# Preface

As I was growing up in Singapore, I maintained a strong curiosity about why there were so few Malay role models for young Malays like me, why the Malay community persistently remained along the socio-economic margins of society in the ostensibly meritocratic and multiracial oasis of Singapore, and why Malay youths were not called up for 'compulsory' national service among other whys related to Malays. I was not satisfied with the prevailing culturalist view that Malays were marginal because they were not sufficiently hardworking, motivated, industrious, and numerous other non-affirming 'were not's'. Intuitively, I always knew that this perspective was too simplistic, smacked of racism, and represented a truncated explanation to a complex phenomenon. Accepting this prevailing view also meant that I, as a Malay from a supposedly deficient cultural tradition, would then also have to accept that I possessed these unflattering attributes. Like many Malay Singaporeans living under the weight and shadow of these negative ethnic stereotypes, my sense of identity, self-esteem, and rootedness in the land of my birth was shaken. The danger of having to carry this negative identity baggage is that it can tragically become a self-fulfilling prophecy. Sadly, this may, to some extent, have transpired within the Singapore Malay community. This research was therefore initiated in response to these burning concerns that I have long contemplated. It was in a sense a purposeful journey in search for meaning to these questions.

Towards this end, the political motivations and ideological premises of the dominant explanations, perceptions, and prescriptions of the Malay marginality are examined. The extent to which the Malay socio-economic and educational marginality is a manifestation of a constellation of complex political, structural, and class-based factors is considered. In attempting to extend the boundaries of understanding on the Malay marginality, this study has focused on the ideological and institutional processes that have contributed to the Malay community's socio-economic and educational status. It has concentrated on the education system as it is actively promoted by the People's Action Party (PAP) government as the most effective means of social mobility for the Malays in Singapore's ostensibly meritocratic and multiracial society. The ideological premises, shifting political motives shaping the course of education policies and their impact on the Malays and other socially disadvantaged Singaporeans, are analysed. The relationship between the community's electoral and political weakness and the ability of PAP Malay politicians to effectively articulate and represent Malay concerns is another area of focus.

The reliance on a single grand theory to explain the Malay socio-economic marginality was avoided in view of the highly complex and multifaceted nature of the phenomenon. Instead, a holistically integrated or eclectic conceptual framework that is appreciative of the complexity of social life and that allows for a fluid and dialectical relationship between theory, evidence, and practice was favoured. Owing to the eclectic framework of the study and the relatively wide spectrum of issues ranging from political leadership, education policies, welfare policies, and the PAP ideology, theoretical and conceptual discussions have largely been incorporated in the relevant sections of each chapter. This allows for the author and reader to more readily synthesize and relate the conceptual framework to the empirical data and discussion.

The study does not make any pretensions of having provided a definitive 'grand solution' to the socio-economic marginality of the Malay community. A more modest objective of raising pertinent questions, challenging and interrogating the dominant myths, and (by doing so) raising critical consciousness and holistically broadening the discourse on the Malay marginality has been sought. In metaphoric terms, I have attempted to look at the situation from different lenses and with the perspective of fresh eyes.

The research for this book, initially embarked upon as a doctoral thesis, was undertaken over a period of many years, including lengthy periods of field research in Singapore. Lengthier periods were spent sorting out material and writing in Sydney. This was followed by a year of teaching and 'soul searching' in Penang, Malaysia, and subsequently my current teaching position at the Economic History Department, University of Sydney. This phase of my life has been the most challenging in personal, intellectual, political, and spiritual terms. It was a varied and at times meandering journey of discovery and rediscovery. Despite the many trials and tribulations of this journey, I feel very enriched by the experience for impressing upon me the larger purpose of life.

Suffice to say, I humbly accept full responsibility for the shortcomings of this research endeavour.

*Sydney*  LILY ZUBAIDAH RAHIM
*February 1998*

# Acknowledgements

THERE are numerous people whose intellectual and moral support has been a source of inspiration and sustained my belief in the contribution of this project towards furthering the ideals of equity, justice, and democracy in Singapore.

Many *terima kasih* are due to Professor Michael Leigh who rendered generous assistance and encouragement, Associate Professor Rodney Tiffen for his constructive suggestions, and Professor Harold Crouch and Dr Barbara Leigh for their helpful comments which helped to keep me 'on track'. Other colleagues whose camaraderie and intellectual stimulation warrant due acknowledgement include Dr John Mettam, Dr Gerard Sullivan, Professor Peter King, Associate Professor Ben Tipton, and Associate Professor Robert Adrich.

I am gratefully indebted to the generous assistance of the staff at the Institute of South-East Asian Studies (ISEAS) during my terms as an ISEAS Research Fellow in 1990 and a Research Associate in 1992. The library facilities and intellectual support at ISEAS allowed me to initiate a substantial bulk of the research while I was there. The staff at Mendaki were particularly helpful in providing information and inviting me to participate in the numerous seminars and educational programmes conducted in 1990 and 1992.

To the numerous Singaporeans who kindly agreed to be interviewed and participated in the survey, I extend my deepest appreciation for their frank and honest comments. My interaction with Singaporeans during the field study has strengthened my belief in the courage and conviction of many Singaporean warriors who, often at considerable personal cost, are working towards strengthening the foundations of a democratic, multiracial, and humane Singapore.

I am greatly indebted to Vanessa Forest, Deborah Stodhart, Haresh Chabbra, and Misleah Sulaiman for their friendship. Vanessa's deep commitment to social justice and equity, both at the personal and professional level, has been a great source of inspiration. That our friendship has endured the often complicated travails and meanderings of personal, political, and spiritual growth has served as a constant reminder of the beauty and larger purpose of life. She is my soul sister!

My parents and siblings have supported me through the years in ways that perhaps only a family can best appreciate. They have taught me the meaning of unconditional love, the importance of adopting a serious yet light-hearted approach towards life, and the appreciation of the dance of life in all its rhythms and contours.

Finally, my heartfelt thanks to Mark John Keevers, who was always there to lend me support and reassurance at every stage of the research. Mark has been an immeasurable source of intellectual, emotional, and spiritual enrichment even at the most trying of periods. He has always maintained an open and compassionate heart and I am most fortunate to have had my life touched by him.

# Contents

|   |   |
|---|---|
| *Preface* | *vii* |
| *Acknowledgements* | *ix* |
| *Tables* | *xiv* |
| *Appendices* | *xv* |
| *Abbreviations* | *xvi* |

**1 Introduction**   *1*
Aims of the Study   *4*
Methodological Approaches   *5*
Research Constraints   *7*

PART I IDENTITY AND IDEOLOGY   *11*

**2 Indigeneity, Islam, and Living on the Margins of Society**   *13*
Indigenous Pan-Malay Identity   *13*
The Islamic Identity   *17*
Living on the Margins of Society   *19*
Relative Deprivation   *23*

**3 The PAP's Vision for Singapore**   *29*
Maintaining the Ideological Hegemony of the PAP   *29*
The PAP Leadership's Perception of Social Inequality   *36*
Survival of the Fittest, Servility of the Weakest   *39*

**4 Perceptions of the Malay Marginality**   *49*
The Legacy of Orientalist and Colonial Perceptions of the Malay Community   *49*
The Impact of the Cultural Deficit Thesis on 'Culturally Deficient Communities'   *52*
The PAP Leadership's Perceptions of the Malay Marginality   *53*
Non-Malay Perceptions of the Malay Marginality   *57*
Malay Perceptions of the Malay Marginality   *59*

## PART II  CONTAINMENT OF MALAY POLITICS — 65

### 5  Minimizing the Political Resources of the Malay Community — 67
Political Resources and Strategies — 67
Maintaining the Numerical Minority Status of Malays — 70
Diluting the Electoral Clout of the Malay Community — 73

### 6  Political Representation of Malay Interests — 82
Dilemmas Confronting Ethnic Minority Leaders — 82
The Tenuous Position of the PAP Malay MP in the PAP Government — 85
The Tenuous Position of the PAP Malay MP as a National Leader — 89
The Tenuous Position of the PAP Malay MP as a Malay Leader — 92

## PART III  EDUCATION AND INEQUALITY — 115

### 7  The Institutionalization of Educational Élitism — 117

THE TREND TOWARDS EDUCATIONAL ÉLITISM — 117
The Ascendancy of the Neo-Conservative Educational Agenda — 117
Localizing the Conservative Educational Agenda — 119
Educational Policy Making in Singapore — 120
The New Education Policy — 123
The NEP's Early Streaming Policy — 124
The Special Assistance Plan — 128
The Gifted Education Programme — 131
The Independent School Concept — 134
Fine-tuning the Educational Élitism of the NEP — 137

THE IMPACT OF EDUCATIONAL ÉLITISM ON EQUAL EDUCATIONAL OPPORTUNITY — 140
The Rise of Parentocracy — 140
Increasing Costs of Education — 141
Competition for Entrance into the Élite Schools — 145
An Escape Route for the 'Less Meritorious' with Financial Resources — 147
Educational Opportunities for Special Education Students — 147

### 8  The Politicization of the Education System — 159
Ideological and Political Socialization — 159
The Construction of Morality — 161
The Construction of History — 163
Racial Quotas for Malays in Schools — 166

|  |  |  |
|---|---|---|
| | Linguistic Bias towards Mandarin | *168* |
| | The Revival of Monoethnic Schools | *169* |
| | Reviving Ethnic/Linguistic Based Language Review Committees | *171* |
| | Population Policies and the Education System | *173* |
| | The 'Meritocratic' Tertiary Education Sector | *176* |
| **9** | **Understanding the Malay Educational Marginality** | *184* |
| | The Educational Marginality of Ethnic Minority Communities | *184* |
| | Explaining the Malay Educational Malaise | *185* |
| | The Promotion and Subsequent Demotion of Malay-medium Education | *188* |
| | Educational (Under)achievement, Socio-economic Status, and Cultural Capital | *191* |
| | The NEP and Malay Educational Progress in the 1980s and Early 1990s | *198* |
| | Has the Educational Gap Narrowed? | *200* |
| | Student Responses to School | *202* |
| | Perceptions of Bias | *205* |
| **10** | **The Inherent Limitations of Mendaki** | *211* |
| | The Political and Ideological Underpinnings of Mendaki | *211* |
| | The Restructuring of Mendaki | *213* |
| | The Perceived Politicization of Mendaki | *215* |
| | Awarding the 'Meritorious' Malay/Muslim Student | *217* |
| | Nurturing the 'Meritorious' Malay/Muslim Student | *217* |
| | The Salience of Parental/Class Background and Cultural Capital in the Educational Achievement of MEP Students | *220* |
| | Career Aspirations of MEP Students | *221* |
| | Mendaki's S1 Project for Normal Stream Students | *222* |
| | Career Aspirations of S1 Project Students | *224* |
| **11** | **The Ethnic Based Self-help Paradigm** | *232* |
| | Motivations and Premises Guiding the Ethnic Based Self-help Paradigm | *232* |
| | Inter-ethnic and Intra-ethnic Social Divisions | *235* |
| | The Unequal Engines of Assistance | *237* |
| | Obfuscating the Structural and Institutional Sources of Underachievement | *239* |
| | Communal Welfarism | *241* |
| | **Conclusion** | *247* |
| | *Appendices* | *253* |
| | *Bibliography* | *261* |
| | *Index* | *293* |

# Tables

| | | |
|---|---|---|
| 2.1 | Census Breakdown of Malay and Sub-Malay Groups in Singapore | 16 |
| 2.2 | Malay and Chinese Working Males Aged Ten Years and Over by Occupation | 20 |
| 2.3 | Distribution of Occupations by Ethnic Group | 20 |
| 2.4 | Monthly Income of Employed Male Malays and Chinese | 21 |
| 2.5 | Monthly Head-of-Household Income by Ethnic Group, 1980 and 1990 | 22 |
| 2.6 | Percentage of Each Ethnic Group Attending University | 23 |
| 2.7 | Absolute Progress Made by Malays | 23 |
| 5.1 | Ethnic Population of Singapore | 70 |
| 5.2 | Electoral Performance of the PKMS | 78 |
| 6.1 | Numerical Representation of Malay MPs in Parliament, 1960–1991 | 86 |
| 6.2 | Ethnic Representation in Government, 1992 | 87 |
| 6.3 | Electoral Constituencies with the Highest Number of Malay Voters | 90 |
| 7.1 | Decreasing Popularity of Chinese Stream Schools | 129 |
| 7.2 | Fee Increases in Independent Schools, 1990–1991 | 142 |
| 7.3 | University Fees, 1990–1992 | 143 |
| 8.1 | Enrolments in Singapore Schools by Language Stream | 169 |
| 9.1 | Enrolment Decline in Malay Schools, 1968–1980 | 190 |
| 9.2 | Special Malay Bursaries Awarded, 1966–1970 | 191 |
| 9.3 | Average Monthly Household Income by Ethnic Group | 192 |
| 9.4 | Languages Spoken at Home | 194 |
| 9.5 | Languages Predominantly Spoken by Malay/Muslim Students at Home | 195 |
| 9.6 | PSLE Passes in English and Mathematics, 1984 and 1991 | 195 |
| 9.7 | Correlation between Housing Type and Tuition Subjects Chosen | 196 |
| 9.8 | Educational Standing of Mothers and the Streaming of Their Children in the Extended and Monolingual Streams | 197 |
| 9.9 | Malay Student Enrolment at the National University of Singapore | 199 |

| | | |
|---|---|---|
| 9.10 | Malay Student Enrolment at the Nanyang Technological University | *200* |
| 9.11 | PSLE Examination Results | *201* |
| 9.12 | PSLE Passes in Mathematics | *201* |
| 9.13 | Students Obtaining a Minimum of 3 '0' Levels by Ethnic Group | *202* |
| 9.14 | Students' Response to Survey Question: Do You Enjoy School? | *205* |
| 10.1 | Occupational Status of Parents of MEP Students Surveyed | *220* |
| 10.2 | Language Use of MEP Students Surveyed | *221* |
| 10.3 | Career Aspirations of MEP Students Surveyed | *222* |
| 10.4 | Occupational Status of Parents of S1 Project Students Surveyed | *223* |
| 10.5 | Usage of English at Home of S1 Project Students Surveyed | *223* |
| 10.6 | Career Aspirations of S1 Project Students Surveyed | *224* |

# Appendices

| | | |
|---|---|---|
| 1 | Interview with Dr Ahmad Mattar, Former Minister of Environment and Malay/Muslim Affairs, Chairperson of Mendaki, October 1990 | *253* |
| 2 | Interview with Abdullah Tarmugi, Minister of Community Development and Malay/Muslim Affairs, August 1990 | *257* |

# Abbreviations

| | |
|---|---|
| 'A' | Advanced |
| ACIE | Action Committee for Indian Education |
| AMP | Association of Malay/Muslim Professionals |
| ASEAN | Association of South-East Asian Nations |
| AWARE | Association of Women for Action and Research |
| *BH* | *Berita Harian* |
| *BT* | *Business Times* |
| CATS | Committee for Attracting Talent to Singapore |
| CCC | Citizen Consultative Committee |
| CDAC | Chinese Development Assistance Council |
| CDC | Community Development Council |
| CL1 | Chinese Language 1 |
| CL2 | Chinese Language 2 |
| CLRC | Chinese Language Review Committee |
| CPF | Central Provident Fund |
| CPI | Consumer Price Index |
| CRC | Cost Review Committee |
| EL1 | English Language 1 |
| EM1 | English/Mother Tongue 1 |
| EM2 | English/Mother Tongue 2 |
| EM3 | English/Mother Tongue 3 |
| EOI | Export Oriented Industrialization |
| ESN | Educationally Subnormal |
| FAS | Financial Assistance Scheme |
| *FEER* | *Far Eastern Economic Review* |
| GCE | General Certificate of Education |
| GDP | Gross Domestic Product |
| GEP | Gifted Education Programme |
| GNP | Gross National Product |
| GPC | Government Parliamentary Committee |
| GRC | Group Representative Constituency |
| GST | Goods and Services Tax |
| HDB | Housing Development Board |
| HSC | Higher School Certificate |
| IE | Institute of Education |
| *IHT* | *International Herald Tribune* |

| | |
|---|---|
| IMF | International Monetary Fund |
| *IQRA* | Mendaki Enrichment Programme Newsletter |
| ISA | Internal Security Act |
| KGMS | Kesatuan Guru-guru Melayu Singapura or Singapore Malay Teachers Union |
| KMM | Kesatuan Melayu Muda |
| L1 | First Language |
| LBKM | Prophet Muhammad Memorial Fund Board |
| MAB | Malay Affairs Bureau |
| MAS | Mendaki Amanah Saham |
| MCA | Malaysian Chinese Association |
| MCE | Malaysian Certificate of Education |
| MCP | Malaysian Communist Party |
| MEP | Mendaki Enrichment Programme |
| MHE | Minimum Household Expenditure |
| MIC | Malaysian Indian Congress |
| MNP | Malaysian Nationalist Party |
| MOE | Ministry of Education |
| MP | Member of Parliament |
| MPAJA | Malayan People's Anti-Japanese Association |
| MSC | Malaysian Solidarity Convention |
| MUIS | Majlis Ugama Islam Singapura |
| NCMP | Non-Constituency Member of Parliament |
| NCSMMP | National Convention of Singapore Malay/Muslim Professionals |
| NEP | New Education Policy |
| NES | New Education System |
| NIC | Newly Industrializing Country |
| NIE | National Institute of Education |
| NMP | Nominated Member of Parliament |
| *NST* | *New Straits Times* |
| NTU | Nanyang Technological University |
| NTUC | National Trade Union Congress |
| 'O' | Ordinary |
| OECD | Organization for Economic Co-operation and Development |
| PA | People's Association |
| PA | Public Assistance |
| PAP | People's Action Party |
| PITK | Association for Muslim Welfare |
| PKMS | Pertubohan Kebangsaan Melayu Singapura |
| PP | Progressive Party |
| PRM | Party Raayat Malaya |
| PSLE | Primary School Leaving Examination |
| PUB | Public Utilities Board |
| RC | Resident Committee |
| SAF | Singapore Armed Forces |
| SAP | Special Assistance Plan |
| SBC | Singapore Broadcasting Corporation |

| | |
|---|---|
| SCCCI | Singapore Chinese Chamber of Commerce and Industry |
| SCSS | Singapore Council of Social Services |
| SDP | Singapore Democratic Party |
| SDS | Social Development Section |
| SDU | Social Development Unit |
| SFCCA | Singapore Federation of Chinese Clan Associations |
| SIF | Singapore International Foundation |
| SINDA | Singapore Indian Development Association |
| SMNO | Singapore Malays National Organization |
| SPS | Social Promotion Section |
| *ST* | *Straits Times* |
| STU | Singapore Teachers Union |
| *ST WOE* | *Straits Times Weekly Overseas Edition* |
| TI | Technical Institute |
| UMNO | United Malays National Organization |
| VITB | Vocational Institute and Training Board |

# 1
# Introduction

SINGAPORE is arguably one of the most impressive economic success stories in Asia. Lacking in natural resources and limited in physical size, the island state has triumphed against formidable odds not only to become South-East Asia's first Newly Industrializing Country (NIC) but also to be classified as a developed economy from 1996 by the Organization for Economic Co-operation and Development (OECD).[1] It has also been credited with the distinction of being the most economically competitive NIC[2] and has long remained the financial centre of the region. Enjoying sustained levels of high Gross Domestic Product (GDP) growth since independence, and the reputation of having the highest home ownership rates in the world, with 90 per cent of the population owning their homes, Singaporeans are poised to experience a standard of living comparable to that of Switzerland by the year 2000. The island's impressive economic credentials are a source of national pride to Singaporeans and go some way towards explaining the continued political hegemony of the People's Action Party (PAP) since its election to office in 1959.

However, a deeper analysis of the island's economic success story reveals some distinct anomalies and contradictions that appear to be at odds with its reputation as an efficiently governed multiracial society ordered along the principles of meritocracy and equal opportunity. What emerges is a strongly socially engineered society that is governed by a political party intent on maintaining high levels of economic growth, preserving its political hegemony, and so convinced of the judiciousness of its political philosophy that dissenting beliefs are barely tolerated.

After more than thirty-five years in office, the PAP leadership has been relatively successful in relegating politics to the realms of technocratic problem solving. Autonomous political participation has been limited to activities such as voting every few years on the assumption that too much democracy is counterproductive to political stability and economic development (Rahim, 1993: 21). Problems that are inherently political have been neatly presented as economic problems requiring economic solutions. Characteristic of technocratic governance, economic considerations take priority over other considerations. As Goh Chok Tong (*ST*, 23 September 1991) has frankly acknowledged, 'I always prefer to get the right economic decision first and then worry about the political and social problems later.'

Conflating the nation's impressive economic record with 'good government', the PAP leadership generally formulates public policy in a top-down manner and initiates social engineering policies which impinge upon the personal affairs[3] of Singaporeans with minimal public consultation.[4] When consultations are ostensibly undertaken via state sponsored forums, the discussions do not centre around principles and goals but focus on fine-tuning policies already determined by the government. The almost characteristic modifications, reformulations, and policy changes within relatively short periods of time in the education sector, with minimal input from educators in the 'frontline', students, and parents, have taken their toll. The poor morale and alienation of teachers from the education system (Goh Report, 1979: 3–7) is demonstrated by their high attrition rates from the profession ('Friday Background', SBC, 17 June 1992). Public discontent with the highly competitive education system and the capricious nature of education policies is also manifested by the high emigration levels[5] of professional Singaporeans (Sullivan and Gunasekaran, 1993). A 1997 survey revealed that 20 per cent of Singaporeans wished to emigrate and a third would like their children to be educated overseas.[6]

The PAP government's management of the persistent socio-economic and educational marginality of the indigenous Malay community, who make up 14 per cent of the total population,[7] represents one of the glaring examples of the contradictions between the theory and practice of equal opportunity, meritocracy, and multiracialism in Singapore. Having denounced communalism and ethnic privilege after the island's expulsion from Malaysia in 1965, the PAP leadership was convinced that its brand of meritocracy and multiracialism would eventually improve the relative material position of the Malay community and other socially disadvantaged Singaporeans. This would prove the superiority of the PAP's multiracial meritocratic philosophy, based on the assumption of equal opportunities and rights for the various ethnic communities, over the Malaysian government's assumption of unequal opportunities and the need for special assistance for the economically disadvantaged *bumiputra* (indigenous)[8] community. No doubt, the PAP leadership's reluctance in granting special assistance to the Malays was predicated on the belief that this could have been perceived by the dominant Chinese community as unfair and activate the ire of the Chinese chauvinists (Khoo, 1988: 38). Thus, despite the constitutional responsibilities of the government,[9] a minimalist approach was adopted towards the socio-economic and educational marginality of the Malay community. The only tangible form of assistance was the continuation of the policy of free education for Malays which was originally initiated by the British colonial authorities.

As the relative socio-economic and educational position of Malays not only showed negligible signs of improvement but had in fact deteriorated by the 1960s, 1970s, and 1980s (Li, 1989; NCSMMP, 1990) and it became increasingly evident that the PAPs brand of meritocracy and multiracialism had failed the Malays, the cultural deficit thesis began to be increasingly relied upon by the PAP government to explain the intractability of the Malay marginality. This approach has served to deflect criticism against the efficacy and judiciousness of its minimalist, multiracial, and meritocratic stance.

The cultural deficit thesis essentially posits that socially disadvantaged ethnic communities have remained economically and educationally marginal primarily because of their negative values and generally moribund attitudes which in turn create the material conditions that reproduce their social disadvantage. As the culturally deficient communities are largely responsible for their marginality, the onus is thus placed on them to reform their negative values and attitudes. Such a discourse absolves the state from implementing structural reforms and actively assisting the marginal community with the aim of narrowing the socio-economic and educational disparity between the ethnic communities. As the problem is supposed to lie with the marginal ethnic community, the solutions are expected to emanate from the community.

Mendaki's inability to appreciably improve the relative socio-economic and educational standing of the Malay community after more than a decade since its establishment, as well as its reluctance to critically question the propriety of education policies that have not promoted the interests of ethnic minorities and the value of eugenics based policies such as early streaming, has precipitated a growing level of frustration and sense of relative deprivation within the Malay community. Their 'lived reality' has enabled them to be acutely cognizant of the contradictions in the cultural deficit thesis, the salience of institutional factors in contributing to their socio-economic, educational, and political marginality, and the contradiction of the otherwise strong interventionist approach towards assisting the cultural development of the Chinese community whilst adopting a minimalist approach towards the Malay community's socio-economic malaise. Articulating the community's frustration with the PAP government's double standards, Malay community activist Kassim Yang Razali (1990: 113) noted that

in the eyes of many Malays, official response has fallen short of their expectations. Some thought it rather half-hearted, ... the Malays see a stark contrast in the way the government introduced and promoted with vigour the Speak Mandarin Campaign and Confucianism, and allowed substantial immigration of Chinese from Hong Kong in what they see as an attempt to make up for the falling birth rate of the majority community. The Malays ... have found it hard to accept what they regard as inconsistency in treatment of the different races and what they perceive to be a drift away from multiracialism.

As more Malays begin to challenge the premises of cultural deficit explanations and articulate their grievances within the national ideals of equal opportunity, multiracialism, and democracy, the PAP government has come under increasing pressure to address the Malay marginality as a serious national problem requiring national rather than ethnic based solutions. However, it has responded to this pressure by continuing to promote the cultural deficit thesis in an ideological alliance with eugenics/biological determinist explanations and by implementing various electoral and institutional measures which have limited the electoral clout of the Malay community. The political marginality of the Malays has allowed the PAP leadership to strengthen its political base within the Chinese community and to promote the nation as a Chinese-dominated Confucian society. The long-term political, social, and geo-political ramifications of a Sinicized Singapore in a Malay region are alarming and form an important theme running through the thesis.

## Aims of the Study

In critically evaluating the impact of ideological and institutional factors on the socio-economic, educational, and political standing of the Malay community, the study has attempted to provide a holistic understanding of the Malay marginality. This is undertaken by challenging the dominant assumptions and exposing the contradictions underpinning the cultural deficit thesis and the practice of multiracialism and equal opportunity in Singapore. Particular attention is paid to the following questions:

1. Has the PAP government's understanding as well as handling of the Malay marginality primarily within the cultural deficit paradigm contributed to the relegation of the Malay community to the socio-economic and educational fringes of society?
2. Why have the PAP Malay politicians not been particularly effective in representing the concerns and interests of the Malay community? Is there a link between the weak political clout of the Malay community and their persistent socio-economic and educational marginality?
3. How equitable is the education system in Singapore? Have institutional factors such as education policies and the nature of the education system contributed towards maintaining the educational marginality of the Malay community?
4. How effective have Mendaki and the ethnic self-help paradigm been in ameliorating the socio-economic and educational marginality of the Malay community? How much is the Malay marginality a class-based problem?

Interlinked to these central questions is the important theme of the contradictions between the theory and practice of multiracialism, meritocracy, and equal opportunity. Pertinent considerations of whether all Singaporeans enjoy equal opportunities in the ostensibly 'meritocratic' education system, as well as the inherent tension and contradiction between the PAP government's élitist and eugenics ideological orientation are addressed.

The Malay marginality is not only a pertinent factor in the socio-political and economic fabric of the island republic but also an important factor in her relations with the neighbouring Malay nations. The persistence of the Singapore Malay marginality serves to sustain the

INTRODUCTION 5

Singapore Chinese community's sense of vulnerability arising from their 'majority with a minority mentality complex' that appears to be typical of immigrant settler societies.[10] This sense of vulnerability by the Chinese community has bred suspicion against the motives of Malays in Singapore and the region, and goes some way towards explaining the island's fragile relations with her Malay Muslim neighbours.

## Methodological Approaches

In establishing the salience of ideological and institutional factors in maintaining and perpetuating the Malay marginality, the PAP's world-view, the efficacy of the political representation of Malay concerns, and the role of the education system have been selected for examination.

The PAP leadership's ideological world-view has strongly shaped and influenced the character and complexion of state and civil institutions in Singapore. This has assisted in maintaining the political hegemony of the PAP without regular recourse to coercive and repressive measures. Coupled with consent attained through the high levels of economic growth, the PAP's ostensible commitment to the ideals of meritocracy, multiracialism, and equal opportunity has provided some credence to its 'good government' image. In an ostensibly equitable socio-political milieu, socially marginal communities such as the Malays are thus perceived as having failed to take advantage of the opportunities for social mobility readily available to them due to their cultural deficits.

The chapter on Malay politics—Chapter 5—has attempted to establish the relationship between the weak electoral clout of the Malay community, the tenuous representation of Malay concerns by PAP Members of Parliament (MPs), and the community's socio-economic and educational marginality. Towards this end, the constellation of electoral engineering mechanisms, resettlement, population, and public housing policies are examined. The ramifications of the conflicting demands of PAP Malay MPs as national leaders, PAP leaders, and Malay leaders, and their representation of the community's aspirations and concerns, are considered.

The education system has long been promoted by the PAP government as the embodiment of the nation's multiracial and meritocratic ideal. Characteristic of the high regard accorded to educational credentials in strongly technocratic-oriented societies (Habermas, 1971: 111), the Malay community has been constantly reminded that education is the key to improving their marginal status in society. Due to the prescriptive status of education in the Malay marginality, an analysis of the education system and education policies has thus been undertaken to measure the efficacy of the education system as the vehicle of social mobility. The education system's meritocratic and multiracial credentials are also analysed. The education system's role in maintaining the political hegemony of the PAP through the processes of ideological socialization is another area of examination.

A survey of 291 Malay/Muslim secondary students was undertaken in

1992. In order to maintain confidentiality and encourage frank responses to some of the more sensitive questions in the survey, students were not required to state their names in the survey. In addition to information gained from the quantitative survey, a qualitative participant/observer ethnographic approach was also undertaken during the author's field-trips to Singapore in 1990 and 1992. Such an approach—listening whilst others talked and observing what often is overlooked—was found to be fruitful as it allowed for ambiguity in the pursuit of complexity. During the course of approximately two months as a relief teacher in two secondary government schools in 1992, the author, by 'getting inside the school', was able to directly experience and witness the cultural nuances, negotiations, manifestations of student resistance, interethnic relations between students, student coping mechanisms, teacher/student relations, teacher attitudes to students and teaching, and thereby gain a better understanding of the complexity of the work schools perform as sites of ideological production and contestation. Such an ethnographic participant/observer approach has served to foreshadow the temptation to ascribe simplistically to the reproductive view of schools as 'black boxes'.[11] It assisted in exposing students and teachers as important actors with a significant level of autonomy in the education system and in understanding the culture found within schools.

Numerous Mendaki seminars, workshops, and tutorials attended by the author provided the opportunity to engage in open-ended discussions with students in Mendaki's programmes for the 'academically talented' and academic 'underachievers'. Several discussions were also conducted with several senior Mendaki and Association of Malay/Muslim Professionals (AMP) administrators who provided invaluable insights into the ideological premises underpinning their educational programmes and the political parameters which guide their policy making. The author also observed and participated in numerous serminars organized by the Malay community on topics pertaining to education, politics, and economics.

A broadly structured interview format covering a wide spectrum of issues was conducted with former and current PAP Malay leaders such as Ahmad Mattar (former Minister of Environment and Malay/Muslim Affairs), Sidek Saniff (Minister of State for Education), and Abdullah Tarmugi (Minister for Community Development and Malay/Muslim Affairs).[12] Interviews with the leaders of the Malay-based opposition party Pertubohan Kebangsaan Melayu Singapura (PKMS), Chiam See Tong (former Secretary-General of the Singapore Democratic Party (SDP) and MP for Potong Pasir), and Juffrie Mahmood (Workers Party politician) were also conducted. Approximately thirty non-Malay and Malay grass roots activists, educationalists, social workers, students, and professionals were interviewed. Owing to the political sensitivity of many of the issues discussed, the names of those interviewed, other than politicians from the PAP and opposition parties, have been kept confidential.

The author was sensitive to the totalizing ambition of a grand theory in claiming more explanatory power than it actually possesses and the propensity to extend the domain of its concepts to answer questions that it is actually unable to deal with satisfactorily. Grand theories also tend to encourage confrontation rather than a search for dialogue or conceptual synthesis. The relational and eclectic approach (Di Stefano, 1991: 152) is generally better equipped to explain the socio-economic, educational, and political marginality of a particular ethnic community as integral to a complex set of processes whose origin encompasses a much wider set of variables beyond ethnicity (Wilson, 1989: 132). More concerned about an accurate explanatory framework than theoretical neatness, such a dialogic and eclectic approach draws on the strengths of the different theoretical paradigms and disciplines within the social sciences. The various theories which are critical strive towards non-authoritarian social relations and share an emancipatory goal that is premised on the principles of equity and justice.

There is also a good case to be made for transcending the compartmentalized, disciplinary epistemologies by integrating the different social science disciplines closer together and encouraging intellectual 'border crossings' (Giroux, 1992a). Such an approach enables the researcher to understand different aspects of a particular phenomenon from various conceptual perspectives. The 'border crossings' approach endeavours to strengthen the utility and value of the social sciences as a method of research and thwart the fragmentation of knowledge and social reality associated with the strictly disciplinary approach. Importantly, it serves to 'challenge, remap, renegotiate' (Giroux, 1992a: 26) the boundaries of knowledge that are hegemonic as well as 'objective' representations of reality. It also assists in questioning and challenging the hegemonic ideas, values, beliefs, and practices that have not been seriously questioned and challenged.[13] This tradition of critical social science serves to facilitate the process of critical discourse, intellectual development, and empowerment.

## Research Constraints

Other than the documents, reports (Sharom and Wong, 1974; NCSMMP, 1990; Blake, 1991), and academic dissertations (Yang Razali Kassim, 1979; Hashimah Johari, 1984; Nurliza Yusuf, 1986; Shaari bin Tadin, 1987) that have incorporated some class, historical, and institutional perspectives in analysing various aspects of the Singapore Malay marginality, a more systematic class and institutional analysis which highlighted the contradictions in the practice of meritocracy and multi-racialism, and questioned the validity of the cultural deficit thesis was undertaken by non-Singaporean researchers Bedlington (1974) and Li (1989).

Bedlington's (1974) study was the first comprehensive research on the Singapore Malay community in post-independence Singapore. Li's (1989) synthesis of the dynamic relationship between structural and ethnographic perspectives represented a systematic paradigm shift from the orthodox cultural deficit thesis. Her study has provided students of ethnic studies with illuminating insights into Malay patterns of marriage, socialization of children, budgeting, and domestic labour. Li's discussion of discrimination faced by Malays in the workforce and the impact of the PAP government's policy of excluding Malay youth from 'compulsory' national service on the socio-economic position of Malays has rendered her research a valuable contribution to knowledge and essential reading for students of ethnicity and Singapore society.

Instructively, little has been written from a systemic and critical perspective about the socio-economic, educational, and political marginality of Malays by Singaporean academics from the tertiary institutions in Singapore. The limited research in this area may be due to its political sensitivity, particularly if the conclusions drawn are critical of the PAP government's handling of the marginality of the Malays and other disadvantaged groups. The politically sensitive nature of research on areas pertaining to the poor and socially marginal springs from the belief promoted by the PAP government that the poor are essentially responsible for their individual failings or cultural deficiencies.

There exists a general practice of self-censorship and lack of serious intellectual critique when writing on Singapore, particularly by social scientists employed at Singaporean tertiary institutions. The dismissal of the Deputy Secretary General of the SDP, Chee Soon Juan, from the Psychology and Social Work Department at the National University of Singapore, on relatively minor charges in 1992, is likely to have reinforced the culture of academic self-censorship. Academics and postgraduate students from Singaporean institutions are inclined to steer away from conducting research on sensitive issues such as the Gifted Education Programme and the early streaming system (Gopinathan and Gremli, 1988: 161, 162, 171). Expatriate academics tend to refrain from publishing articles critical of the PAP government fearing that their short-term teaching contracts would not be renewed. The insecurity of not having their contracts renewed has been made real by the experiences of expatriate academics who have been detained for questioning and sued for defamation or have not had their contracts renewed for daring to publish articles critical of the PAP government (Asiawatch, 1990; *IHT*, 2 August 1993). Because of the political constraints on academic research in Singapore, the bulk of social science research in Singapore tends to be overly concerned with quantitative methodology (Clammer, 1985: 164), data gathering, and data analysis without systematically addressing issues of theoretical interest or challenging the ideological premises of government policies.

---

1. In 1997, the Geneva-based International Institute for Management Development has ranked Singapore the world's second most competitive economy after the United States (*ST*, 26 March 1997).

2. The World Competitiveness Report was conducted by the Geneva-based International Institute for Management Development and the World Economic Forum (*ST WOE*, June 1991).

3. In justifying the state's intrusions into the private sphere, Lee Kuan Yew stated at a 1987 National Day Rally, 'I am often accused of interfering in the private lives of citizens ... if I did not, had not done that, we wouldn't be here today ... we would not have made economic progress, if we had not intervened on very personal matters—who your neighbour is, how you live, the noise you make, how you spit ... or what language you use.... We decide what is right. Never mind what the people think. That's another problem' (cf. Bello and Rosenfeld, 1992: 318).

4. Most of the technocratic 'new guard' PAP leaders such as Prime Minister Goh Chok Tong, Deputy Prime Minister Lee Hsien Loong, and Minister for Information George Yeo were culled from the Civil Service and had minimal political experience prior to their co-optation into the PAP. Traditionally, many of the PAP Ministers have been economists and possess academic credentials in the non-social sciences (Yeo, 1982: 27).

5. An estimated 100,000 Singaporeans have emigrated (*Sunday Times*, 28 June 1992).

6. The survey was conducted by Mastercard International's 'Asian Ideals' survey of thirteen Asia–Pacific countries (*ST*, 17 April 1997).

7. The Chinese community make up 78 per cent whilst the Indian community 7 per cent of the total population (*ST WOE*, 25 May 1991) of nearly 3 million.

8. In contrast to the PAP, the Malaysian leadership's approach towards multiracialism and equity for the Malays was articulated cogently by Mahathir Mohamad (1970: 68): 'To be equal is to be accepted into every strata of society socially, economically and politically to a degree which more or less reflects the proportion of the population made up of the various groups.'

9. Section 152 of the Singapore Constitution states: 'It shall be a deliberate and conscious policy of the Government of Singapore at all times to recognize the special position of the Malays who are the indigenous people of the island and who are in most need of assistance and accordingly it shall be the responsibility of the Government of Singapore to protect, support, foster and promote their political, educational, religious, economic, social and cultural interests and the Malay Language.'

10. In such societies, the dominant ethnic community suffers from a sense of vulnerability and insecurity as they constitute a minority ethnic community in the region.

11. The orthodox conflict theorists of education (Bowles and Gintis, 1976) tended to underestimate the potential of the education sector as an arena of social reform and resistance. They maintained that schools only served to reproduce existing class, gender, and ethnic divisions and performed a stabilizing function for the economic and political order.

12. The author's interviews with Ahmad Mattar and Abdullah Tarmugi have been included in the Appendix.

13. As Wirth (1960: 36) has aptly stated, 'The most important things ... we can know about a man [*sic*] is what he takes for granted, and the most seldom debated are generally regarded as settled.'

# PART I
# IDENTITY AND IDEOLOGY

# 2
# Indigeneity, Islam, and Living on the Margins of Society

It shall be a deliberate and conscious policy of the Government of Singapore at all times to recognize the special position of the Malays who are the indigenous people of the island and who are in most need of assistance and accordingly, it shall be the responsibility of the Government of Singapore to protect, support, foster, and promote their political, educational, religious, economic, social, and cultural interests, and the Malay language (Section 152, Singapore Constitution).

THE Pan-Malay regional identity, Islamic consciousness, and the socio-economic marginality of the Malay community constitute the predominant interweaving threads which have shaped the Singapore Malay identity. This chapter locates the community's indigenous status within a regional context, the nature of their Pan-Malay identity, and relationship with other Malays in the Malay World. The significance of Islam in shaping Malay identity is also considered. Islam has served to strengthen Pan-Malay identity but has also contributed towards attenuating the indigenous component of Malay identity. The fluctuating importance of Islam and indigeneity in shaping the Malay identity has been influenced by the socio-political circumstances in the region and within the respective nations in the Malay World. The persistence and extent of the socio-economic and educational marginality of the Malay community is discussed with the aim of contextualizing the community's acute sense of relative deprivation. An appreciation of the community's indigeneity, Islamic identity, and socio-economic, educational, and political marginality provides the basis for understanding who the Malays are, where they stand in society, and assists in identifying their concerns and aspirations.

## Indigenous Pan-Malay Identity

The Malays of Singapore share a 'myth' of common descent,[1] elements of a shared cultural tradition, a historical association with a particular region or territory (Smith, 1988; Connor, 1992), and a linguistic affinity with the more than 200 million indigenous inhabitants in the Malay Archipelago (commonly referred to as 'Nusantara' or 'Alam Melayu' [Malay World] by Malays). The regional 'Nusantara' cultural community, generally includes the relatively recent colonial and post-colonial political constructs that have been more recently referred to as Indonesia, Malaysia, Brunei, Singapore, the Philippines, and the southern provinces of Thailand.[2]

Historical records suggest that the Malays initially migrated to the Malay Archipelago from the Asian mainland between 2,000 and 5,000 BC (Bellwood, 1985: 120). Within the Archipelago, historians have recorded extensive movement of indigenous Malays from one *rumpun* (group; region within the larger 'Nusantara') to another. The extensive movement or internal migration to other *rumpun* within the Archipelago was facilitated by trading activities, the rise and fall of dynastic centres of power, and a sense of organic regional identity (Andaya and Andaya, 1982). The fact that a Majapahit Hindu prince, Sang Nila Utama, and his descendants could establish royal houses in Temasek and Malacca from the thirteenth century and then base themselves in the Riau Islands is illustrative of the relative ease in the cultural integration and mobility of Malays from one *rumpun* within the 'Nusantara' to another. The history of Temasek as part of the Srivijaya, Majapahit, and Johore Riau royal houses symbolizes this organic cultural link.

As the indigenous populace of the 'Nusantara' began to be increasingly conscious of their weakening numerical and social standing with the onslaught of Western colonialism, the tribal subethnic *rumpun* identity began to be increasingly overshadowed by a homogenizing Pan-Malay identity. The strengthening of the Pan-Malay indigenous identity occurred despite the fragmentation of the 'Nusantara' by the British, Dutch, and Spanish colonial regimes. In Peninsular Malaya and Singapore, the Pan-Malay identity provided a sense of security against the massive infusions of Chinese and Indian immigrants[3] which served to further weaken their confidence.

The latent Pan-Malay 'Nusantara' consciousness found expression in the anti-colonial nationalist struggle. The reunification of the Dutch East Indies and British Malaya under the banner of 'Melayu Raya' was a popular clarion call particularly amongst early Malay nationalists in Malaya and Singapore.[4] Impassioned by their anti-colonial sentiments, Malay students at the Al-Azhar University in Cairo and the Sultan Idris Training College in Perak in the 1920s nationalistically championed the concept of 'Melayu Raya' (Jarvis, 1991: xcviii). The intermeshing of nationalist and Pan-Malay sentiments was commonly expressed in Malay newspapers such as *Utusan Melayu* and *Majlis* (ibid). In addition to the moral support extended to the Indonesian independence struggle in the post-war era, Singapore Malays played a significant role in assisting Indonesian nationalists based in Singapore. Indeed, the anti-colonial struggles of the Indonesian nationalists, like a 'baptism of fire', acted to heighten the Pan-Malay bond across the Malacca Straits.

Inspired by radical Indonesian nationalists, leftist Malay nationalists such as Burhanuddin, Ibrahim Yaacob, Ahmad Boestamam, and Ishak Haji Muhammad also shared the vision of a unified and strong 'Melayu Raya' in the hope of forging a more egalitarian society. Malay political parties such as the Malay Nationalist Party (MNP) and the Party Raayat Malaya (PRM) were similarly inspired by the concept of a 'Melayu Raya'. This Pan-Malay consciousness was cemented and symbolized when Malayan nationalists such as Ibrahim Yaacob met with the Indonesian nationalists Sukarno and Hatta in Taiping, Perak in 1945 and pledged their loyalty to the single motherland of Malaya and Indonesia (Soenarno, 1959: 234).

The adoption of Bahasa as the national language by Indonesian nationalists not only played a significant role in unifying the diverse linguistic communities in the Dutch East Indies but also served to strengthen ties with Malays who spoke Bahasa in British Malaya. The rise in literacy levels aided in bolstering the Pan-Malay identity as more Malays began to read newspaper and journal articles about the humiliation and injustices suffered by Malays and Indonesians under Western colonial rule.

The failure of the arbitrary colonial boundary divisions in substantially diluting the Pan-Malay identity in Singapore in the immediate decades after the Second World War was noted by Djamour (1959) in her pioneering research on Malay kinship on the island. Djamour noted that despite their regional differences, there existed a strong in-group solidarity amongst Singapore Malays.[5] This in-group solidarity was particularly obvious in Malay interaction with the non-Malay communities. Bedlington (1974: 12) has similarly observed the strong 'Nusantara' identity amongst Singapore Malays who saw their community as a microcosm of the surrounding 'Nusantara'. The strong in-group Singapore Malay solidarity was further intensified by their collective adherence to Islam, their unique status as numerical ethnic minorities in the 'Nusantara', and importantly, their sense of insecurity stemming from their socio-economic marginality in the Chinese dominated island. In a study pertaining to Singapore Malay identity, Nurliza Yusuf (1986: 5–6) observed that Singapore Malays possessed a strong indigenous and regional identity that emanates from their acute consciousness of Singapore's place in the 'Nusantara' or Malay World. This Pan-Malay consciousness was aptly articulated by one of her informants in the following way: 'The Malay Archipelago is like a big house. The Malays in Singapore *hanya tukar bilik dan bukan tukar rumah* (are merely changing rooms and not changing houses).

The process of subsuming the sub-Malay identity in favour of the larger Pan-Malay identity by Singapore Malays is evidenced by their racial identification in the Population Census. As Table 2.1 indicates, the number of Malays who identified as Malays has increased substantially from 1931 to 1980. However, the rise in sub-Malay (tribal) identification in the 1990 Population Census can be attributed to the method by which the 1990 Census Malay categorization breakdown was constructed. Unlike previous years where Census field workers just relied on information given by their respondents as to their ethnic affiliation, the 1990 Census for the first time included the breakdown of Malay, Javanese, Bugis, and Boyanese (*Sunday Times*, 28 June 1992).

TABLE 2.1
Census Breakdown of Malay and Sub-Malay Groups in Singapore

| Malay Groups | 1931 | 1947 | 1957 | 1970 | 1980 | 1990 |
|---|---|---|---|---|---|---|
| Malay | 57.5 | 61.8 | 68.8 | 86.1 | 89.0 | 68.3 |
| Javanese | 24.5 | 21.7 | 18.3 | 7.7 | 6.0 | 17.2 |
| Boyanese | 14.4 | 13.5 | 11.3 | 5.5 | 4.1 | 11.3 |
| Bugis | 1.2 | 0.6 | 0.5 | 0.2 | 0.1 | 0.4 |
| Banjarese | 0.7 | 0.3 | 0.2 | 0.1 | n.a. | n.a. |
| Other Malays and Indonesians | 1.7 | 2.1 | 0.9 | 0.4 | 0.8 | 2.9 |

Sources: Pang, 1984: Appendix m; Sunday Times, 28 June 1992.

The potency of the Pan-Malay 'Nusantara' consciousness amongst Singaporean Malays is demonstrated by their efforts in forging regional links through the promotion of regional forums in Singapore. The Singapore Kemunting Society organized a three-nation (Singapore, Malaysia, and Indonesia) ASEAN drama meeting and the 'Nusantara' Drama Festival in the early 1980s. The Singapore Malay Teachers Union (KGMS) organized the 'Nusantara' Teachers meeting in 1985 whilst the Singapore Malay Journalists Union organized the Nusantara Journalists meeting in 1988 (ST, 11 February 1992). The 'Nusantara' consciousness of Indonesians was demonstrated when they hosted a Malay cultural festival in Batam in 1992. Participants included cultural troupes from Malaysia, Singapore, Brunei, and Indonesia, modern-day state polities which are historically and culturally connected to one another. A six-member Serumpun Chamber of Commerce made up of Malay business chambers from Singapore, Brunei, Penang, Johore, Jakarta, and Batam was formed in 1992. These joint 'Nusantara' activities and initiatives have served to provide Singapore Malays with the cultural security, commercial networks, and psychological morale arising from their identity that is historically and culturally interconnected to the Malay majority in the region.

The organic historical, ethnic, and cultural linkages between the *bumiputra* Malays, the significance underpinning the internal migration of Malays from one *rumpun* of the 'Nusantara' to another, coupled with the fact that modern Malaysia and Singapore have historically evolved from a Malay polity, appears not to be understood by elements within the non-Malay communities. A manifestation of this lack of understanding is the perennial questioning of the indigenous status of Malays in Malaysia and Singapore. During the tumultuous merger period, Lee Kuan Yew (ST, 5 May 1965) challenged the special constitutional position and privileges of Malays in Malaysia by alleging that Malays were no more indigenous than the Chinese, Indians, and other immigrant communities. Motivated either by a political agenda geared towards advancing the political interests of the PAP or sheer ignorance of the region's history, culture, and indigenous populace, Lee referred to

Malaysian Malays of Indonesian descent as immigrants who should be on the same footing as the other immigrant communities[6] (Mauzy, 1983: 32). Similar inferences which cast doubt on the indigeneity of Malays continue to be made by non-Malay Singaporeans and some non-Malay politicians in Malaysia.

## The Islamic Identity

It is generally accepted that Malays in the 'Nusantara' were introduced to Islam after contact with Indian Muslim traders in the thirteenth century (Wertheim, 1959; Fatimi, 1963). However, it was only during the period of the Malacca Empire in the fifteenth century that the conversion of Malays to Islam occurred in large numbers. Thus, for a period of nearly 1,000 years prior to the spread of Islam in the 'Nusantara', Malay rulers and their subjects were predominantly Hindus (Nurliza Yusuf, 1986: 49). In historical terms, most Malays in the 'Nusantara' have thus been Hindus much longer than they have been Muslims. It is within this context that the persisting remnants of Hinduism extant in contemporary Malay cultural practices (or *adat*) and the strength of their ethnic consciousness expressed by many Malays can be profitably understood.

It was only by the turn of the twentieth century that Islamic consciousness began to take on significant political and social manifestations in the 'Nusantara'. Malay political consciousness and nationalist sentiments appeared to inspire and be inspired by the surge in Islamic consciousness. By the early decades of the twentieth century, Islam became an increasingly significant mobilizing ideology shaping Malay nationalism and identity in the face of the large influx of immigrants and the continued imposition of colonial rule. Malay Muslims were not only a dominant ethnic community but also the dominant religious community in the Archipelago.[7] The rising Islamic consciousness, coupled with an increasingly assertive Malay identity, culminated in the signing of the Federation of Malaya Agreement in 1948, which for the first time formally recognized Islam as an essential component of Malayness (Mohamed Suffian, 1972: 291). This set a precedent for the conflation of Malay identity with Islam.[8] Henceforth, to be formally considered a Malay (in Malaysia and Singapore), one must be a Muslim, speak Malay, and observe the traditions of the Malay culture. Indigeneity was, at least in the formal sense, relegated to secondary status in this construction of Malayness.[9] Interestingly, some writers (Nagata, 1979; Hussin Mutalib, 1990: 310) have asserted that when the two gravities of identification (Islam and Malay ethnicity) interact, the Malay identity often emerges as the more potent force of identification.

Some observers (Mohammad, *ST*, 14 May 1989; Hussin Mutalib, 1990: 158) are of the view that the strong ethnic consciousness and traditional pre-Islamic cultural practices of Malays have tainted the Islamic revival, compromised the community's Islamic consciousness, and retarded their socio-economic development. On this basis, they have called for the eradication of the pre-Islamic Malay cultural practices.[10] Such an attitude reveals a lack of appreciation of the fact that the practice of Islam by any community is shaped by specific historical, political, cultural, economic, and social forces that have 'localized' the religion. Just as there are different ways of being Malay and asserting Malayness, there are similarly a variety of ways of being Muslim (Mariam Mohd. Ali, 1990: 129),[11] asserting Muslim identity, and interpreting Islam.[12] For example, the Islamic resurgence in Indonesia tends to be strongly oriented towards issues of poverty and income disparities whilst in Malaysia and Singapore, Islam is more oriented towards questions of ethnic identity (Muzaffar, 1986: 151). Similarly, the practice and interpretation of Islam by Arabs in the Middle East is highly heterogeneous and varies from state to state, with pre-Islamic Arab cultural practices incorporated into contemporary Arabic Islamic customs.

This relatively recent construction of 'Melayu' (that is wedded to Islam) has denied the status of 'Melayu' to non-Muslim indigenous *bumiputra* in the 'Nusantara' such as the Christian Bataks[13] but made it easier for non-indigenous Muslims such as Indian Muslims and Arabs to be theoretically considered as 'Melayu'.[14] However, the persisting importance attached to indigeneity over Islam by Malays has been verified in studies (Nagata, 1979; Nurliza Yusuf, 1986: 57; Long, 1989) which found that those embracing Islam or '*masuk* Islam' are not automatically accepted or considered as '*masuk* Melayu' (to be Malay). Other than a recognition of Malays as the indigenous people of Singapore, the absence of a constitutional definition of a Malay in Singapore has contributed to the salience of indigeneity criteria in the understanding of 'Melayu' by the Malay community.

The ambivalence surrounding the boundary markers of a Malay is exemplified in the numerous administrative definitions and criteria of a Malay in Singapore.[15] For example, the Public Service Circular classification of Malay students eligible for free tuition clearly attached importance to indigeneity by specifically excluding non-indigenous Muslims who are not of 'Malay parentage' and those who 'profess the Islamic faith and are of Pakistan, Arab or Indian origin' (cf. Chew Oon-Ai, 1978: 177). The 1980 Census of Population nebulously defined Malays as 'persons of Malay or Indonesian origin such as Javanese' without reference to Islam. Despite the recommendation of nine Malay MPs to the Select Committee on the Group Representative Constituency (GRC) to include the criteria of Islam in the definition of a Malay (*ST*, 3 February 1988), the Select Committee eventually defined a Malay in non-Islamic terms. According to the Select Committee, a Malay is 'someone who is Malay, Javanese, Boyanese, Bugis, Arab or any other person who is generally accepted as a member of the Malay community by that community' (*ST*, 11 May 1988).[16]

The strong undercurrent of support for raising the significance of the indigeneity criteria in the definition of a Malay in Malaysia was articulated by the former Malaysian Foreign Minister Tan Sri Ghazali Shafie (*ST*, 8 October 1991) at a forum in Kuala Lumpur entitled 'From

Malayan Union to 2020' in October 1991. Ghazali maintained that the current definition of a Malay (wedded to Islam) was too rigid as it excluded other non-Muslim Malays from the Malay World. At United Malays National Organization (UMNO) gathering in Perlis a month earlier, Defence Minister Datuk Seri Najib Tun Razak (*ST*, 8 October 1991) called on the members to look at the concept of an 'archipelago Malay' in a wider sense. Consistent with this inclusive 'Nusantara' identity, it was not altogether surprising that by the mid-1990s UMNO became a *bumiputra* rather than a Malay-based party when non-Muslim *bumiputra* were authorized to become members of the party. It has also become increasingly common for the Malaysian government to refer to the concept of *serumpun* (people of the same stock) in describing its relationship with Indonesia and other Malays in the region. This *serumpun* concept, with its stress on indigeneity, represents an emerging political will to come to terms with and accord greater recognition to the atavistic pre-Islamic relationship, cultural, and linguistic affinities of the Malay people in the region.

### Living on the Margins of Society

Throughout the duration of colonial rule in Singapore, the Malay community persistently remained on the socio-economic, educational, and political margins of society.[17] In the closing decade of the twentieth century, after nearly thirty years since Singapore attained political independence, their status has not changed. This has contributed to the mosaic-like Malay identity that is not only Singaporean, indigenous, and Muslim but also marginal in socio-economic, educational, and political terms. Between the late 1950s and 1982 when the Malay/Muslim self-help body, Mendaki, was established, the PAP government adopted a minimalist approach towards the socio-economic and educational malaise confronting the Malay community while the socio-economic and educational gap between the Malays and Chinese widened significantly (Table 2.2).

As Table 2.2 indicates, the gap between Malays and Chinese in the two highest occupational categories was 2.3 per cent in 1957, which increased to 4.1 per cent in 1970 and 9.6 per cent in 1980.[18] Whereas there was approximately the same proportion of Malays and Chinese in the lower manual category in 1957, by 1980 there were 10 per cent more Malays in this occupational grouping. In the 1980s, the Chinese community continued to enjoy greater occupational mobility relative to the Malay and Indian communities (Table 2.3).

While there was a decrease of 25.3 per cent of Chinese male workers in the income category of less than $400 per month between 1975 and 1980, the proportion of Malays in that income category actually increased by 1.5 per cent in the same period. Whereas there was an increase of 5.9 per cent Chinese male workers in the income bracket of more than $1,000 per month between 1975 and 1980, the increase for Malays was only 1.9 per cent (Table 2.4). During the 1980s, the relative

TABLE 2.2
Malay and Chinese Working Males Aged Ten Years and Over by Occupation (percentage)

|  | 1957 |  | 1970 |  | 1980 |  |
|---|---|---|---|---|---|---|
| Occupation | Malay | Chinese | Malay | Chinese | Malay | Chinese |
| Professional & Technical | 2.8 | 3.6 | 4.4 | 6.7 | 4.6 | 8.3 |
| Admin. & Managerial | 0.3 | 1.8 | 0.3 | 2.1 | 0.8 | 6.7 |
| Clerical | 15.0 | 11.5 | 13.9 | 11.2 | 13.0 | 8.5 |
| Sales | 3.0 | 23.8 | 3.7 | 20.0 | 3.1 | 15.4 |
| Services | 13.7 | 9.0 | 21.6 | 7.6 | 18.0 | 6.2 |
| Agriculture & Fisheries | 10.0 | 7.6 | 5.9 | 4.6 | 3.1 | 2.5 |
| Production & Transport | 42.1 | 42.3 | 45.4 | 43.2 | 53.5 | 43.2 |
| Not classified | 13.1 | 0.4 | 4.8 | 4.6 | 3.7 | 9.1 |
| Total | 100.0 | 100.0 | 100.0 | 100.0 | 100.0 | 100.0 |

Source: Li, 1989: 102.

income levels of the Malay community were discouraging. In 1980, the average Malay household income was 73.8 per cent of the average Chinese household income (Table 2.5). By 1990, the income gap widened as the average Malay household income dropped to 69.8 per cent of the average Chinese household income[19] (Jesudason, 1993: 16).

In the 1980s, the educational gap between Malays and Chinese showed negligible signs of narrowing and in many cases actually widened. At the tertiary education level (Table 2.6), the Chinese appeared to make the most progress with a 2.9 per cent increase of those within this community attending university between 1980 and 1990 compared to an increase

TABLE 2.3
Distribution of Occupations by Ethnic Group (percentage)

|  | Chinese |  | Malays |  | Indians |  |
|---|---|---|---|---|---|---|
| Occupation | 1980 | 1990 | 1980 | 1990 | 1980 | 1990 |
| Professional & Technical | 9.0 | 17.5 | 4.8 | 6.6 | 8.8 | 12.0 |
| Admin. & Managerial | 5.2 | 9.6 | 0.5 | 0.9 | 3.6 | 5.4 |
| Clerical | 16.0 | 13.4 | 14.3 | 15.3 | 13.8 | 11.9 |
| Sales & Services | 22.6 | 14.0 | 20.8 | 14.2 | 28.5 | 12.9 |
| Agriculture & Fisheries | 1.9 | 0.3 | 2.3 | 0.2 | 1.3 | 0.0 |
| Production | 38.6 | 38.3 | 54.2 | 54.8 | 36.0 | 51.3 |

Source: Jesudason, 1993: 17.

TABLE 2.4
Monthly Income of Employed Male Malays and Chinese (percentage)

| Year | Earning <$400 Malay | Chinese | Earning >$1000 Malay | Chinese |
|---|---|---|---|---|
| 1975 | 62.6 | 67.1 | 0.8 | 7.0 |
| 1978 | 78.8 | 53.3 | 1.8 | 8.9 |
| 1980 | 64.1 | 41.8 | 2.7 | 12.9 |

Sources: Ministry of Labor, *Report on the Labor Force Survey*, 1975, 1978, 1980; Li, 1989: 103.

of 1.7 per cent for Indians and a modest 0.8 per cent increase for Malays. Significantly, a majority (55 per cent) of Malay students at university in 1990 were enrolled in the Arts faculty compared to 35.5 per cent for Indians and 25.7 per cent for Chinese. In 1990, only 2.4 per cent of Malay university students were enrolled in the medical faculty compared to 8.2 per cent for Indian students and 6 per cent for Chinese university students (*ST WOE*, 1 May 1992).

The educational gap between Malays and non-Malays is more alarming when the percentage of graduate household heads for each ethnic community is considered. Whilst only 1.4 per cent of Malay households in 1990 were headed[20] by a person with tertiary qualifications, the figure was 9.6 per cent for Chinese households and 6.4 per cent for Indian households (*ST*, 28 November 1992). At the primary and secondary level, the educational gap also appears to have widened between Malays and non-Malays for most of the 1980s. In the 1980s, the percentage of Malay passes, relative to the Chinese, at the Primary School Leaving Examination (PSLE) and the General Certificate of Education (GCE 'O' levels) widened by 3–5 per cent (NCSMMP, 1990: 104). By the early 1990s, the only sign of a narrowing in the educational gap was the 1992 PSLE results where Malay students achieved a 6.5 per cent point increase from their 1991 PSLE results compared to a 1 per cent point increase for Chinese students and a 5 per cent point increase for Indian students (*ST WOE*, July 1993).

The socio-economic disparity between Malay and non-Malay communities is reflected in the level of ethnic representation in non-public housing dwellings. The exclusivity of private dwellings is illustrated by the fact that in 1990, the average monthly income per household in a private dwelling was $6,423, more than double the national average income per household of $3,076 (*ST*, 28 November 1992). The exclusivity of private dwellings is made more germane in view of the fact that 85.7 per cent of the total population in 1990 were living in public housing provided by the Housing Development Board (HDB) (*ST WOE*, 25 May 1991). Only 1.4 per cent of Malays were living in private dwellings in 1990 compared to 11.8 per cent of Chinese and 9.3 per cent of Indians (*ST WOE*, 25 May 1991).

TABLE 2.5
Monthly Head-of-Household Income by Ethnic Group, 1980 and 1990 (percentage)

|  | Total 1980 | Total 1990 | Chinese 1980 | Chinese 1990 | Malays 1980 | Malays 1990 | Indians 1980 | Indians 1990 | Others 1980 | Others 1990 |
|---|---|---|---|---|---|---|---|---|---|---|
| Below 1,000 | 57.6 | 16.0 | 56.9 | 15.7 | 67.7 | 17.0 | 61.6 | 16.7 | 23.2 | 16.6 |
| 1,000–1,499 | 16.7 | 13.6 | 17.1 | 12.8 | 17.5 | 18.7 | 15.3 | 14.4 | 7.8 | 10.8 |
| 1,500–1,999 | 9.6 | 13.5 | 9.9 | 12.7 | 8.5 | 18.3 | 8.8 | 14.2 | 7.2 | 9.3 |
| 2,000–2,999 | 8.6 | 20.1 | 9.1 | 19.6 | 4.8 | 23.4 | 8.1 | 21.6 | 14.6 | 16.4 |
| 3,000–3,999 | 3.5 | 13.0 | 3.6 | 13.3 | 0.9 | 11.6 | 3.0 | 13.0 | 13.1 | 11.8 |
| 4,000–4,999 | 1.7 | 8.2 | 1.6 | 8.6 | 0.3 | 5.6 | 1.3 | 7.4 | 10.6 | 8.9 |
| >5,000 | 2.3 | 15.6 | 1.8 | 17.3 | 0.3 | 5.4 | 1.9 | 12.7 | 23.5 | 26.2 |
| Total | 100.0 | 100.0 | 100.0 | 100.0 | 100.0 | 100.0 | 100.0 | 100.0 | 100.0 | 100.0 |
| Average ($) | 1,228 | 3,076 | 1,213 | 3,213 | 896 | 2,246 | 1,133 | 2,859 | 3,225 | 3,885 |

*Source:* Jesudason, 1993: 17.

TABLE 2.6
Percentage of Each Ethnic Group Attending University

| Ethnic Group | 1980 | 1990 |
|---|---|---|
| Chinese | 1.5 | 4.4 |
| Malays | 0.2 | 1.0 |
| Indians | 1.4 | 3.1 |
| Others | 2.2 | 3.2 |

Source: ST WOE, 1 May 1992.

## Relative Deprivation

To be sure, Malays have made absolute socio-economic and educational gains since the nation's independence in 1965 (Table 2.7). Since the early 1990s, the issue of the community's absolute gains and 'profound achievements' has been regularly emphasized by the PAP leadership and the media (Goh Chok Tong, ST, 16 April 1991; A. Mattar, 16 April 1991). Articles applauding the success stories of individual Malays, coupled with data on the educational and occupational progress, have been a regular feature in the local newspapers (ST, 12 October 1992; ST, 16 May 1993).

Whilst highlighting the considerable absolute gains made by the Malay community, the latter have been repeatedly reminded by PAP leaders not to make interethnic comparisons on the grounds that it was an 'unnecessary distraction' (ST editorial, 8 July 1987), 'counterproductive' (Mattar, ST, 16 April 1991; ST, 11 June 1995), and a 'psychological trap' (Lee Kuan Yew, ST, 7 July 1987) which would only serve to dishearten Malays as they were 'still the same as before or maybe even worse off' (ST, 5 February 1990). In other words, Malays are expected to be content with the community's absolute gains even though they

TABLE 2.7
Absolute Progress Made by Malays (percentage)

| | 1980 | 1990 |
|---|---|---|
| Education | | |
| Children (6–16 years) in school | 85 | 93 |
| PSLE pass rate | 72 | 74 |
| 3 'O' level passes | 48 | 77 |
| Housing | | |
| Home owners | 49 | 92 |
| Living in 4-room or larger HDB flats | 8 | 40 |
| Jobs | | |
| Professional, technical, and managerial | 7 | 11 |

Source: ST, 12 October 1992.

have not made significant gains in narrowing the socio-economic and educational gap with the non-Malay communities. As will be discussed in greater detail in Chapter 4, the PAP leadership's caution against interethnic comparisons is strongly premised on their adherence to the cultural deficit thesis and to a lesser extent to the biological determinist perspective which essentially places blame on the deficient cultural values and innate intellectual limitations of the ethnic community for their marginal status in society.

The PAP government's endeavours towards engendering Malay satisfaction with the absolute gains made and discouraging interethnic comparisons has not attenuated the acute sense of relative deprivation generally felt by the Malay community with their persisting place in the socio-economic margins of society (Nurliza Yusuf, 1986; Li, 1989; Kassim Yang Razali, 1990). As Kassim Yang Razali (1990: 113) put it, 'As a people, they are still far from happy. They do not feel they have arrived.... While the socio-economic statistics might show that they have made progress in relation to themselves over the years, it is when they look at how the Chinese are surging even further ahead that they perceive themselves as not having moved at all. And the perception is what lingers on in their consciousness.' The community's sense of relative deprivation has also been heightened by the unmet expectations of narrowing the socio-economic and educational gap after more than a decade since the establishment of Mendaki in 1982.

That ethnic communities are prone to evaluate their achievements by comparing their socio-economic status with other ethnic/reference groups, who are often better off and in close proximity, is a familiar social phenomenon in multiethnic societies (Martin, 1981: 53–197; Horowitz, 1985: 144) and not at all unique to Malays. As Runciman (1966: 9) observed, as long as a community is aware of the prosperity of another community in society, they will remain discontented and feel relatively deprived until they have caught up with the reference group.[21] The feeling of relative deprivation can be intensified when expectations are heightened under conditions such as a robust economic environment and rises in social mobility rates without any appreciable improvement in the relative position of the marginal community (Runciman, 1966: 19). In a highly competitive society such as Singapore, the level of relative deprivation felt by socially marginal communities is more readily enhanced. Additionally, exposure to ideals such as social justice, equality, and equity have no doubt contributed significantly to feelings of relative deprivation (Horowitz, 1985: 5).

The sense of relative deprivation is just as strongly felt by highly educated and professional ethnic minorities particularly when faced with difficulties in attaining high status jobs and promotions despite their academic credentials (Blau and Duncan, 1967; Wilson, 1978; Marable, 1985; Brennan and McGeevor, 1990).[22] Disheartened by repeated setbacks, they are more likely to be cognizant of the subtle institutional barriers to social mobility, consciously or sometimes subconsciously, practised by members of the dominant ethnic community. The difficulties confronting Malay professionals particularly when seeking employment in local Chinese firms (Bedlington, 1974: 354) may perhaps explain their stronger representation in the civil service and Western multinational corporations. The prevalence of negative stereotyping of Malays (Leong, 1978; Abu Bakar, *ST*, 25 September 1993), when translated into practice, has meant that a Malay job applicant has to be much better qualified than a competing Chinese applicant to be seriously considered for a job in a local firm (NCSMMP, 1990: 84).

Concerned that ethnic minorities have been deprived of fair and equal opportunities in the work-force, many minority professionals have begun to seriously question the contradictions between the theory and practice of the multiracial and meritocratic ideal in the work-force (NCSMMP, 1990: 17; *ST WOE*, 7 December 1991). The frustration of Malay professionals with perceived discrimination and unequal job opportunities in the work-force was articulated by participants at the National Convention of Singapore Malay/Muslim Professionals in October 1990. At the Congress, suggestions were also made for the implementation of anti-discrimination laws and the establishment of a body to monitor discriminatory practices in society. To date, the government has not acknowledged that discrimination against minorities in the work-force is a problem that needs to be seriously addressed in order to preserve the integrity of the nation's meritocratic and multiracial ideal. Preferring to see Singapore as a model meritocratic society, despite grievances of unequal employment opportunities from women's organizations such as the Association of Women for Action and Research (AWARE) (*ST*, 17 November 1993) and ethnic minority communities, PAP leaders such as Lee Kuan Yew (*ST*, 18 August 1987) have commented 'the absence of discrimination on the basis of class, race, language, and religion.... How far one can go in life largely depends on the drive and ability imbued in the individual.' This point has been regularly reiterated by other members of the PAP leadership at public forums and assiduously promoted by the local press.

* * *

The process of ethnic boundary maintenance is dynamic and is subject to the forces of social, economic, and political change and thus varies over time. The formula of Islam, culture, and language in defining the ethnic boundaries in Singapore and Malaysia has conflicted with the historical Malay identity that is strongly regional rather than religious in base. The strong emphasis on Islam in the construction of the Malay identity, particularly since the first half of the twentieth century, appears to have been somewhat attenuated in favour of regional Malay indigenous identity in more recent times. As discussed in greater detail in Chapter 6, this organic regional identity felt by Singapore Malays is not fully understood or appreciated by many within the non-indigenous communities and has been exploited for political purposes. The lack of understanding of the organic nature of the regional Malay identity has also contributed to the questioning of the indigenous status of Malays, despite the constitutional recognition of their indigeneity, and attempts to categorize them as immigrants on par with the other immigrant communities.

Despite the advice of the PAP government to the Malay community to be content with their absolute material gains, the Malays continue to feel an acute sense of relative deprivation stemming from their socio-economic and educational marginality. The government's promotion of the cultural deficit thesis has not been particularly effective as it conflicts with the 'lived realities' of many within the community who are confronted with unequal employment and education opportunities. Indeed, experiences of discrimination and the PAP government's inaction in addressing the issue and its minimalist approach towards addressing the Malay socio-economic marginality, despite a constitutional obligation to do so, may have strengthened the Malay community's sense of relative deprivation and formed the basis of their tenuous relationship with the PAP government.

1. This 'myth' of common descent rarely corresponds with factual history. There is hardly a nation that is not found to be of several ethnic strains (Connor, 1992: 48).

2. Malays particularly in the northern states of Malaysia and those in the southern provinces of Thailand have long shared a sense of cultural and historical bond. This Pan-Malay aspiration was propagated by the MNP during the colonial era. It pronounced 'the right of the Malays in the four southern provinces of Thailand to determine their own future' (cf. Suhrke and Noble, 1977). Early Indonesian nationalists like Sukarno supported the self-determination struggle of the Malay/Muslims of southern Thailand (Pitsuwan, 1990: 162).

3. Singapore Malays were the dominant numerical community until the mid-1830s when the Chinese population began to supersede them in numerical terms (Saw, 1969: 39).

4. The 'Melayu Raya' concept was not particularly well received by Indonesian nationalists for reasons of political expediency during the Indonesian war of independence. Explaining the Indonesian nationalist stance, prominent Indonesian nationalist leader A. H. Nasution stated, 'The union idea including Malaya is not convenient, as we would have to fight both the British and Dutch at the same time' (cf. Cheah, 1983: 265).

5. They commonly referred to themselves as '*saya* Melayu Minang' or '*saya* Melayu Jawa' (Djamour, 1959: 4–6). In this context, 'Melayu' refers to their ethnic group whilst 'Minang' and 'Jawa' refer to their regional ethnic grouping.

6. If this line of argument is logically pursued, some of the northern Chinese dialect groups such as the Hakka who internally migrated to the southern provinces of China should also be conferred immigrant rather than internal migrant status. Similarly, a Tasmanian Aboriginal living on the mainland of Australia would also be an immigrant.

7. Muslim population in ASEAN, 1977.

| Country | Total Population (million) | Muslim Population (million) | % of Muslims |
|---|---|---|---|
| Indonesia | 136.9 | 123.2 | 90.0 |
| Malaysia | 12.6 | 5.5 | 44.0 |
| Philippines | 44.3 | 2.3 | 5.3 |
| Singapore | 2.3 | 0.3 | 15.0 |
| Thailand | 44.4 | 1.7 | 4.0 |
| Total | 240.5 | 133.0 | 55.3 |

*Source*: Weeks, 1978: 499.

8. In the 1891 Population Census of the Straits Settlements, the racial categories were divided up under the headings 'Europeans', 'Eurasians', 'Chinese', 'Malays and other natives of the Archipelago', 'other nationalities', and 'Tamils and other natives of India'. The classification of 'Malays and other natives of the Archipelago', despite the differences in language and religion, illustrates the official recognition of the kinship between Malay peoples (Hirschman, 1987: 562). However, in the 1931 Census, the Achinese, Bataks, Minangkabau, Jambis, and Banjarese were categorized separately from Malays. The Superintendent of the 1931 Census admitted that this breakdown of the sub-Malay communities was based on political considerations as Indonesia and Malaya were colonized by different European powers. Significantly, the children of those listed as Achinese, Bataks, Minangkabaus, Jambis, and Banjarese were classified as Malay (Vlieland, 1932: 84).

9. Indonesia does not have a constitutional definition of a pribumi or Malay.

10. The limited appreciation by some Malays of the fundamental spirit of Islam beyond rituals and outward appearances can be attributed to the agenda of the religious élite and the dominant political forces. To maintain their hegemony, it may indeed be in the interest of the religious and political élite to maintain a conservative and orthodox approach towards Islam which has not incorporated the interpretations of progressive Islamic philosophers and contemporary ideas of social science (Muzaffar, 1986: 185).

11. In her study on Islam in Singapore, Mariam Mohd. Ali (1990: 129) found that Muslims in Singapore are not a homogeneous grouping. They belong to various sects based on different interpretations and constructions of Islam.

12. The major Islamic sects are the Sunni and the Shia. Islamic philosophical schools of thought include the modernists, traditionalists, Islamists, and secularists.

13. Christian Bataks in Singapore are an example of a community that prefers to be identified as Malay despite their non-Islamic status (Nurliza Yusuf, 1986: 56).

14. Many Malays did not identify strongly with the Arab and Indian Muslim community who often acted as representatives and leaders of the Malay/Muslim community during the colonial era. So strong was the Malay resentment against Arabs and Indian Muslims acting as leaders of the Malays that the first Malay political party in Malaya and Singapore, the Kesatuan Melayu Singapura, attempted to resist non-Malay representation of Malay affairs (Andaya and Andaya, 1982: 249). Malays have also remained wary of the situational ethnicities held by these groups, i.e. they were Malays when it benefited them to be Malays (Nagata, 1974).

15. In Singapore, 98 per cent of Malays are Muslims. Malays make up 99.3 per cent of the total Muslim population in Singapore (1980 Population Census of Singapore, Department of Statistics).

16. In an interview with the *Straits Times*, an unnamed community leader stated that the GRC's definition of a Malay, which excluded Islam, may be related to Article 152 of the Singapore Constitution which bestows Malays special privileges such as free education. The government, in excluding Islam, appears to be careful in not extending this privilege to Indians and Arabs (*ST*, 11 December 1987).

17. The Indonesian nationalist Tan Malaka noted that when Raffles first arrived in Singapore, the Malays controlled activities such as industry, sailing, fishing, and trade. In his numerous visits to Singapore in the first half of the twentieth century, Tan Malaka observed the fast deteriorating socio-economic standing of the Malay community relative to the other ethnic groups (cf. Jarvis, 1991: 102–95).

18. In the tumultuous but brief merger and post-merger period from 1963 to 1965, a substantial number of professional, middle-class Malays migrated to Malaysia (Pang, 1984: 123). A large number of Malays lost their jobs when the British military forces pulled out of Singapore in the early 1970s. A disproportionate number of Malays were employed by the British military establishment. The PAP government's policy of minimizing Malay participation in the defence establishment meant that Malays previously employed in the British military establishment could not easily seek employment in the Singaporean military establishment.

19. The household income of the Indian community relative to the Chinese community also fell during this period. In 1980, the average Indian household income was 93.4 per cent and in 1990 it was 88.9 per cent of the average Chinese household income (Jesudason, 1993: 16).

20. The anomalous title of 'head' in the government compiled census data refers to the father or single parent.

21. Unlike the Malay/Muslim self-help body Mendaki, the Indian self-help body Singapore Indian Development Association (SINDA) has clearly cited the more socially and economically successful Chinese community as the reference group for the Indian community. SINDA's goal is for Indian students to match the performance of Chinese students in the major school examinations in twenty years (*ST*, 20 July 1991).

22. Blau and Duncan (1967) have noted that the African-American and white occupational differentials increased at each educational level. In other words, the gap between the occupational levels for the two ethnic communities increased with educational attainments. A tertiary educated African-American tends to be further behind in occupational status than a similarly educated white American.

# 3
# The PAP's Vision for Singapore

What we see depends on how we look, patterns of matter reflect the patterns of our mind.... (Capra, 1987).

THIS chapter investigates the nature, function, and political uses of ideology in maintaining the PAP government's political hegemony in Singapore. In addition to the ideological processes which facilitate consent, the role of coercion and constitutional engineering is also considered. The increasingly conservative ideological orientation of the PAP leadership since the late 1970s, its influence on social welfare policies and impact on lower income Singaporeans is analysed. Importantly, the ideological consistency and linkage between the PAP government's minimalist approach towards social welfare and its minimalist approach towards the socio-economic marginality of the Malay community are highlighted.

### Maintaining the Ideological Hegemony of the PAP

One of the most potent forms of exercising power and maintaining hegemony is the ability to manufacture consent by defining the conceptions, priorities, interests, and desires of the masses and the larger society (Lukes, 1978: 669; Rorty, 1992: 2). In this way, the crude mechanisms of brute force and coercion are bypassed in favour of the subtle ideological and political processes of consent creation. However, in semi-democratic and authoritarian societies such as Singapore, a combination of consent, coercion, and constitutional engineering has been commonly used by governments to maintain their hegemony.

In Singapore, consent is strongly facilitated by the state control of information and knowledge dissemination channels such as the media[1] and education system. This ensures that the social reality, belief systems, and policies promoted by the PAP government are not easily contested. The potential of foreign newspaper and journal publications critically appraising local issues has been restrained by periodic recourse to legal proceedings for publishing offending articles. As financial considerations strongly impact on an editorial policy of newspapers and journals, foreign journalists, like their Singaporean counterparts, have increasingly resorted to self-censorship as a means of avoiding legal tussles with the PAP government. More specifically, the 1986 amendment to the

Newspaper and Printing Presses Act allows the government to renew their annual licence only under stringent conditions. The elaborate licensing laws on publications, broadcasts, and public forums have ensured that opposition parties do not have ready public access to publicize their views. Such laws and regulations have allowed the PAP government to dominate the construction of social reality by penalizing any newspaper or periodical published outside Singapore that contradicts its version of reality.[2] Journals that have fallen foul of the 1986 Act include the *Far Eastern Economic Review*, *Asiaweek*, *Asian Wall Street Journal*, *The Economist*, *Time*, and the *International Herald Tribune*.[3]

In schools, consent is generated through the moral education curriculum which inculcates selected aspects of 'Asian values' to students. Instructively, the 'Asian values' that are strongly emphasized possess a strong Confucian orientation. They include values such as the unquestioning reverence for higher authorities, and respect for scholars and the state (Gomez, 1992: 57). The inculcation of young Singaporeans with conservative and authoritarian values is an effective means of shielding Singaporeans from liberal democratic values commonly accepted in Western democracies.

Confucian values which complement the PAP's 'good government' philosophy have been institutionalized by the adoption of the national 'shared values' in 1991. They include the ideals of nation before community and society before self, family as a basic unit of society, regard and community support for the individual, consensus instead of contention, and racial and religious harmony. In this way, Singaporeans have been encouraged to subscribe to the view that patriotic citizens are those who identify with the 'shared values' which are based on compliance rather than active resistance, and support of a paternalistic style of governance rather than challenging the government (Birch, 1991: 14). As these national values are promoted as non-ideological, attention is deflected away from potentially divisive issues such as class (Clammer, 1991: 7). It is instructive that the values of democracy, social justice, and the rule of law have not been incorporated within the national 'shared values'.

The sheer longevity of the PAP in government, its omnipresence in both public and personal realms, and its political reconstruction from a political party to a national movement in 1982 has facilitated its self-anointment as the creator and embodiment of modern Singapore. The PAP government's corporatist promotion of itself as the organic embodiment of modern Singapore was frankly acknowledged in 1982 in the PAP's journal *Petir*:

The PAP is, of course, a registered political association. But it is more than that. It is not concerned just with winning elections. It is not concerned with political posturing and playing to the gallery. It is concerned with our nation, with our people, with our future and our survival.... The PAP is the vital nerve centre of the entire nation.... Without the PAP, there will be no Singapore as we know it today, as the Secretary General Comrade Lee Kuan Yew has stated, 'I make no apologies that the PAP is the government and the government is the PAP.'[4]

In reaffirming the organic relationship between the PAP and the state, Minister of Information and the Arts George Yeo (*ST WOE*, 8 May 1993) announced at an address to PAP activists in 1993, 'Without the PAP, we would not have been able to complete the last lap. Without the PAP, we will not be able to run the next lap.' The promotion of the organic relationship between the PAP, the state, and the people epitomizes the PAP as the embodiment of the state and the people.

The PAP's purposeful blurring of the boundaries between the state and civil society has provided it with the ability to effectively dominate and control the state, promote its ideological world-view, and fashion the nation according to the lines of a corporatist state (Deyo, 1981; Brown, 1989a; Jesudason, 1993). Characteristic of many corporatist societies, the state is promoted as being independent of class and interest group bias, as understanding and representing the common good (Panitch, 1980: 157–87), and thus accorded with the legitimacy to command loyalty from its citizens. This allows the state to articulate the ideology for the masses rather than reflecting the values of the latter (Carnoy, 1984: 39). The corporatist state framework also allows the PAP to define the national interest from a technocratic and economistic perspective.[5] In this way, politics is kept within the realms of technocratic problem-solving and primarily concerned with issues pertaining to the economy (Jesudason, 1993: 4). Autonomous political participation by civil society is restricted to activities such as voting every few years on the assumption that too much democracy is counter-productive to political stability and economic development.

The efficacy of the Singaporean style corporatist state in executing its political functions has been facilitated by the success and depth of its economic activities. State commercial activities account for 45 per cent of GDP and employ close to 25 per cent of the work-force (Clad, 1989: 143). By the 1980s, the state controlled 42 per cent of the island's retail trade, owned or jointly owned 450 companies capitalized at S$10 billion (ibid), and held reserves of S$52 billion in 1991 (*FEER*, 14 November 1991: 75). The state-run HDB houses 88 per cent of the population and owns two thirds of the nation's land area (Paul, 1993: 295). A strong, intrusive, and extensive state structure is perceived by the PAP leadership as instrumental to the maintenance of national unity and cordial interethnic relations. As the Minister of Information and the Arts George Yeo (1993) put it to delegates at the African Leadership Forum in November 1993, 'A strong state can use force to suppress tribal conflicts but force is a temporary solution. Witness the Soviet Union, Ireland, Yugoslavia, and South Africa. Indeed, the problem today is the decline of strong states.... As the power of the state weakens, tribal divisions naturally reassert themselves.'

In its management and surveillance of the political arena, the corporatist state commonly creates officially established channels where the major segments of civil society can articulate their concerns and demands. This allows the state to exert significant influence over the leadership, agenda, and internal governance of the various corporatized segments in civil society (Collier and Collier, 1979: 493). Public interest groups in civil society that take on issues which are critical of the government are barely tolerated. When the leadership of the Law Society in 1986 offered dissenting views on the Newspaper and Printing Presses (Amendment) Act, which would facilitate the restriction of foreign publications, the PAP government introduced the Legal Profession (Amendment) Bill to force a change in leadership and disciplinary procedures against the Law Society (Tremewan, 1994: 197). In essence, dissenting political activity within civil society is deemed as subversive to the PAP leadership. The control of the National Trade Union Congress (NTUC), various state sponsored ethnic based self-help organizations, and community based bodies such as the People's Association (PA) and the Citizens' Consultative Committees (CCC), exemplifies the subordination of civil society according to the dictates of the PAP government. The positioning of PAP Ministers Lim Boon Heng as the NTUC's Secretary-General and Abdullah Tarmugi as chairperson of Mendaki, and the state monopoly of the local newspaper, television, and radio services exemplifies the corporatist state's subordination of civil society.

This Singaporean corporatist structure presents dissenting community based organizations outside the corporatist paradigm as illegitimate and vulnerable to allegations of subverting national prosperity, being communal or communist inspired. Sustained criticism of government policies is only tolerated by registered political parties and treated with contempt when it is directed by elements within civil society. The PAP government's lack of tolerance for those who have strayed beyond 'acceptable' political and ideological parameters has been acknowledged by Goh Chok Tong (cf. Vasil, 1992: 205–6): 'No matter how well-meaning a person may be, if his [sic] idea is dangerous, it must be clobbered. The protagonist of the idea may also be hurt in the process.' It thus appears that the consultation and consensus formation initiatives under Goh's leadership may not have translated into a qualitative remoulding of the PAP's basic political philosophy. It merely reflects the PAP leadership's recognition of the increasing political sophistication of the general public and the need to invest greater effort in 'selling' its policies.

In typically paternalistic fashion, the PAP leadership has also promoted itself as the moral guardian and preserver of Asian values which have been identified as coming under assault from decadent Western values such as individualism and lack of collective mindedness. These negative Western values if left unfettered are supposed to weaken the social and moral fabric of the fragile 'Singaporean family'. This paternalistic style of governance has been legitimized by relying on Confucianist precepts which bestow political legitimacy to benevolent but authoritarian rule.[6] The PAP leadership's Confucian interpretation and cultural discourse is thus based on 'the forging of an identity from the past and not from the future—and from a past that the majority of Singaporeans have never experienced' (Birch, 1993: 6). Such a discourse serves to guide behaviour by screening and determining the acceptability of ideas and messages derived from overseas (Lowe, 1987: 57). As the state and its political office-bearers are supposed to possess greater wisdom than the general populace, they are deemed to be in a position to determine what the best interests of the public are. Their greater wisdom is often correlated with their impressive academic credentials, management, and administrative record rather than their proven community service experience and political skills.[7] Operating on this logic, the well-educated technocratic members of the PAP leadership, in the tradition of the Confucian Mandarin scholar, are prone to lecture Singaporeans on a wide spectrum of issues ranging from 'the principles of good government' (*ST*, 19 November 1984), 'what is life and society about?' (*ST*, 17 August 1984), to dispensing advice on personal matters such as how many children families should have and what language to speak at home. Issues that are inherently political are regularly presented by the technocrat-cum-politician PAP 'new guard' as primarily economic problems requiring economic solutions to be resolved by the 'experts' rather than the less informed and subjective public.

The implementation of unpopular policies has been rationalized by exploiting the discourse of crisis/survivalism and the discounting of ideology in guiding public policy making. Encouraging other nations to adopt the PAP government's 'non-ideological' approach to public policy, Minister for Information and the Arts George Yeo (1993) stated, at an address to the African Leadership Forum, that 'we try not to get taken in by ideological fads, whether of the socialist or liberal variety. Old fashioned values have served our forefathers well over the cycles of history and enabled them to survive war, flood, and famine. We stick to them.' The ability of the PAP leadership in elevating their 'non-ideological' discourse to the reified status of 'common sense' has been assisted by exploiting the insecurities felt by Singaporeans. Constant reminders of the island's small size, limited pool of talent, lack of natural resources, economic vulnerabilities, cultural contamination from the West, and the inherent vulnerability of a predominantly affluent Chinese nation in a potentially hostile Malay region has assuaged the insecurities of Singaporeans. Time and time again, Singaporeans have been reminded not to take the island's economic well-being for granted, that the 'road ahead is difficult and tough, and there is no certainty that we will win ... it is quite possible that we will lose' (Lee Kuan Yew, *Sunday Times*, 3 January 1993) in the increasingly competitive international and regional economic race. Crisis-laden statements such as 'If we make a mistake there is no safety net underneath' (Lee Kuan Yew, *The Mirror*, Vol. 2, No. 29, 1966), 'What took 25 years to build could be destroyed in 2 minutes' (Lee Kuan Yew, *ST*, 9 June 1990), 'overnight, an oasis may become a desert' (Lee Hsien Loong, cf. Clad, 1989: 144) and Lee Kuan Yew's raising the possibility of a re-merger with Malaysia in June 1996 are periodically enunciated by the PAP leadership. The island's inherent physical limitations and the manipulation of ostensibly non-ideological terms such as 'pragmatism' and 'survivalism' have allowed the PAP government to rationalize policies that are particularly controversial and unpopular (Chua, 1985).

The PAP government's crisis discourse has not only served to maintain a tight leash on the media and civil society but has legitimized the high levels of military spending[8] and the maintenance of a highly sophisticated military arsenal (Huxley, 1991) that has accorded the island the reputation of being the most militarized state in the region. The crisis atmosphere has been maintained by regular military oriented community emergency exercises which include water and food rationing, the construction of underground bomb shelters under housing blocks, and air raid sirens in all neighbourhoods (Tremewan, 1994: 223). In addition to the two-year compulsory military service, the existence of a large civilian reservist force, and the promotion of paramilitary bodies in schools have served to foster militaristic values such as deference to authority, acceptance of directives from higher authority, and an uncritical acceptance of the élitist and hierarchical social structure. Such values complement and legitimize the paternalistic and authoritarian nature of the PAP government.

Singaporeans have been periodically besieged by political crisis in the form of Marxist conspiracies instigated by Christian priests manipulated by exiled Marxists, and American attempts to undermine national stability and communal/religious tensions.[9] An intelligence depletion crisis with the potential of undermining the nation's economic progress was forebodingly announced by Lee Kuan Yew in a 1983 National Day Rally speech. Drawing on eugenics logic, Lee warned of the crucial importance in enhancing the poor procreation patterns of tertiary educated women relative to their less educated counterparts in order to maintain the island's limited talent pool. A language and cultural crisis has also been identified since the late 1970s thereby justifying the ongoing 'Speak Mandarin Campaign' and the promotion of Confucian values. The PAP government's ongoing crisis discourse and its emphasis on the fragility of the state and its economy has nurtured a latent psychosis of insecurity and uncertainty. As the ostensible averter of numerous crises which have threatened to tear away the nation's social fabric, the crisis discourse has arguably served as one of the more effective strategies in maintaining the PAP government's political hegemony. Importantly, it has also facilitated the PAP's monopoly in determining the national interest and engendered the belief that the PAP's political survival is inextricably linked to Singapore's survival (Rodan, 1989: 88).

The PAP government has also been able to sustain a significant level of legitimacy and consent due to the relatively high levels of economic growth, improved standards of living, and material achievements that have been consistently sustained during the post-independence period. For example, between 1965 and 1989, Singapore's GNP per capita increased at an annual rate of 7 per cent in contrast to the world average of only 1.6 per cent. Singapore's official foreign reserves were valued at S$48.5 billion in 1990 (Asher, 1991: 26). Singapore has the highest home ownership rates in the world with 90 per cent of the population owning their homes in 1990 (Census of Population, 1990: 31). Notwithstanding the crisis discourse, Singaporeans have been told to look forward to a standard of living comparable to Switzerland by the year 2000 if the island maintains its high levels of economic growth (Ho, 1989: 68). Particularly in the decades of the 1960s and 1970s, its competent record of economic management invoked a high level of 'pragmatic acquiescence' from the masses.[10] This 'pragmatic acquiescence' has, to some extent, contributed to the focus on a consumerist culture which can have a socially integrative but depoliticizing effect (Gane, 1991: 5). The 'pragmatic acquiescence' and consumerist compulsions which encourage greater readiness to sacrifice democratic participation for material gain is reinforced by the view promoted by the PAP leadership that there is no viable alternative to the PAP's 'good government'. Added to this, the middle classes in Singapore are quite unlike their more liberal oriented and politically motivated counterparts in many parts of Asia. The lack of political savvy of the Singaporean middle classes can be attributed to the fact that up to 40 per cent of educated élite are employees of the state (Brown, 1994: 73). Many appear to be as caught up in materialistic pursuits, accruing status symbols and imbued with *kiasu* (competitive selfish anxiety) traits (ibid.). As most Singaporeans are relatively recent immigrants dating back to only few generations, material and social well-being under PAP rule has, for most Singaporeans, been better than any other time. This is well understood and exploited by the PAP leadership who regularly remind Singaporeans of the years of socio-economic malaise and political turbulence prior to their ascendancy to public office.

The PAP's reliance on the processes of co-optation, and the politicization and stringent surveillance of sections of civil society such as the media, trade unions,[11] schools, and religious bodies (through the 1990 Maintenance of Religious Harmony Bill), has served to emasculate these civic elements which otherwise have the potential of exacting greater political pressure on the PAP government. The periodic use of the Internal Security Act (ISA) and the vindictive treatment of the PAP government's critics, such as Chia Thia Poh,[12] Workers Party chairperson J. B. Jeyaratnam,[13] Dr Bin,[14] Juffrie Mahmood,[15] and Tang Liang Hong[16] (also of the Workers Party), Francis Seow,[17] and Chee Soon Juan from the SDP,[18] have effectively dissuaded many Singaporeans from engaging in political activity that challenges PAP hegemony.

Since the relative electoral decline of the PAP in the 1980s, a spate of constitutional and other political initiatives have resulted in substantial changes to the formal rules in the political system and generating a uniquely Singaporean form of guided democracy. The Non-Constituency Member of Parliament (NCMP),[19] Nominated Member of Parliament (NMP),[20] Group Representative Constituency (GRC),[21] and Elected Presidency[22] initiatives represent a significant reconstruction of the political rules. In 1996, the Community Development Council (CDC) concept,[23] which is expected to divide the island into ten to fifteen geographical regions, was announced by Goh Chok Tong. The above initiatives have been justified by the government on the grounds that they have secured minority political representation, ensured independent political perspectives in parliament, allowed for greater opposition participation in parliament, and facilitated a sound mechanism for the protection of the state's national reserves. However, critics of these initiatives see it as essentially a means of creating a controlled 'opposition' which would undermine the electoral performance of the political opposition.

The hegemony of the PAP has thus been maintained by its reliance on a combination of consent, coercion, and constitutional engineering mechanisms. This approach has been relatively effective because of the ability of the PAP government to sustain high levels of economic growth and material standards of living. However, with the increasing levels of political sophistication and educational attainments of Singaporeans, there appears to be an increasing reliance by the PAP on consent and constitutional engineering mechanisms to maintain its hegemony (Rahim, 1993).

## The PAP Leadership's Perception of Social Inequality

During the tumultuous colonial and post-colonial era, many non-Western political leaders and parties were inclined towards professing a commitment to socialist and social democratic ideals. Concepts of modernity, equity, justice, and science were particularly attractive to indigenous political activists as representing an ideological alternative to archaic manifestations of tradition, economic exploitation, and social inequity associated with colonial capitalist rule. The identification with socialist and social democratic principles was also a means of distinguishing them from the colonial regime and the feudal élite that generally benefited from colonial rule. Many post-colonial leaders such as Lee Kuan Yew were also inspired by and participated in the intellectual discourses during their years as students in the West.

Since the PAP's inception in 1955, its democratic socialist label has always been vague and restricted to generic terms such as establishing 'a more just and equal society' and the creation of employment, subsidized housing, health, educational services, equitable distribution of income, and the improvement in the status of workers and women.[24] In the early years of the PAP's formation, its democratic socialist credentials were particularly expedient as it facilitated considerable organizational and electoral support from the formidable left-wing unions, left-leaning organizations, and their supporters.

Once in office, the PAP did deliver many of its democratic socialist promises. For example, it set out with expeditious zeal to materialize its promise of low cost housing by accommodating 23.2 per cent of Singaporeans with public housing in 1965. Flat rentals were subsidized and fixed at no more than 20 per cent of the average wage earners monthly income (Tan, 1983: 30). Literacy levels improved considerably as free education was provided to each child for the first ten years of schooling and health services were substantially upgraded and heavily subsidized. The PAP's commitment towards expanding educational services was evident in the increased enrolment in government and government aided primary schools from 261,000 to 360,000 between 1959 and 1965 (ibid.: 32). The impressively high level of economic growth in the decades of the 1960s and 1970s was also accompanied by a decline in income inequality (Islam and Kirkpatrick, 1986: 20).

However, the PAP's impressive initiative towards providing social services such as education, health, and housing has been counterbalanced by the implementation of draconian measures such as the 1968 Employment and Industrial Relations (Amendment) Act. Put simply, the Act effectively reduced the rights and benefits of workers whilst enhancing the powers of employers, particularly in matters of recruitment and dismissal.[25] At the same time, the continued detention without trial of those alleged as communists and other political dissidents under the ISA outwardly contravened democratic socialist principles and contributed to the PAP's resignation-cum-expulsion from the Socialist International in 1976.[26]

Particularly after Singapore's expulsion from Malaysia in 1965,[27] the PAP government began to gravitate from its earlier democratic socialist platform which aimed 'to abolish the inequality of wealth' (Petir, 1958: 2) towards the doctrine of economic rationalism which extends market principles to as many aspects of human life as possible. Issues pertaining to social equality and fair distribution of wealth were now of secondary importance. The then Deputy Prime Minister Goh Keng Swee (1972: 285), architect of Singapore's earlier economic industrialization programme,[28] frankly rationalized the nation's priorities in pragmatic terms: 'Our main concern was to generate fast economic growth by any and every possible means.... If unequal distribution of income induced greater savings and investment ... then this must be accepted as the price of fighting unemployment.' By the mid-1960s, reference to the earlier PAP ideals of eliminating social and economic inequalities was conspicuously missing in PAP manifestos and speeches by party leaders. In its place, utilitarian notions of rewarding diligence, merit, and talent to further the nation's economic development became commonplace. Social inequality has also been sanctioned as inevitable, natural, and in the larger interests of society. At a Socialist International meeting in Zurich in 1967, Lee Kuan Yew[29] proclaimed that 'the younger generation in Asia is no longer stirred by the simple slogans of an egalitarian society; more and more, the young are showing that they can strive to be unequal'. Singaporeans have since been encouraged to adhere to the precept 'From each his best, to each his worth' which according to Lee (ST, 9 February 1977) 'has been the basis of our progress'. Indicative of its ideological metamorphosis, the PAP's democratic socialist ideal of creating 'a more just and equal society' was formally discarded in the party constitution in 1982.

Notwithstanding the PAP's ideological metamorphosis, the uneasy amalgamation between the ideals of socialism and the free-market[30] has been affirmed as the central philosophical tenet of the PAP at its annual conventions in the last few years.[31] Employing conservative economic jargon, the PAP's brand of socialism has been rhetorically redefined by Minister of Information, Brigadier-General George Yeo (*ST WOE*, 8 May 1993), at an address to PAP activists in 1993, as a 'supply side socialism which tries to maximize the ability of all human beings and not a demand side socialism which subsidizes and reduces the incentive to effort ... a socialism based on rights and duties and not on rights alone'. Notwithstanding Yeo's affirmation of a 'supply side' socialism, the more frequently touted constellation of affirmations since the 1980s include the ideals of meritocracy, free market, competition, and self-reliance.

Egalitarian ideals have since been unreservedly dismissed as being detrimental to economic and social progress whilst social inequality has been unabashedly lauded in functional terms. In an address to students at the National University of Singapore in 1990, Lee Kuan Yew (*ST*, 25 July 1990) warned of the economic disadvantages arising from an egalitarian society: 'If you want a society which is compassionate, where everybody is entitled to the same medical treatment and the same social benefits ... then you are not going to have a competitive society, which means you are not going to have a productive economy.' He has similarly dismissed those who are concerned with issues pertaining to income distribution and poverty as 'wandering towards peripheral problems' (*Sunday Times*, 3 January 1993) and likening the discourse on equity to 'concentrating on our navels' (ibid.). Lee has warned that the nation's economic prosperity would be jeopardized by a continued focus on such unimportant matters.

Prone to reciting the statements and views of conservative ideologues such as M. Friedman and F. Hayek,[32] Prime Minister Goh Chok Tong and other PAP leaders have consistently reiterated the conservative dogma of accepting social inequality as a necessary outcome of economic development and personal initiative. If social disparities and unequal rewards did not exist, Goh (*ST*, 5 January 1991) has warned that those with initiative, hard work, and skills 'will lose the incentive to contribute their utmost to the economy. Then everybody will be poorer off. Do not grudge them their higher earnings ... for getting the big prizes in the free market.'[33] Such a world-view accepts social inequality as a mechanism to ensure that the most 'capable' and 'talented' hold the vital positions in society. Innovation and initiative are believed to accrue from the competitive drive which inequality generates. The pursuit of selfish individualistic goals will somehow reap benefits for the larger society. Such a perspective justifies economic disparities as a consequence of differences in individual abilities and efforts. The socially disadvantaged are perceived as being afflicted with individual deficiencies, inept value and cultural systems, or maligned by some innate biological deficiency. Little, if any, serious recognition is attributed to institutional, structural, and historical forces which have undermined the opportunities of the socially disadvantaged to compete on an equal footing with other competitors in the 'race' for social mobility.

Despite the significant body of evidence which strongly suggests the importance of material wealth in attaining academic success (Domhoff, 1983; Useem, 1984; Heng Siew Hwee, 1985), and the strong perception of discrimination and unequal opportunities, particularly in the form of the 'glass ceiling', in the workplace by ethnic minorities (Nurliza Yusuf, 1986; Li, 1989; NCSMMP, 1990) and women (*ST WOE*, 19 June 1993), the PAP leadership has none the less persisted with its meritocratic rhetoric which purports that all Singaporeans compete on an equal footing in the meritocratic society. However, their ostensibly dogged commitment to meritocratic principles of fair play has been contradicted by the deliberate policy of excluding Malays, for nearly twenty years, from national service and its continued policy of excluding Malays from the 'sensitive' units of the Singapore Armed Forces (SAF).[34] As will be discussed in Chapters 4, 5, and 6, the existence of numerous cultural, linguistic, and educational affirmative action policies has revealed the contradictions in the meritocratic rhetoric of Singapore's 'level playing field'.

Compared to the parsimonious social welfare expenditure of the state (Ramesh, 1992), its generous spending on various élite programmes has been justified in cold instrumentalist terms. The state's generous funding of élitist programmes for the academically 'able' and well-educated has been metaphorically described by PAP leaders as 'yeast' which helps to 'raise the overall performance of society' (Wong Kan Seng, *Sunday Times*, 19 January, 1992) and a good 'investment' which promises to reap a 'higher than average return' for the country (Goh Chok Tong, *ST WOE*, 18 January 1992). The granting of generous government scholarships that are not means tested to the 'meritorious' is justified as a profitable 'investment' (Lee Hsien Loong, 1992: 18). Consistent with such views, the trickle down theory is regularly evoked on the premise that the net result of having 'invested in the more able' leads to all Singaporeans progressing more rapidly (Lee Hsien Loong, 1992: 22). This instrumentalist conception of society in cold investment terms helps explain the allocation of state resources to the various segments of society. Quite simply, those that are expected to reap 'profitable' investment returns for the nation have been generally accorded greater priority in resource allocation.

## Survival of the Fittest, Servility of the Weakest

The PAP government's economic strategies have reaped relatively high rates of economic growth,[35] impressive per capita income levels,[36] price stability, high employment, a strong balance of payments, impressive levels of official foreign reserves, and established the island as one of the best investment locations in the world.[37] Average monthly household earnings have increased from $692 in 1980 to $1,557 in 1990 (*ST*, 13 July 1991). If such economic indicators are used as a yardstick to measure the success of a nation, then Singapore would be considered a resounding success.

However, a discerning analysis of these impressive economic indicators does reveal that the economic distribution of the island's 'economic miracle' has been somewhat lopsided. After a period of decline in income inequality in the 1960s and early 1970s (Islam and Kirkpatrick, 1986: 20), the income gap between the bottom 20 per cent and the remaining 80 per cent began to widen by the mid-1970s (*ST*, 10 September 1991).[38] Despite the fact that the island's GNP per capita was an impressive $12,765 per month in 1990 (Bello and Rosenfeld, 1992: 1), 75 per cent of the work-force in that year earned less than $1,000 per month (*ST WOE*, 19 October 1991), 54.5 per cent earned less than $800 per month,[39] whilst an estimated 20 per cent earned less than $400 a month (*ST*, 2 July 1990).[40] The 1993 Cost Review Committee (CRC) Report revealed that in absolute dollar terms, the income gap between the top 20 per cent and the bottom 20 per cent had widened from $3,710 per month in 1980 to $6,760 in 1990 (*ST WOE*, 2 October 1993). Singapore's Chief Statistician, Paul Cheung (W. Fernandez, *ST*, 9 October 1993), has suggested that the wage gap is likely to widen in the future because of the globalization of the labour market. This has allowed Singaporean skilled workers to be in a strong bargaining position to command salaries offered in the West whilst unskilled workers have had their wages held down by competition from the poorly paid unskilled foreign workers in Singapore and the less economically developed nations. Added to this, the systematic move towards the structural upgrading of Singapore's technological industrial base has substantially weakened the economic position and bargaining power of the less skilled worker.

Frustration with such income disparities, particularly amongst sections of the lower middle class[41] and low income groups, was acknowledged by Prime Minister Goh at a National Day rally speech in 1991. Citing a government survey, Goh indicated that only 65 per cent of Singaporeans felt that they had benefited from Singapore's economic development whilst 20 per cent said that they had not and 12 per cent did not respond either way (*ST*, 12 August 1991). Despite the sustained levels of economic growth, government surveys conducted from 1990 to 1995 revealed that 50 per cent of Singaporeans felt that their lives had not improved (*ST*, 11 February 1995).

The existence of poverty amidst plenty is acknowledged in Singapore's economic miracle.[42] However, it is not discussed and publicly debated beyond a superficial level. The poor are stereotypically perceived as those who are physically or mentally handicapped, widowed, the aged who have no relatives to care for them, and culturally marred or social deviants who are able-bodied but refuse to extricate themselves from poverty. The latter are commonly perceived to have only themselves to blame for their poverty whilst the former are sympathized with but primarily assisted by their families or private charitable organizations.

Little if any recognition is accorded to the possibility that, other than age, personal tragedy, mental or physical incapacity, and explanations of poverty within the individual and cultural deficit perspective, there may

be an institutional and structural basis which contributes to and helps perpetuate poverty. The absence of this institutional basis to poverty in the public discourse was clearly exemplified by the government sponsored Committee on Destitute Families (1989) which characteristically limited the causes of poverty as being identified with:
1. physical, intellectual, and mental dysfunction;
2. socio-psychological dysfunction, and;
3. family structure dysfunction.

That socio-psychological dysfunction may be a symptom rather than a cause of poverty is not seriously acknowledged. These assumptions have however been contradicted by studies (Cheah, 1977; Asher, 1991; Blake, 1991; Ramesh, 1992) which have highlighted the significance of institutional and structural factors in contributing to and perpetuating poverty in Singapore.

Cheah Hock Beng's (1977: 42, 77) insightful study of poverty in Singapore revealed that poverty actually increased three and a half times between 1954 and 1973. As Singapore was building up its reputation as an economic success story par excellence, 33 per cent of Singaporean households did not have incomes which sufficiently provided basic needs and were living in poverty in 1973.[43] By 1985, one in six Singaporeans lived on a combined family income of less than $500 per month with 16 per cent living below the official minimum household assistance or poverty line.[44] Of particular concern was Cheah's disclosure that the poor were not primarily those restricted to the aged, widowed, and handicapped but that the majority were in fact the working poor. They tended to be those who did not have a Central Provident Fund (CPF) savings account to fall back on, due to their part-time or casual employment status, and other low wage workers such as domestic servants whose wages often fall below the poverty line but are not protected by a minimum wage law. Myrna Blake's (1991: 5) study of poverty in the Malay community similarly found that many Malay families in poverty were working but earned wages below the poverty line. They often opted for casual and part-time employment primarily because of the higher non-CPF[45] deduction wages, even though the long-term financial security of their family upon their retirement was jeopardized.

Only the absolutely destitute who are chronically ill, aged, handicapped, or vagrant are entitled to minimal assistance from the state, consistently below the Minimum Household Expenditure (MHE) or poverty line, offered by the Ministry of Community Development's Public Assistance (PA) scheme.[46] For example, in 1988 the PA rates for more than one-person households were about 25 per cent lower than the MHE (*ST*, 25 March 1988). Further, the PA's stringent criteria assures that it is understood by the general community not as a scheme which provides benefits to all poor families. In 1989 only 53 per cent of PA applicants were successful (*ST*, 24 March 1990). The stringent eligibility criteria and gross inadequacy of PA rates have even been criticized by then PAP MP for Ulu Pandan Dixie Tan (*ST*, 21 June 1987) for not doing credit to a country of Singapore's affluence.

The government's rendering of welfare assistance only to those deemed to be destitute and in chronic financial distress has meant that privately funded welfare bodies such as the Singapore Council of Social Services[47] (SCSS) have had to cater for the bulk of the needs of the poor. This is borne out by the fact that the government spent $3.4 million on PA whilst $8.6 million were spent by private charitable organizations in 1987 (Ramesh, 1992: 5). Recent trends in the social welfare arena suggest that the PAP government is not only minimizing but systematically privatizing its welfare services. In its place, the family, national community, ethnic community, and the market (Ramesh, 1992: 1) have been spurred to take on the responsibility of addressing the needs of the poor. The diminution of the state's responsibilities towards the needy is clearly demonstrated by the decline in expenditure on social security[48] as a proportion of total government expenditures from 8.3 per cent in 1972 to 6.8 per cent in 1989 (IMF, 1990, 1991). The privatization initiative in the health sector has also led to a drop in the government's share in the total health expenditure from 40.1 per cent in 1970 to 27.4 per cent in 1989 (Phua, 1990: 20), and a reduction in subsidy levels and the share of low and non-paying beds in government hospitals (Asher, 1991b: 13).

The trend towards the privatization of welfare and social security services[49] rests on the PAP leadership's conviction that Singaporeans have been too dependent on the state for their basic needs. They assert that this dependence has adversely effected the productivity of workers and loyalty to employers (Lim, 1989: 81). The PAP government has also rejected the view that it is primarily the responsibility of the state to assist the disadvantaged by arguing that state responsibility was better directed at providing conditions for full employment and educational infrastructure which would then allow the populace to acquire marketable skills (Asher, 1991b: 4). Welfare programmes are to be kept to a minimum in the belief that the alternative would spell social and economic disaster for the resource poor island.[50] In addition to welfare being presented as a catalyst of social and economic calamity, it has been said to go against the natural 'instinct to look after oneself' (Lee Kuan Yew, *ST WOE*, 23 March 1991). Using a combination of the 'survival of the fittest' and 'charity' logic, Lee has frankly stated that there will always be losers in society and that it was the altruistic amongst the successful, rather than the government, who should assist the losers. So committed is the PAP leadership towards ensuring that a future government does not attempt to use the state's assets to finance a more generous welfare programme that the provisions attached to the 1991 Elected Presidency Bill have, *inter alia*, allowed for the President to veto excessive government spending on social welfare.

Since the 1980s, the trend towards the privatization and decentralization of social services has been explained by Lim (1983: 759) as a means of divesting the government from the loss making functions of government such as health care, education, and subsidized housing. The emphasis now is not to view these social services as a social investment but as a commodity to be sold in the market place for profit (Lim, 1989: 173). As the overseas experience shows, the privatization and decentralization of social services and health care generally results in a spiralling of health costs.[51] Singapore's experience with the privatization of health services has proved to be no different in terms of the appreciable cost spiral. Between 1984 and 1989, medical costs rose annually by 3.5 per cent and total expenditure on health by 11 per cent, compared to the Consumer Price Index (CPI) increase of only 1 per cent (Phua, 1990: 19). Suffice to say, these cost rises have caused hardships and a heightened sense of insecurity particularly amongst the aged and lower income groups.

The imposition of the 5 per cent Goods and Services Tax (GST) from 1994 is likely to further undermine the economic standing of the aged and low income families. Touted as a means of making the island's economy more competitive by reducing corporate and income tax[52] without running into deficit, the reduced corporate tax is expected to improve Singapore's appeal particularly to foreign investors.[53] With the GST, the tax burden has been shifted from the corporate sector to the ordinary citizen who will now have to contend with higher prices for many essential items and general goods and services. Widespread public requests to exempt essential items such as food, transportation, and medical charges in the low class hospital wards so as to relieve some of the financial pressure on poorer Singaporeans have been rejected by the government (*ST WOE*, 6 March 1993). In justifying the government's intractable stance, S. Dhanabalan (Minister of Trade and Industry) stated that the GST was a means of reminding people that they could not pressure the government to provide social services without shouldering the financial costs through higher taxes (*ST WOE*, 6 March 1993). Despite the provision of some compensatory tax rebates designed to offset the effects of the GST,[54] the aged and those who are not economically active[55] are expected to be adversely affected by the higher cost of living with the GST (Ibrahim, *ST WOE*, 27 February 1993). The tax rebates are also of minimal significance to the aged and those not engaged in paid work as most pay little or no income tax and do not greatly benefit from the higher reliefs promised by the government (ibid.).

\* \* \*

The PAP's ideological orientation appears to have increasingly gravitated from an ostensible commitment to democratic socialist principles in the late 1950s and 1960s towards a more ideological conservative worldview as its political hegemony became more entrenched from the 1970s. In addition to the processes of coercion and constitutional engineering, the PAP government has been able to maintain its hegemony by assiduously deploying a conservative ideological world-view which rationalizes its paternalistic style of governance. In particular, the deployment of concepts such as the superiority of (East) Asian cultural values over

Western cultural values, the prioritization of economics over politics, and the crisis discourse have effectively served the political interests of the PAP government.

Its promotion of the philosophy of self-help, anti-welfare discourse, and the trend towards privatizing social welfare has established the ideological foundations for minimizing social welfare spending and assistance to the needy. Far from being non-ideological and pragmatic, the PAP government's social welfare policies are distinctly ideological and consistent with its conservative philosophical world-view. Its ideological discourses have had the effect of systematically legitimizing the social marginality of individuals, the poorly educated, the disabled, the aged, and communities like the Malays who, after more than thirty years of PAP rule, have remained on the socio-economic and educational fringes of society.

1. Since the early 1980s, the local print media has been under the control of the Singapore Press Holdings of which the government is a major shareholder. Local journalists tend to exercise self-censorship on sensitive issues (Asiawatch, 1990: 47).

2. Singaporean journalists must seek permission from their employer to publish in a foreign publication and their employer must then inform the appropriate government ministry (Birch, 1993: 34).

3. In 1985, contempt charges were filed against the *Asian Wall Street Journal*. In 1987, the *FEER*'s circulation was reduced from 9,000 to 500 because of a report concerning the ISA detentions that year. The *Asian Wall Street Journal*'s circulation was also restricted from 5,000 copies to 400 in 1987 (Asiawatch, 1990: 51). In 1986, *Time*'s circulation was restricted and in 1987, *Asiaweek*'s circulation was reduced from 10,000 to 500 (ibid.). In 1993, *The Economist* suffered the same fate as the others whilst the *International Herald Tribune* in August 1995 was ordered by the Singapore High Court to pay S$950,000 over an article it published in August 1994 alleging the existence of 'dynastic politics' in Singapore. In January 1995, it was also found to be in contempt of court over an article it published in October 1994 by Singapore-based academic Christopher Lingle which suggested that the judiciary in some Asian countries was 'compliant' (*ST*, 7 August 1995).

4. *Petir*, Editorial, December 1982: 3.

5. The submerging of political issues within economic realms was acknowledged by Lee (1962: 83) in the early 1960s: 'Political problems ultimately mean the problem of how we make our living, how we can give everyone a fair go and equal chance to study and work and have a full life.'

6. The Confucianist theory of government generally sees the ruler as acting according to *li* (the rules of proper conduct) and *ren* (benevolent love) whose subjects obey and emulate the ruler. It dictates that reforms come from the capable subordinates appointed by the righteous ruler (*FEER*, 26 October 1979).

7. MacDougall (1975: 37–8) has noted that technocrats are commonly placed in ministerial positions in authoritarian societies as they do not possess a strong political constituency, often lack political ambition, and are loyal to those who co-opted them into politics.

8. The state spends nearly US $1 billion a year in defence (Clad, 1989: 144). Singapore's military budget as a percentage of GDP is higher than that of the neighbouring military dominated regimes of Indonesia and Thailand (Vatikiotis, 1993: 62).

9. In 1987, twenty-two Singaporeans were detained under the ISA for their alleged involvement in a Marxist-style conspiracy against the state. Many of those arrested were Christian community activists.

10. Hill (1990: 3) has argued that the foundation of social stability in advanced capitalist societies has been non-normative and largely economic in character.

11. The symbiotic relationship between the NTUC and the PAP government is openly acknowledged. Eight out of twenty members in the Executive Committee of the NTUC are PAP MPs. Until September 1993, the Deputy Secretary-General of the NTUC was PAP Minister Lim Boon Heng whilst the Secretary-General of the NTUC was the Deputy Prime Minister Ong Teng Cheong (Rosa, 1990: 492). Ong's elevation to the presidency paved the way for Lim's appointment as Secretary-General of the NTUC. Opposition party activists have been prevented from remaining as officials of NTUC branches. For example, two taxi drivers with the NTUC taxi co-operative were forced to resign because they stood as opposition candidates in the 1988 general elections and thus did not fully comply with the NTUC by-laws forbidding members from being involved with any organization whose aims were deemed to be incompatible and prejudicial to the NTUC (ibid.: 495).

12. A founding member of the now defunct Barisan Socialis, Chia had been detained without trial under the ISA for thirty years. According to Amnesty International, he is one of the longest serving political prisoners in the world. 'Released' to Sentosa Island in 1989, the PAP government's case against Chia is questionable as it has not provided any concrete evidence to back its claim that Chia had plotted to partake in unconstitutional acts to subvert the state (Asiawatch, 1990: 12). He has recently been allowed to travel overseas but under stringent terms.

13. He was debarred from Parliament in 1985 following his conviction for perjury. The Privy Council has found him innocent of the charges, stating that 'they [Jeyaratnam] have been fined, imprisoned and publicly disgraced for offences of which they were not guilty' (cf. Asiawatch, 1990: 59). Not surprisingly, the Privy Council's judgement was ignored by the PAP government. As with other opposition politicians, he has been subjected to numerous libel suits initiated by PAP politicians for remarks made against the PAP during election rallies.

14. A leading member of the Workers Party, Dr Bin narrowly lost the Changi seat in the 1991 general elections. He has since been debarred from practising medicine in 1992 on the grounds that he had over-prescribed sedatives to his patients.

15. He has been accused of being a Malay chauvinist and communalist in the 1991 elections when he stood in a Workers Party GRC team in Eunos against the PAP.

16. During the January 1997 elections, the PAP leadership accused Workers Party candidate for Cheng San GRC Tang Liang Hong of being an anti-Christian Chinese chauvinist. Shortly after the elections, Tang, fearing that he would be detained under the Iinternal Security Act, fled the country but was promptly served with a series of defamation suits by leading PAP politicians.

17. Former Solicitor-General Francis Seow was detained under the ISA, convicted of tax evasion and susequently fined and disqualified from taking up an NCMP seat after he narrowly lost in the Eunos PAP GRC team in the 1991 general elections. Seow served as a counsel for two of the twenty-two arrested under the ISA in 1987. In May 1988, Seow was detained on the grounds that he was in 'close contact' with US diplomat E. Hendrickson. As with the other ISA arrests, no concrete evidence was advanced to substantiate the government's allegations that Seow acted improperly in his contacts with Hendrickson. For a detailed account of Seow's detention, read F. Seow's, *To Catch A Tartar* (1994).

18. National University of Singapore lecturer and Secretary-General of the Singapore Democratic Party, Chee Soon Juan stood against the PAP GRC Marine Parade team in the 1992 by-elections. He was sacked from his university position in April 1993 for allegedly misusing his research funds.

19. The Constitution was amended in July 1984 to provide for the creation of the NCMP. Up to three parliamentary seats were from then on available to the highest opposition losers in the general elections.

20. Legislatively created in 1989, six NMPs were to be appointed by the President on the advice of a Special Select Committee appointed by Parliament.

21. The GRC Bill was introduced in 1987. Voters would have to choose among a team

of MPs in the GRC constituencies. At least one member of the GRC team has to be an ethnic minority.

22. The Bill affords wide powers to the elected President such as the ability to veto budgets, reject appointees to senior posts such as the Chief Justice, Attorney-General, Auditor-General, members of the Public Service Commission, and Chief of the Defence Force. The President is given the powers to oversee the national reserves, the administration of the Internal Security Act, the Maintenance of Religious Harmony Bill (1990), and the Corrupt Practices Investigation Bureau. The stringent qualifications for the office of the President effectively rule out Singaporeans not from the PAP or the establishment.

23. Goh claimed that the CDCs would help to revive the community spirit of mutual help found in early Singapore when the kampong *penghulu* (chief) and clan leaders looked after the welfare of their constituents. The CDC is expected to serve as an umbrella body, overseeing existing grass roots bodies such as the Citizens' Consultative Committees, the Community Centre Management Committees and the Residents' Committees (RC). The CDC chairperson will be conferred the title of mayor if he or she heads a town council in charge of more than 150,000 residents and is an elected MP (*ST WOE*, 31 August 1996). Opposition MP Chiam See Tong has suggested that the CDC proposal is essentially a means of entrenching PAP control (ibid).

24. Refer to the PAP's manifesto, 'The Tasks Ahead' (1959).

25. It increased working hours, reduced public holidays, paid holidays, rest days, and sick leave. Trade union powers were curtailed as promotions, transfers, retrenchments, dismissals, reinstatements, and work assignments were excluded from collective bargaining (Rodan, 1989).

26. Refer to Devan Nair's 1976 'Socialism That Works: The Singapore Way' (1976), for a spirited defence of the PAP's democratic socialist credentials. After his 'departure' from Singapore amidst an acrimonious stream of allegations against him by the PAP leadership, Nair's perception of the PAP is less savoury. In Seow's book (1994: xx, xxvii) on his detention under the ISA, Nair wrote, 'Today I an obliged to eat a good number of words I uttered in London in 1976 ... his (Lee Kuan Yew) most unpardonable failure is the crass betrayal of the ideal which launched the People's Action Party into political orbit—that of an equal, multiracial, democratic society.'

27. The PAP government was faced with the formidable task of resolving the high unemployment levels which averaged between 7 to 12 per cent by the mid 1960s. This was further compounded by the fact that new jobs had to be created to meet the labour force growth of 3.5 per cent per annum between 1966 to 1976 largely as a result of school leavers entering the work-force (*ST*, 16 December 1966). The disclosure by the British government in 1968 of its intention to withdraw its bases, which contributed to 20 per cent of Singapore's GDP and employed 40,000 workers, meant that the island's already high unemployment levels would be further compounded (*FEER*, 5 August 1972) and further complicated the PAP government's task of economic reconstruction.

28. He continues to play an influential role in economic policy making and holds important executive positions in government statutory bodies.

29. Speech at the 1967 Council Meeting at the Socialist International, Zurich, Singapore: Ministry of Culture, 1967.

30. Singapore is more aptly characterized as a system based on command capitalism rather than free-market capitalism.

31. The other philosophical tenets affirmed at the PAP's 1992 convention included democracy, multiracialism, and international co-operation (Henson, 'PAP Convention Is No Party', *ST WOE*, 23 November 1991).

32. However, conservative free-marketeers such as Hayek are firmly opposed to a large and interventionist role of the state in the social and economic spheres. This is characteristic of the PAP-dominated state in Singapore.

33. While the élite administrative service received salary increases ranging from 13 to 20 per cent in 1989, other civil servants received increments of 4 per cent. However, Cabinet Ministers received larger salary increases of 60 per cent (Rosa, 1990: 502). The Prime Minister of Singapore earns US$365,000 per annum. This is 50 per cent more than the annual salary of the President of the United States of America (ibid.). By 1993, the

Singaporean Prime Minister's salary had increased to S$96,000 per month or S$1,152,000 a year (*ST*, 4 December 1993). The gross monthly salary of Ministers and senior civil servants as of 1993 are as follows:

| Position | Salary (S$) | Position | Salary (S$) |
| --- | --- | --- | --- |
| Prime Minister | 96,000 | Superscale D | 20,000 |
| Deputy Prime Minister | 84,000 | Superscale E1 | 16,000 |
| Minister | 64,000 | Superscale E | 15,000 |
| Superscale C | 29,000 | Superscale F | 14,000 |

*Source*: *ST*, 4 December 1993.

34. This issue will be discussed in greater detail in Chapter 4.

35. Average GDP growth has been around 9 per cent since independence (Wong, 1990: 3). Economic growth of 5 per cent is predicted for the decade of the 1990s (Huxley, 1992: 283).

36. Per capita income rose from S$1,330 in 1960 to S$9,293 in 1980 (Chen, 1984). In 1990, GNP per capita stood at US$11,300 (Huxley, 1992: 282). Singapore is also the financial centre of the region with a foreign exchange turnover of approximately $24 billion per day (Coplin et al., 1990).

37. In 1991, Singapore retained its top spot as the most competitive NIC for the third consecutive year in the World Competitiveness Report. The Report is carried out by the Geneva-based International Management Development Institute and the World Economic Forum (*ST WOE*, 22 June 1991).

38. By 1983, the average income of administrative and managerial personnel was five times more than those of production and service personnel (Islam and Kirkpatrick, 1986; 120–1).

39. Singapore, Ministry of Labour (1990), *Report on the Labour Force Survey of Singapore, 1989*.

40. The average hourly rate of Singapore's production workers is S$3.50 (Bello and Rosenfeld, 1992: 313). Singapore's trend towards widening income gaps and social inequality parallels similar trends in other NICs such as Korea. In the case of the latter, income inequality declined in the first phase of the Export Oriented Industrialization (EOI) programme in the 1960s leading to greater opportunities for social mobility. Thereafter, the increasingly sophisticated nature of the economy saw greater differentials in skills and remuneration (Khoo, 1985: 129–48).

41. The emergence of the 'middle class squeeze' has been asserted by academic Tan Kong Yam. He has claimed that this class comprises 20 per cent of the population who earn too much to benefit from the subsidies, yet too little to outbid the top 10 per cent for private property, cars, and other limited resources. The rises in education and health costs have also adversely impacted on them (*ST*, 29 July 1991). For example, whilst the consumer price index rose by 3.8 per cent for the first half of 1991, cost in public transport rose by 19 per cent, health charges by 9.9 per cent and educational charges by 6.8 per cent (*FEER*, 10 October 1991).

42. In 1990, Prime Minister Goh Chok Tong frankly stated that the poor or 'underclass' comprised 10–15 per cent of the population (*ST*, 12 February 1990).

43. It has been estimated that as high as 30 per cent of households in Singapore lived below the poverty line in the 1980s (Clammer, 1987: 192).

44. The government has calculated that the minimum household subsistence for a family of four amounts to $365 per month in 1985 (*ST*, 21 April 1985).

45. The CPF is a superannuation scheme which is the primary means of income maintenance for retired workers. It is a tax-free compulsory savings scheme which requires employers and employees to contribute a fixed percentage of their wages to a CPF account. In 1992, the CPF contribution was 18 per cent for employers and 22 per cent for employees. Withdrawal is permitted at fifty-five years or for the purchase of housing and approved investment incomes.

46. A 1988 Ministry of Community Development sponsored Report by the Committee on Destitute Families frankly acknowledged that the existing PA allowance was grossly insufficient as it fell below the already conservative MHE. As of 1991, it was set at $140 per month for a single person, $270 per month for a family of three adults, and $345 per month for a family of one adult and two children (*ST*, 26 February 1991).

47. The SCSS established the Community Chest in 1983 as a financial basket which centralizes the collection and allocation of funds to private welfare organizations.

48. Its share of the total health expenditure also fell from 39 per cent in 1960, 37.4 per cent in 1985 to 27.4 per cent in 1989 (Singapore, Department of Statistics, *Yearbook of Statistics*, 1990).

49. Social security refers to services aimed at maintaining income and assisting the costs of receiving health care and raising children. It does not include education and housing programmes (Ramesh, 1991: 1).

50. Wilensky's (1981: 191–2) survey of the relationship between social welfare spending and social security revealed that the bigger welfare spenders and taxers such as Germany, the Netherlands, Norway, and Belgium were in the better performing half of the nineteen richest democracies from 1950 to 1974. They enjoyed good average annual growth per capita, low unemployment, and medium to low inflation. By contrast, the lower welfare spending nations such as the United States, Canada, Australia, United Kingdom, and New Zealand all suffered low growth per capita and a mixed performance by other measures.

51. Organization for Economic Co-operation and Development, *Reforming Public Pensions*, Social Policy Studies No. 5, Paris: OECD, 1988, p. 36.

52. The corporate tax was reduced from 30 per cent to 27 per cent and income tax reduced by 3 per cent.

53. The corporate tax in Hong Kong is 17.5 per cent, Taiwan 25 per cent, Thailand 25 per cent, and Brazil 25 per cent. However, countries with higher corporate taxes include China at 33 per cent, Malaysia 34 per cent, and Mexico 35 per cent (*ST WOE*, 27 February 1993).

54. The offsets include rebates for properties with annual values of less than $10,000, 5 per cent tax on domestic telephone bills were removed, Public Utilities Board (PUB) bill reduced from 5 to 2 per cent, entertainment duty removed, rebates on service and conservancy charges for one, two- and three-room flats, rebates on HDB flat rentals, Edusave grants (vouchers) increased from $50 to $100 per year per student, Public Allowance up by $5 to $15, and financial aid to the poor through the Citizen Consultative Committees (CCC) (*ST WOE*, 27 February 1993).

55. Eight out of ten of those above sixty years are economically inactive (that is, not engaged in paid work).

# 4
# Perceptions of the Malay Marginality

The eyes of the ... least advantaged are the eyes that matter when it comes to looking at justice (K. Marx).

THIS chapter explores the political motivations, socio-cultural orientation, and ideological biases of the proponents of the cultural deficit thesis from the British colonial era to more contemporary times. The cultural deficit thesis has also acted as an ideological springboard for the PAP leadership's eugenics and biological determinist ideas. Such ideas serve to further rationalize the minimalist social assistance approach of the PAP government towards the Malay community and other socially disadvantaged Singaporeans. Importantly, the cultural deficit discourse has strengthened long-held negative stereotypes by the non-Malay communities towards the Malays and engendered limited public empathy for the Malay marginality.

## The Legacy of Orientalist and Colonial Perceptions of the Malay Community

Contemporary perceptions of Malay society have been strongly influenced and shaped by colonial and orientalist discourse on Malays.[1] The negative cultural stereotypes promoted by colonial administrators and orientalist scholars commonly characterized Malays as endowed with traits of complacency, indolence, apathy,[2] infused with a love of leisure, and an absence of motivation and discipline. They were generally deemed to be lacking in the highly esteemed material pursuits of commercial enterprise which the immigrant communities possessed.[3]

Such unflattering cultural characterizations served to justify the 'white man's burden' associated with colonial rule and obscure the pivotal role of colonial policies in marginalizing the Malay community in socio-economic and educational terms.[4] Orientalist historiography has generally failed to highlight the fact that Malays were discouraged by the colonial authorities to cultivate cash crops such as rubber by the implementation of a 'no rubber' clause imposed as a condition in the alienation of agricultural land to Malays (Shaharuddin Ma'arof, 1988: 51).

They generally accorded scant recognition to the existence of successful Malay trading communities, such as the Bugis and the Minangkabau, who commercially dominated the prosperous ancient trading ports of Temasek and Malacca centuries prior to the advent of colonialism. Orientalist historiography has also failed to acknowledge the vigour of Malay urban institutions and organizations in areas such as Kota Baru in Kelantan where colonial rule was less intrusive and the immigrant population smaller (Nagata, 1979: 82). It is particularly instructive that Malay traders, entrepreneurs, and professionals were also more successful in such areas compared to the cities on the west coast (ibid.: 83).

The ideology of Malay cultural deficiency gained added currency when prominent Arab and Indian dominated Muslim community organizations embraced it. Generally stationed above Malays in the colonial social hierarchy and often on cordial terms with the colonial authorities, many non-Malays who held leadership positions in the Muslim community were prone to criticize Malays for being lazy, quarrelsome, and complacent. Exemplifying their patronizing attitude towards Malays, the Arab-run Malay language paper *Al-Imam* in 1907 called on Malays to be better Muslims in order to elevate their weak socio-economic standing (Weyland, 1991: 225).

During the colonial era, notable Malay personalities such as Zainal Abidin bin Ahmad (or Za'aba) (1923) conferred credibility on the ideology of Malay cultural inferiority by incorporating its logic in their writings. Having internalized the colonial discourse on Malays, they severely chastised Malays for their deficient cultural values. Not surprisingly, their critiques of Malay culture and attitudes were warmly received by the colonial authorities as they served to legitimize the colonization of Malaya (Shaharuddin Ma'arof, 1988: 25). Articles by notable personalities such as Za'aba (1923) commonly appeared in the local press contemptuously castigating Malays for being 'poor in money, poor in education, poor in intellectual equipment and moral qualities.... Their literature is poor and unelevating ... their outlook in life is poor.... In short, the Malays cut poor figures in every department of life.'[5] Others like Abdullah Munshi were particularly lavish in their critique of the negative influences of feudalism in Malay society but conveniently ignored the role of British colonialism in preserving Malay feudalism and its adverse impact on the socio-economic development of Malays (Shaharuddin Ma'arof, 1988: 76).[6]

This tradition of self-vilification and self-condemnation by some Malays during the colonial era has been sustained in the more recent works of UMNO and PAP Malay politicians such as Senu Abdullah's *Revolusi Mental* (1971),[7] Mahathir Mohamad's *The Malay Dilemma* (1970), and Wan Hussein Zoohri's *The Singapore Malays: The Dilemma of Development* (1990). In echoing and perpetuating the ideology of Malay inferiority, they revealed their acute inferiority complex (Shaharuddin Ma'arof, 1988: 62).

The ideology of Malay cultural inferiority has not only engraved an indelible imprint on sections of the Malay community but has also served to shape non-Malay perceptions during the colonial era.[8] The pillarized social structure of the colonial plural society, whereby the different ethnic communities superficially coexisted in the public sphere and even less superficially in the private sphere, contributed significantly towards generating negative ethnic stereotypes.

Ethnic stereotyping was fostered by the greater participation of the non-Malays in the colonial economy which in turn engendered a sense of superiority towards Malays (Abraham, 1986: 16–17). Such attitudes tended to promote the belief that the wealth of their community and Malay poverty were the natural consequence of immigrant industry, thrift, and adaptability to modern ways compared to the indolence and rigidity of Malays (Silcock, 1959: 183). For example, Rupert Emerson (1964: 18) noted that in the 1930s there was 'a common European and Chinese complaint that Malays are a lazy and shiftless people' who refused to exploit the bountiful economic opportunities under colonial rule.

The ready acceptance of the ideology of Malay cultural inferiority by Malays and non-Malays from the post-colonial era was given an added boost by the promotion of cultural deficit explanations by Western writers and academics (Lewis, 1961; Banfield, 1970). They asserted that the persisting socio-economic marginality of certain ethnic communities such as African–Americans stemmed from their inept cultural values and attitudes. Such communities were supposed to be afflicted by negative characteristics such as inertia, complacency, unstable family units, prone towards seeking immediate gratification, and a failure to seize available opportunities. These cultural deficiencies were thus supposed to create the material conditions which reproduce poverty and social inequality.

The cultural deficit thesis is thus very much based on a discourse that racializes poverty and social inequality. The discourse allows socially marginal ethnic communities to be projected as being undeserving of assistance, lazy, dull, and suffering from an identity crisis. By pathologizing the problems confronting ethnic minorities, their disadvantaged class position is obscured. Importantly, by locating the source of the 'problem' firmly within the marginal ethnic community, the racial discourse disentangles the significance of structural, institutional, and historical factors in contributing to their poverty. As the culturally deficient ethnic communities are largely responsible for their socio-economic malaise, the onus is thus firmly on them to reform their 'deviant' and deficient ways. This logic absolves the state from actively assisting socially disadvantaged communities on the rationale that it would only create a welfare or crutch mentality, increase crime, single-parent families (Murray, 1984), and threaten the well-being of the free-market economy.

The cultural deficit thesis has thus provided a convenient explanation for the continued socio-economic marginalization of the Malay community in Singapore. Moreover, it has provided the PAP government with the rationale for adopting a minimalist approach towards the Malay marginality, particularly in the decades of the 1960s and 1970s. Even with the establishment of the Malay/Muslim self-help body Mendaki in

1982, the cultural deficit thesis is still looked upon by the Malay leadership in the PAP government as the major explanation of the Malay community's socio-economic and educational marginality.

## The Impact of the Cultural Deficit Thesis on 'Culturally Deficient Communities'

Ethnic minority writers and activists such as Frantz Fanon (1967), Malcolm X (1965), and William Du Bois (1969) were particularly concerned about the impact of marginalized communities internalizing negative self-images of themselves which could well result in a self-fulfilling prophecy. They were thus concerned not only with the economic but also the psychological state of their community, believing that the two realms symbiotically interacted and influenced each other. Believing that the ultimate form of control was that of the mind, it was important to circumvent the situation where the subordinated psychologically builds their own prison and becomes both prisoner and warder (Baker, 1983. 41). This is likely to occur when members of the stereotyped community look at themselves 'through the eyes of others' (Du Bois, 1969: 115). To overcome the internalization of negative self-images and ideological colonization, it was imperative that the socially marginal community regain their pride and self-esteem and challenge existing notions of their cultural inferiority. The 'black is beautiful' and 'black power' slogans of the American civil rights movement in the 1960s are illustrative of the attempt by African–Americans to regain their pride and self-esteem.

In addition to the process of thought control, the compliance of the subordinate community has been achieved by utilizing the 'carrot and stick' approach (Baker, 1983: 60). The 'carrot' approach is facilitated by giving financial concessions, providing jobs to the élite within the minority community and extending other forms of material resources. On the other hand, the 'stick' approach is exercised by withdrawing resources and other benefits previously rendered to force compliance. As discussed in Chapter 6, the PAP government has on various occasions resorted to the 'carrot and stick' approach in its dealings with the Malay community.

Musgrove (1977) has posited that those who are susceptible to internalizing the dominant ideology tend to be the socially mobile and élite segments of the marginal community. While the ethnic élite are likely to accept the dominant world-view and to attribute their successes to their personal efforts and abilities (Kluegel and Smith, 1986: 24), those that have managed to break away from their disadvantaged social status are prone to be unsympathetic towards others who have not been able to follow suit. Their quest for social mobility is often individualistic rather than group-oriented (Dworkin and Dworkin, 1976: 39–41). Put in another way, they were more concerned about their own individual mobility than their ethnic community's aggregate social mobility.

In uncritically acceding to the ideology of cultural inferiority and by adopting an individualist meritocratic orientation, many will attempt to emulate and identify with the dominant ethnic community (Dworkin and Dworkin, 1976: 40) and often react by urging others in the community to adopt new cultural models and values. This commonly results in a diminution of ethnic solidarity and pride (Bonancich, 1980: 584). As more of the social élite become co-opted into the system and alienated from their own community, the ethnic community suffers a shortfall in representatives who possess the resources, skills, and commitment to effectively articulate and represent the minority community's grievances to the larger society (Femia, 1981: 48).

The influence of the dominant world-view over socially marginal ethnic minorities is not altogether without its underlying tensions and possibilities of resistance. As in the case of women and other marginal communities, some ethnic minorities who have attained social mobility but still experience discrimination in the work-force in the course of their daily experiences recognize the limitations in the meritocracy and equal opportunity thesis. As their 'lived reality' differs from the rhetoric of the dominant world-view, they are able to recognize the contradictory 'cracks' in the dominant world-view. Rothchild (1981: 117) has posited that as more minority group members achieve social mobility, ethnic group solidarity tends to be strengthened. Enamoured by this psychological boost, they are more likely to be critical of the *status quo*, begin to assertively challenge and expose the contradictions in the dominant world-view, and forcefully articulate the concerns of their ethnic community.

## The PAP Leadership's Perceptions of the Malay Marginality

The ideology of Malay inferiority, conceptualized in cultural deficit terms, has been accorded greater legitimacy and prominence in post-independence Singapore due primarily to its promotion as the major tool of analysis in explaining the socio-economic marginality of the Malay, and to a lesser extent Indian,[9] community. Firmly ensconced within this mode of analysis, Malays have been counselled by the PAP leadership to 'work hard', 'help yourself', 'change your outlook' (Othman Wok, *ST*, 20 May 1965), 'study hard', and 'be more competitive'. Their perceived cultural deficit has even been referred to by PAP leaders as a psychological dysfunction, the clear inference being that the problem lies with Malays. As Lee Kuan Yew claimed, 'problem is psychological ... if they try hard enough and long enough, then the education gap between them and the Chinese, or them and the Indians, would close.... Progress or achievement depends on ability and effort' (*ST*, 7 July 1987). Other than the continuance of the free education policy for Malays, initially instituted by the colonial authorities, special assistance to Malays as a socially marginal community was firmly rejected on the grounds that it would create a crutch mentality, promote communal divisions, and undermine the principles of meritocracy.

Much like the colonial authorities before them, the PAP government's eager acceptance of the cultural deficit thesis provided a powerful and convenient justification for adopting a minimalist stance towards the socio-economic and educational marginality of Malays despite their constitutional responsibility to do otherwise.[10] Having challenged UMNO's adherence to Malay political dominance, communal politics, and the special position and rights of indigenous Malaysians under the banner of a 'Malaysian Malaysia' during Singapore's brief but tumultuous period of merger with Malaysia,[11] the PAP leadership was committed to the establishment of a 'Singaporean Singapore' multiracial society where all citizens would enjoy equal privileges.[12] The twin principles of multiracialism and meritocracy were promoted as the guiding ideological ground rules of the newly independent island state.[13] Thus any calls made by Malay community leaders for greater government assistance to the community tended to be viewed by the PAP leadership in the context of its dispute with the Malaysian government about the special privileges enjoyed by the Malays in Malaysia (NCSMMP, 1990: 56).

Committed to the view that all Singaporeans were accorded equal access to resources and were competing in the 'meritocratic race' on an equal footing, the PAP was indifferent to the significance of historical and institutional factors and the salience of ethnicity, class, and gender on social mobility. Lee Kuan Yew (*ST*, 25 October 1989) was firmly of the view that in multiracial and meritocratic Singapore, social mobility and material advancement primarily sprang from a person's ability and diligence. The ostensibly strict adherence to the 'survival of the fittest' meritocratic principle was also perceived to be a means of maintaining the competitive spirit and achieving high economic development. Embedded in this world-view, the PAP government was opposed to initiating concrete measures to improve the standing of the socially marginal.

Consistent with the PAP leadership's commitment to its meritocratic beliefs, the nation building decades of the 1960s and 1970s were conspicuous for their absence of any concrete programme to address and ameliorate the persisting socio-economic and educational marginality of the Malay community. During this period, the Malay marginality issue was accorded an almost phantom like status and it appeared to be a matter only of concern to the Malay community. Quite simply, the PAP leadership was not willing to concede that historical, institutional, and structural factors had continued to impede the socio-economic and educational progress of Malays.

With the establishment of Mendaki in 1982, some PAP leaders such as George Yeo (Minister of Information and the Arts) have attempted to give a more sophisticated cast to the cultural deficit explanation of the Malay marginality. At a community dinner in 1991, Yeo postulated that Malays have remained socially marginal because of the adverse effects of their relocation from traditional to semi-rural village style settlements into modern high-rise housing units. Despite the allure of this explanation, such a view does not stand up well against empirical scrutiny. Indeed, there is little evidence to support Yeo's thesis that Malays are more traditional and rural oriented than the other ethnic communities. Rodney Tan's (1972) and Riaz Hassan's (1977) studies have revealed that the problems of relocated low-income families were generally similar regardless of ethnicity. Indeed, they found that Malays generally had a higher level of satisfaction and coped better with the economics of high-rise living than their Chinese neighbours.

The PAP leadership's generally unsympathetic attitude towards the socio-economic and educational marginality of Malays is better appreciated when contextualized within the eugenics and biological determinist beliefs of Singapore's long-serving Prime Minister and current Senior Minister Lee Kuan Yew. Proponents of such beliefs (Galton, 1959; Jensen, 1969) essentially endorse social inequality as a natural human phenomenon endowed by nature. Nature rather than nurture is the principal determining factor of material success. Such beliefs serve to undermine ideals and social programmes in favour of social equity on the grounds that they fly in the face of the 'natural givens' of life. A concrete public policy manifestation of the PAP leadership's eugenics beliefs was evident in the 1970s when the low-profile Eugenics Board was commissioned to analyse cases during the initial period of legalized abortion in Singapore (Benjamin, 1976: 126).

By the early 1980s, the hitherto low-profile eugenics beliefs of the PAP leadership took on a more overt form. In a 1983 National Day address, Lee Kuan Yew made public his long-held eugenic beliefs by purporting that 80 per cent of talent and intelligence was inherited while only 20 per cent was nurtured (*ST*, 15 August 1983).[14] With this caveat, he ruefully lamented that if the present population trend continued, with the poorer and less educated having larger families than the well educated, the already limited talent pool in Singapore would continue to shrink. This shrinking of the talent pool would endanger the island's long term economic prosperity (*FEER*, 8 October 1983).

Concerned that the gene pool of Singaporeans be safeguarded from the genetic pollution of the large number of unskilled foreign workers, Singaporeans are forbidden from marrying the latter without obtaining permission. If permission is granted, both husband and wife have to agree to be sterilized after the second child so as to prevent a lowering in the intellectual quality of the nation (Tremewan, 1994: 113). Failure to abide by this injunction leads to the immediate cancellation of the unskilled foreign worker's work permit, their deportation and permanent entry ban to the island (Bello and Rosenfeld, 1992: 312). To counter the possibility of unskilled female foreign workers having children out of wedlock during their stay in Singapore, they are required to undergo a pregnancy test once every six months. If they are found to be pregnant, they will be immediately repatriated and their employer punished by forfeiting their unskilled workers bond held by the government (ibid.: 313). The fact that these draconian laws were tailored for the largely non-Chinese[15] unskilled foreign worker highlights the racist undertones of the government's population policy. This is exemplified by the liberal labour laws for foreign workers from 'new sources', most of whom are ethnic Chinese and other East Asians from Hong Kong, Macau, Taiwan, and South Korea (Lee Tsao Yuan, 1987: 188).

Another fervent eugenicist, former Deputy Prime Minister Goh Keng Swee, has justified the highly unpopular and élitist Graduate Mothers Policy[16] on the grounds that graduate mothers produced nine times the number of gifted children compared to the non-graduate population.[17] The introduction of the 1979 New Education Policy's early school streaming was another manifestation of the PAP leadership's eugenicist convictions. To stem the lopsided procreation pattern, a matchmaking body for university graduates euphemistically called the Social Development Unit (SDU) was established in 1982. Indicative of the élitist belief in the social segregation of society according to intelligence, the Social Development Section (SDS) was established in 1985 to cater for unmarried Singaporeans who have GCE 'O' levels and the Social Promotion Section (SPS) for those without GCE 'O' levels (*ST WOE*, 13 February 1993).

The eugenics beliefs and policies of the PAP government are particularly offensive to Malays who have long been disproportionately represented amongst the poorly educated and lower income strata of society. If talent and ability is predominantly innate, as suggested by eugenicists, then the genetic and intellectual standing of the socially marginal Malay community must also be deficient. Exposing such assumptions, Lee Kuan Yew (*ST*, 26 June 1992) has publicly announced that Malays could never perform better than the Chinese in Mathematics: 'If you pretend that the problem does not exist, and that in fact (the Malays) can score as well as the Chinese in Maths, then you have created yourself an enormous myth which you will be stuck with.'[18]

In contrast to the allegedly deficient cultural and intellectual traits of Malays, the Chinese have been commended for possessing a myriad of positive cultural traits such as diligence, discipline, industry, communitarianism, being consensus, and achievement oriented (Josey, 1968: 572; Lee Kuan Yew, *ST WOE*, 2 November 1991). The economic success of Singapore, the East Asian NICs, and Japan, have been attributed to the positive Confucianist values of the Chinese and East Asians[19] (*ST*, 4 February 1982; Goh Chok Tong, *ST*, 29 October 1988). In justifying the government's racially biased immigration policy and the active promotion of Mandarin and Confucianism, Goh Chok Tong (*ST WOE*, 27 July 1991) questioned 'whether Singapore could survive without these core values of thrift, hard work, and group cohesion which are strongly identified in Chinese culture'.

The PAP leadership's promotion of Malay cultural inferiority and Chinese cultural superiority has been politically useful. *Inter alia*, it has served to strengthen the portrayal of the dynamic Confucian island precariously located in a poorer, less diligent, and potentially hostile Malay region (Minchin, 1986: 165). Importantly, such a conception justifies the continuance of the island's relatively high military spending (Huxley, 1991) and assists in projecting the image of the PAP as the guardian of the Chinese. It also obliquely legitimizes the Chinese political, social, and economic dominance of Singapore.

Recognizing the importance of attenuating the Malay community's frustration with their persisting marginalization and the political tension arising from it, the PAP leadership has strenuously urged Malays against the 'psychological trap' of measuring their socio-economic and educational standing against that of other ethnic communities. Instead they have been advised to realistically measure their progress against their past socio-economic and educational standing (Lee Kuan Yew, *ST*, 7 July 1987). In his first address to the Malay community as Prime Minister, Goh Chok Tong (*ST*, 8 February 1991) advised Malays not to be too concerned about 'catching up' with the other communities but to 're-define the challenge and set new targets. Instead of chasing a moving target, set fixed targets for yourselves, independent of how the other communities perform.' Malays are thus expected to be content with their marginality and grateful about the absolute gains achieved. Premised on this logic, PAP Malay MP Harun Abdul Ghani advised the Malays that 'trailing behind the Chinese does not mean that the Malays are losing out. They are improving themselves' (*ST*, 24 July 1992). Malays are therefore expected to tolerate their socio-economic and educational marginality as a permanent fixture with stoic resignation.

### Non-Malay Perceptions of the Malay Marginality

The ideology of Malay cultural inferiority, initially promoted by the British colonial administrators and orientalists and reinvigorated by the PAP government, has assisted in perpetuating negative ethnic stereotyping and prejudice against Malays. Such negative stereotypes are particularly susceptible in highly urbanized and competitive social environments where people are commonly assessed according to their material worth. Malays are expected to hold menial and low status jobs, be poorly educated, lack motivation, not be particularly intelligent, prone to having large families, drug addiction, and divorce. Such stereotypical generalizations serve to crudely explain, rationalize, and blame Malays for their marginal socio-economic and educational status in society.

If contact with Malays by the average non-Malay Singaporean living in public housing estates is superficial (Hassan, 1976), that of the social élite who live in private residential estates where a negligible number of Malays reside, would be even more limited. Contact of non-Malays from senior executive and professional levels in the work-force with Malays would commonly be restricted to the 'office/messenger boy', cleaner, or receptionist in the office. Similarly, contact with Malays in the private sphere may be limited to other subordinates such as the Malay washerwoman, driver, or domestic servant. Ongoing professional and personal relationships which centre on the Chinese as the superior and the Malay the subordinate serve to reify the ideology of Malay cultural inferiority, strengthen negative stereotypes, and further fortify class and ethnic prejudices.

The salience of the ideology of Malay inferiority amongst non-Malays was revealed in Leong Choon Cheong's (1978) study of youth in the army. In the study, Malays were described as lazy, unintelligent, unhygienic, and aggressive by Chinese national servicemen. A 1989 survey on Singaporean attitudes to race by the Institute of Policy Studies found that 15 per cent of Chinese thought that Malays were characteristically 'lazy' compared to only a 6 per cent Chinese perception of Indians in that unflattering light (*Sunday Times*, 23 September 1990). Significantly, laziness was the second most common Malay trait identified by the Chinese after 'friendly' (ibid.).[20] The rhetoric that Singapore is a meritocratic society where equal opportunities are available to all has also served to add legitimacy to the cultural deficit thesis which infers that Malays have not been able to make it in a meritocratic society because they have not worked hard enough and thus have only themselves to blame. Indeed, the negative stereotyping of Malays is so deeply embedded in society that it has been reified and often left uncontested.

It is worth noting that the Singaporean studies and surveys on interethnic perceptions cited above appear to corroborate American studies (Converse, 1980; Hochschild, 1988) on interethnic perceptions. Hochschild (1988) found that the dominant European–American community tended to accept the view that the socially disadvantaged status of African–Americans was primarily attributed to their personal and cultural shortcomings.[21] Ethnic majorities tend to be less aware, empathetic, and sensitive to the weight of historical and structural factors and the forces of discrimination that have impeded the social mobility of ethnic minorities (Marable, 1992). In contrast to the generally unsympathetic perception of ethnic minority marginality, the issue of discrimination, unequal opportunities, and the phenomenon of the 'glass ceiling' faced by women in the work-force is accorded greater acknowledgement and tends to receive wider positive media coverage and public empathy (*ST*, 8 March 1993; *ST WOE*, 20 March 1993).

Negative stereotyping of Malays can also be attributed to the promotion of cultural deficit perspectives by the state controlled electronic and print media. Articles in the local dailies which depict Malays as lacking in motivation, industry, diligence, and being socially deviant (*ST*, 12 September 1990; *ST*, 10 August 1993), generally highlight the myriad cultural shortcomings of Malays as a cause of the community's socioeconomic marginality.[22] Similarly, the media has promoted the dominant meritocratic thesis by highlighting the success stories of middle-class professional Malays (*Sunday Times*, 27 September 1992; *ST*, 10 October 1992) who, from humble childhood beginnings of selling *goreng pisang* (fried bananas) and cleaning stables in their youth, eventually achieved professional and financial success due to their hard work and dogged determination to 'make it' in life.

Significantly, the myriad institutional and structural difficulties involved in 'making it' and impediments such as discrimination in the workplace are accorded scant attention in these media instigated success stories. This is because the primary objective of such articles is to promote the meritocratic ideal which posits that 'how far one can go in life largely depends on the drive and ability imbued in the individual. This is the egalitarianism as we know it to be in Singapore' (*ST*,

Editorial, 18 August 1987). Just as meritocracy is applauded for its practical relevance, articles authored by notable conservative foreign scholars such as Thomas Sowell (*ST*, 12 March 1990; *ST*, 1 June 1990) denouncing affirmative action programmes and downplaying the significance of discrimination against ethnic minorities have been periodically featured in the *Straits Times*.

## Malay Perceptions of the Malay Marginality

Firmly committed to the PAP leadership's ideological world-view, PAP Malay MPs have consistently affirmed their subscription to the cultural deficit perspective when explaining the socio-economic and educational marginality of Malays. In frank and unambiguous terms, they have chastised Malays for manifesting a 'nagging and begging mentality' (Sidek Saniff, *ST*, 26 February 1988), a 'crutch mentality' (Sidek Saniff, *ST*, 3 October 1984), for selfishly expecting the government to 'do this and that for them' (Yatiman Yusof, *ST*, 3 October 1984), for being entrapped in a 'minority syndrome' (Wan Hussein Zoohri, 1990), and for being afflicted by the 'lethargy and psychological burdens of the past' (A. Tarmugi, *ST*, 18 December 1992).[23] Malays have been advised to make Malay culture more dynamic by discarding 'old ways, old views and past practices which have outlived their usefulness' (Zulkifli Mohammed, *ST*, 14 May 1989).

The ideology of Malay cultural inferiority has also been uncritically endorsed by sections of the Malay middle and professional class. Having attained high educational credentials, material success, and social mobility, the meritocratic discourse advocated by the PAP leadership serves to flatter their achievements and accords them the esteemed status as role models of exceptional qualities. Their socio-economic distance from the general Malay community and their ethnic difference from the non-Malay community places them in a position of double alienation. This profound level of alienation has rendered the Malay middle class socially vulnerable and susceptible towards uncritically accepting the cultural deficit thesis which gratifies their ego for having extricated themselves from the negative cultural attributes afflicting the Malay community.

Their uncritical acceptance of the ideology of Malay cultural deficit can also be attributed to the fact that a significant proportion of the Malay middle and professional classes are civil servants.[24] Public articulations of dissent against the dominant ideology are likely to jeopardize their careers in the civil service. Interestingly, a few senior Malay civil servants have not only publicly supported the dominant ideology of Malay cultural inferiority and meritocracy but have, in the tradition of Malays such as Za'aba and PAP Malay MPs, been quick to criticize their ethnic community. For example, a Malay diplomat (cf. Ibrahim, *ST*, 10 October 1992) has alleged that Malays 'fail to learn the virtues of competition and so fail to rise through the educational ladder because they slide into a kind of cultural comfort' and emanate from a 'soft society, where standards or difficult goals are not thought to be worth the effort' (ibid.). Others have attributed the alleged Malay values of fatalism or *rezeki*,[25] satisfaction with short-term results, passive resignation, and a retarded scientific orientation to the community's erroneous interpretation of Islam and adherence to pre-Islamic cultural values (Kassim Yang Razali, 1979: 33).

Despite the acceptance of the ideology of Malay cultural inferiority by segments of the Malay middle class, the cultural deficit thesis and its *ubah sikap*[26] prescriptions have been critically discounted by writers such as Ungku Aziz (1959; 1974), Syed Hussein Alatas (1977), Syed Husin Ali (1984), and Muzaffar (1989a). Factors such as colonial policies, government policies, and limited opportunities in the private sector have been cited to explain the Malay marginality. Within the context of the Singapore Malay marginality, Li (1989), Nurliza Yusuf (1986), and the National Convention of Singapore Malay/Muslim Professionals (NCSMMP) (1990) have highlighted the salience of institutional factors such as education policies, poor political leadership, and discrimination in the private and public sector. The Malay based political party, the Pertubohan Kebangsaan Melayu Singapura (PKMS), has also vigorously rejected the cultural deficit thesis. They have pointed to the weak Malay leadership's representation of Malay interests in government as the major factor contributing to the Singapore Malay marginality (*Message*, 9 January 1990).

The 'lived reality' or day-to-day experiences of the Malay masses have significantly mediated the dominance of the meritocratic and dominant cultural deficit discourse. This 'lived reality' is based on their awareness of the persistence of discrimination and unequal opportunities in the work-force despite the promotion of Singapore as a meritocratic and multiracial society par excellence. Nearly all of the working histories of Malays collected by Li (1989: 110) included detailed accounts of perceived discriminatory practices by Chinese employers. The perceived discriminatory practices cited included recruitment, pay, working conditions, and opportunities for training and advancement. Similarly, Aljunied (1980), Nurliza Yusuf (1986), Lai (1995), and the AMP's (NCSMMP, 1990) study highlighted Malay perceptions of unequal opportunities often in the form of 'glass ceilings' in the work-force. In the face of their less than meritocratic 'lived reality', the discourse of the PAP leadership, Malay MPs, and sections of the Malay élite is viewed cynically.

As members of a socially marginal community, this 'lived reality', coupled with an acute sense of relative deprivation, has allowed many Malays to critically view meritocracy as an inherently unjust principle which favours those who are socially advantaged (Nurliza Yusuf, 1986). This is fuelled by the belief that factors such as ethnicity and socio-economic status hinder many from competing on an equal footing in the 'meritocratic race' (Nurliza Yusuf, 1986: 12; Li, 1989: 111). Research by Aljuneid (1980), Hashimah Johari (1984), Nurliza Yusuf (1986), and Li (1989) have consistently demonstrated that Malays are generally more inclined towards attributing historical, institutional, and structural explanations for the community's socio-economic marginality.

The Singaporean findings have corroborated numerous foreign studies (Huber and Form, 1973; Moorehouse, 1973; Hewstone and Jaspars, 1982; Gallie, 1983) which indicate that those who experience the greatest barriers to social mobility are more cognizant of the institutional inequities and showed least support for the dominant ideology. Social inequality has thus been reluctantly endured rather than accepted as a norm. The inconsistencies and contradictions between the dominant ideology of meritocracy and equal opportunity and the 'lived reality' of relative deprivation, discrimination, and unequal opportunities have aided in the demystification and creation of cracks in the dominant ideology. This provides the foundation for future ideological contestations and challenges to the PAP leadership's ideological constructions.

\* \* \*

The cultural deficit thesis has served to legitimize the interests of colonial capitalism and justify the PAP government's minimalist approach towards assisting the socially marginal ethnic communities. By individualizing the 'failure' of some members of the dominant ethnic community but culturalizing the 'failure' of ethnic minority communities, a coherent rationale for the existing social and ethnic inequalities is provided.

In failing to recognize the impact of socio-historical, structural, and institutional factors on the socio-economic and educational marginality of Malays, the community's supposed cultural deficiencies and biological shortcomings have instead been highlighted by the PAP leadership and the mainstream media. Singaporeans have thus been encouraged to believe that the Malays are deserving of their marginality and are likely to remain marginal. As Mano Subrani (*ST*, 31 October 1988) has cautioned, 'what is said in public often does not reflect the private thoughts of many Singaporeans. I find that more and more, at least recently, people are beginning to think that nature intended it such that some sections of society, particularly the Malays, will always be lagging behind ... it is like giving yourself an excuse to think that nothing much can be done.'

Like a self-fulfilling prophecy, the dominant understanding of the Malay marginality that is informed by the cultural deficit and, to a lesser extent, biological determinist ideology may well prove to be a major contributor to the persisting socio-economic and educational marginality of the Malay community.

1. Refer to Swettenham (1900) and Winstedt (1929).
2. *Tidak apa* in Malay means not to care or take things seriously.
3. For an insightful account of Malay society by colonial authorities and orientalists, refer to Syed Hussein Alatas, *The Myth of the Lazy Native*, London: Frank Cass, 1977. Edward Said's *Orientalism* (Harmondsworth: Penguin, 1978) provides an illuminating exposition of the role of Orientalist literature in shaping contemporary perceptions of formerly colonized communities.
4. The British actively discouraged Malays in switching from agricultural production to

the more lucrative cash crops. Education for Malays was 'to make the son of a fisherman or peasant a more intelligent fisherman or peasant than his father had been' (British Director of Education in 1929, cited from Roff, 1980: 138).

5. 'The Poverty of the Malays', *Malay Mail*, 1 December 1923. Cited from *Prosa Melayu Moden*, London: Longman, Green, 1959.

6. Shaharuddin Ma'arof (1988: 27) has contextualized the socio-economic malaise of the Malay masses as symptomatic of the moral and intellectual decay of the feudal élite. Their oppressive actions such as the seizing of food and other forms of material surplus from the populace tended to diminish any incentive for hard work. The system of *kerah* or forced labour also imposed a heavy burden on the Malay community and deprived them of the opportunity to seriously and successfully engage in entrepreneurial activities.

7. It should be noted that Senu Abdullah, like many other UMNO politicians who adopted the cultural deficit perspective, was a businessman who benefited substantially from the existing system.

8. The Straits Chinese paper *Bintang Timor* published a series of eleven articles in October 1934 which exposed a strong cultural deficit bias. The articles were instructively entitled 'Mengapa Melayu Layu?' [Why Are the Malays in a State of Inertia?].

9. Cultural deficit perspectives have also been commonly cited to explain the weak socio-economic and educational position of the Indian community. PAP Indian MP Dr Vasoo has cited Hinduism and its 'karmatic fixation' as contributing to many Indians being 'resigned to their fates' (*ST*, 22 June 1991).

10. However, the Malay community were assured by the PAP leadership just after separation that the government would abide by their constitutional responsibility in rendering assistance to the community. As Lee (*ST*, 14 August 1965) put it, 'There will be built-in provisions to ensure that any elected government must continue ... to raise the economic and educational level of Malays as embodied in Article 152 of the Constitution' (*ST*, 14 August 1965). This was affirmed again in 1967 when Lee (quoted by Mattar, 1979: 82) stated that 'the government, with the support of the non-Malays, are prepared to concentrate more than the average share of their resources on our Malay citizens'. Despite these pronouncements, the only tangible form of assistance was the policy of free education for Malays. This policy was broken in 1990 when Malays were made to pay for their tertiary education.

11. Using the Malaysian Solidarity Convention as a platform, the PAP leadership championed the establishment of a 'Malaysian Malaysia' whereupon all Malaysians would be treated equally regardless of their ethnicity, indigeneity, class or gender. This position was generally adopted by the non-Malay left political parties and organizations such as the Malayan Communist Party (MCP) and the Malayan People's Anti-Japanese Association (MPAJA). In contrast, left-wing Malay organizations such as the Malay Nationalist Party (MNP) and Kesatuan Melayu Muda (KMM) since the pre-war era believed that the *bumiputra* had a special position in the country. For an engaging analysis of the differences between the Malay and non-Malay left in Malaya, refer to Muhammad Ikmal Said (1992).

12. The PAP's ostensibly non-communal approach was not unique in Singapore as most political parties had adopted multiracialism as a platform (Yeo, 1969: 140–1). Betts (1975: 72) has suggested that a reason for the lack of obvious communal political orientation by political parties in Singapore was because the Chinese, as the strongest socio-economic and political force in Singapore, did not have to organize along ethnic lines. The non-communal multiracial veneer of the PAP served to de-emphasize the Chinese-based nature of the party membership. Particularly in the earlier years, the PAP found it difficult to get the English-educated Indians and Malays to join the party. Most of the party activists were Chinese-educated and branch meetings were often conducted in Chinese (Vasil, 1992: 45).

13. Despite the PAP's multiracial meritocratic rhetoric, Lee was to affirm on 11 August 1965 that 'the government's multiracial policy would be written into the Singapore Constitution with safeguards for minorities and steps to raise the economic and educational standards of the Malays' (Colony of Singapore, *Annual Report*, Singapore, 1966: 4). Only a few days earlier Lee (*ST*, 10 August 1965) was reported to have promised that 'we (the government) will continue helping the Malays in competition with UMNO'.

14. To lend credibility to Lee's eugenics ideas, the state controlled television station Singapore Broadcasting Corporation (SBC) interviewed the well-known eugenicist Hans Eysenck on the inheritance of intelligence. Eysenck noted that 'if the bright don't reproduce at the same rate as the duller, then the gene pool will decline in quality' (*ST*, 17 September 1983).

15. Most of them are ethnic Malays from Indonesia, Malaysia, and the Philippines whilst the others are from Thailand, Sri Lanka, and India.

16. As will be discussed in greater detail in Chapters 7 and 8, the policy gave numerous preferences such as school registration priority to the third child of graduate mothers.

17. 'Classless Societies a Myth', Parliamentary speech by First Deputy Prime Minister Goh Keng Swee, cited in the *Singapore Bulletin*, Vol. 12, No. 7 (March 1984).

18. Lee has also made offensive comments which allude to the cultural deficit of the Indians. He has alleged that South Asians tend to be 'contentious' and make decisions on the basis of argumentation as opposed to the East Asians who make decisions on the basis of consensus. This he claimed was the reason why the East Asians prospered economically and the South Asians did not (*ST*, 26 May 1992).

19. Woodwiss (1990: 102) has argued that the notion of the cultural uniqueness of Confucianist East Asian societies such as Japan is largely a product of European/American orientalist studies of Japan. He has purported that Confucianism has not been a dominant ideology in its own right since the Tokugawa period. By the post-war period, Confucianism had been subject to displacement and become a capitalist discourse. It appears that the PAP leadership has readily accepted this Orientalist discourse as it legitimizes their social and political programme.

20. IPS 1989 survey of Chinese perception of Malays.

| Community Characteristics | % | Community Characteristics | % |
|---|---|---|---|
| Friendly | 36 | Co-operative | 6 |
| Lazy | 15 | Racialistic | 6 |
| United | 10 | Hardworking | 3 |
| Helpful | 9 | Easy-going | 3 |
| Religious | 7 | Selfish | 3 |

*Source*: *Sunday Times*, 23 September 1990.

21. In contrast to the less than empathetic European/American perceptions, African-Americans believed that prejudice and discrimination rather than personal shortcomings was the major factor contributing to their socially disadvantaged status.

22. For example, the opening paragraphs of a *Straits Times* article by R. Tan (10 August 1993) entitled 'Malay Singaporeans Come to Grips with Delinquency in Community' was as follows: 'A teenage gang of tattooed Malay girls recently beat up primary school boys to extort money from them. The girls' parents found out about the incident only after the school complained and the teenagers were hauled up for a stern ticking-off by the police.... And the main reason for such delinquent behaviour is bad parenting arising from high divorce rates.... It is also the reason why a growing number of students join gangs, take drugs and drop out of school.'

23. This interpretation was cited by the Deputy Speaker of Parliament and MP for Siglap at a 1992 NUS address. He claimed that Singapore's separation from Malaysia left the Malays 'confused and somewhat disoriented'. The trauma of separation was supposed to have adversely affected the community's socio-economic progress.

24. As civil servants, they are likely to be acutely conscious of the PAP government's ideological preferences.

25. The concept of *rezeki* (belief in predetermined outcome based on fate) appears not to be unique to Malays and is also found in Chinese culture (Wee, 1976; Leong, 1978: 119). Li (1989: 171) also did not find the concept of *rezeki* to be particularly prominent in Malay thinking on economic matters.

26. *Ubah sikap* means to change one's attitudes.

# PART II
# CONTAINMENT OF MALAY POLITICS

# 5
# Minimizing the Political Resources of the Malay Community

THIS chapter examines the means by which the political and electoral clout of the Malay community has been blunted by a myriad of political engineering initiatives which have permanently locked them into the position of an electoral minority in all electoral constituencies. Their numerical minority status at the national level has also been secured by the population/immigration policy of 'maintaining the ethnic balance' which in practical terms serves to maintain the Chinese numerical dominance in Singapore. The weak electoral and political clout of the Malay community has allowed the PAP government to remain relatively unresponsive to the concerns and sensitivities of the community without absorbing damaging electoral repercussions. Malay concerns have been articulated within the ideological and political parameters constructed by the PAP government and its Malay MPs. Importantly, the political marginality of the Malay community has resulted in a trend towards communal politicking as the major political parties are increasingly focused on articulating the concerns and capturing the support of the electorally commanding Chinese community.

## Political Resources and Strategies

Dominant political forces are more inclined to negotiate, make concessions, and are generally more accommodating to a minority community when it is lobbying from a position of political strength that is supported by a formidable raft of political resources and mobilization capacities. Put simply, the greater the political resources a group has at its disposal, the better are their prospects in realizing their objectives. Conversely, the fewer political resources a group possesses, the less likely their demands will be seriously considered. Thus, group relations are akin to contests where power resources are mobilized and developed with the aim of gaining influence or control over societal structures (Baker, 1983: 41) which determine and shape the political course pursued by the state.

The political strategies that can be effectively utilized by minority

communities when attempting to strengthen their bargaining position include:
1. Mobilizing the community's collective numerical strength for various forms of protest action and civil disobedience.
2. Mobilizing its collective electoral clout during elections at the local and national level in support or rejection of particular candidates and parties.
3. Developing a strong and visionary leadership that has the support and confidence of the community and is supported by an effective organizational network and a community that is socially cohesive.
4. Procuring a broader base of support from other progressive segments and disadvantaged groups in the wider community, by linking up their 'cause' with other social issues to win public support and cooperation in a 'rainbow coalition', that is, a coalition of other minority groups and progressive elements in society. In this way, the latter's understanding of the ethnic minority's problems will be better understood. The electoral potency of this 'rainbow coalition' will also serve to enhance the election to public office of politically liberal and reformist oriented politicians (Wilson, 1973: 51).
5. Invoking moral support and empathy from ethnic brethren in neighbouring countries as well as from international organizations such as the United Nations and human rights agencies.
6. Developing sufficient financial and human resources to sustain the independence of community based organizations (ibid.).
7. Delegitimizing the dominant ideologies and myths that have served to justify the socially disadvantaged status of the minority community and other socially disadvantaged groups (Deutsch, 1985: 58).

Some of these mentioned power resources and political strategies have been effectively utilized by organizations such as the trade union movement, feminist organizations, ethnic and indigenous minorities, human rights groups, and the environmentalist movement. Importantly, major concessions won by such groups have been achieved not by passively waiting for the altruistic impulses of the dominant forces but by resorting to various forms of political activity that directly challenge and question the values, presuppositions, and paradigms of the *status quo*.

In societies where elections are regularly held and genuinely administered, ethnic minorities have been able to effectively mobilize their collective electoral strength with the objective of initiating political reforms that are likely to address their concerns. The strategy of harnessing the collective political power of a community has been employed by economically marginal ethnic communities such as African–Americans, indigenous Malaysians, and indigenous South Africans. For example, the African–American civil rights protests of the 1960s successfully ushered forth numerous civil rights reforms which, *inter alia*, sought to eliminate forms of institutional discrimination and improve the socioeconomic standing of the African–American and other discriminated groups. Recognizing the long-term goal of the civil rights movement, civil rights leader Martin Luther King (1964: 104) noted that 'political power may well, in the days to come, be the most effective tool of the Negro's liberation'. King (ibid.) believed that the collective electoral power of African–Americans was a potent catalyst of political power and that voting was 'the foundation stone for political action'.[1] Similarly, the more radical African–American political activists such as Malcolm X saw the community's electoral strength as a potent political resource which would help extricate racists out of public office thereby facilitating more equitable socio-economic opportunities for African–Americans (Harding, 1968).

The aggregate numerical strength of an ethnic community in a particular locality or at the national level can act as a potent reservoir of political power. The sheer numerical strength of the community can by itself strongly facilitate the long-term success of the community's extra-parliamentary or parliamentary struggle for equity and self-determination. For example, the preponderance of indigenous South Africans has assisted them in ultimately dismembering the oppressive system of apartheid which had maintained the economic and political hegemony of minority European rule. Similarly, the political struggles of the New Zealand Maori, who constitute approximately 15 per cent of the total population, for land rights and political representation has been more successful than the numerically weak Australian Aborigines across the Tasman.[2] Demographic projections which estimate that African–Americans and Hispanic Americans will constitute a numerical majority in nearly one third of the fifty largest cities in the United States (Marable, 1993: 124) means that they are more likely to be able to effectively challenge ethnocentric attitudes and other forms of institutionalized discrimination in the future. In contrast to the promising political struggles of the indigenous South Africans and the New Zealand Maori, the struggle of numerically weak indigenous minorities such as the Australian Aborigines and the American Indians, who constitute less than 5 per cent of the total population, for justice and self-determination seem more formidable. Their numerically weak status has rendered them a feeble electoral and political force at national and local levels. As a corollary of their insubstantial electoral base, they are not able to negotiate from a forceful position without strong moral support from the wider national community.

When the dominant community perceive their hegemony to be seriously threatened, they may resort to undermining the resources of the subordinate communities through constitutional, legislative, and institutional means. Baker (1983) has referred to communities who behave as though their way of life and culture is under threat as 'siege culture communities'. Feeling under perpetual siege, they are likely to be rigid and dogmatic in their beliefs, often believing the myths and propaganda they have spun of the community under suspicion. Examples of 'siege culture communities' include the Europeans of South Africa, the Israelis, and the Chinese of South-East Asia.

The preponderance of ethnic minorities in particular electoral localities can be counteracted by the implementation of electoral measures which dilute their electoral power with the purpose of preventing them from participating assertively in the political process. Apart from the system of apartheid that was practised in South Africa, the United States practised a form of ethnic gerrymandering (Parker, 1984: 107) which submerged and diluted minority electoral strength by incorporating ethnic minority strongholds with ethnic majority districts under the multi-member slating system. Other ingenious forms of vote dilution commonly practised include the gerrymandering or the redrawing of boundaries, candidate diminution,[3] and overconcentrating the minority community into a single electoral district in excess of the percentage needed for minority voters to elect candidates of their choice.[4]

When the dominant ethnic community feels threatened by the increasing number of minority communities, they have responded by enacting immigration and population policies which are geared towards restricting the numerical position of ethnic minorities (Baker, 1983: 17). Such initiatives serve to undermine the political and electoral resources of the latter. Population policies such as Australia's White Australia Policy, Britain's Nationality Act, Israel's immigration policy which is overly biased towards Jews but discriminates against Palestinians, and Singapore's population policy of 'maintaining the racial balance' are examples of the institutionalization of ethnic majority dominance.

## Maintaining the Numerical Minority Status of Malays

Turnbull (1977: 5) has estimated that when the British established Singapore as a trading port in 1819, the island was populated by up to 1,000 Malays and subethnic Malay groups such as the Orang Kallang, Orang Seletar, Orang Gelam, and Orang Laut. In addition to the indigenous populace, there existed a scattering of twenty to thirty Chinese gambier planters.[5] By 1836, the indigenous Malay communities were reduced to the status of a numerical minority owing to the rapid influx of foreign labour from China and India needed to work in the tin mines and plantations in the Malay States and the Straits Settlements[6] (Table 5.1). Initially, the numerical diminution of Malays in Singapore and Penang did not particularly alarm the Malay community as they continued to perceive the island as an integral part of the larger hinterland on the

TABLE 5.1
Ethnic Population of Singapore

| Ethnicity | 1824 | 1836 | 1891 | 1970 | 1980 | 1990 |
|---|---|---|---|---|---|---|
| Malay | 60.0 | 41.8 | 19.8 | 15.0 | 14.4 | 14.1 |
| Chinese | 31.0 | 45.8 | 67.1 | 76.2 | 78.3 | 77.7 |
| Indian | 7.1 | 9.8 | 8.8 | 7.8 | 6.3 | 7.1 |

*Sources*: Saw, 1969: 39; 1970 Census of Population; *Yearbook of Statistics*, Singapore, 1987; *ST WOE*, 25 May 1991.

mainland where Malays remained numerically dominant. Foreign Chinese and Indian labourers were also believed to be sojourners who would, after accumulating enough money, eventually return to their respective homelands.

During the period of this rapid human influx into Singapore in the nineteenth century, Malay communities from the 'Nusantara' settled in Singapore not as sojourners but largely to 'set up home' on the island. As noted by demographer Saw Swee Hock (1969: 57), the permanent settlement of Malays on the island was reflected in the community's relatively balanced sex ratio: 'They have at no time exhibited the great excess of males which characterized the other two communities, their sex ratio remained constantly normal.' Malays have for centuries been 'internally migrating' from one *rumpun* of the 'Nusantara' to another for economic and, to a lesser extent, political reasons. The demographic cycles of the island's ancient history, from a population of several thousands in the era when it was a thriving trading port called Temasek[7] in the eleventh century to only a thousand or so inhabitants in 1819, exemplifies the atavistic *merantau* (internal migration) tradition of Malay migration within the 'Nusantara'. As elaborated in Chapter 2, Singapore Malays are acutely conscious of and take pride in Singapore's integral historical relationship with the 'Nusantara' and the island's ancient Malay heritage (Bedlington, 1974). As Singapore is embedded in the heartland of the 'Nusantara' homeland, the Singapore Malay community thus consider themselves as indigenous to the island. The Malay saying, *Di mana bumi dipijak, di situlah langit dijunjong* (on whatever soil we find ourselves, there we will hold up the sky)[8] exemplifies the organic Singapore Malay identification with the 'Nusantara', of which Singapore is inextricably a part.

The numerical decline of the Malay community, which occurred rapidly in the nineteenth century, corresponded with their economic and political eclipse[9] in colonial Singapore. In their 'Nusantara' homeland, Malays found themselves numerically, economically, politically, and socially submerged in 'a European ruled Chinese city' (Turnbull, 1977: 100) with limited opportunities for social mobility in the harshly competitive pioneering society. The correlation between the community's declining numerical status and their corresponding political and economic decline has long been of considerable concern to the indigenous community.

The PAP leadership has always been acutely aware of the salience of a nation's ethnic numerical composition in shaping its political complexion. Indeed, it was the island's numerical Chinese majority status that caused the Malay-dominated Alliance government of Tunku Abdul Rahman to hold strong reservations about upsetting mainland Malaya's racial balance by including Singapore in the newly created Malaysian Federation in 1963. However, once admitted into Malaysia the PAP leadership initiated the Malaysian Solidarity Convention (MSC) in 1964 with the primary objective of challenging the Alliance government's policy of according special status to the indigenous communities. In championing the ideal of a 'Malaysian Malaysia', the MSC, under the tutelage of the PAP leadership, challenged the Alliance government's political philosophy which was centred on Malay political dominance. In rejecting the the existing political equation and the special position of the Malays, the PAP may have according to Hua (1983: 142) expediently attempted 'to appeal to the communalist sentiments of the non-Malays in its attempt to extend its political base in the mainland' and in the process 'created a highly charged atmosphere of communalism within Malaysia'.

Following Singapore's expulsion from the Federation on 7 August 1965, the PAP leadership set out to establish the MSC's brand of multiracialism. In the spirit of its failed 'Malaysian Malaysia' ideal, the island was to be governed strictly along the 'Singaporean Singapore' principle where ethnic- or communal-style politics and the dominance of a particular ethnic community was ostensibly rejected. However, the more obvious contradictions in the PAP government's commitment to the multiracial 'Singaporean Singapore' ideal emerged in the early 1980s when the policy of maintaining Chinese numerical dominance on the island was facilitated by establishing the Committee for Attracting Talent to Singapore (CATS) in Hong Kong to attract overseas Chinese to immigrate to Singapore (*FEER*, 6 October 1983). Skilled workers who were ethnic Chinese or East Asian were encouraged to apply for permanent residency, and from 1984, Hong Kong, Korea, and Macau were accorded the status of 'traditional sources' of foreign labour. Such a status would ensure that skilled workers from these countries would be easily recruited by employers in Singapore (Lim and Pang, 1986: 62). In contrast to the liberal policy towards non-Singaporean Chinese workers, Malaysian Malays have faced considerable difficulty in attaining work permits to Singapore (*ST*, 7 March 1991).[10] At a National University of Singapore forum in 1986, Prime Minister Lee Kuan Yew (*ST*, 15 December 1986) revealed the PAP government's intention to maintain the Chinese numerical dominance on the island when he expressed grave concerns about the declining birth-rate of the Chinese compared to the higher fertility rates of the ethnic minority communities.

The PAP government's preoccupation with maintaining the Chinese numerical dominance became a national priority when Lee Kuan Yew, in the 1988 National Day rally speech, identified the declining birth rate of the Chinese as one of the three pressing national problems (the others being education and the growing number of unmarried graduates) that required urgent redress.[11] Having outlined the problematic nature of the ethnic fertility trend, Lee disclosed that the government was attempting to increase the Chinese population by significantly widening its immigration intake of Chinese, especially those from Hong Kong.[12] By 1988, 4,707 families (approximately 80 per cent Chinese) had emigrated to the island. In 1990, the PAP government revealed that it would admit up to 25,000 Hong Kong families over the next five to eight years (*NST*, 24 February 1990).

Anticipating ethnic minority discontent with the racially oriented population policy and criticisms that such a policy contradicted the state ideal of multiracialism, the PAP government pledged that the curent racial balance would be steadfastly maintained. It promised that this would be guaranteed by permitting more Indian and Malay immigrants[13] to the island if the Chinese population should exceed 76 per cent of the total population. However, despite assurances to the minority communities of 'maintaining the racial balance', ethnic minorities are generally cognizant that the PAP's population policy of 'maintaining the ethnic balance' is essentially geared towards maintaining the numerical dominance of the Chinese community and thus contradicts the ideal of multiracialism.

The PAP leadership's policy of 'maintaining the racial balance' is premised on the belief that the cultural dynamism of the East Asian Chinese is responsible for the political stability and economic dynamism of the island. As far back as 1968, Lee propagated the belief that 'climate and diet may have given East Asians a cultural edge over South East Asians in coping with modern economic development'.[14] In contrast to the dynamism of East Asians, Lee has described indigenous South East Asians as 'a jolly people, they sing, they dance, [characteristics which are] unsettling on the local (Chinese) population'[15] and thus likely to upset the East Asian Confucianist values of thrift and diligence.

Lee's cultural deficit beliefs infer that the relatively high fertility rate of the Malays if allowed to continue unabated, coupled with a corresponding decrease in the Chinese population as a result of their high levels of emigration[16] and low fertility rates, would potentially serve to undermine the continued economic dynamism of the island. Moreover, any change in the racial balance in favour of Malays would also be potentially damaging to the PAP, in electoral terms, as the PAP leadership has long believed that Malays have, in large numbers, persistently rejected the party at the polls.[17] Lee Kuan Yew (*ST*, 6 April 1987) has alleged that the PAP has never won more than 50 per cent of the Malay vote. Maintaining the racial balance for the PAP government thus appears to be an adjunct of its general strategy of maintaining the political *status quo* in post-independence Singapore. This *status quo* is one based on a political dominance that has been underwritten by the numerically dominant Chinese community.

## Diluting the Electoral Clout of the Malay Community

*Urban Resettlement Programmes*

The PAP leadership has on numerous occasions publicly acknowledged that the PAP has always found it difficult to garner strong Malay electoral support.[18] Their weak support from the Malay community can be attributed to the community's perception of the PAP as a Chinese-based party whose multiracial ideology was little more than rhetoric.

It was only in the pre-merger elections of 1963 that the PAP managed to narrowly wrest electoral control of traditional Malay strongholds such as Geylang Serai, Kampong Kembangan, and the Southern Islands from

Malay based parties. Bedlington (1974: 190) has suggested that these seats were only narrowly won by the PAP not by any resounding support from the Malays but largely because of the strong backing it received from the Chinese community. The latter's support for the PAP is likely to have been strongly motivated by a fear of Malay based parties and Malay political dominance in the likely event of Singapore's merger with the Malay dominated mainland. MacDougall (1968: 204) has also posited that the PAP's electoral success in the traditional Malay stronghold of Kampong Kembangan in the 1963 elections, (previously a Singapore Malays National Organization (SMNO) stronghold) is attributed to its urban resettlement policies which had significantly reduced the Malay population in that seat. The Malay vote may have also been sharply split by the severe internal divisions suffered by SMNO when some of its prominent members such as Ya'acob Mohammed and Rahmat Kenap defected to the PAP just before the elections (ibid.). The PAP's 1963 narrow electoral successes in the Malay electoral strongholds thus cannot be convincingly attributed to a significant shift in Malay support for the party. Appreciative of their tenuous electoral support from the Malay community, the PAP leadership recognized that as long as Malay electoral strongholds remained, their future electoral successes there could not be secured. Coupled with that, Malay based parties would remain politically menacing because of their formidable electoral force in these constituencies.

The PAP's solution to this 'problem' lay in the ambitious urban resettlement programmes and public housing policies which splintered the Malay electoral strongholds by dispersing the Malay community into the newly established public housing estates throughout the island. The PAP government's urban resettlement and public housing programmes[19] eroded the electoral base of Malay based parties such as the PKMS (formerly SMNO) and has prevented them from winning a single seat since its 1963 electoral losses to the PAP. The PKMS has since been reduced to an impotent electoral force with bleak hopes of ever gaining a seat under the existing demographic set-up.[20] The purposeful erosion of the PKMS's electoral base through the urban resettlement and public housing initiatives in the 1960s and 1970s was acknowledged by James Fu (*ST*, 4 March 1988), the Prime Minister's Press Secretary, in a letter to the *Straits Times* Forum page: 'Today with resettlement, every constituency is racially integrated. PKMS can no longer win anywhere in Singapore.'

The PAP's precarious electoral victories in the 1959 and 1963 general elections, where it only attained 53.4 per cent and 46.4 per cent of the votes (*FEER*, 12 September 1991: 11), strengthened the PAP leadership's resolve to utilize its urban renewal and public housing programmes as a means of improving the housing standards of Singaporeans, generating economic activity, and providing employment opportunities.[21] It was hoped that such initiatives would strengthen their electoral base at the national level. The demolition of kampongs, where the PAP tended to have weaker electoral support, also presented itself as an opportunity to disperse lower income Singaporeans who tended to be strong supporters of opposition parties such as the Barisan Socialis. The eruption of the 1964 racial riots on the island and the 1969 riots in Malaysia provided an added impetus to dilute the residential clustering of Malays. The riots reinforced the PAP leadership's belief that Malay residential enclaves constituted a potential source of political instability which could easily erupt into civil unrest as opposition parties vied for Malay support (*ST*, 23 Jannary 1988).

The breakup of Malay electoral strongholds decisively undermined the collective electoral clout of the community and denied them the ability to act as a salient force in determining the electoral outcome in any electoral constituency, much less unseat a PAP candidate. In addition to the resettlement programmes, gerrymandering or the electoral reapportionment of traditional Malay strongholds such as Pasir Panjang, Geylang Serai, and Kaki Bukit into larger electoral divisions had the intended effect of further diluting the electoral and political clout of the community (Kassim Yang Razali, 1979: 88).

Having established the demographic preconditions for the electoral eclipse of the PKMS, PAP Malay MPs now emerged as the unchallenged political representatives of the Malay community in public office. Malay interests would from then on be primarily articulated and represented within the parameters defined by the PAP government and its Malay MPs. Its minimalist approach towards the socio-economic marginality of the Malay community could now be safely executed without the PAP government and its Malay MPs incurring serious electoral repercussions from the Malay community.

*Ethnic Residential Quotas*

By the 1980s, the splintering of Malay residential strongholds via the urban resettlement and public housing programmes was circumvented by the gravitation of Malays back to the traditional Malay residential areas around Geylang Serai, Bedok, and other east coast districts. Many Malays were buying public housing flats in these districts from non-Malays who were upgrading to the newly established housing estates. By moving into traditional Malay areas, these Malays were able to recreate kampong networks in flats, form informal associations, inform each other of religious functions, and assist one another during social events at the block level. If allowed to persist, the trend towards Malay resettlement in traditional Malay areas would culminate in Malays constituting up to 40 per cent of the total population in the east coast constituencies such as Bedok by 1999 (*FEER*, 9 March 1989).

The PAP leadership was acutely conscious that, if unrestrained, the trend would eventually result in the Malay community re-emerging as a salient electoral force in certain constituencies. This would enable them to be in a position to exert their collective electoral strength as a political bargaining tool. Indeed, glimpses of this probable future scenario appeared to be crystallizing in the narrow 1988 electoral successes of PAP candidates in the seats of Bedok and Eunos where Malays constituted nearly 30 per cent of the electorate (*ST*, 22 January 1988). It was of particular alarm to the PAP that in Eunos, the strongest opposition team mustered an impressive 49.1 per cent of the total vote whilst in Bedok, they polled 45 per cent of the total vote (ibid.).

Determined to short-circuit this residential trend, ethnic residential quotas for public housing estates were introduced in 1989. Such quotas ensured that Malays did not constitute more than 20 per cent of the total population in any constituency and 22 per cent of the total population in any public housing block. For the Chinese community, the quota dictated a maximum of 80 per cent in a constituency and 87 per cent in a public housing block. The quota was effectively enforced by prohibiting non-Malays from selling their flat to a Malay, and vice versa, in districts where the Malay population had already satisfied the maximum limits of the quota (*ST*, 22 January 1988). As nearly 86 per cent of Singaporeans reside in public housing estates, such quotas have been effective in ensuring the dilution of the Malay community's collective electoral power base.

The official rationale for the quotas was that it would ensure 'a balanced racial mix' (*ST WOE*, 18 February 1988) and therefore prevent the re-emergence of ethnic residential enclaves which were deemed as detrimental to the maintenance of interethnic integration and the nurturing of healthy interethnic relations. However, in reality, the ethnic residential quotas have ensured that the Chinese remained the numerically and electorally dominant community in all constituencies. Far from establishing a multiracial environment in public housing estates, constituencies such as Hougang, where the Chinese make up approximately 80 per cent of the total population, have been allowed to remain Chinese residential enclaves.[22] The contradictory logic underpinning the ethnic residential quotas was noted by Tremewan (1994: 66): 'By this logic, a block which has 87 per cent Chinese residents is not a racial enclave but a block which has 26 per cent Malay residents is a racial enclave.' Whilst the emerging Malay residential enclaves have been vigilantly nipped in the bud in the name of multiracialism, the strong Chinese residential enclaves in public housing estates like Hougang have remained. Moreover, the exclusive private residential estates off Holland Road and Bukit Timah Road where Malays are negligibly represented have not been the focus of the government's concern. The policy also contradicts the PAP government's exhortations for greater family support, filial piety, and the maintenance of traditional culture as the quotas can hinder those who wish to live near their families (Lai, 1995: 124). Suffice to say, the contradictions inherent in the multiracial rationale for the ethnic residential quotas have rendered more transparent the political engineering aims of the policy.

The government's rationale for the quotas has been made more questionable in the face of numerous academic studies on interethnic urban attitudes and relations. For example, Rabushka's (1971: 91–107) study found that it was common for people living in ethnically homogeneous areas to adopt favourable attitudes towards other ethnic groups. Further, people who resided in ethnically mixed areas but did not mix with other ethnic groups also were found to hold negative attitudes towards others. He postulated that physical proximity coupled with superficial interaction across ethnic lines may in fact lead to heightened contempt for other ethnic groups. Urban studies (Fischer, 1976) have similarly found that close physical distance of different ethnic groups does not necessarily result in narrowing the social distance between the communities. Indeed, physical ethnic proximity in large cities may well engender 'mutual revulsion' and a heightening of ethnocentrism. These research findings have been corroborated by several Singaporean studies (Hassan, 1977; Lai, 1995) which have found interethnic relations in the ethnically integrated public housing flats to be relatively superficial.

Amir, Ben-Ari, and Bizman's study (1986) of interethnic relations similarly found that physical contact between different ethnic groups was necessary but not a sufficient precondition for the attenuation of prejudice. For this to effectively occur, it was crucial that members of the different ethnic communities perceive one another respectfully as social equals. Without the acceptance of equality in social status, negative attitudes and other forms of pernicious stereotyping and discrimination are likely to persist. This study is particularly relevant to the Singapore context where the government has assiduously maintained ethnically integrated housing estates but yet have not been particularly concerned with the poor ethnic integration and representation at the higher socio-economic echelons of society. As a community that is at the lowest socio-economic and educational rungs of society, Malays are anything but the social equals of the Chinese and the Indian communities. Amir et al.'s (1986) study of interethnic relations suggests that the social preconditions of engendering and fostering meaningful interethnic harmony may not be particularly robust in Singapore. The empirical evidence indicates that policies which impose ethnic quota regulations at the housing estate level, without eliminating the marginal social status of Malays, will not successfully create the preconditions required to build a harmonious multiracial society.

*Group Representative Constituency*

Implemented just before the 1988 general elections, the GRC system represented a significant change in the electoral system with the integration of thirty-nine constituencies into thirteen electoral wards.[23] As each GRC ward was constituted from three adjoining constituencies, each voter in a GRC ward would be voting not for a candidate but for a team or slate of candidates from a political party. Rationalized by the PAP leadership as an electoral reform that would ensure a multiracial parliament, each GRC team had to include an ethnic minority.

Given the reliance of the Malay based party PKMS on Malay electoral support, the GRC requirement has effectively prevented the party from contesting in the GRC constituencies. Its electoral fortunes appeared even bleaker when the more 'troublesome' constituencies such as Eunos, Bedok, and Kampong Kembangan, where Malays constitute a significant electoral force, were incorporated into GRC wards. Unable to produce a multiethnic GRC team, the PKMS has, since the 1988 elections, resorted to contesting in single constituency seats despite the weak Malay numerical base in such seats. As a consequence, the PKMS's percentage of votes in seats contested has dropped to less than half the electoral support it received in the 1984 elections (Table 5.2).

The GRC system has tended to discourage ethnic minority candidates in the GRC team from raising politically sensitive issues specific to the ethnic minority community in order to avoid accusations of ethnic chauvinism and weaken their GRC team's electoral support from the dominant ethnic community. Thus, under the multiethnic slating regime, ethnic minority candidates tend to be pressurized into focusing on neutral national issues that are not specific to the concerns of the ethnic minority community (Davidson and Fraga, 1984: 139). The GRC slating system could well be reduced to a form of political tokenism as the inclusion of a minority candidate in the team ensures the appearance, rather than the substance, of being sensitive to the aspirations of the minority community. So as not to alienate the dominant ethnic community, the minority candidate chosen is often a 'safe' candidate who is not likely to assertively champion the aspirations and concerns of the minority community (ibid.: 139). For example, during the 1991 electoral campaign in the marginal Eunos GRC, the Workers Party candidate Juffrie Mahmood was accused by the PAP leadership and the media of pandering to communal politics and ethnic chauvinism when he vehemently criticized the efficacy of PAP Malay MPs in representing Malay interests. Such accusations aroused public suspicion against Juffrie and contributed to the narrow defeat of the Workers Party GRC Team in Eunos. Prime Minister Goh Chok Tong and Deputy Prime Minister Lee Hsien Loong have acknowledged that their allegations of communalism against Juffrie helped to clinch the critical votes required to win the marginal Eunos ward. Justifying the PAP's raising of the communal spectre in the name of safeguarding multiracialism Lee claimed, 'If we had not done it, I think we would clearly have lost Eunos GRC and the consequences would have been worse for Singapore' (*ST*, 2 September 1991).

In addition to undermining the electoral standing of the Malay based

TABLE 5.2
Electoral Performance of the PKMS

|  | 1976 | 1980 | 1984 | 1988 | 1991 |
| --- | --- | --- | --- | --- | --- |
| Seats contested | 2 | 4 | 1 | 4 | 4 |
| Percentage of votes in seats contested | 28.3 | 19.5 | 36.3 | 16.6 | 16.9 |

Source: *ST*, 1 September 1991.

party PKMS and Malays in opposition parties who assertively articulate Malay concerns, the GRC has made it particularly difficult for the opposition parties to successfully contest in the GRC ward as they have always found it difficult to field electorally appealing ethnic minority candidates (*FEER*, 12 September 1991: 11) with impressive educational credentials and political experience. Their electoral position was made more tenuous when, under the GRC regime, constituencies that were opposition strongholds, such as Anson and Eunos, have been split up and incorporated into other constituencies. In a further move to reconfigurate the GRC system, the PAP government in the lead up to the 1997 elections increased the number of wards in a GRC to as many as six and reduced the minimum number of single seats to eight. Suffice to say, this move has served to further strengthen the electoral standing of the PAP. In view of the obstacles presented by the GRC, it is thus not particularly surprising that opposition parties such as the SDP and the PKMS had, until the 1997 elections, boycotted GRC wards. To date, no opposition party has successfully contested in a GRC ward.[24]

\* \* \*

Urban resettlement and public housing programmes, immigration and population policies, ethnic residential quotas, and the GRC have contributed in varying degrees towards diluting the electoral and political resources available to the Malay community. These formidable institutional barriers 'placed, like hurdles on a race track, at many different points' (Davidson, 1972: 75) are political engineering measures aimed at blunting and neutralizing the collective electoral potential of the Malay community. Their diluted political resources and weak bargaining position has in a sense frozen the community into the status of a permanent political minority who are unable to lobby the PAP government from a position of strength.

As the Malay community is unable to determine the electoral outcome of any constituency, the PAP government has been able to remain relatively unresponsive to Malay concerns without absorbing damaging electoral repercussions. This highly unequal power relationship has also allowed the PAP to maintain their paternalistic, top–down relationship with the community.

The numerical weakness of the Malay community has also allowed the major opposition parties to remain relatively unresponsive and reluctant to assiduously take on specific Malay concerns so as not to alienate the numerically commanding Chinese vote.[25] When Malay concerns were taken up by the Workers Party Eunos GRC candidate Juffrie Mahmood in the 1991 general elections, the PAP was able to successfully exploit non-Malay insecurities by accusing him of being a Malay chauvinist and communalist. It is most instructive that in the 1991 elections, the highest vote getting opposition party, the SDP, fielded only Chinese candidates. Significantly, the ten opposition candidates with the highest votes and all four opposition candidates elected were Chinese (Singh, 1992a: 103). In view of the allegations of communalism hurled by PAP politicians against Juffrie in the 1991 elections, it was not surprising that specific Malay concerns related to language, religion, and ethnicity were not highlighted by opposition candidates during the 1997 elections.

By minimizing the political and electoral clout of the Malay community and instituting the various political engineering mechanisms discussed, the PAP government has not only been able to safeguard its political dominance but also the position of the PAP Malay MPs as the primary political representatives of the Malay community.

1. Cited in Morris, 1984: 271.
2. Indigenous Australians constitute less than 2 per cent of the total population in contemporary Australia. When the first 1,000 European settlers arrived in 1788, they were vastly outnumbered by approximately 300,000 Aborigines. By 1901, the Aboriginal population had declined to 100,000 whilst the European population had increased to 4 million.
3. This process occurs when the candidates representing the interests of a group of voters are prevented or discouraged from running for office by means such as high bonding fees and the intimidation of candidates by threats.
4. This electoral device is a means of depriving ethnic minority voters the opportunity to influence the outcome of elections in adjoining districts (Parker, 1984: 96).
5. Despite the concrete evidence available, government publications and school history textbooks tend to gloss over the island's pre-1819 history as a thriving trading port that was linked to the Sri Vijaya and Majapahit empires. Instead, pre-1819 Singapore has been commonly referred to in historical terms as an island of a few villagers devoid of a past worth mentioning. Refer to the Curriculum Development Institute of Singapore's (1984) school text, *Social and Economic History of Modern Singapore*, for secondary two and three students.
6. By the early nineteenth century, Singapore became a centre for the importation of immigrant labour, especially from the poverty stricken provinces of South India and South China, to work as cheap labour in the rubber estates, tin mines, and other business undertakings established by Western and Chinese business interests. Refer to Roff (1980) and Turnbull (1977) for a detailed account.
7. Between the eleventh and thirteenth century, Temasek was part of the ancient Sri Vijayan empire. Temasek was renamed Singapura after it was established in the thirteenth century by Sang Nila Utama (Parameswara), who was a prince from the royal house in Palembang. The island subsequently became part of the Malaccan empire and then moved its base to the Riau–Lingga region after the Portuguese invasion of Malacca in 1644.
8. 'Wherever the Malays find themselves in the "Nusantara", they will thank God for having a home' (a translated essence and meaning of the saying).
9. The Malay community suffered from an absence of a traditional leader after the death of Sultan Hussein in 1835 and the subsequent resettlement of Temenggong Ibrahim to Johore. Sultan Hussein's heirs were stripped of the sultanship by the British after the signing of the 1824 Treaty. For an insightful account of Sultan Hussein and the fate of his descendants, refer to Pang Keng Fong (1983).
10. This was revealed by the chairperson of Johore's Science, Technology, and Resources Committee Chua Soi Lek (*ST*, 7 March 1991).
11. In his speech, Lee lamented that as early as 1977, the number of live births for each race and the proportion of births that were the fourth or higher birth-order child were higher for Malays and Indians than for the Chinese (*ST*, 16 August 1988). In 1988, the Indians and Malays were replacing themselves. However, the Chinese were only 'producing' 1.8 babies per Chinese woman. The Malay fertility rate was 2 per cent in 1986 and 2.3 per cent in 1988. For Indians, it was 1.9 per cent in 1986 and 2.1 per cent in 1988. By

contrast, the Chinese fertility rate was 1.3 per cent in 1986 and 1.8 per cent in 1988 (*ST*, 16 August 1988).

12. It appears that the government is not particularly concerned with just attracting skilled Chinese migrants to Singapore as nearly 50 per cent of permanent residents in 1989 (mainly from Hong Kong) had only primary education or less (*ST WOE*, 16 February 1991). A popular rationale used to justify 'maintaining the racial balance' includes the survivalist argument that a vulnerable nation like Singapore should stick to the ethnic numerical formula which has maintained interethnic harmony and high levels of economic growth ('Editorial', *ST*, 19 February 1991).

13. In April 1990, Minister for National Development, S. Dhanabalan revealed the government's intention of recruiting 'talented' foreign Indians to replace the relatively large numbers of Indians that had emigrated (*ST*, 23 April 1990).

14. Gabriel Silver Memorial Lecture, Columbia University, NY. December 1968. Quoted in the *Eastern Sun*, 23 December 1968.

15. Interview with BBC World Service radio programme, 'Peoples of the Pacific Century', BBC, 1984.

16. The 1990 Census estimates that the number of Singaporeans living overseas was 36,000. However, the Director of the Singapore International Foundation (specifically established by the government to maintain close links with Singaporeans living overseas) Professor Chan Heng Chee has suggested that the more accurate figure is closer to 100,000 (*Sunday Times*, 28 June 1992). The majority of Singaporeans living overseas are Chinese.

17. Goh Chok Tong (*ST*, 26 September 1988) similarly claimed that straw polls taken during the 1988 elections revealed that Malay support for the PAP lagged 5–10 per cent behind that of the Chinese.

18. However, during and after the 1991 elections Goh Chok Tong confidently announced that Malay electoral support for the PAP had significantly improved. In a post-election statement, he noted that 'the Malay ground (in the 1991 elections) was relatively sweeter than in 1988' (*ST*, 2 September 1991).

19. When the PAP assumed office in 1959, a large proportion of the population was living in substandard housing conditions. By 1974, 43 per cent of the population was residing in flats built by the statutory body set up by the PAP government, the Housing Development Board (HDB) (Hassan, 1976: 240). The contribution of public housing construction to the GDP between 1960 and 1970 more than doubled to 5.4 per cent (ibid.: 248).

20. By the mid-1960s the PKMS clearly foresaw its electoral eclipse with the implementation of the urban resettlement policies (*ST*, 17 November 1967).

21. Between 1960 and 1970, employment increased by 7 per cent as a direct result of the extensive public housing programme (Hassan, 1976: 248).

22. Despite Hougang's overwhelmingly Chinese population, the PAP lost the seat to the Workers Party candidate Low Thia Khiang in the 1991 elections. This contradicts the PAP assumption that it is generally the strong Malay constituencies that are more of a potential electoral threat to the PAP. Malays constitute a small 8 per cent of the population in Hougang (*ST*, 11 September 1991).

23. In the 1988 elections, the thirteen selected GRC's included thirty-nine constituencies. They were Aljunied, Bedok, Brickworks, Chen San, Eunos, Hong Kah, Jalan Besar, Marine Parade, Pasir Panjang, Sembawang, Tampines, Tiong Bahru, and Toa Payoh. Just prior to the 1991 general elections, another two GRCs were created with the number of constituencies in a GRC increasing from three to four.

24. In the 1991 general elections, the opposition unsuccessfully contested only five of the fifteen GRCs. However, in the twenty single wards fought, the PAP lost four and had its margin of victory reduced in nine compared to the 1988 elections (*FEER*, 12 September 1991).

25. In an interview with the founder and then chairperson of the SDP, Chiam See Tong, in 1990, the latter acknowledged that there have been pressures on him by party supporters not to spend too much time on issues specific to the Malay community.

# 6
# Political Representation of Malay Interests

THE weak electoral clout of the Malay community has limited the ability of the PAP Malay MP in effectively representing and articulating the concerns and interests of the Malay community. The political constraints of the PAP Malay MP have been exacerbated by the difficulties in balancing the conflicting demands of a PAP politician, national leader, and Malay leader. The linkage between the electoral weakness of the Malay community, the weakness of the PAP Malay MP in representing Malay concerns, and the persistence of the socio-economic and educational marginality of the Malay community is established in this chapter. The contradictions in the PAP's rhetoric and practice of multiracialism in the political arena are highlighted.

## Dilemmas Confronting Ethnic Minority Leaders

Ethnic minority politicians working within a mainstream political party that is dominated by members of the dominant ethnic community tend to be placed in a tenuous position of political brokering, balancing, and compromising the divergent and often conflicting demands of the party and their ethnic minority constituents. Working within a multiethnic political framework, ethnic minority politicians have to somehow skilfully appear not to be too ethnic centred or easily inclined to accede to the dominant political forces (Rothchild, 1981: 142). If they appear to be making too many compromises, in order to procure the party's support for specific minority causes and programmes, support from their ethnic constituents will weaken. Stigmatized as 'Uncle Toms', their weak electoral appeal within the ethnic community further weakens their political influence particularly when their political usefulness to the party is uncertain.

On the other hand, if they are perceived by the ethnic majority community to be championing minority causes too vociferously, they are likely to be stigmatized as ethnic chauvinists and being single-issue centred. If the stigma persists, they will be an electoral and political liability and are likely to lose influence within the party. The political stagnation, resignation, or expulsion of the more radical and militant ethnic minority politicians from the mainstream political party is often a consequence of having overstepped the acceptable political parameters for ethnic minority leaders.

As party members, minority leaders are thus captive to the party's political philosophy and directives even though the public policy manifestations of these directives may not be perceived by their ethnic constituents to be in the community's long-term interest. Burning issues of concern to the minority community that are deemed to be too sensitive to the wider community are often relegated to 'backroom deals', 'horse-trading', and other forms of negotiation held out of public purview. Minority leaders are generally cognizant that the demands of their ethnic constituents will not be entirely satisfied within the mainstream political process. None the less, they may choose to work within the existing framework in the belief that it will reap some concessions from the government and include minority perspectives in the decision-making process.

Minority leaders working in mainstream political parties may also play an instrumental role in ensuring that certain politically sensitive issues are dismissed outright and rendered 'non-decisions'. This is facilitated by the exclusion of politically sensitive issues from the party's political agenda and the relevant decision-making arenas. For example, the constitutionally recognized special position of indigenous Malays in Singapore and the government's responsibility to assist the community were 'non-decision' issues particularly in the 1960s and 1970s. Dench (1986: 138) has referred to such minority leaders as 'captive leaders' who are continually under great pressure to 'demonstrate that they are not single-issue activists ... [yet are] ... expected to voice their communal constituent sentiments ... [but] ... will be discouraged from giving too great a priority to them as this would be electorally damaging to the party'. In complying with these contradictory and conflicting tasks, initially well-meaning minority leaders may find themselves reduced to party 'cheer-leaders' (ibid.: 10) who have failed to genuinely articulate and represent the aspirations of their minority constituents.

The way in which minority leaders are recruited to public life and the institutional constraints under which they operate have an indelible imprint on their representation of minority interests. Dworkin and Dworkin (1976) have pointed out that minority leaders are often co-opted into a mainstream political party primarily because of the political and electoral benefits that they are likely to deliver to the party rather than any genuine inclination to improve the representation of minority interests. The co-optation of highly respected and dynamic minority grass roots leaders has also served to attenuate and moderate the demands of the minority community. Acting as 'buffers' between the dominant community and the ethnic minority community, they help deflect potential protest and create the impression that the problems of discrimination and economic deprivation are accorded high priority by the political party (Werbner and Anwar, 1991: 116). The presence of minority leaders also provides the mainstream political party with the symbolic appearance of ethnic minority representation and the public impression that it is sensitive to the concerns of the minority community. By minimally conceding to some of the demands of the minority community, often accompanied by considerable fanfare and publicity, the political party effectively gives the impression to the minority community that it is willing to compromise its larger concerns, without actually committing and delivering too much. The achievement of some concessions by the minority community may also serve to dissipate some of the community's frustration and encourage them to lapse into a quietist political profile.

In more authoritarian societies, the subjugation of ethnic minorities and the neutralization of minority leaders who have not been successfully co-opted by the dominant political parties can be facilitated through more coercive measures. They include the detention without trial of the more radical minority leaders and the introduction of institutional mechanisms which act to subvert the political resources of the minority community. Minority political and electoral power can also be effectively circumscribed by the process of gerrymandering or redrawing of electoral boundaries and the dispersal of minority residential strongholds to ensure that minorities are not in a position to collectively harness their electoral clout to elect independent minority political candidates to public office. Other measures employed to diffuse minority discontent and undermine their political clout include the manipulation of information through avenues such as the education system, media, and the promotion of particular ideological perspectives to explain the socio-economic problems confronting minorities. By promoting ideological perspectives such as the cultural deficit thesis, socially marginal minority communities are commonly perceived by the general public to have only themselves to blame for their marginality. The vilification of prominent and respected community organizations and minority leaders who have refused to work within the boundaries dictated by the mainstream political parties and have been overtly critical of government policies is commonly resorted to. Such measures are employed to ensure that they do not seriously challenge the credibility of the co-opted minority leader.

An effective means of obfuscating the structural and institutional factors which contribute to the socio-economic and educational marginality of minority communities is facilitated by the promotion of ethnic based self-help initiatives. Such ethnic based initiatives help create a class of small but noticeable minority of well-educated and economically successful members (Wilson, 1989). Having materially benefited from the existing system, they tend to uphold political and social values which reflect a 'bargaining culture' (Girling, 1981: 4). They are also held up as exemplifying the meritocratic philosophy which posits that all members of the national community have equal opportunities, thereby leaving the economically marginal with only themselves to blame for their predicament. Minority militancy is thus effectively attenuated by promoting the ideal of individual achievement rather than group mobility (Wenger, 1980: 69). The existence of this élite minority group also tends to widen the social and political divisions within the community and consequently its cohesiveness. This is beneficial to the dominant community as a divided ethnic community is politically weak and represents less of a threat to the *status quo*.

Numerous writers (Fanon, 1967; Dillingham, 1981; Rothchild, 1981) have noted that the credibility of the 'bargaining culture' is likely to suffer when there is a critical mass of better educated and socially mobile ethnic minority members. The widening of this social base is likely to boost the morale and confidence of the community. This psychological boost is often transformed into a more assertive articulation and representation of community concerns by the upwardly mobile members of the community. Their empathy for others who have remained socially marginal may be generated by feelings of relative deprivation arising from their own experiences with the 'glass ceiling' in the work-force. Dillingham's (1981) study of middle-class African–Americans revealed that their ethnic consciousness and solidarity were reinvigorated when they were not accepted on equal terms by Americans of European descent from a similar class and experienced discrimination in the workforce. Thus despite having attained a level of social mobility and professional status, they have not been able to escape from the invidious forces of racial discrimination deeply embedded in society. In their baptism of bitter disappointments and set-backs, many become politicized, emerge as radical representatives of the ethnic community, and challenge the political approaches of the more accommodative ethnic leaders. Their knowledge of the political system, material resources, social and political links with the wider community equip them to challenge the perceived institutional inequities and its legitimizing ideologies.

Thus, one of the greatest threats to the mainstream political parties and its co-opted minority representatives may well come from those who have achieved some degree of social mobility but in the process of attaining social mobility have encountered discrimination and unequal opportunities. The emergence of the AMP in 1990 is an example of the politicized and upwardly mobile Malays. In the early years of its formation, the AMP represented a potential challenge to the accommodative and bargaining culture of the co-opted Malay leaders in the PAP government.

## The Tenuous Position of the PAP Malay MP in the PAP Government

In the politically turbulent years preceding Singapore's merger with Malaysia in 1963, the PAP government enthusiastically immersed itself in a Malayanization campaign with the aim of courting the Malay dominated Alliance government to accept the predominantly Chinese Singapore into the Malaysian Federation. By successfully co-opting a significant number of Malays into the PAP leadership and conferring high priority to the Malay language, Malay medium education, and other Malay based issues, the PAP's image as a multiracial rather than a Chinese based party was further enhanced. As a politically independent

Singapore was perceived as a 'foolish and absurd proposition' (Lee Kuan Yew, cf. Drysdale, 1984: 249), merger with Malaysia was thought to be the most viable means of ensuring the island's 'survival'. Importantly, during those uncertain pre-merger and merger years, the political influence of the Singapore Malay community was somewhat strengthened by their ethnic affiliation with the politically dominant Malay community on the mainland. In Singapore's legislative chambers, Malays constituted a formidable 20 per cent of the total number of MPs (Kassim Yang Razali, 1979: 14).

The relatively strong level of Malay legislative representation (Table 6.1) during the merger and immediate post-merger years can also be attributed to the numerical majority status of Malays in electoral constituencies such as Kampong Kembangan, Geylang Serai, and the Southern Islands. These constituencies were traditional Malay residential settlements since the advent of British colonization. As discussed in Chapter 5, these Malay electoral strongholds were splintered by the PAP government's urban resettlement programmes which effectively dispersed the community into the newly established housing estates scattered throughout the island. By the mid-1970s, the urban resettlement programmes systematically reduced the Malay community to the status of a numerical minority in all electoral constituencies and weakened the community's electoral potency. Consequently, they also became less important to the political and electoral livelihood of the PAP. As Malays were reduced to numerical minority status in all constituencies, the Chinese were conversely elevated to the status of a numerical majority in all electoral constituencies, thus enhancing the latter's electoral clout even further.

Coinciding with the weakening electoral clout of the Malay community, Malay legislative representation dropped to 13 per cent by 1974 (see Table 6.1). At the ministerial level, Malay political representation suffered even more depressing fortunes. Whereas there was one Malay/Muslim Cabinet Minister and two Malay Ministers of State up till 1984, by 1990 there remained only one Muslim Cabinet Minister

TABLE 6.1
Numerical Representation of Malay MPs in Parliament, 1960–1991

| Year | Total Number of MPs | Total Number of Malay MPs | % of Malay MPs |
|---|---|---|---|
| 1960 | 50 | 10 | 20.0 |
| 1963 | 50 | 8 | 16.0 |
| 1968 | 58 | 9 | 16.0 |
| 1974 | 64 | 8 | 13.0 |
| 1980 | 75 | 10 | 13.0 |
| 1984 | 79 | 9 | 11.3 |
| 1988 | 81 | 10 | 12.3 |
| 1991 | 81 | 8 | 9.8 |

*Sources*: Yang Razali Kassim, 1979: 14; Hashimah Johari, 1984: 90; *ST*, 26 September 1988; *ST*, 22 August 1991.

(Table 6.2).[1] Thus, with the diminution of Malay electoral power as a consequence of the urban resettlement policies, Malay political representation in the PAP government, at the executive and legislative arms of government, steadily declined. In contrast to the atrophied state of Malay representation at the executive and legislative levels, Chinese and Indian representation have remained disproportionately higher than their communities' numerical composition at the national level (see Table 6.2).

The declining levels of Malay political representation in the PAP government, paradoxically at a time when there is a larger pool of Malay graduates to co-opt into the party, has been a source of some concern to the community and heatedly debated at major community forums.[2] In justifying the poor Malay numerical representation at the Cabinet level, Prime Minister Goh Chok Tong (*ST*, 22 July 1991) claimed that the PAP government was not in the practice of allocating Cabinet positions according to racial quotas but did so on the basis of merit alone. This implied that, apart from Ahmad Mattar, there was no other Malay MP of Cabinet material.[3] Notwithstanding Goh's explanation, the correlation between the numerical decline in Malay political representation and their limited electoral clout as a consequence of policies such as the urban resettlement programmes and the 1989 ethnic residential quotas in public housing estates is conspicuous.

It has to be acknowledged that a high proportion of Malay representation at the legislative and executive levels does not necessarily guarantee an effective representation of the community's concerns. Indeed, it is possible for community interests to be effectively represented by the few Malay representatives, or even by the non-Malays, in government if they were perceived by the community to be representing them effectively. It could also be argued that despite its shortcomings, the current proportion of representation has thus far provided Singapore with the political stability and business confidence required for sustained economic growth and development. However, the logic of democracy and multiracialism requires that political representation in public office be a social microcosm that fairly reflects the various social elements and multiracial composition of society (Pitkin, 1967: 63). As Gunnar Sjoblom (1988: 197) put it, 'the more representative the parties are in relation to their

TABLE 6.2
Ethnic Representation in Government, 1992

|  | Total Number | Chinese Number | % | Malays Number | % | Indians Number | % |
| --- | --- | --- | --- | --- | --- | --- | --- |
| Cabinet | 14 | 11 | 79 | 1 | 7 | 2 | 14 |
| MPs | 82 | 66 | 81 | 10 | 12 | 6 | 7 |

Sources: *ST*, 28 November 1990; *Petir*, various issues.

(respective) voters, the higher the degree of democracy. The "representative body" (parliament, or the like) shall, ideally, be a miniature of the electorate in terms of interests, opinions, and demands, and their distribution; in that way different interests will get a chance of being publicly expressed, discussed and assessed in the formation of public policies.'

The disproportionately low numerical representation of Malays in the PAP government over the past two decades has been made even more conspicuous by the absence of Malays in the more sensitive and important Cabinet portfolios such as Defence, Home Affairs, Foreign Affairs, and Trade and Industry. The late Ahmad Ibrahim held the portfolio of Minister of Health, Othman Wok was Minister of Social Affairs, and Ahmad Mattar has served as Minister of Social Affairs, Environment and Muslim Affairs until his retirement in June 1993.[4] In reaffirming the unlikelihood of Malays in the more senior positions, Prime Minister Goh (cf. *ST*, 11 June 1991) frankly stated in an interview with *Asiaweek*, that it was highly unlikely that a Malay would be prime minister of Singapore in the near future.

The election of ex-Deputy Prime Minister Ong Teng Cheong as the first elected president in August 1993 and the fifth president of Singapore has further served to strengthen Malay suspicions that their community's political standing is in a general state of eclipse in an increasingly Sinicized island state. The succession of Ong as president, after Wee Kim Wee's two terms in office, has clearly revealed that the PAP government has disregarded its implicit arrangement made during the merger period that each ethnic group would take turns in representing the office of the Head of State.[5] With the Head of State, Prime Minister, Deputy Prime Minister, and Foreign Minister[6] uniformly held by members of the dominant Chinese community, ethnic minorities are acutely conscious of their marginal political status.

The weakening Malay representation in the PAP government can also be attributed to the PAP leadership's belief that the electorally dominant Chinese community has traditionally voted along communal lines and tend to support a Chinese over a Malay or ethnic minority candidate. Lee Kuan Yew's Press Secretary, James Fu, has also used this claim to justify the GRC proposal (*ST*, 4 March 1988). Wrote Fu: 'Time and again, Malay MPs, even with the back-up of the PAP organization, were unable to reach out to the Chinese ground. Then the PM would receive requests to field a Chinese candidate the next time. So some MPs had to be moved.... In several cases, such Malay MPs had to be dropped. The fact is, other things being equal, Chinese voters prefer a Chinese to a Malay MP.' However, no concrete evidence has been put forward by the PAP leadership to substantiate the proposition that Chinese Singaporeans strongly vote along ethnic lines.

C. C. Tan, a former leader of the Progressive Party (PP) who was elected to public office in the 1948 and 1951 elections, has refuted the PAP leadership's assertions of Chinese electoral bias by stating that a candidate's success was not strongly determined by race (*ST*, 11 March 1988). Singapore's first Chief Minister, the late David Marshall,[7] was popularly elected to office despite being a member of one of the smallest ethnic communities. Furthermore, the electoral success of J. B. Jeyaratnam (Secretary-General of the Workers Party) in the 1981 and 1984 general elections against Chinese PAP candidates in the seat of Anson casts grave doubts on the credibility of the PAP leadership's claims of Chinese voting bias.

The PAP's less than decisive support of their Malay colleagues when the latter's performance came under strong criticism by the AMP,[8] prior to and during its inaugural congress in October 1990, has served as another reminder of the weak position of the Malay MPs within the PAP government. Instead of supporting their beleaguered Malay MPs, the AMP was publicly praised by the members of the PAP leadership such as Lee Kuan Yew as a 'positive development' (*ST*, 16 July 1990). Against the advice of PAP Malay MPs not to support the AMP (*ST*, 23 August 1991), the latter was not only accorded legitimacy by the PAP leadership but granted financial assistance to execute its welfare programmes (*ST*, 15 February 1991). The PAP leadership's eagerness to establish cordial relations with the AMP leadership, pre-empt them from engaging in dissenting politics, and maintain its inclusive corporatist strategy was apparent when they granted financial assistance to the organization even though its programmes would be in direct competition with the body established and closely identified with the PAP Malay MPs, Mendaki.[9]

## The Tenuous Position of the PAP Malay MP as a National Leader

As Malays have become a numerical minority in all electoral constituencies, Malay MPs are elected to public office largely on the weight of non-Malay electoral support. Their reliance on non-Malay electoral support dictates that they maintain a strong public profile as a national leader representing national interests. However, this task has been made arduous by their added responsibility as Malay community leaders who are expected to address and oversee issues directly affecting the Malays. Thus, unlike most of their Chinese colleagues, Malay MPs have been uniformly conferred the tenuous and often conflicting task of fulfilling the roles of a national leader and a Malay leader.[10]

As Table 6.3 indicates, the absence of Malay residential strongholds has meant that the electoral and political survival of the Malay MPs is primarily contingent upon their credibility as a national leader to the wider community. Mindful of this reality, specific Malay issues and community self-help initiatives are not promoted too enthusiastically so as to avoid becoming stereotyped as being too Malay centred. PAP Malay MP Sidek Saniff (*ST*, 16 August 1987) has frankly acknowledged that if confidence and support of the electorally decisive majority community were to be attained, it was more important to project an image as a national leader rather than that of an ethnic community leader.[11] On the other hand, PAP Malay MPs are also cognizant that if they are not

TABLE 6.3
Electoral Constituencies with the Highest Number of Malay Voters

| Constituency | % of Malay Voters |
| --- | --- |
| New Kaki Bukit | 29.09 |
| Kampong Kembangan | 28.21 |
| Changi | 27.93 |
| Jurong | 27.44 |
| Bedok | 26.61 |
| Kampong Ubi | 26.21 |
| Ayer Rajah | 23.58 |
| Pasir Panjang | 22.00 |

Source: ST, 22 January 1988.

perceived by the Malay community to be championing Malay concerns energetically, their credibility as a Malay leader would be tarnished. In acknowledging the difficult task of delicately balancing the often conflicting roles of Malay MPs as a national and a Malay leader, GRC MP (Marine Parade) Othman Haron Eusofe (ST WOE, 22 July 1995) stated, 'we walk on a tightrope ... the (Malay) community expects you to go and press for its rights. But other people may misunderstand and say this chap is only concerned with sectoral interests.'

As such, PAP Malay MPs who have articulated Malay concerns assertively have had their political careers prematurely short-circuited or have not managed to climb very far in the PAP hierarchy. The resignation of Ahmad Halim (MP for Telok Blangah) in 1977 fuelled speculation that his political career was short-circuited after he raised in Parliament the politically sensitive and, at that time, implicitly taboo issue of the PAP government's limited recruitment of Malays into the 'compulsory' National Service programme. Embarrassing the PAP government even further, he argued that this exclusionary policy adversely effected the socio-economic standing of the Malay community.[12] The relatively early political retirement of the first tertiary educated PAP Malay MP, Shaari Tadin, in 1980 similarly fuelled Malay suspicions that his active involvement in Malay community organizations and in helping to organize the historic 1971 seminar on 'Malay Participation in National Development' at a time when the PAP government adopted a minimalist stance towards this politically sensitive issue may have placed him out of step and favour with the PAP leadership. His relatively brief political career may have also been prompted by the perception of his non-Malay electoral constituents that he was too preoccupied with Malay issues and therefore fell short of his responsibilities as a national leader. In justifying the need for the GRC to ostensibly ensure minority political representation, Lee Kuan Yew (ST, 14 February 1988) pointed to Shaari Tadin as an example of a PAP Malay leader who had difficulty getting support from his non-Malay constituents. Lee alleged that Shaari

Tadin's weak support from his non-Malay constituents caused the PAP to relocate him from Chai Chee to Bedok constituency where the Malay population was higher (ibid.).

The short-lived political careers of Ahmad Halim and Shaari Tadin are commonly perceived by the Malay community as testimonies of the political casualties suffered by the more gutsy PAP Malay MPs who attempted to directly address the politically sensitive concerns of the community but, in doing so, antagonized the PAP leadership and weakened their standing as national leaders. In contrast to Ahmad Halim and Shaari Tadin, PAP Malay MPs who have successfully climbed the party hierarchy and served lengthy terms in public office have generally avoided making public statements on the more politically sensitive issues such as the government's exclusionist SAF policy towards Malays. They have also acted to soften the tone of Malay grievances particularly when it conflicts with the general orientation of the PAP leadership's philosophical beliefs. Not wishing to alienate their non-Malay electoral constituents and suffer the same fate as Malay MPs who have been 'dropped', they have expediently adopted an accommodationist and incrementalist approach when representing Malay community concerns to the PAP leadership and the wider society.

Despite the vigilant efforts of Malay MPs to enhance their national standing, their credibility as national leaders may have been ironically undermined by the PAP leadership during the 1987 GRC debate. In presenting the GRC proposal primarily as a means of ensuring continued ethnic minority representation, Lee Kuan Yew alleged, without substantive evidence, that in the last two elections, Singaporeans were voting for the best qualified MP which included, among other things, the ability to converse in the dialect or Mandarin.[13] Because of this supposed communal voting pattern, Lee (*ST*, 17 August 1987) claimed that 'Malay candidates will find it difficult' to garner electoral support from Chinese constituents. The relatively poor performance of Sidek Saniff in the 1984 elections, garnering only 57.9 per cent of the total votes[14] in the predominantly working class constituency of Kolam Ayer, was cited as an example of the weak electoral appeal of Malay candidates (*ST*, 30 January 1984).

Upon closer scrutiny, Lee's assertions do not appear to be very convincing particularly when Sidek's poor electoral performance is placed within the broader electoral performance of the PAP. For example, Sidek's relatively poor performance in the 1984 elections was not unique and generally equalled the percentage of votes garnered by fifteen, largely non-Malay, MPs who faced strong opposition candidates from the Workers Party. Little publicity was also accorded to the fact that in percentage terms, Sidek Saniff fared better than his five Chinese colleagues in the 1984 elections (*ST*, 31 January 1983).[15]

The claims made by Lee Kuan Yew and other PAP leaders about the weak electoral appeal of their Malay colleagues have contributed towards undermining the political credibility and stature of the Malay MP as a national leader to their non-Malay constituents. Such assertions serve to fuel the public perception that the Malay MP can only be safely elected to office via the coat-tails of their non-Malay colleagues. With the introduction of the GRC system in 1988, PAP MPs are generally perceived to have been elected to office only because of the collective weight of their GRC team members. By excluding all PAP Malay MPs from contesting in the non-GRC single member constituencies in the 1988 and 1991 elections, thereby eliminating the possibility of some PAP Malay MPs being elected on their own electoral steam, the PAP leadership may have transformed their claim of the weak electoral appeal of Malay candidates into a self-perpetuating prophecy.

It is of particular significance that the rationale for the GRC represents a gross contradiction of the PAP's political philosophy which champions the ideal of meritocracy. This philosophical inconsistency has been highlighted by opposition politicians such as Chiam See Tong (*ST*, 30 August 1991) who have argued that the GRC system, far from institutionalizing multiracialism in politics, may in fact be institutionalizing communal politics.[16]

PAP Malay leaders have thus been placed with the tenuous task of having to primarily project themselves as national leaders in a multiracial society, yet are expected to take an active lead in representing Malay concerns not through inclusive national based initiatives and multiracial programmes, but through exclusive ethnic based initiatives such as Mendaki. This ethnic based welfare approach, coupled with allegations by their non-Malay colleagues of their weak electoral appeal and relatively lightweight positions in the PAP hierarchy, has ultimately undermined their stature as national leaders to their non-Malay constituents. The relatively high profile of many PAP MPs as leaders of Malay grass roots organizations, prior to their co-optation into the PAP, has contributed further to the perception by their non-Malay constituents of them primarily as Malay leaders rather than national leaders. This perception has been further reinforced by the tendency of many Malay MPs to address Malay centred issues in Parliament and conduct their parliamentary speeches in Malay, as opposed to the more politically neutral language of English.

### The Tenuous Position of the PAP Malay MP as a Malay Leader

Minority leaders require strong support from their ethnic constituents if they are to have the political resources to bargain effectively on behalf of the latter. For a relationship of trust and confidence to develop, ethnic leaders must be perceived by their ethnic constituents not to be making too many compromises which appear to be 'selling out' the community.

It is commonly acknowledged that PAP Malay MPs generally have endured weak support from the Malay community. In turn, their anaemic community support has further weakened their political bargaining and brokering position within the PAP government. This dilemma has been publicly acknowledged by Prime Minister Goh (*BT*, 8 February 1991) at a dinner hosted by Malay community organizations in February 1991. Goh took this opportunity to urge more community support for Malay MPs so that their political clout within the PAP would be enhanced. Advised Goh (ibid.), 'If Malay leaders lose some of their influence with the Malays when they join the government, then they also lose their influence with the government ... the more support Malay MPs get from members of their community, the more influence they would have with the leadership, provided they can also win the support of their non-Malay constituents.' Reiterating the same message in a 1991 Hari Raya address some months later, Goh (*ST*, 16 April 1991) urged Malays to extend greater support to PAP Malay MPs if they wanted to ensure that the community made greater progress.

Why have PAP Malay MPs received such weak support from their ethnic constituents? An analysis of their politics of accommodation, corporatist domination of leadership positions in Malay grass roots organizations, management of controversial issues and events, the 'strings attached' attitude of the PAP government towards Malays, the discriminatory policies against Malays in the SAF, the PAP's 'separation syndrome' and 'Malay phobia', and the emergence of an increasingly critical Malay middle class will be undertaken to explain the Malay community's perception of the PAP Malay MP, what they stand for, and whose interests they ultimately represent.

*The Politics of Accommodation*

Bunce (1981: 26) has observed that accommodationist politicking has been commonly adopted by mainstream politicians who are products of 'a socialization process that emphasizes compromise and extols the benefits of making small changes at the margin'. This style of politicking is also characteristic in societies dominated by a particular ethnic community. For example, 'moderate' African–American leaders in pre-civil rights America practised this form of politics in the belief that the weak political resources of the minority community demand that they do most of the compromising in order to gain some concessions (ibid.).

The process of bargaining, brokering, and compromising by PAP Malay MPs has been referred to as the 'Politics of Accommodation' (*ST*, 5 April 1988). This style of politics is premised on an acute consciousness of the community's weak political resources stemming from their limited electoral muscle. Furthermore, this accommodationist approach is deemed to be pragmatic in view of the political and ideological orientation of the PAP leadership. In a 1988 Tinjuan[17] interview (*ST*, 5 April 1988), PAP Malay MPs Zulkifli Mohammed (MP for Eunos GRC, Political Secretary at the Ministry of Community Development), Sidek Saniff (MP for Kolam Ayer, then Parliamentary Secretary at the Ministry for Education), and Yatiman Yusof (MP for Kampong Kembangan GRC, Political Secretary for the Ministry of Foreign Affairs) collectively affirmed their subscription to accommodationist politicking as the most practical and effective approach in representing Malay interests.

This form of politicking has been rationalized as having succeeded in 'winning some battles' and getting some concessions rather than getting nothing at all. PAP MP Sidek Saniff (*ST*, 3 January 1988) has regularly expounded this logic in the following way: 'Of course we don't get 100 per cent of our demands, but getting 50 per cent of them is better than 100 per cent of nothing.' Despite the positive self-assessment by PAP Malay MPs of their style of bargaining and accommodationist politics,[18] many within the community are cynical about its efficacy. Articulating this cynicism, then chairperson of the AMP Hussin Mutalib (*ST*, 31 October 1988) observed: 'I think the Malay perception is one of inadequacy, if not ineffectualness of the Malay MPs to represent their interests.... In politics, to say that "yes we have done a lot of work behind the scenes" is not convincing enough to the masses.'

Untrammelled by their tenuous community support, PAP Malay MPs have remained firmly convinced of the correctness of their political approach and the value of representing Malay interests within the confines of the party's political philosophy. In rationalizing their poor community support, PAP MP Yatiman Yusof (*ST*, 31 October 1988) stated: 'Malay political leaders who are working within the system find it difficult to get support from the entire community ... in history there is no minority, which works with the majority that can gain full support from the minority. That being the basic consideration, the ... expectations of getting more than 70 per cent of Malay support for the ruling party can be ruled out as a matter of reality.' The 'I know what's best' attitude of PAP Malay MPs can be better understood if it is located within the context of the PAP leadership's style of governance which does not hesitate to override the general will of the public on an unpopular policy if it strongly believes the unpopular policy is in the nation's long-term interest.

A particularly unpopular manifestation of the PAP Malay MPs' politics of accommodation is the 'behind closed doors' discussions of issues that are politically sensitive and potentially controversial. At a theoretical level, this form of decision-making contravenes the democratic spirit of accountability which generally demands that those who have power should be accountable and those who are accountable should have power (Sjoblom, 1988: 189). It also breaches the democratic principle which demands that political representatives be accountable to their constituents and dictates that constituents should have some control over the political agenda (Pitkin, 1967: 232). This covert style of decision-making also keeps the community ignorant of the bargaining and decision-making process. Concessions accrued from this form of decision-making may not be particularly effective in terms of policy implementation due to the absence of strong community consensus and support. The limitations arising from this form of decision-making were exemplified in the difficulties surrounding the establishment of Mendaki 2 in 1989 after Goh Chok Tong's 'proposal' at the inauguration of the body that it be partly financed by funds derived from the tertiary education fees paid by Malay university students. Goh's 'proposal' was highly unpopular with the Malay community as it meant that the policy of free tertiary education for Malays would be effectively terminated. Despite vociferous community protests against the 'proposal', it was enthusiastically supported by PAP Malay MPs and eventually adopted.

It became increasingly obvious to the Malay community that when the 'proposal' was first mooted, it was a *fait accompli* that had already been sealed by a 'behind closed doors' deal trade-off made by PAP Malay MPs in return for the PAP leadership's support of the reconstituted and enlarged Mendaki 2. Angered by the steamrolling of community feelings and the 'shadow acting' by PAP Malay MPs, calls were made at the inaugural congress of the AMP in 1990 for Mendaki 2 to be more accountable and include greater community input into the body's decision-making process (NCSMMP, 1990). To ensure that Mendaki remained politically independent and free of manipulation by politicians with a concealed political agenda, AMP leaders recommended that PAP Malay MPs and other politicians be excluded from holding executive positions in the body.

The inherent limitations and potentially counterproductive nature of this covert style of bargaining has been acknowledged by former PAP Malay MP (Pasir Panjang) Major Abbas Abu Amin (*ST*, 9 April 1987). He admitted that Malay MPs had for many years unsuccessfully pressured the government to change its policy of excluding Malays from sensitive positions in the SAF but because this lobbying was done 'behind closed doors', the community was not fully aware and thus unappreciative of their strenuous efforts. However, it could also be argued that if the repeated failures of Malay MPs on the issue of Malay discrimination in the SAF had been publicly known, their weak bargaining position with the PAP leadership would have been embarrassingly transparent and would only have undermined their credibility further. Thus, both the covert and overt approaches present their own set of dilemmas for the PAP Malay MP.

Community resentment against the PAP government for compelling Malay MPs to work within the confines of covert politicking and deal making, merely to obtain assistance in improving the community's marginal socio-economic and educational position, is better understood when set against the constitutional responsibilities of the PAP government. They are acutely aware of the government's obligation in safeguarding the well-being of the indigenous community as specifically stated in Section 152 of the Singapore Constitution. That Malay MPs have to bargain, compromise, broker, and engage in trade-offs behind 'closed doors' despite Section 152 is commonly perceived as a clear example of the PAP government's abdication of its constitutional responsibility towards the Malay community.

*Procuring Leadership Positions in Community Organizations*

Weak community support has been a phenomenon that has persistently dogged PAP Malay MPs since the earliest days of the party's formation. Despite their impressive political credentials in the anti-colonial struggle, 'old guard' PAP Malay MPs such as Othman Wok, Ya'acob Mohammed, and Rahim Ishak[19] had to contend with the Malay community's generally distrustful perception of the PAP as an essentially Chinese based party[20] that had questioned the indigenous status and rights of Malays during the tumultuous merger period. In the post-independence years, PAP Malay MPs were strongly chastised for being little more than *alat pemerentah* (government agents) of the Chinese dominated PAP government. The former Cabinet Minister Othman Wok (*Petir*, May 1981: 44) frankly acknowledged this: 'We were rejected by the Malay community in Singapore ... were branded as Malay traitors and did not get a warm welcome from the Malays.... Although there were Malay party members who were loyal to the PAP, their number was small.'

The stature of the 'old guard' PAP Malay MPs was not made easier by the absence of a coherent programme geared towards addressing the socio-economic and educational marginality of the Malay community. The absence of a prescriptive plan of action can be attributed to their belief that the PAP government's multiracial and meritocratic political and social framework, coupled with the policy of free education for Malay students, would improve the community's socio-economic and educational standing (*Petir*, May, 1981: 44). However, despite their weak support base within the Malay community, the absence of a high-profile community self-help programme and their election to public office without the GRC system, may have strengthened their credibility as national leaders.

The limitations of the minimalist approach towards the Malay marginality was exposed by the 1980 census which clearly revealed the dire socio-economic and educational position of the Malay community. Jolted by the census findings, greater recognition was now accorded by the 'new guard' Malay MPs to the importance of preventing the community from sliding even deeper into a socio-economic and educational morass. They recognized the importance of improving their support base within the community, thereby strengthening their influence within the PAP government. The need to integrate the Malay community further into the mainstream of society and enhance Singapore's relationship with its regional Malay nations was another consideration.

In attempting to strengthen links with the Malay masses, greater efforts were directed at establishing relations with community based organizations by co-opting some of its prominent leaders into the PAP government. Sidek Saniff (ex-KGMS President co-opted into the PAP in 1976), Wan Hussein Zoohri (ex-KGMS President co-opted in 1982), Yatiman Yusof (ex-KGMS President co-opted in 1984), Zulkifli Mohammed (Majlis Pusat President co-opted in 1984), Mohd. Maidin Packer (Taman Bacaan activist co-opted in 1991), and Zainul Abidin Rasheed (ex-CEO of Mendaki co-opted in 1996) were some of the prominent grass roots activists who were co-opted into the PAP government. In particular, the re-election of Zulkifli Mohammed as Majlis Pusat President in 1984, despite his election as a PAP MP that year, clearly signalled the emergence of the corporatist-style relationship between Malay community grass roots organizations, PAP Malay MPs, and the PAP government.[21] The commanding positions held by Malay MPs in major community organizations has assisted in neutralizing community organizations when unpopular government policies are proposed and subsequently implemented. The acquiescent position adopted by PAP dominated organizations like Mendaki, Majlis Pusat, and Taman Bacaan, during the controversial 1989 tertiary education debate, illustrates the efficacy of this corporatist relationship for the PAP government.

However, the short-term benefits accrued from this corporatist approach may, like a double-edged sword, incur negative long-term ramifications particularly when the community becomes increasingly cognizant of the potential conflict of interest faced by community organizations led by PAP MPs and their supporters. Community disquiet over the issue of conflict of interest and the politicization of community organizations has been repeatedly articulated at Majlis Pusat forums and the inaugural AMP Congress in 1990 (NCSMMP, 1990: 21). The leadership positions held by Malay MPs in community grass roots organizations contributed to fissures between those who value the importance of community organizations maintaining a non-partisan stance and those who pragmatically accept the political and financial benefits of having PAP Malay MPs in leadership positions. Those in favour of the autonomy of community organizations tend to view PAP Malay MPs as PAP 'trojan horses' whose political agenda includes neutralizing and reducing the community based organizations to the status of 'toothless tigers' that are unable to effectively mobilize the community's collective strength or mount a formidable challenge against government policies. This perception is fuelled by an appreciation of the PAP government's preference in maintaining corporatist relations with other sectors of society such as the trade union movement,[22] the PA, the CCC, and the RC. As discussed earlier, the compliant stances adopted by organizations such as Majlis Pusat, Taman Bacaan,[23] and Mendaki[24] over Prime Minister Goh Chok Tong's 1989 'proposed' termination of free tertiary education for Malays, despite the community's overt displeasure, is generally recognized as a typical response of the corporatist community structure. This corporatist relationship was evident during the August 1991 elections when sixteen Malay grass roots organizations, led by PAP MPs and their supporters, took the unprecedented step of publicly supporting the PAP and endorsing Goh's brand of leadership (*ST*, 24 August 1991). Support for Ong Teng Cheong's candidature during the August 1993 presidential elections by thirteen Malay community organizations (*ST*, 28 August 1993) is also illustrative of the politicization of community organizations.

The numerous resignations and awkwardly handled expulsions of respected community activists from organizations such as Majlis Pusat and those affiliated to Majlis Pusat, after they criticized PAP policies and questioned the propriety of PAP Malay MPs holding leadership positions in community organizations, have further tarnished the credibility of PAP Malay MPs and weakened community support for the community organizations they are associated with.[25] The presence of Malay MPs in leadership positions in community organizations has had the effect of discouraging many members in the community from actively participating in grass roots organizations (NCSMMP, 1990: 21; *ST*, 22 June 1991). The numerous challenges and resistance against the corporatist nature of community organizations expose the tenuous nature of its foundations.

The PAP's co-optation strategy and the corporatist relationship with Malay/Muslim grass roots organizations has thus been fraught with difficulties. This has impaired the ability of PAP Malay MPs and their supporters in community organizations to accurately represent and articulate the concerns and aspirations of the Malay community. Consequently, the credibility of PAP Malay MPs as community leaders and PAP-dominated community organizations has suffered.

*Preference for the Malay MP with Stronger National Appeal*

The corporatist initiatives geared towards forging closer links between PAP Malay MPs and the community have been made more tenuous by the appointment of Malay MPs with poor grass roots experience and support as Cabinet Ministers. For example, Ahmad Mattar (ex-Minister of Environment) and Abdullah Tarmugi (Minister for Community Development and Malay/Muslim Affairs) were not actively involved in community based grass roots organizations before their co-optation into the PAP.[26] Not having the experience of assertively championing Malay grass roots concerns, they appear to be more attuned to working within the political parameters acceptable to the PAP leadership when lobbying for Malay interests. Their political style generally complements the English-educated technocratic leadership of the PAP government.

The impressive political ascendancy of Abdullah Tarmugi[27] in the 1980s exemplifies the PAP leadership's preference for the English-educated Malay politicians with technocratic skills and national appeal despite their limited community grass roots experience. Tarmugi's appointments as deputy speaker of Parliament, chairperson of the Government Parliamentary Committee on community development, chairperson of the Malay Affairs Bureau in 1991, plus his fluency in English, impressive academic credentials, and membership in the Mendaki Board of Directors fuelled community speculation that he was being groomed to succeed Mattar. Tarmugi's eventual promotion as Minister of State (Environment and Malay/Muslim Affairs), after Mattar's resignation in July 1993, confirmed the PAP leadership's technocratic preferences. Much like his predecessors, Tarmugi's limited community support base has meant that he will continue to encounter difficulties in mobilizing grass roots support particularly when promoting unpopular government policies. Ultimately, his efficacy is contingent upon how adept he is in articulating Malay concerns, overcoming community suspicions of being a PAP *alat pemerentah*, and creatively balancing the tenuous roles of a Malay leader, national leader, and PAP leader.

An appreciation of the PAP leadership's preference for the technocratic Malay Cabinet Minister with strong national appeal explains the less impressive political careers of Malay MPs such as the late Ya'acob Mohammed, who held relatively credible grass roots links before and after his co-optation into the PAP (from the Malay based party of UMNO). He retired not as a Cabinet Minister but as a minister of state (Prime Minister's office). Similarly, Sidek Saniff's established links with grass roots organizations have not assisted in hastening his rise through the party's ranks. After fifteen years as a Political and Parliamentary Secretary, he was finally appointed as Minister of State (Education) in 1991, after persistent calls by the community for greater Malay representation at the ministerial level. Other Malay MPs co-opted from the grass roots such as Harun Abdul Ghani (Hong Kah GRC)[28] and Yatiman Yusof have endured sluggish political careers in the PAP hierarchy.

The Malay MPs' past or present image as community grass roots leaders with mobilization skills may in fact be counterproductive to their rise in the ranks of the PAP. This can be attributed to the higher regard PAP leaders have for well-educated technocrats with proven administrative skills. The inherent weaknesses of the technocrat-cum-politician, such as their weaker political acumen and lack of a deep understanding of the aspirations of the masses (Milne and Mauzy, 1990: 417),[29] appears not to be a major consideration to the PAP leadership.

It cannot be denied that the interventionist approach of the 'new guard' PAP Malay MPs has contributed towards generating a greater degree of dialogue, discussion, and general awareness of issues pertaining to the socio-economic and educational marginality of the Malay community. This has been facilitated by the numerous forums, conventions, and dialogue sessions organized by community organizations and PAP MPs since the 1980s.[30] The efforts of Malay MPs have in no small measure contributed to the material support Mendaki receives from the PAP government.[31] Additionally, the Malay Affairs Bureau (MAB) appears to have been rejuvenated and, since the 1980s, focused more sharply on socio-economic and educational issues, improving linkages with the community, enhancing the image of PAP Malay MPs, and recruiting professional Malays into the PAP (*ST*, 14 June 1991).[32] The cascade of forums and greater media coverage centred on issues pertaining to the Malay marginality has provided a conduit for professionals, community activists, and concerned members of the community to articulate their views. Importantly, this climate of debate and discussion has generated greater community expectations and developed political confidence and empowerment within the community.

Like a double-edged sword, the climate of greater 'openness' under Goh Chok Tong's prime ministership has not only provided greater leverage in the discussion of politically sensitive issues but has allowed greater discussion on the efficacy of Malay MPs in representing the concerns of the Malay community. For example, the performance of Malay MPs in representing and articulating Malay/Muslim concerns over the Israeli President's visit to Singapore in November 1986,[33] dented their credibility. That they failed to advise their colleagues against inviting the Israeli President, in order to avoid antagonizing both domestic and regional Muslim sensitivities, was generally perceived by the community to be indicative of the frailty of Malay MPs in shaping and setting the important areas of policy making. That more importance was accorded to preserving goodwill to Israel, a nation that was diplomatically snubbed by other Association of South-East Asian Nations (ASEAN) nations because of its occupation of the West Bank and Gaza Strip, than towards maintaining goodwill with its local Muslim populace, was taken as an insult to the Muslim community and starkly symbolized the political marginality of the community in relation to the PAP government's priorities.

Shortly after the Hertzog visit, the debate over Malay loyalty to the state was triggered by Lee Kuan Yew's statement that polls taken before and after the Hertzog visit revealed that Malays behaved more as Malay Muslims than as loyal Singaporeans (*ST*, 20 July 1987). Lee's controversial inferences of Malay disloyalty were aggravated when the younger Lee (*ST*, 20 July 1987) took this opportunity to confirm long-held Malay suspicions that certain posts in the SAF had been closed to Malays for 'national security' reasons. He claimed that this policy was implemented to avoid placing Malays in an awkward position when loyalty to the nation and religion came into conflict (ibid.). The shock waves that reverberated through the community arising from Lee Hsien Loong's inferences of potential Malay disloyalty to the nation so soon after the Israeli President's visit to Singapore caused Malays to feel victimized and alienated. They also felt betrayed by PAP Malay MPs who appeared not to be willing to frankly articulate the concerns of the community at a time when it felt humiliated and under siege. The muted and reticent attitude of Malay MPs during the debate on Malay loyalty was regarded as indicative of the paramount allegiance of PAP Malay MP's, as veritable *alat pemerentah*, to the PAP government. Frankly acknowledging the community's general state of despondency during this episode, MP for Siglap and Deputy Speaker Abdullah Tarmugi (*FEER*, 8 February 1989) stated in a parliamentary address, 'It appeared that we (Malays) did nothing right. It seemed that we were singled out for regular unmeritorious mention ... some members of my own community were on the verge of disowning my parliamentary colleagues and I [*sic*] for not openly championing their interests or challenging strongly enough the perceived indignities aimed at the community.'

In stark contrast to the guarded stance of PAP Malay MPs, opposition parties such as the SDP and the PKMS were uninhibited in chastising the PAP leadership for questioning Malay loyalty to the state and maintaining their exclusionist policy against Malays in the SAF. In a parliamentary address, opposition MP Chiam See Tong (*ST*, 18 March

1987) criticized the government's SAF policy towards Malays as discriminatory and out of step with the spirit of regional co-operation and harmony. Politicians from the opposition parties have also been more prepared to articulate Muslim concerns when they criticized the government's Maintenance of Religious Harmony Bill (1990) which prevents religious authorities from involvement in domestic politics.[34] They have highlighted the double standards inherent in the PAP government's interpretation of the Bill owing to PAP MP and Minister of Environment Ahmad Mattar's position as Minister of Malay/Muslim Affairs. Mattar's Malay/Muslim Affairs portfolio has been commonly cited, during the author's interviews with opposition politicians and community activists, as a clear example of the PAP government's fusion of religion and politics. The Bill is also perceived particularly by many Muslims as fundamentally contravening the Islamic *ad-deen* (complete way of life) principle which views Islam as a religion which encompasses all aspects of life.[35]

*Quid pro quo Relations between the PAP Government and the Malay Community*

The PAP government and the Singapore Malay community have endured a relationship of mutual suspicion and distrust dating from the pre-merger and merger period. The PAP leadership's vociferous questioning of Malay special rights under the 'Malaysian Malaysia' banner was cynically perceived by Malays across both sides of the causeway as a political exercise that was primarily intended to shore up its popularity with the non-Malay community in the federation. The Malay community's distrust of the PAP leadership was reinforced when promises made during the merger and post-merger period to 'strengthen their competitive position in society in general and in the economic sphere in particular ... (Lee Kuan Yew, cf. Josey, 1968: 309) ... not only because of the special position of Malays, recognized in the Singapore Constitution, but also because harm will be done to the unity and integrity of the nation if one section of the community is lagging behind' (Lee Kuan Yew, cf. Bedlington, 1974: 289) did not materialize. The only form of assistance accorded to the socially marginal community was the continuation of the free education policy for Malays initiated by the colonial authorities. To justify their minimalist approach, the cultural deficit thesis, which posits that the problem and thus solution lies within the Malay community, was actively promoted. The PAP government's minimalist stance generated Malay anger and a feeling of being 'cheated' by the 'Chinese dominated government'[36] (*ST WOE*, 2 March 1991). For nearly two decades after independence, appeals by Malay community activists to the PAP government for more assistance to the community struck an unresponsive chord.

The alarming findings of the 1980 census, which indicated that the Malay socio-economic and educational position was weakening relative to the other ethnic communities, finally jolted PAP Malay MPs to establish the ethnic self-help body Mendaki in 1982. Importantly, Mendaki's establishment was an implicit acknowledgement that the minimalist approach of the 1960s and 1970s had failed and that an interventionist approach had to be taken if the Malay community was to be prevented from trailing further behind the other ethnic communities.

Notwithstanding the establishment of Mendaki in 1982, the PAP government's assistance to the community soon proved to be of a conditional nature. This was demonstrated by Goh Chok Tong's (*ST*, 24 September 1988) threat of terminating support for Mendaki after he was heckled by a group of Malay opposition supporters at a polling station during the 1988 elections. In a *Berita Harian* interview a few days later, a more composed Goh (*ST*, 26 September 1988) justified his threats to the Malay community on the grounds that straw polls conducted during the elections revealed that Malay support for the PAP lagged 5–10 per cent behind the Chinese. He then stated that the PAP government would henceforth be reassessing its past approach of assisting 'all regardless of whether they openly support us, are neutral or against us' (ibid.) on the rationale that this policy of blanket support did not reap the electoral dividends to warrant its continuance. In establishing the quid pro quo terms required for the government's continued assistance to the Malay community, Goh further warned that 'if they (Malays) commit themselves to another party, they should turn to that party to advance their interests' (ibid.).[37] This quid pro quo mentality was rationalized by a *Straits Times* editorial (29 September 1988) in machiavellian terms: 'The outcome for the Malays or, for that matter, any other community which spurns the PAP could be to become a less important consideration in the party's order of priorities. The reality is, in politics, as in any other business, an old principle applies. It is called quid pro quo.'[38]

Many Malays were angered and disappointed by the ferocity of Goh's threats against the community (*ST*, 24 September 1988). His threats also served to reinforce the long held Malay suspicion that the PAP government was not genuinely committed to assisting the community resolve its socio-economic and educational marginality. Their conditional approach was also perceived as an abrogation of the PAP government's constitutional responsibility. In articulating the indignant Malay attitude, a *Berita Harian* editorial noted (cited in *ST*, 25 September 1988), 'To the Malays, the government is responsible for the progress of citizens who are lagging behind in the fields of economy and education. Hence, to link the support and votes for the PAP to the government's support and assistance for the Malays is not a convincing argument.'

Some three years after Goh's quid pro quo caveat, the community was once again reminded of it in his first address as Prime Minister to the community in February 1991. In announcing the government's offer of up to $10 million, over a period of five years, to assist the programmes and initiatives of community based organizations,[39] the Prime Minister hastened to remind the community, once again, of the counter-productive nature of its 'ambivalent attitude' towards the PAP (*ST*, 8 February 1991). Cautioned Goh, 'Many Malays want the government to do more for them and yet they want to keep a distance from the PAP ... the ambivalent attitude of these Malays towards the government is unhelpful to themselves. Surely, if you want someone to help you, you have to work closely with that person. Otherwise, how can he help you?' (ibid.)

Somewhat heartened by the PAP government's financial assistance to the community, there nevertheless remained a general sense of disquiet over the PAP leadership's numerous references to its conditional assistance. This disquiet springs largely from the community's understanding that any properly elected government is constitutionally obligated to assist the Malay community as long as it remains on the socio-economic margins of society. Additionally, the much trumpeted instances of conditional government assistance to the community has been contrasted with the unconditional and enthusiastic government assistance to the Chinese community in alleviating the supposedly weakening cultural attributes via the promotion of Mandarin through the more than decade old 'Speak Mandarin Campaign',[40] promotion of Confucianist philosophy,[41] and the Special Assistance Plan (SAP) programme in Chinese premier schools.[42]

The empathetic response of the PAP leadership to its acknowledged loss of electoral support from the Chinese-educated in the 1991 elections has been contrasted with Goh's threats to the Malay community for not supporting the PAP in the 1988 elections. Instead of threatening to withdraw assistance from the Chinese-educated, as Goh had done to the Malays after the 1988 elections, PAP leaders pledged greater sensitivity and attention to their needs and problems. Then Deputy Prime Minister Ong Teng Cheong (*ST*, 18 September 1991) claimed that the Chinese-educated had been neglected by the government because it was paying too much attention to the English-educated. Ong went on to add that the Chinese-educated were disadvantaged in the work-force due to their poor English and that this adversely impacted on their social mobility (ibid.). The different approaches of the PAP leadership toward the Malay and the Chinese electorates reflect the different electoral resources of both communities. As the PAP government is dependent on the Chinese community for its political survival, they have been treated with more sensitivity and magnanimity.

Another incident which contributed to the souring of relations between the PAP government and the Malay community was the debate over the GRC proposal in 1988. As discussed in an earlier section of this chapter, the PAP leaders such as Lee Kuan Yew asserted that the GRC system was introduced to ensure the continued parliamentary presence of ethnic minorities which was threatened by the supposed tendency of the Chinese to vote for a Chinese candidate (*ST*, 4 March 1988). Notwithstanding the PAP government's seemingly laudable intentions, many Malays perceived the GRC as primarily a means of undermining the opposition parties who have always found it difficult to recruit electorally appealing ethnic minority candidates.[43] As a Malay professional succinctly put it, 'Does the government implement the system purely to ensure Malay representation in parliament ... or is the system a means of perpetuating their rule?' (*ST*, 2 September 1987).

Malay suspicions about the actual agenda underpinning the GRC were acknowledged by grass roots activists Mohd. Maidin Packer, Abdul Halim Kadir, and Salim Osman (*ST*, 10 March 1988) in the GRC Parliamentary Select Committee hearing in March 1988. They (ibid.) stated that under the GRC system, the status of Malay MPs would be diminished to 'second class' MPs and perceived as unable to be elected on their own steam.[44] Harbouring reservations towards the government's rationale for the GRC, PAP 'old guard' and former Minister of State Ya'acob Mohammed (*ST*, 10 January 1988) stated that it was not just ethnic minority parliamentary representation but effective ethnic minority representation that was more crucial to Malays. As Ya'acob (*ST*, 10 January 1988) put it, 'If Malay MPs are not seen to be performing an effective role, we might as well not have any of them.'

Malay suspicions of the PAP leadership's motives for the GRC have been hardened by the declining levels of Malay representation at the parliamentary and ministerial level in the PAP government particularly since the 1960s (see Tables 6.1 and 6.2). This has caused the community to feel that they have been used as an alibi to mask the government's primary objective of undermining the electoral clout of the opposition. This cynicism has been augmented by the PAP's selective concern with upholding multiracial representation at the parliamentary level when it has generally shown scant concern for Malay underrepresentation in the higher levels of the civil service, statutory bodies, tertiary educational institutions, and executive positions in the private sector.

### *The PAP Leadership's Separation Syndrome and Malay Phobia*

The PAP government's brief but bitter experiences with the Malay-dominated alliance government during the merger period and confrontation with Indonesia has left an indelible psychological mark on the PAP leadership. This is manifested by the PAP leadership's generally suspicious attitude towards the Malay/Muslim community in Singapore and neighbouring countries. Lee Kuan Yew's distrust and low regard for Malays in the surrounding region was exposed as far back as 1966 when he described the region as a 'milieu of poverty, intolerance, and xenophobia' compared to the 'sane, stable, tolerant, and prosperous society' of the predominantly Chinese Singapore (cf. Minchin, 1986: 165). Contextualized in historical terms, Lee's condescending attitude towards Malays in the region may be reflective of a collective South-East Asian Chinese siege mentality which has been described by Regnier (1991: 195) as a 'latent psychosis of insecurity, which is passed on from one generation to the next' induced by the numerous pogroms suffered by the Chinese in South-East Asia.[45] This siege mentality may have been augmented by the PAP leadership's poor understanding of Malay political history and nationalism. The predominantly Chinese support base of the PAP and the Chinese dominance of the island has shielded the PAP leadership from developing a deeper understanding of Malay cultural attitudes, Malay political orientations, and economic aspirations (Pillay, 1974: 282).

The intentions of non-PAP Malay political and grass roots activists who have assertively articulated the concerns of the Malay community are generally viewed with intense suspicion and perceived in communal terms. Trenchant criticism has been directed at Workers Party politician Juffrie Mahmood when he criticized the PAP Malay leadership for 'selling out' Malay interests and compromising their religious integrity by supporting the Maintenance of Religious Harmony Bill (1990) during the 1991 general elections.[46] Promptly responding to Juffrie's criticism of Saniff, Goh Chok Tong (Prime Minister), Lee Hsien Loong (Deputy Prime Minister), Ong Teng Cheong (ex-Deputy Prime Minister), and Wong Kan Seng (Minister of Foreign Affairs) condemned Juffrie for being communalistic, indulging in extremist politics, agitating the Malay ground (*ST*, 30 August 1991), and radicalizing the political climate (*ST*, 28 August 1991). The only evidence forwarded by the PAP leadership to substantiate their allegations was Juffrie's usage of the generic Islamic terms *Insya'allah* (God willing), *Alhumdulillah* (All praise to God), and 'if you vote me, I will not disappoint you' (*ST*, 29 August 1991) in his election rally speeches.[47]

In characterizing Juffrie as a dangerous extremist and communalist, PAP leaders expediently raised the spectre of the 1951 and 1964 racial riots and urged the electorate in the marginal Eunos GRC to support moderate politics and moderate PAP politicians to prevent the 'radicalization of politics' (*ST*, 27 August; *ST*, 28 August 1991) by politicians like Juffrie. Graphically reminding Singaporeans of the dire consequences of communalist politics and politicians, the media published various photos of the 1951 and 1964 racial riots (Singh, 1992a: 76). By making communalism a major election issue, the PAP was able to 'persuade' enough people not to vote for the Workers Party GRC team and it managed to hold Eunos GRC by a narrow margin (ibid.: 128). In frankly acknowledging the PAP's decision to deliberately make communalism an election issue in order to win Eunos GRC, Lee Hsien Loong (*ST*, 2 September 1991) stated after the elections, 'If we had not done it, I think we would clearly have lost Eunos GRC.' For many Malays, the PAP leadership's allegations of communalism betrayed the PAP leadership's distrust and dread of formidable non-PAP Malay politicians and their generally shallow understanding of Malay/Muslim culture. Such an impoverished understanding of Islam has made the Muslim community even less confident of the PAP government's ability to impartially and judiciously interpret and execute the Religious Harmony law.

Johan Jaaffar's[48] (*ST*, 24 March 1997) and Geoffrey Robertson's[49] (*FEER*, 26 October 1989: 11) observations that Lee Kuan Yew had relied on PAP's unhappy merger experiences to interpret and understand many contemporary events relating to neighbouring nations and the Singapore Malay community help explain his diplomatically disastrous statements in March 1997 which described Johore as a 'place notorious for shootings, muggings and car-jackings' (*ST*, 11 March 1997).[50] It also explains the logic underpinning the PAP government's policies such as the ethnic housing quotas, exclusion of Malays from National Service for nearly twenty years, their continued limited inclusion into certain units of the SAF such as the air force, population policies geared towards maintaining the 'racial balance', the questioning of Malay loyalty to the state, and Malay threats against the community. Writers such as George (1974), Minchin (1986), and Huxley (1991) have suggested that the PAP leadership's separation syndrome and Malay phobia is manifested in a siege mentality which renders them generally suspicious of the Singapore Malay community and the intentions of the other Malay/Muslim communities in the surrounding region. Huxley (1991) has argued that the major reason for Singapore's military vigilance has more to do with perceived threats by its immediate neighbours than with extra-regional threats.[51] Importantly, Singapore's preoccupation with armouring itself, its exclusionist policy towards Singaporean Malays in the armed forces, and inviting the United States to locate its military facilities on the island may have raised regional tensions as neighbouring Malay nations recognize the barely concealed motive underpinning the PAP government's stance. Voicing concern with the island's acts of 'neighbourliness', Malaysian politician Datuk Abdullah (cf. *ST WOE*, 2 September 1989) noted:

When you want to host U.S. facilities here and when we perceive that you see us as a threat to your existence and your stability, then of course we see that the offer is directed as a deterrence against us. [What] you ... see is this sea of hostile Malays surrounding you and you are saying: 'Hey, don't meddle with us, we have the Americans behind us.' We feel a little hurt, a little suspicious of your intentions and motives, a little doubtful of your sense of commitment to ASEAN and the concept of the Zone of Peace Freedom and Neutrality (ZOPFAN) and your sense of good neighbourliness.

The state visit of the Israeli President Chaim Hertzog to Singapore in 1986, despite overt protests from the Muslim community in Singapore and the region,[52] coupled with the subsequent questioning of Malay loyalty, was perceived by many Malays as further evidence of the PAP government's deep-seated suspicion and insensitivity towards the Malays in Singapore and the region.[53] In regional terms, Hertzog's visit raised questions about Singapore's commitment to the ASEAN member principles of consultation and consideration of each member's sensitivities (Rolls, 1991: 315–29). The PAP leadership's questioning of the Malay community's loyalty to the state revealed its subtle promotion of the Malays as a potential source of threat and instability to the nation and as a community that could not be relied upon in a conflict with a neighbouring Malay nation (Khoo, 1988: 53). It also served to justify the PAP government's exclusionist policy against Malays in the armed forces.

The vocal opposition by many Malay organizations and individuals to the Hertzog visit was perceived by the PAP leadership as a vindication of their long-held suspicion of Malay loyalty to Singapore and affinity with the neighbouring Malay nations. The absence of any Singaporean Malay protests against the burning of the Singapore flag and effigy of Lee Kuan Yew in Malaysia was viewed suspiciously by the PAP leadership. Relating the PAP leadership's uneasiness towards the Malay community's response during the Hertzog incident, Ahmad Mattar noted in an interview with the author in 1990:[54]

After they saw Muslim groups in KL staging demonstrations, burning effigies of the PM, the Singapore flag, this is when the (Singapore) Muslims should have drawn the line by coming out to say, 'Look we agree with you as Muslims, we don't like Hertzog to visit Singapore, but we end there'.... The leadership then formed certain conclusions. They asked themselves, 'Are the Muslims in Singapore taking the cues from the Muslims in Malaysia?' The Muslims in Singapore began to be more vocal after the Muslims in Malaysia staged demonstrations.... They could have seized the opportunity during the Hertzog visit by stating their disapproval of Malaysian actions against Singapore.

The PAP leadership's deep-rooted distrust of its Malay neighbours was once again revealed when Goh Chok Tong (*ST*, 6 August 1990) likened Singapore's vulnerability to the wealthy small nation of Kuwait shortly after the latter's invasion by the less wealthy but bigger neighbouring nation of Iraq in August 1990.[55] Additionally, Goh's comments served to reconfirm Malay community suspicions that the PAP government has long viewed Singapore Malays as a potential fifth column in the event of military hostilities with one of its immediate neighbours.[56] The spectre of Malay disloyalty was afforded greater poignancy with the publication of the results of a series of 1991 *Straits Times* surveys on the responses of the different ethnic groups to the Gulf War. The polls revealed that more Malay Muslims disapproved of the American-led attack on Iraq than the Indians or Chinese.[57]

It is significant that the PAP leadership's deep-seated suspicion of Malay loyalty has prevailed despite the substantial body of academic research on ethnic attitudes to the nation which indicates that Malay loyalty to the nation is stronger than the other ethnic communities. Studies by the Institute of Policy Studies (cf. *ST*, 30 September 1990) and Chew (1987) have revealed that the Malay community possess a stronger sense of national pride and identification compared to the other major ethnic groups.[58] In view of the above-mentioned studies, it would appear that the PAP government has mistaken Malay political alienation and dissent for disloyalty. The high level of Malay political alienation has been borne out by Chiew's (1990) survey which found that Malays had the highest levels of political alienation (57 per cent) compared with Indians (52 per cent) and Chinese (41 per cent ).

\* \* \*

As long as the questioning of Malay loyalty persists, discriminatory policies remain, conditional assistance is maintained, and the community remains in the socio-economic and educational margins of society, their relationship with the PAP government and its Malay representatives will remain tenuous.

The reciprocal nature of this quid pro quo relationship based on mutual distrust and suspicion is ultimately counterproductive to both parties, particularly in terms of forging a healthy multiracial society. It is likely to reinforce long-held insecurities felt by the dominant Singaporean Chinese community who are minorities in the Malay region and Malay alienation and insecurity based on their relegation to the socio-economic, political, and educational margins of society.

The weakening electoral and political clout of the Malay community as a consequence of the PAP's political engineering initiatives (discussed in Chapter 5) has resulted in the PAP being more dependent on the Chinese community to maintain their political hegemony. This has contributed towards the trend of raising ethnic consciousness and the deliverance of symbolic cultural goods such as the promotion of Mandarin, Confucianism, and other aspects of Chinese culture by the PAP government. Since the PAP's electoral losses in the predominantly Chinese working class constituencies in the 1991 elections, the PAP leadership has revealed its intention to keep closer contacts with the Chinese grass roots as 'they represent a larger segment of the population' (Lee Kuan Yew, cf. *FEER*, 10 October 1991). Also, Lee's belief that the Chinese-educated want 'firm government; all they want is steady progress and prosperity. They do not care how we are running the place' (cf. *Australian Financial Review*, 6 September 1991) has contributed further to the PAP leadership's commitment towards maintaining a Chinese-dominated society. Lee Kuan Yew (ibid.) has also suggested that ministers who read Mandarin and keep in close contact with the Chinese grass roots 'must be given more weight' (ibid.). The important portfolios held by the more conservative PAP leadership with Chinese grass roots links such as the newly elected President Ong Teng Cheong, Deputy Prime Minister Lee Hsien Loong, Foreign Minister Wong Kan Seng, and MP Ow Chin Hock as the chairperson of the Feedback Unit, strengthens the PAP government's orientation in courting the Chinese community to recapture lost electoral ground.

In offsetting this flirtation with communal politicking, Prime Minister Goh Chok Tong's consultative approach to politics represents a political opportunity for the Malay community. Goh's attendance at the AMP Congress in October 1990 despite the latter's trenchant criticism of PAP Malay MPs (NCSMMP, 1990) is indicative of the widening political opportunity for Malays. However, in exploiting this political opportunity, the Malay community cannot afford to remain insular but need to skilfully form alliances with other interest groups who are concerned with issues pertaining to socio-economic equity, multiracialism, and democracy.

PAP Malay MPs have clearly recognized the political opportunity presented by Goh's leadership. The author's discussions with PAP Malay leaders and grass roots activists suggest that they see Goh's leadership as a buffer against the more conservative and Chinese-centred politicians in the PAP. Expressions of concern about the future of the Malay community should a member of the more conservative and Chinese-centred PAP leadership succeed Goh as Prime Minister suggests that Malay interests in the PAP would be best represented by the 'liberal' faction in the PAP. Notwithstanding the widened political opportunity structure under Goh's leadership, PAP Malay MPs are cognizant that in balancing the corporatist functions and demands of a national leader, Malay leader, and PAP leader, their standing particularly within the Malay community has suffered. Their weak political base and brokering power in all three constituencies has meant that they have not been able to effectively represent the interests and concerns of the Malay community. Working within the current political and institutional framework, their representation of Malay community concerns and interests has been primarily of a delayed, reactive, and attenuated nature.

After nearly more than three decades of independence and more than a decade after the establishment of the ethnic based self-help body Mendaki, PAP Malay MPs have not been particularly successful in qualitatively alleviating the socio-economic and educational marginality of the Malay community. By contrast, they have been more effective in representing the political interests of the PAP government by providing it with Malay representatives willing to work within the prescribed political parameters and help facilitate the public impression that the PAP government is kept sensitive to the concerns of Singapore's indigenous community. Their representation of Malay concerns is likely to come under increasing scrutiny as the number of professional Malays who are not employed in the civil service expands. Unlike Malays who have traditionally relied on the civil service for their livelihood and thus become more susceptible to the process of co-optation and compromise, these professional Malays have more scope to criticize PAP Malay MPs and government policies which impact on Malays, and clearly articulate community concerns without relying on the politics of accommodation. Having greater social and professional contact with the wider community, their credibility and support base is likely to be stronger. More importantly, their confidence and political independence will help to engender a renewed pride in being Malay and mount ideological challenges against the cultural deficit thesis.

1. Between December 1980 to January 1985, no Malay Cabinet Minister was appointed after the retirement of Othman Wok. During this period, Dr Mattar served as the Acting Minister for Social Affairs.
2. This issue was heatedly debated at the Majlis Pusat forum in 1984 and 1988.
3. Goh's inference discredits the standing of the other nine Malay MPs who, going by Goh's claim, are not competent enough to warrant promotion to Cabinet ministerial status.

4. PAP government Ministers have generally risen swiftly through the PAP hierarchy. Goh Chok Tong, Lee Hsien Loong, S. Jayakumar, and Tony Tan attained ministerial and Cabinet portfolios shortly after their election to Parliament. After only three years in Parliament, Brigadier-General George Yeo, Seet Ai Mee, and Mah Bow Tan were promoted to Cabinet status in July 1991 (*ST WOE*, 6 July 1991). By contrast, Ahmad Mattar was appointed Parliamentary Secretary in 1972 and was finally elevated to a Cabinet position in 1984 (*ST*, 31 May 1984).

5. Since the death of President Yusoff Ishak (a Malay) in 1970, Benjamin Sheares (a Eurasian), Devan Nair (an Indian), Wee Kim Wee (a Chinese), and Ong Teng Cheong (a Chinese) have held the presidency.

6. The first Foreign Minister in the PAP government was S. Rajaratnam. He was succeeded by S. Dhanabalan.

7. *The Mirror*, Vol. 24 No. 1, 1 January 1988.

8. The ineffectual leadership of the PAP Malay leaders was cited as a major factor in contributing to the community's sense of alienation. Refer to the AMP's journal *Forging a Vision* (1990) for more detail on the association's views of the Malay political leadership.

9. Unlike other Malay organizations, the AMP will not be required to get Mendaki's approval for its plans to assist the Malay community. A special government committee has been appointed to assess whether AMP's community assistance programmes qualify for government funds (*ST*, 10 March 1991). Mendaki's Executive Secretary Zainul Abidin Rasheed expressed reservations about granting AMP this special status. He felt that it was much better for Mendaki to oversee the management of five-year plans from all Malay community organizations, including the AMP (ibid.).

10. In contrast, not all Chinese PAP MPs are expected to be representing the interests of the Chinese community. However, there are some Chinese MPs such as Ow Chin Hock who have a high public profile in promoting issues pertaining to Chinese language and culture. Ow is notable for triggering the 1989–90 free tertiary education debate for Malays when he questioned the fairness of such a policy in Parliament. He is commonly identified as one of the more influential leaders of the conservative Chinese lobby in the PAP government.

11. Refer to the author's interview with Malay MP Abdullah Tarmugi in the Appendix for the latter's views on the importance of Malay MPs projecting an image of a national leader.

12. Hansard, 19 February 1977, Col. 144. It was only in the late 1980s that the PAP government publicly admitted that it had limited Malay participation in the Singapore Armed Forces on the basis of their 'dubious' loyalty.

13. Opposition parties have claimed that the GRC was a deliberate strategy by the PAP government to further undermine them by changing the political groundrules.

14. However, in the 1984 elections, there was a relatively strong electoral swing against the PAP with its electoral support dropping to a low 64.8 per cent of the total vote. The opposition parties received an impressive total of 35.2 per cent of the national vote with two opposition leaders Chiam See Tong (Singapore Democratic Party) and J. B. Jeyaratnam (Workers Party) elected to Parliament.

15. They were Ng Pock Too (Anson) 43.2 per cent, Heng Chiang Meng (Jalan Kayu) 51.2 per cent, Chng Hee Kok (Radin Mas) 54 per cent, Tang See Chim (Chua Chu Kang) 54.8 per cent, and Koh Lam Son (Telok Blangah) 55 per cent.

16. Under the GRC, non-Chinese Singaporean candidates in a GRC ward must appear before a committee to certify that they are indeed a bona-fide member of a particular ethnic minority community. The leader of the Singapore Democratic Party, Chiam See Tong, has criticized this certification of ethnicity as an unnecessary indignity and warned of the long-term dangers of institutionalizing communal politics (*ST*, 30 August 1991).

17. 'Tinjuan' is a weekly Malay current affairs television programme.

18. PAP Malay MPs have often cited the establishment of the Mosque Building Fund and Mendaki as tangible examples of the gains accrued from their style of accommodationist politicking.

19. Many of the 'old guard' PAP Malay MPs are respected for their political activism

during the colonial era when the political winds were fraught with uncertainty. Long before joining the PAP, they were associated with various anti-colonial organizations and struggles. Rahmat Kenap and Ya'acob Mohammad were UMNO political activists while others like Roslan Hassan, Buang Omar Junid, and Mahmud Awang were trade union activists. Othman Wok and Rahim Ishak were journalists for the Malay daily *Utusan Melayu* which adopted an overtly anti-colonial orientation. Their committed political activism coupled with their multiracial political orientation represented a great asset to the image of the PAP as a party committed to multiracialism.

20. Until 1961, Malay membership in the PAP only amounted to 4.1 per cent (Pang, 1971: 173).

21. Until the early 1980s, Malay community leaders who were co-opted into the PAP commonly resigned from their executive positions in grass roots organizations (*ST*, 2 May 1985). For example, PAP Malay MP Shaari Tadin was instrumental in the formation of Majlis Pusat in 1968 but did not hold any executive position in the organization to avoid any perceived conflict of interest.

22. Until his election to the presidency in September 1993, Deputy Prime Minister Ong Teng Cheong was Secretary-General of the National Trade Union Congress (NTUC). For many years, PAP MP and Minister of Trade Lim Boon Heng was Deputy Secretary-General of the NTUC. He has since succeeded Ong as Secretary General of the NTUC. Other PAP MPs such as Haron Yusuff, John Chen, and Yu Foo Yee Shoon hold executive positions in the NTUC.

23. The long-serving President of Taman Bacaan is an Indian Muslim who is a PAP member.

24. Until a few years ago, all Malay MPs were Mendaki council members (*ST*, 2 May 1985).

25. In 1987, Perdaus (Adult Muslim Religious Students Association), Pergas (Singapore Muslim Religious Teachers Association), and PITK (Association for Muslim Welfare) elected to withdraw from Majlis Pusat. Perdaus leader Embek Ali cited his organization's concern that politicians leading Majlis Pusat were promoting government policies (*ST*, 12 September 1987). Pergas and PITK cited similar reasons for withdrawing from Majlis Pusat. The expulsion of respected community activist Suratman Markassan from the deputy presidency of Majlis Pusat has further strengthened community suspicions about the politicization of the organization. Bustanol Arifin Association was also expelled by the Majlis Pusat leadership after some of its leaders made public its disagreement with the former over their handling of the free tertiary education debate. In 1991, Perkasa (a social welfare group) questioned the constitutionality and motives of Majlis Pusat leaders in expelling Bustanol without the assent of its members in a general meeting (*ST*, 22 June 1991). Perkasa and Taman Bacaan were sacked from Majlis Pusat in August 1992 for allegedly damaging the image of Majlis Pusat by their criticisms of the body. The leaders of both organizations unsuccessfully attempted to oust Zulkifli Mohammed from the Presidency of Majlis Pusat at the 1992 annual general meeting.

26. Their weak community support is often compensated by the appointment of Malays with a stronger grass roots base in the more junior portfolios.

27. Abdullah Tarmugi holds a BA (Hons.) degree from NUS and a Diploma in Town Planning from England. Until his appointment as Minister in July 1993, he held an executive position with the *Straits Times* in addition to other public offices.

28. He was Secretary-General of the Singapore Malay Teachers Union and chairperson of the Malay Teachers Multipurpose Cooperative. He was the oldest PAP MP to contest in the 1991 elections for the first time (*ST*, 28 July 1992).

29. The 'new guard' PAP leaders such as Goh Chok Tong, Lee Hsien Loong, George Yeo, and Tony Tan had limited political experience at the grass roots level before entering the domain of politics.

30. In September 1984 and April 1988, major Majlis Pusat seminars were organized. In 1985, the Kemas Congress was held to discuss ways by which Malay Muslims could improve their economic standing. Mendaki was formally inaugurated in 1982 while Mendaki 2 was convened in May 1989.

31. In February 1991, Goh Chok Tong promised a grant of $10 million over a period

of five years to Mendaki and other community organizations with viable proposals and programmes to elevate the socio-economic position of the community. Prior to that, Mendaki had been receiving an annual grant of approximately $250,000 and staff administrative secondment from the civil service.

32. The MAB was established in 1954 initially as an advisory body and feedback channel to the largely non-Malay PAP leadership. In the 1960s and 1970s, the MAB primarily focused its attention on issues pertaining to Majlis Ugama Islam Singapura (MUIS), mosque building, the recruitment of Malays into the PAP, articulating government policies to the community and providing feedback to the government on community attitudes towards government policies (*Petir*, March 1989). In promoting a higher profile for itself, the MAB has since July 1991 launched a series of dialogue sessions to gather feedback on issues affecting the Malay community and to bring the party closer to the Malays. Professionals, grass root leaders, and unionists have been invited to the sessions organized by the MAB. The increasing scope and importance in its functions is reflected in the appointment to the MAB of some grass roots leaders and non-Malay Ministers such as Tay Eng Soon and George Yeo in 1989 (ibid.).

33. Many Malays were sorely disappointed with some Malay MPs, including the Minister for Muslim Affairs Ahmad Mattar, who chose to holiday overseas instead of standing by the community during the Israeli President's visit to Singapore.

34. Opponents of the Religious Harmony Bill see it as another device instituted by the government to silence its critics from religious quarters. Shortly after detaining several Christian activists in 1987 under the ISA, Lee Kuan Yew (*ST*, August. 1987), in a National Day rally speech, warned that he would not tolerate religious groups from venturing into the political arena: '... priests better stay out of espousing a form of economic system, or challenge the way we do things, social policy or theory'. In 1987, four Muslim preachers from India, Malaysia, and Indonesia were banned from entering Singapore on the grounds that they were attempting to incite Muslim feeling and civil disorder (*ST*, 2 September 1987). The governing body on Islamic issues, MUIS, is administered at the highest levels by men such as Zainul Abidin Rasheed and Ridzwan Dzafir who are not known to be critical of government policies such as the Maintenance of Religious Harmony Bill (1990). The Mufti has also regularly made public statements in support of controversial government policies such as the Maintenance of Religious Harmony Bill (1990). Under the Bill, *ulama* and other religious figures who are opposed to government policies and practices are not allowed to speak publicly against them even if they believe that they contravene the principles of the religion.

35. The failure of PAP Malay MPs in persuading the government to allow female Muslim public servants in certain security posts to wear head scarves is perceived as further evidence of the weak position of PAP Malay MPs in the PAP.

36. These views were stated by a participant at the 1991 Singapore Malay Teachers Union (KGMS) forum.

37. The earnestness of the PAP government's conditional strings attached approach was reiterated by President Wee Kim Wee in his 1989 address to Parliament. He stated (1989: 5) that government assistance would be extended 'so long as the members of the community support these government policies by openly identifying themselves with them'.

38. Soon after Goh's remarks on the government's quid pro quo approach, his 1989 'proposal' for the abolition of free tertiary education for Malays has been viewed as an execution of the threat.

39. Goh's offer has been referred to as a 'turning point' in PAP government/Malay community relations and a greater commitment from the government to assist the community (*Sunday Times*, 10 March 1991). To help finance Mendaki and other community initiated programmes, Goh offered the community to match dollar for dollar (of up to $10 million) of the community's financial donations over the next five years. Malay/Muslim contributions are largely derived from the monthly financial contributions of Malays in the paid work-force facilitated by the CPF check-off system.

40. Malays are deeply unhappy with the declining importance of the Malay language despite its formal status as the national language of Singapore. Next to English, Mandarin

has become the most important official language as a consequence of the government's assiduous promotion of the language as the lingua franca amongst the Chinese.

41. The promotion of Confucianist philosophy by the PAP government has generally been perceived by ethnic minorities as an example of the Sinicization of the nation.

42. Initially established in 1979, Chinese students who scored impressive results in the PSLE are encouraged to enrol in SAP schools which offer Chinese and English as first languages. Minorities perceive this to be a case of unequal treatment as a corresponding school system where Malay and Indian students can learn their 'mother tongue' and English as a first language has not been established.

43. These suspicions were aroused by the inconsistent rationales forwarded to justify the implementation of a GRC. The concept was first broached by then MP for Kebun Bahru Lim Boon Heng in January 1987. He saw the GRC proposal as a means of ensuring the smooth running of the multi-constituency councils that would eventually take over the administration of all HDB estates (*ST*, 30 December 1987). However, Lee Kuan Yew (*ST*, 4 March 1988) later claimed that the GRC proposal was a means of ensuring the continued representation of minority races, especially Malays. He purported, without concrete evidence, that there was a trend towards voting along communal lines and that ... 'other things being equal, Chinese voters prefer a Chinese to a Malay MP' (ibid.). SDP leader Chiam See Tong (*ST*, 6 December 1987), has, however, alleged that the GRC is a PAP strategy to perpetuate its dominance and undermine the existing electoral system.

44. In their joint submission to the Select Committee hearing on the GRC, they expressed concern over the quality of the PAP Malay leadership and asserted that Malays were not 'fully satisfied' with the quality of the performance of some of the Malay MPs in Parliament (*ST*, 10 March 1988).

45. The Chinese have been an object of persecution in South-East Asia primarily because of indigenous antagonisms arising from their dominance of the urban economy. Their middleman role in the colonial economy contributed to the perception of them as parasites. Because of their perceived clannishness, their loyalty to the nation has been held in suspicion (Regnier, 1991: 194).

46. Juffrie also criticized Saniff for not opposing the screening of R-rated movies (Singh, 1992a: 76).

47. The PAP leadership's allegations against Juffrie's improper usage of the terms *Insya'allah* and *Alhumdullilah* during election rallies were contradicted by the President of the MUIS, Zainul Abidin Rasheed. He publicly stated that the PAP leadership had misinterpreted Juffrie's usage of the two Islamic phrases as a means of agitating Muslims (*ST*, 8 September 1991). After the elections, Sidek Saniff similarly noted that the two Islamic phrases can be used for all occasions, including political rallies (*ST*, 5 September 1991). The statements by Rasheed and Saniff clearly contradicted the PAP leadership's condemnation of Juffrie as a communalist agitator.

48. Johan is the Group Editor of the Malaysian daily *Utusan Melayu*. Commenting on Lee Kuan Yew's controversial statements about Johore in March 1997, Johan stated that Lee 'has lived far too long in his past ... we should sympathize with his inability to understand the new realities' (quoted in *ST*, 24 March 1997).

49. Robertson is a prominent human rights barrister.

50. The Malaysian government has responded firmly to Lee's statements about Johore by issuing a statement on 26 March, that it would be freezing indefinitely all new bilateral ties with Singapore. Importantly, the decision by the Malaysian Cabinet jeopardizes Singapore's participation in a number of Malaysian megaprojects such as the Multimedia Super Corridor.

51. Compared to other ASEAN nations, Singapore makes the highest contribution in military spending per inhabitant at US$330 (Regnier, 1991: 256). The island has an army of 50,000 soldiers and a pool of 200,000 reservists. In 1987, its annual military budget was US$869 million or 21 per cent of the public expenditure.

52. Most Malays interviewed by *Berita Harian* said that they opposed the Israeli President's visit primarily because of the Israeli government's intransigent and aggressive postures in the Middle East and its unjust treatment of the Palestinians (*ST*, 17 January 1987). They were thus taking a moral stand.

53. The PAP government did not seriously heed the advice of Malay Muslim organizations like Jamiyah (Muslim Missionary Society) and PKMS against inviting the Israeli President. Both organizations forewarned the government of the likely domestic and geopolitical response of the Muslim community in the region if Hertzog were to visit Singapore.

54. Refer to the interview with Ahmad Mattar in Appendix 1.

55. The Indonesian and the Malaysian press strongly criticized Goh's remarks on the grounds that it was highly inappropriate and callous for an ASEAN leader to raise doubts about the sincerity of its neighbours (*ST*, 12 August 1990). Shortly after the incident, Indonesian MPs frankly informed their Singaporean counterparts who were on a visit to Indonesia that Singapore's leaders should be more aware of neighbouring sensitivities when making public statements (*ST*, 19 August 1990).

56. Goh's remarks also cast doubt on his claim, upon succeeding Lee Kuan Yew as Prime Minister, that he did not carry 'the emotional baggage' of the past and was not interested in 'balancing the accounts' (quoted in Ganesan, 1992: 190).

57. The first *ST* poll revealed that while 80 per cent of Singaporeans supported the US-led Allied offensive against Iraq while 65 per cent of Malays disapproved of it (*ST WOE*, 2 February 1991). Another poll conducted eighteen days after Iraq agreed to a ceasefire revealed that 50 per cent of the Malays surveyed supported the military attack on Iraq compared to 80 per cent of non-Malays (*ST WOE*, 13 April 1991).

58. Chew's (1987) study of ethnic and national identification found that Malays have the highest sense of national identification (86–98 per cent) compared with 85–90 per cent for Indians and 30–61 per cent for Chinese; 69–95 per cent of Malays are proud to be Singaporeans compared with 54–74 per cent of Chinese. A 1989 Institute of Policy Studies Survey further revealed that 94 per cent of Malays were happy to be Singaporeans compared compared with 81 per cent of Chinese and 91 per cent of Indians (cited in *ST*, 30 September 1990).

# PART III
# EDUCATION AND INEQUALITY

# 7
# The Institutionalization of Educational Élitism

> Knowledge is the process of gaining information, wisdom is the process of understanding the interconnections of life with compassion and humility.

THIS chapter analyses the trend towards educational élitism and its implications for equal educational opportunity and multiracialism in Singapore. Particularly since the late 1970s, the PAP government's technocratic approach towards educational policy-making has been influenced by the conservative educational philosophy from the West. The 1979 New Education Policy (NEP) and post-NEP policies such as early streaming, the establishment of independent, autonomous and monoethnic schools, the rising costs of education, and their impact on equal educational opportunity are examined. The increasing importance of class in educational achievement and its impact on ethnic minorities, special education students, and others from socially disadvantaged backgrounds is the central focus of the final section of the chapter. Importantly, the contradictions between the rhetoric and practice of equal educational opportunity, meritocracy, and multiracialism in the education system are highlighted.

## THE TREND TOWARDS EDUCATIONAL ÉLITISM

### The Ascendancy of the Neo-Conservative Educational Agenda

In the decades of relative economic prosperity following the Second World War, the social democratic educational agenda which promoted the ideals of educational expansion, equity, accessibility, and compensatory education was institutionalized in many Western industrialized nations.[1] However, the severe economic recession of the 1970s resulted in the ideological pendulum shifting away from the social democratic educational agenda towards a more conservative one. Social democratic educational reforms were criticized for being out of tune with the needs of industry, failing to sustain the economic momentum of the previous decades and provide solutions to the economic crisis of the 1970s.[2]

Swept along by this conservative offensive, the educational agenda, which had earlier focused on issues of equity, comprehensiveness, and compensatory initiatives, had now become increasingly centred on notions of excellence, merit, streaming, privatization, talent, competition, and choice.[3] Committed to the human capital and economic rationalist approach to education which views education primarily as an economic resource to be utilized and invested for the economic development of the nation, these conservative reforms essentially subordinated education to the overriding interests of the market economy. While public funding was accepted as necessary, more private resources in the form of fees and tuition would be required especially at the higher levels of education and training. By broadening the resource base, students would be required to pay a greater proportion of the financial cost of their education. This logic is largely grounded on the economic rationalist assumption that education is a commodity that should be more market-oriented (Marginson, 1993: 56). The rising costs of school and university fees in Singapore in the last few years can be explained from the context of the human capital theory and economic rationalist approach to education.

Paradoxically, the conservative educational offensives in the 1970s and 1980s were made easier by the orthodox conflict theorists (Bowles and Gintis, 1976) who tended to underestimate the potential of the education sector as an arena of social reform and resistance. They maintained that schools only served to reproduce existing class, gender, and ethnic divisions and performed a stabilizing function for the economic and political order. Social democratic educational reforms were dismissed as a Gramscian 'passive revolution' where the state implements reforms in order to prevent revolution and create an environment where passive popular consent is secured (Hall, 1989: 126).[4]

Social democratic reforms were also under attack by conservative think-tank organizations (Hillgate Group, Institute of Economic Affairs, National Association of Scholars) and scholars such as Allan Bloom (1987) and Milton Friedman (1980). Conservatives criticized multicultural education for its supposed divisiveness and discredited the struggles waged by minority groups for social justice whilst Friedman (1980) called for the termination of publicly funded primary and secondary education. Social democratic educational reforms were also criticized for failing to meet the academic needs of students, fulfil the requirements of industry, and contributing significantly to the uncompetitive nature of the economy.[5] Its sluggishness was diagnosed as a corollary of the education sector not being dictated by competitive free market forces. They assumed that the quality of the education system would sharply improve as individual schools competed with one another for students, particularly the 'better' students, thereby providing better educational choices for the public to select from. In this way, the conservative educational paradigm ostensibly provided the incentive to steer schools towards running more like efficient business enterprises where the 'customer' is the parent and the pupil the 'product'. The quality of the 'product' is gauged by the schools' average performance in national tests. Dictated by the free market logic, schools would be encouraged to compete for funds from the alumni, parents, and business community, and to engage in various fund-raising activities (Jones, 1989: 48).

In addition to eroding academic standards, social democratic educational reforms have been accused of centralization and limiting the role of parents in taking an informed interest in their children's schooling (Chubb and Moe, 1986). These reforms have also been chastised for penalizing the more 'gifted' and 'talented' students on the grounds that these largely catered to the 'average' student. Instead, separate curriculums and streams have been proposed for the 'talented', 'average', and 'slow' students so as to foster excellence (Waltrous, 1984: 13).[6] Those who have been classified as 'talented' are accorded greater educational resources.

Proponents of the conservative educational agenda generally do not seriously consider the view that a student's socio-economic background and the quality of education strongly determine academic achievement as this contradicts their assumption that sheer hard work and fortuitous genetic endowment are the key determinants of success.[7] The lack of academic success of some students is not linked to the structural weaknesses of the education system but purported to be the fault of their genes and/or indolence. Research which demonstrates that standardized achievement (IQ) tests discriminate against socially disadvantaged and minority students is generally discounted as it contradicts their belief in the neutrality and fairness of the education system. Similarly, studies which suggest that academic test performance bears a weak relation to job performance are also discounted (Collins, 1979).

## Localizing the Conservative Educational Agenda

In the first two decades of PAP rule (1959–79), Singapore's education system was oriented towards a quantitative[8] and socially integrative course. An intensive programme of school building and a quantitative-based teachers' training course were launched to cater to the high demand for teachers. Education was accorded high priority in the human capital assumption that an educated work-force is an effective ingredient in enhancing economic development and engendering a socially cohesive Singaporean identity. This integrative approach towards education was deemed to be imperative in view of the socially fragmented and ethnically segregated education system inherited from the colonial administration.[9] Whilst maintaining the 6–4–2 British system,[10] the education system become more socially integrated when students from all language streams were required to study English and to sit for the Cambridge General Certificate of Education (GCE 'O' levels) from 1970. Greater ethnic and social integration was engendered as more students began to attend English schools, civics classes, and study from textbooks that were standardized. For the first time Singapore history was offered as a subject in its own right.[11] Bilingualism was also made compulsory for all students from Primary 1 to Pre-University 2. The bilingual policy enabled parents to choose, in addition to English, any of the four official languages as the medium of instruction for their children, with one language as the first language (L1).[12]

The PAP leadership's educational philosophy has long been influenced by eugenics notions that intelligence was predominantly determined by genetic makeup. Believing that the innately 'talented' constituted a small minority, the limited resources and the survival of Singapore dictated that they be invested with a disproportionate amount of the state's resources. As early as 1966, Lee Kuan Yew (1966) advocated the importance of 'nurturing a generation at the very top of society that has all the qualities needed to lead and give the people the inspiration and drive to succeed. In short, the élite.' Committed to the importance of nurturing the 'talented' few and the benefits of educational differentiation, a system of streaming which channelled students into the academic, technical, and vocational institutes was implemented in 1969 (Milne and Mauzy, 1990: 18).[13] Élite institutions called junior colleges emerged in the early 1970s to cater to students who performed particularly well in the GCE examinations.

Since the early 1980s, Singapore's Ministry of Education (MOE) has adopted much of the conservative educational discourse and agenda advanced in the West. This conservative educational agenda was warmly received as it complemented the PAP leadership's ideological orientation and eugenics biases. It also provided ready made explanations for the shortcomings of past educational policies and solutions to rectify these weaknesses.[14] In justifying the marked shift in educational policy making, social democratic educational reforms have been regularly criticized as being inappropriate for Singapore on the grounds that 'we have so few talented students and cannot afford to waste them like the British' (Lee Kuan Yew, *ST*, 14 September 1986).

The institutionalization of the neo-conservative educational agenda was manifested by the implementation of the NEP's early streaming policy. This was consolidated by the privatization of the premier educational institutions into independent schools in the late 1980s. In announcing the establishment of independent schools at the opening of a pre-university seminar, Education Minister Tony Tan (*ST*, 23 June 1987) referred to the North American research by educational conservatives J. Chubb and T. Moe (1986 and 1990). The latter are avid promoters of the view that private schools operating through the marketplace enhance the academic performance of students, are more responsive to the concerns of parents, and foster excellence.

### Educational Policy Making in Singapore

Before examining the various education policies emanating from the 1979 NEP, a brief review of educational policy making in Singapore is in order. This allows important factors such as the educational bureaucratic processes and the salience of political and ideological dictates on educational policy making to be better appreciated.

Long before the receptive borrowing of neo-conservative educational ideas from the West, it was standard practice for education policies and the school curriculum to be developed overseas and formulated by visiting experts, consultants, and expatriate staff.[15] The strong reliance on foreign input on policy formulation has produced a lack of locally standardized tests and an overreliance on the findings of educational research carried out in the United States and Great Britain which may not be particularly relevant to the problems and progress of Singaporean children and schools (Taylor, 1980).[16] As will be discussed in greater detail in Chapter 8, educational policy making is often strongly influenced by political rather than educational considerations. This could perhaps explain the capriciousness of education policies which tend to be formulated and reformulated, invoked and revoked, structured and restructured with disconcerting frequency. Coupled with this, the relatively short stewardship of education ministers[17] has assisted in sustaining the chequered nature of education policy making.

The recommendations of the Goh Report's 1979 NEP and the 1991 New Education System (NES) clearly exemplify the technocratic, ideological, and political orientation of educational policy making in Singapore. The recommendations of the Goh Report were premised on assumptions that were consistent with the PAP leadership's ideological world-view.[18] A social impact study of its myriad recommendations was not undertaken. This is hardly surprising in view of the fact that the Goh Team was largely made up of systems analysts and economists who unabashedly acknowledged that 'none of us possess much knowledge or expertise on education' (Goh Report, 1979: 1). Social scientists and educationalists were deliberately excluded from the team by Education Minister Goh Keng Swee as he had little regard for their expertise. Goh's contempt for their expertise was made public when he frankly stated that he had 'no confidence in social scientists' (*New Nation*, 10 September 1979). The depth of the all-Chinese team's sensitivity towards the ethnic minorities was illustrated by its recommendation of the SAP scheme for Chinese students. Despite their superficial understanding of educational issues, the Goh Team only took six months to complete their wide-ranging report which boldly recommended radical changes to the educational system.

As the NEP was designed by economists, systems engineers, and technocrats, their approach was characteristically technocratic and indelibly shaped by the dominant ideological preferences of the day.[19] The impact of education policies on ethnic minorities and the socially disadvantaged were not on the agenda for serious consideration. This policy making approach towards education was consistent with the strongly élitist and instrumentalist attitude of the senior bureaucrats at the MOE (Naronha, 1981). Thus, the technocratic approach of the Goh Team did not represent a breach of conventional practice but a continuation of the style and substance of past educational policy making by technocrats who generally had scant practical experience or academic expertise in education.[20] As with other areas of public policy making, rarely are major educational reforms and policies germinated from the ground, that is, from the collective recommendations of teachers, principals, parents, and students. This top-down approach in education policy making has been acknowledged by the Goh Team, citing policies such as the 1978 Revised Secondary Education System, Language Exposure Time, and the Pre-University Options project as emanating from the Prime Minister's Office (Goh Report, 1979: 5–4).

The paucity of in-depth social impact studies prior to the remodification or implementation of a major education policy is exemplified by the implementation of the SAP scheme in 1980. No social and political impact study of the monoethnic scheme on minority communities and ethnic relations prior to its implementation was undertaken. The NEP's controversial and highly unpopular monolingual stream[21] was finally abolished by the NES (1991/2) leaving thousands of monolingual stream students without the secondary education important for social mobility.[22] Despite the absence of a public apology, the short-sightedness of the NEP's monolingual stream and early streaming policy was acknowledged by the Minister of Education, Tony Tan, in a public address before his retirement in 1992. He conceded that the monolingual streaming policy was an unsuccessful experiment in educational and economic terms.[23] The Open University concept, announced amidst much publicity in July 1991, was initially scheduled to open its doors as a public tertiary institution in 1993. However, less than a year after the initial announcement (March 1992) the government revealed that the proposed Open University would be run not as a public body but as a private institution.[24] In another complete turnaround, the Chinese language based Nanyang University and the University of Singapore were merged in 1980. Only a decade later, they were reorganized into separate tertiary institutions. Religious Knowledge replaced Civics as a compulsory subject in 1984 but by 1989 its compulsory status was terminated and by 1990 the subject was not examinable. Another short-lived and poorly researched programme was the 1992 Day School Scheme for primary pupils. Poor parental response to the scheme[25] resulted in its termination the following year (*ST*, 2 June 1992).

Changes and minor alterations to particular education policies have been undertaken when they appear to evoke strong public resistance. However, these policy changes and modifications largely represent pragmatic gestures aimed at diffusing public discontent. An example of the changes in education policy as a response to public resistance was the short-lived and highly unpopular graduate mothers policy. The policy offered children of tertiary educated women priority into the school of their choice. Based on eugenics principles, it was a means of encouraging graduate women to have more children to counter the higher procreation patterns of less educated women. Introduced in 1983, the policy was terminated more than a year later after it generated considerable public opposition and posed too much of an electoral liability for the PAP government. Particularly since the mid-1980s, education policy makers have thus learnt to become more politically sensitive and flexible enough to incur minor policy adjustments and fine-tuning to suit the changing economic and social climate. However, the fundamental characteristics and components of the education system such as the eugenics based Gifted Education Programme (GEP), establishment of SAP, early streaming system, and its ethnic/linguistic bias such as the promotion of Mandarin have not been substantively altered despite strong public criticism against many of these programmes.

### The New Education Policy

The Goh Report (1979) represented the first of a series of educational reforms which was inspired by the neo-conservative educational agenda that was taking root in many Western nations by the late 1970s. Its implementation was an educational watershed which clearly signalled the ascendancy of an overtly conservative educational agenda and firmly institutionalized the foundations of educational differentiation primarily through the policy of early streaming.

The three major weaknesses of the education system cited by the Goh Report (1979: 1–4) which warranted a restructuring of the existing education system were:
1. high education 'wastage' levels (high attrition rates);[26]
2. low literacy level of many school leavers;[27] and
3. non-attainment of effective bilingualism.[28]

With only minimal public debate and discussion on the radical recommendations of the Goh Report, it was swiftly implemented under the emblem of the NEP. The most distinctive feature of the NEP was the streaming of nine-year old students in Primary 3 into the
1. normal bilingual stream (60 per cent) — six years of primary education;[29]
2. extended bilingual stream (20 per cent) — eight years of primary education;[30] or the
3. monolingual (pre-vocational) stream (20 per cent) — eight years of terminating primary education.[31]

At the secondary level, students are again streamed into three channels on the basis of their performance in the PSLE. They include the
1. special or gifted stream (top 10 per cent) — four years of secondary education;[32]
2. express stream (next 40 per cent) — four years of secondary education;[33] and the
3. normal stream (bottom 50 per cent) — five years of secondary education.[34]

The principal argument forwarded to justify the hierarchically structured streaming system was that the previous 6-4-2 system, which generally subjected most students to the same syllabus and examination within the same time frame, was unfair and a 'chief defect of our educational system in the past' (Goh Report, 1979: 1–5). Employing egalitarian rhetoric, despite its élitist assumptions, the report alleged that the uniform system favoured the above average but penalized the slow learners as different students possessed different absorption capacities. Early streaming would supposedly rectify this deficiency by identifying the most gifted students and transferring them to a more demanding and intellectually stimulating curriculum, taught in schools with the best educational facilities. Those identified as the intellectually 'weaker' students would be transferred to the extended and monolingual stream which would prepare them for vocational training. Students identified as lying somewhere between the intellectual poles but closer to the latter were to be placed in the extended primary and 'normal' secondary stream. With this educational regime of differentiated curriculums and time frames for those with different 'abilities', students were to be taught 'at the pace at which they can absorb instruction' (Goh Report, 1979: 1–3).

A less publicized but implicit function of streaming was that it would help facilitate the channelling of students from the various educational streams eventually into the varying levels of the occupational hierarchy. The 'less able' monolingual and normal stream students, who constitute approximately 40 per cent of the student population at the primary and secondary level, were to be provided with the basic educational and technical/vocational skills to carry out their future positions as semi-skilled workers in the labour force. The remaining 50 per cent would be expected to complete secondary school and enter the polytechnics and other training institutes. A smaller minority would be elevated to the élite pre-university junior colleges and an even smaller élite would engage in tertiary studies at the university. This streaming regime was expected to minimize 'wastage' in the education system. Instead of offering, as it did in the past, the opportunity for most students to sit for the major examinations, such as the PSLE and GCE 'O' levels, educational resources would instead be disproportionately channelled into the various élite programmes for the educationally 'talented'. This is based on the assumption that the more 'talented' students would reap greater dividends for the economy and the nation in the long run.

## The NEP's Early Streaming Policy

The major rationale advanced by the Goh Report (1979) to justify early streaming was that it would allow students to learn and develop at their own pace. However, students identified as 'less able' were channelled into the non-academic streams where the educational resources, curriculum, and credentials offered were not only different but generally inferior to that offered to students in the academic mainstream. Cramped in classes of up to forty students, they are taught by teachers who are not specially trained to teach 'slower' students. Once channelled to the monolingual stream, the formidable academic and psychological barriers that must be overcome in order to transfer laterally to the better streams virtually condemn these students to a 'path of no return' (STU, 1980: 50). Similarly, lateral transfers for normal stream secondary students to the express stream is just as onerous due to the stringent promotion requirements.[35] Herein lies one of the major contradictions in the Goh Report's ostensible concern for the 'less able' when in practice limited opportunities were made available to them to have real choices, learn and develop at their own pace with the aid of satisfactory resources, and within the mainstream education system.

A substantial body of research has consistently demonstrated that early streaming has a powerful predictive effect on a student's future academic achievement, post-school career opportunities (Ball, 1986: 85) and enhances the influence of family background on academic attainment (Mortimore and Mortimore, 1986: 26). Studies by Barker-Lunn (1970) and Alexander et al. (1978) found that students wrongly streamed tended to assume the academic ability of the stream they were assigned to thereby realizing the self-fulfilling prophecy. Significantly, studies (Calhoun and Elliot, 1977; Dar and Resh, 1986; Gamoran, 1986; Slavin and Madden, 1986; Sorensen and Hallinan, 1986) have indicated that 'slower' learners in unstreamed classes tended to perform much better than 'slow' learners that have been channelled into the slow streams. Contrary to the early streaming logic, good learning environments, positive feedback procedures between student and teacher, and corrective procedures in and out of the classroom have been found to help most children to learn at a very high level. Provided with such an intellectually and emotionally supportive environment, most children learn to develop positive attitudes towards school and to build confidence in their learning ability (ibid.).

Singaporean studies (STU, 1980; Heng, 1985; Saroja, 1987; Mannarlingham 1989) on the slower stream students suggest that streaming has psychologically demoralized students in the slower streams. Feeling dejected, powerless, and on 'the path of no return', many of the students that have been stigmatized as 'slow' and academic failures begin to lose the motivation to study hard and catch up with other students in the faster track streams (Heng, 1985: 39). Failing to get the approval of their peers, parents, and teachers, many decide not to try any longer in the hope that adults will no longer entertain any hopes of their academic redemption thereby relieving themselves of the pressure to succeed. Ever conscious that their future career options are limited, they are prone towards adopting a defeatist 'don't care' attitude (ibid., 1985: 48) as a defence mechanism to cope with their failure and acute sense of frustration with the school system. Feeling denigrated and losing self-esteem, some resort to disruptive anti-social behaviour such as glue-sniffing, smoking, and dressing in an unruly fashion (ibid.: 59) which signal their resistance to the dominant values of the educational system that has so condemned and rejected them. The more perceptive may begin to see their academic failure not so much in terms of their individual weaknesses but the weakness of the educational system itself which has impeded their academic progress (Willis, 1977). However, like the others, they tend to externalize their frustrations through forms of non-constructive behaviour.

The system of streaming and labelling children as 'gifted', 'slow learner', and 'average' is a social construct that is linked to the ideological and educational beliefs of the conservative educational agenda. It is also premised on the highly contentious IQ tests[36] and based on a limited range of knowledge (such as Mathematics and Science) as opposed to a broader range of attributes. Far from being objective and neutral, such forms of labelling legitimize the distribution of different kinds of knowledge and curricula to different students, and serve to divert attention from the structural anomalies and social inequities of the educational system (Apple, 1987: 25, 135). It is a cruel irony that many students who are channelled into the slower streams have their confidence and self-esteem shattered[37] and often come to believe the academic label that they have been stigmatized with. During the author's period as a relief teacher in 1992, it was common to hear self-demeaning statements from normal stream students such as 'we're just stupid' and 'we're only from the normal stream' to explain their poor academic performance. They tend to believe and act out the 'less able' label accorded to them by the streaming system. Confirming the adverse psychological effects of streaming in Singapore, Professor of Social Medicine Nalla Tan (*Asiaweek*, 17 May 1985) noted that it imposes 'severe, neurotic, psychological, and traumatic effects on both children and parents'.

A survey by the National Institute of Education on students revealed that over half of the 4,000 teenagers surveyed suffered from low self-esteem which was directly related to the stressful nature of the educational system (S. Davie, *ST*, 28 July 1992).[38] Further, the eugenics premise underlying the early streaming policy has caused parents to blame themselves for their children's poor academic progress. The pressure on these students is intensified when they are made to feel that they have let the academic standards and image of the school down by their contribution to the number of monolingual and extended classes in the school (Heng, 1985: 18). In the highly competitive educational environment in Singapore, the more 'slow' stream classes in a school the lower its educational standing. These schools would generally rate poorly against élite schools like Raffles Institution which do not offer classes for 'slower' students. Students in these prestigious schools who perform poorly in their studies are often transferred out to 'lesser' schools so as not to lower the academic reputation of the school. The poor self-esteem of normal stream students is further dented by the lack of social interaction with the more 'meritorious' express stream students in the school who tend to develop a superiority complex and hold negative stereotypes of the former (ibid.: 19).

The pressure endured by the slower stream students has been compounded further by the low morale and resentment of teachers assigned to the slower streams. A 1983 survey conducted by MOE to ascertain the experiences of primary school teachers in teaching the monolingual stream found that most teachers expressed a lack of job satisfaction and frustration with being assigned to the slower stream (*ST*, 10 April 1983). This was confirmed by a report presented to the Schools Council in 1982 which affirmed that the 'better' teachers tended to be placed in the faster streams as the academic reputation of a school is contingent upon their student's performance in the final examinations (*ST*, 17 October 1982). The tendency of assigning the younger and better qualified teachers to the express stream and those with less credentials to the normal stream was observed by the author during her period as a relief teacher in government schools in 1992.

Feeling demoted and stigmatized as less competent, teachers assigned to the slower streams, like their students, suffer from low morale. The frustration with having to teach in a stream for which they have not been properly trained tends to have a deleterious impact on their teaching standards. The extent of their stress and disillusionment with the teaching profession was revealed by a 1986 MOE survey of monolingual teachers which alarmingly revealed that 50 per cent had left the teaching profession after being assigned to the monolingual stream (*ST*, 18 April 1987). This high attrition rate of monolingual teachers had exacerbated the staffing problems confronting schools with a high number of monolingual classes. As a consequence of this, many government schools with larger numbers of monolingual and extended stream classes were compelled to rely more on relief teachers who tend not to be professionally trained teachers.

It is of particular concern that the system of educational differentiation and streaming at an early age may have mistakenly diagnosed students with learning difficulties such as dyslexia and assigned them to the slower streams. Particularly in schools with many slow stream classes and where individualized attention is infrequent, the learning disability of such students may never be diagnosed and properly treated. In this way, learning handicaps are quite likely to be transformed into academic failure. Early streaming also ignores the view that academic ability develops and matures at different rates for different children, and that its emphasis on language and mathematics downgrades other cognitive abilities such as creative and artistic skills. The prevalence of negative stereotypical attitudes held by teachers towards students who are poor or socially disadvantaged ethnic minorities, regarding them as 'slow', 'stupid', and generally intellectually inferior, has in no small measure contributed to their overrepresentation in the Educationally Sub-Normal (ESN) stream (Clark, 1965: 131; Dorn, 1985; Apple, 1987: 137). In the United States, and Britain, there is a clear overrepresentation of students of African and Carribean descent that have been erroneously classified under ESN, and a gross underrepresentation in the fast track streams (Tomlinson, 1982; Dorn, 1985: 15). In the Singapore educational context, socially disadvantaged ethnic minorities such as Malays, and to a lesser extent Indians, have been persistently overrepresented in the slower monolingual and normal streams.

The NEP's early streaming policy is arguably one of the most unpopular and politically costly education policies introduced by the PAP government. The widespread unpopularity of the policy is clearly evidenced by dissenting letters to the *Straits Times* forum page (*ST*, 17 March 1990; *ST*, 15 March 1991), the salience of the streaming policy as an electoral issue during election campaigns, and the passionate parliamentary debates on the issue. Even PAP MPs have been known to publicly criticize educational streaming at an early age.[39] A 1981 comprehensive survey of 1,500 teachers from 170 primary and secondary schools by the Singapore Teachers Union (*ST*, 25 March 1981) found that the majority of teachers were opposed to the NEP. Alarmed by the strong level of opposition to the early streaming policy, the Singapore Teachers Union recommended that the policy of streaming at Primary 3 be abolished in favour of the pre-NEP policy of streaming at the end of primary school (*ST*, 25 March 1981). Teachers and parents appear to be apprehensive of the widening educational, infrastructural, and social disparity between schools with more express classes and others with more slower stream classes. This phenomenon is augmented by the tendency for the 'better' schools to attract the more 'talented' students from schools with a lower academic rating and the 'slower' students from the 'better' and prestigious schools to be re-routed to the less academically rated schools. The early streaming system thus serves to intensify the hierarchical relationship between schools.

Despite this groundswell of public unhappiness with early streaming, the PAP government has stood firm in its belief that the early streaming policy is in the long-term educational and economic interest of the nation. Its technocratic top-down approach towards educational policy making was demonstrated when it removed the right of parents to reject their child being channelled to the monolingual stream between the years 1983 and 1985 (Soon, 1988: 22).[40] Confronted with strong public pressure, the policy was skilfully 'softened' without any fundamental changes to the NEP's streaming system in 1992. Parents were from then allowed on behalf of their children to opt for a stream that is different from that recommended by the school at the end of the Primary 4 streaming process. However, at the end of Primary 5 the school's judgement in the streaming of the student could not be challenged (*ST*, 14 October 1992).

## The Special Assistance Plan

The NEP is not only characterized by its élitism but also by its ethnic and linguistic bias with the inception of the monoethnic SAP schools. To ensure its ethnic and academic exclusivity, only the top Chinese PSLE students[41] are eligible for enrolment in the prestigious SAP schools where English and Chinese are taught as a first language. Purportedly the brainchild of then Prime Minister Lee Kuan Yew (Goh Report, 1979: 1–3), the implementation of the Chinese only SAP schools coincided with the initial state sponsorship of the 'Speak Mandarin Campaign' (1979) which was ostensibly aimed at improving the Chinese community's proficiency in Mandarin as their 'mother tongue'.[42] Mandarin is perceived by the PAP leadership as an effective means of transmitting positive Chinese cultural values which are purported to be fast eroding in the Westernizing island state.

The establishment of SAP schools was also a means of stemming the dwindling enrolments, particularly in the 1960s and 1970s, of Chinese language schools (Table 7.1) as more Singaporeans pragmatically recognized the benefits of English education in gaining employment and achieving social mobility. If the trend in the dwindling enrolments was not arrested, Chinese stream schools would eventually have to close their doors, as was the fate of Malay and Tamil stream schools.

The SAP was thus a means of preserving the premier Chinese stream schools and with it the positive Chinese cultural values that are presumably inculcated through Mandarin. In lending further weight to the SAP school concept, Prime Minister Lee Kuan Yew asserted that Chinese education imparted desirable communitarian values such as a desire for social unity and a willingness to sacrifice for the larger community (*ST*, 19 August 1978).

Despite the PAP government's enthusiastic promotion of SAP schools and their superior educational facilities, SAP schools only managed to attract half of the top 8 per cent of PSLE students into the programme in 1979. For most of the 1980s, public enthusiasm for the government sponsored programme did not significantly improve. For example, in 1980 only 37.5 per cent of PSLE students invited to the programme chose to study at SAP schools (*ST*, 23 January 1981). By 1983, 38.8 per cent of the eligible PSLE students opted for the SAP schools (*ST*, 14 August 1983). It appeared that the parents of 'talented' Chinese students may not have been thoroughly convinced of the educational benefits of such a scheme.

Undeterred by the poor student response to the scheme and determined to make the SAP a success, a generous package of concessional inducements was offered to students eligible for the scheme in an attempt to bolster enrolment numbers. These concessions included:

TABLE 7.1
Decreasing Popularity of Chinese Stream Schools

| Year | *English Stream Enrolment* | *Chinese Stream Enrolment* | *Chinese Stream Enrolment as a % of the Total* |
|---|---|---|---|
| 1959 | 28,113 | 27,223 | 45.9 |
| 1962 | 31,580 | 22,669 | 38.4 |
| 1965 | 36,269 | 17,735 | 30.0 |
| 1968 | 34,090 | 18,927 | 33.6 |
| 1971 | 37,505 | 15,731 | 29.0 |
| 1974 | 36,834 | 10,263 | 21.7 |
| 1975 | 35,086 | 9,112 | 20.5 |
| 1976 | 35,035 | 7,478 | 17.5 |
| 1977 | 40,622 | 6,590 | 13.9 |
| 1978 | 41,995 | 5,289 | 11.2 |

*Source*: Goh Report, 1979: 1–1.

1. Granting SAP students an extra two points to their 'O' levels and 'A' level aggregate.
2. Accepting a score of E8 in English and Chinese as first language as equivalent to C6 in English and Chinese as second language.[43]
3. Giving priority for admission to the prestigious junior colleges to those who passed English and Chinese as first language (EL1 and CL1) (*ST*, 23 January 1981).
4. From 1984, allowing Chinese to be studied as a second language (CL2) at Secondary 1 in SAP schools[44] (*ST*, 14 August 1983).
5. From 1990, allowing the SAP schools to offer a special preparatory kindergarten programme which focuses on the teaching of English and Chinese as the first language and the inculcation of core values.

The generous concessions to SAP students[45] coupled with the government's enthusiastic promotion of Mandarin via the 'Speak Mandarin Campaign' have successfully bolstered student enrolments in SAP schools. For example, in 1979 only three out of ten students enrolled at the SAP schools, were from the English stream. By 1986, the figure had jumped to nine out of ten (*ST*, 27 July 1986). The popularity of the SAP schools, in a society where a good grasp of Mandarin has become a distinct social and occupational advantage, is reflected in the strong demand for places in these premier schools by the late 1980s.

Notwithstanding the PAP government's periodic assurances that it has at all times acted to protect and preserve multiracialism, the establishment of the monoethnic SAP scheme has contradicted the multiracial principle of according equal treatment to the non-English language streams. That only the élite Chinese students are offered the opportunity to study English and Mandarin as first languages within the confines of the well-facilitated SAP school environment has rendered the SAP an institutionalized form of ethnic/cultural favouritism.

Disturbed by the perceived breach of multiracial principles in the education sector with the establishment of the SAP, the KGMS newsletter *BAKTI* (December 1978) highlighted the double standards implicit in the PAP government's attempt to save Chinese stream schools from extinction whilst doing little to prevent the demise of Malay and Tamil stream schools, due to dwindling student enrolments, in the late 1970s and early 1980s.

After considerable criticism, particularly by ethnic minority communities, against the perceived unequal treatment of 'mother tongues' in the education system, the PAP government disclosed that by 1986 the top 10 per cent of Malay and Indian students would be offered the opportunity to study Malay/Tamil and English as first language, albeit not on the same terms as their Chinese counterparts in SAP schools. To study their mother tongue as a first language, they had to travel to language centres run by the MOE (*ST*, 25 November 1985) which conducted classes outside the school timetable while SAP students were spared this inconvenience.

This form of unequal treatment is inconsistent with the principles of equal educational opportunity, meritocracy, and multiracialism. Summing up these concerns, the AMP noted: 'Very clearly, the scheme had been conceived for Chinese students. The decision to devote more resources in terms of the best facilities and teachers was perceived as impinging on the policy of equal treatment in education and thereby a setback in the practice of multiracialism which Singapore has committed to since 1959' (NCSMMP, 1990: 108).

The double standard in the PAP government's practice of multiracialism in the education sector becomes more obvious when seen in relation to the breaking up of Malay residential settlements and the dispersal of the community throughout the island in the 1960s and 1970s and the implementation of ethnic housing quotas in the late 1980s. These policies were justified on the grounds that it was unhealthy for Malays to maintain residential ghettos and not integrate with other Singaporeans (discussed in Chapter 5). Yet the possibility that the monoethnic SAP school system may well impede the integration and socialization of Chinese youths in this multiracial society has been ignored. It thus appears that the government has been vigilant in enforcing ethnic integration for the minority Malays but on the other hand has liberally allowed for Chinese youths to be in monoethnic social environments in SAP schools.

Concerned with the potential social and political ramifications of the SAP scheme on the state of multiracialism, PAP MP Chandra Das (GRC Cheng San) has cautioned that the likelihood of SAP students holding important positions in the future portends to 'serious implications in the way Singapore is ruled and run' (*ST*, 10 July 1990). Concerns have also been raised about the monoracial social environments in SAP schools causing their students to have difficulty in interacting with people from other ethnic groups in a later stage of their lives (NCSMMP, 1990: 112; *ST*, 29 April 1990). It is particularly instructive that PAP Ministers such as Lee Hsien Loong (Deputy Prime Minister) and Ong Teng Cheong (former Deputy Prime Minister), who were educated at traditional Chinese stream schools, are the very people in government who are avid promoters of Chinese culture, Mandarin, and the SAP schools.

## The Gifted Education Programme

The elaborate streaming processes of the NEP, coupled with the SAP scheme, have helped to strengthen the institutionalization of educational élitism and the implementation of élitist programmes such as the GEP at four premier schools[46] in 1984. Along with other élitist educational programmes, public funding of the exclusive GEP has been justified on the rationale that Singapore's limited natural resources demand the careful nurturing of the intellectually gifted. This nurturing of 'talent' is purported to be in the nation's long-term interest as the intellectually gifted are expected to be the future political leaders, 'movers and shakers' of society. As Deputy Prime Minister Lee Hsien Loong (1992: 22) put it, 'Because we have invested more in the more able, all Singaporeans have progressed faster.'

As far as the author is aware, no comprehensive local study was undertaken to warrant the GEP's segregated approach for the educationally 'gifted' in preference to other approaches such as the accelerated (for example, double promotion) or enrichment programme approach (extracurricular programmes).[47] To shore up public support for the GEP programme, much media coverage on selected statistical data was highlighted to promote the eugenics proposition that 'gifted children' tended to have highly educated parents.[48]

Student eligibility into the GEP is stringently limited to the top 3 per cent of Primary 3 students who successfully complete a series of IQ tests on language, numerical, and general ability. To ensure that some 'gifted' students have not 'slipped the net', the top 4–5 per cent of Primary 6 students are also invited to participate in a series of IQ tests. After this rigorous process of testing and retesting, only about 0.5 per cent of each cohort in Primary 3 and 6 are eventually invited into the GEP (Tan, 1989: 104).

Unlike the monolingual and extended stream students, GEP students are taught by teachers who have been specially trained and selected.[49] To ensure that each 'gifted' child is endowed with personalized attention, classrooms are limited to twenty-five students (Tan, 1989: 104). This is nearly half the class size in neighbourhood government schools.[50] Unlike the mainstream school curricula which tend to be more rigid and less creative, the GEP curricula emphasizes critical thinking, problem solving, creativity, flexibility, and choice. The development of these skills are believed to be important for the future leaders of society. Camps are regularly held to enable students to further develop their social and leadership skills (ibid.: 105). Talks by experts in the relevant fields are periodically organized and topics studied for Secondary 3 and 4 range from artificial intelligence, cancer research, astronomy to forensic pathology (ibid.). Should these future leaders of society suffer emotional stress, they have ready access to counsellors from the MOE (ibid.: 106). Should they live a long distance from school and thus be deterred from attending the GEP, minibuses are arranged to transport them to and from school (*ST*, 11 December 1983).

In addition to the philosophical and ethical questions stemming from the need for such a programme, there are numerous discrepancies in the GEP which serve to unmask its gender, class, and ethnic bias. Bearing striking resemblance to other programmes for the 'gifted' in other countries, Singapore's GEP caters to a disproportionate number of boys. For example, there were approximately three times more boys than girls that were eligible for the Primary 4 GEP in 1983 (*ST*, 1 December 1983). Similarly in 1987, there were 110 boys as compared to 65 girls in the programme (*ST*, 25 November 1987). Taken at face value, this gross gender imbalance suggests that Singaporean males are somehow more intellectually 'gifted' compared to females.[51] However, there has been no credible scientific data to explain the lower number of intellectually 'gifted' females relative to males. A critical interpretation of this gender imbalance suggests that the educational system favours socially privileged males who have been socialized to develop, at an early age, the confidence and cultural capital required for high academic performance in examinations and IQ tests.

Scant information has been publicly forwarded by the MOE about the precise socio-economic and ethnic composition of the students participating in the GEP presumably due to the sensitive political and ethnic related questions that it is likely to provoke. However, the author's discussions with Mendaki bureaucrats and some Malay/Muslim students in the GEP programme have indicated that just as girls are grossly underrepresented, ethnic minorities are similarly underrepresented whilst ethnic Chinese are overrepresented. For example, less than five Malay students were accepted into the 1990 batch of the GEP at Raffles Institution.

Two philosophically divergent explanations can be used to explain this gender and ethnic discrepancy. The explanation offered by educational conservatives for the underrepresentation of ethnic minorities merely vindicates the eugenics and cultural deficit thesis. They assume that as the socially disadvantaged and the Malays are poorly represented in the GEP, then the problem must lie with the cultural shortcomings or poor genetic make-up of the community rather than the GEP entrance criteria or the educational system. The other explanation asserts that the highly competitive and hierarchical educational system, coupled with programmes such as the GEP, serves to disadvantaged groups that do not have the cultural and material capital to compete on equal terms with a privileged minority who have had a head start in the educational race. As IQ tests are notorious for their cultural bias (Eells ct al. 1951; Chomsky, 1984; Zuckerman, 1990), it is probable that the GEP's IQ tests possess class, ethnic, and cultural biases. The underrepresentation of ethnic minorities and girls warrants a reappraisal of the entrance criteria for the programme in order to preserve the ideals of multiracialism and equity. The ethics underpinning the public financing of such a programme which is tantamount to a transfer of public funds to the 'talented' few, a disproportionate number of whom are also likely to be from socially privileged family backgrounds, is highly contentious.

A further flaw of the GEP is its implicit definition of 'gifted' on the basis of a student's success in the admission tests. Enrolment in the programme requires an 'A' or high distinction in all four subjects (that is, English, 'mother tongue', Mathematics, and Science). Thus a student with a higher total score but with only 3 'A's is not quite considered gifted. Judged by this criteria, those who have extraordinary talents in one field are effectively excluded from the definition of 'gifted' (Lim, 1988: 39). Notable luminaries in their respective fields such as Albert Einstein, Amadeus Mozart, and Bertrand Russell would never have been considered gifted under Singapore's GEP criteria.

## The Independent School Concept

Inspired by the conservative educational innovations in the West, Education Minister Tony Tan led a team of a dozen school principals on a study tour of the United States and the United Kingdom in 1986. With the primary aim of applying the conservative educational innovations in the West to the Singapore educational system, it was therefore hardly coincidental that the bulk of twenty-five secondary schools selected for inspection were élite private schools.[52] Upon their return, the Study Team promptly completed a report entitled 'Towards Excellence in Schools' (1987) which recommended that schools be given more autonomy,[53] selected premier schools be established as private or independent schools, and principals be accorded more policy making and administrative powers.[54] The NEP regime was now carried a step further with the speedy establishment in 1988 of independent schools which would cater to the academically 'meritorious'.[55] Most of the premier government and government aided schools such as Anglo-Chinese School, Chinese High School, Saint Joseph's Institution, Raffles Institution, Singapore Chinese Girls School, Raffles Girls Secondary, and Nanyang Girls School[56] were persuaded to pioneer the independent school system in Singapore.

Like many of the NEP initiatives, the independent school scheme has come under strong public criticism principally for its élitism and precipitation of rapid fee increases. At a 1987 forum organized by the National University of Singapore Society to discuss the proposed independent school system, numerous concerns were expressed about the élitist nature of independent schools and the rendering of a substantial amount of public resources to a select few (*ST*, 21 February 1987). Others expressed the fear, at venues organized by the Feedback Unit, that the independent school system, like the privatized health system, represented an attempt by the government to increasingly shift the cost of education to the public (*ST*, 8 March 1987).

Many in the Malay community are apprehensive with the independent school system as its emphasis on excellence and competition is likely to make it more difficult for the socially disadvantaged but easier for socially privileged students to gain a place in the premier independent schools. The higher fees charged by independent schools and its impact on the socially disadvantaged was another area of concern expressed by Malay parents at a Taman Bacaan forum on independent schools (*ST*, 23 February 1987). Concerned with the likelihood of ethnic underrepresentation at independent schools, the Tamil Teachers Union has urged the MOE to ensure that students from all ethnic communities are proportionately represented there (*ST*, 1 March 1987). However, suggestions to ensure the multiracial social complexion of these premier institutions have not been seriously considered by the MOE.[57]

The PAP government's reaction to the public apprehension with the educational initiatives such as the SAP, GEP, and independent schools has generally been to trivialize criticisms that have been raised. In his

1991 National Day rally speech, Goh Chok Tong dismissed critics of the controvertial educational initiatives as the 'less able' who were 'beginning to envy the success of the more able' (*ST*, 12 August 1991) and claimed that their objections were primarily motivated by the envious knowledge that 'their children cannot make it to independent schools' (ibid.). Far from acceding to public pressure by limiting its élitist educational initiatives, the PAP government has revealed its plans to expand the GEP (Government of Singapore, 1991: 40).

In addition to receiving the same state subsidy per student as government schools (Asher, 1991: 12),[58] independent schools have access to an additional reservoir of funds from the higher school fees charged, donations from their alumni, and parents of students. Thus unlike government schools, which are primarily dependent on government funding, independent schools have access to a larger number of financial reservoirs when upgrading their educational facilities. This allows them to be able to attract better qualified and experienced teachers, offer a greater variety of courses, and have a low pupil–teacher ratio. For example, the teacher–pupil ratio in independent schools is 1:20 compared to 1:40 in government schools. Advantaged by their superior educational environment, it is not altogether surprising that independent and SAP students, who generally begin with a head start due to their privileged socio-economic and cultural capital, perform well in the major examinations.[59] Indeed, research by Jaynes (1989: 332) suggests that the quality of educational facilities in schools strongly determines the achievement level of students.

The link between academic achievement and socio-economic background has been boosted by findings which reveal that a disproportionate number of 'meritorious' independent school students are from middle and upper-middle class backgrounds. For example, two thirds of students from independent schools are from households with incomes (more than $2,000 per month) above the national average income (*ST*, 26 September 1990). Further, 30 per cent of independent school students live in private dwellings even though only 11 per cent of the total population can afford to live in such dwellings (C. George, *ST*, 8 February 1992). It thus appears that the social complexion of independent school students in Singapore generally corresponds with the privileged social make-up of private school students in the United States and Britain.[60]

The trend towards the privatization of premier schools has further contributed to the disparity in educational facilities between the few élite schools and the non-SAP government schools. For example, independent schools such as the Chinese High School offer impressive facilities such as a drama centre, computer centre, art and crafts centre, gymnasium, five lecture theatres, amphitheatre, and a multi-purpose hall (*ST*, 3 September 1990).[61] Students at Raffles Institution have access to facilities such as a computer laboratory, music laboratory, pottery facilities, and the study of esoteric subjects such as Chinese chess and public speaking. To cultivate the talents and develop the personalities of Raffles Institution students into well-rounded 'total students', a Director of Pupil

Development (unheard of in government schools) has been appointed by the school ('Friday Background', SBC, 17 June 1992). St Joseph's Institution offers these facilities plus an array of sports facilities such as two tennis courts and three squash courts (*ST*, 26 October 1990). Raffles Institution, St Joseph's Institution, Chinese High School, and Methodist Girls School have plans of establishing boarding school facilities as part of their programme to develop well-rounded students (*ST*, 18 July 1992).[62] Thus, the move towards 'excellence' in education has resulted in a disproportionate sum of public resources being devoted to a few élite schools which serve an élite minority of the total student population.

Concerned with the widening educational disparity between the non-SAP government schools and the independent schools, PAP MP John Chen (Hong Kah GRC) cautioned that 'the good schools are getting better while the poor schools seem to be getting poorer' (*ST*, 17 March 1990). Many parents have expressed concern over the superior facilities and higher fees at independent schools and have called on the government to spend more of its resources on government schools (*ST*, 14 September 1990). Tan Cheng Bok, MP for Ayer Rajah and former chairperson of the Government Parliamentary Committee (GPC) for Education, has urged the government to spend more money on government schools in order to upgrade their facilities so that parents have an alternative to the more expensive independent schools (ibid.).

The PAP government's response to the strong public demand for an upgrading of educational facilities in non-SAP government schools and the high demand for places in independent schools has been to establish a few semi-independent schools commonly referred to as autonomous schools. Such schools are expected to provide quality education at a cost which is more affordable than independent schools. They are entitled to more funds from the government,[63] enjoy more freedom to select staff and tailor their school programmes, and to function more like independent schools. Six schools became autonomous schools in 1994 and in the next few years there is expected to be ten to fifteen autonomous schools (*ST WOE*, 24 July 1993). Assuring the public that fees in such schools would not be as high as that charged by independent schools,[64] Prime Minister Goh promised that autonomous schools would be given a larger financial subsidy to conduct additional programmes (*ST*, 17 August 1992). It remains to be seen whether the establishment of autonomous schools will help dilute the public stirrings for a more equitable distribution of educational resources between the premier schools and the majority of government neighbourhood schools. Warning signals have however been sounded by some educationalists who have suggested that a vicious cycle could develop with the best teachers and pupils sent to autonomous and independent schools while the majority are left behind in the neighbourhood government schools (W. Fernandez, *ST*, 15 August 1992).

## Fine-tuning the Educational Élitism of the NEP

More than a decade after the implementation of the NEP, modifications were introduced to refashion some of its obvious shortcomings. In political terms, reforms to the NEP were aimed at attenuating some of the apparent public disquiet over the increasingly competitive and hierarchical education system. Guided by the human capital theory approach to education and the increasing need for a highly skilled and competitive workforce, the government recognized that the NEP's policy of excluding a substantial proportion of the population in the monolingual stream from attaining secondary education undermined the goal of upgrading the economy towards a more sophisticated high technological base. This required not only an expansion of the vocational sector but just as importantly, the post-secondary and tertiary sector.

The major educational reforms of the NES at the primary level included:
1. Deferring early streaming from Primary 3 to Primary 4.
    After their Primary 4 examination,[65] pupils would be channelled into:
    (a) EM1 stream—'mother tongue' would be taught as the first language,[66]
    (b) EM2 stream—'mother tongue' would be taught as a second language,[67]
    (c) EM3 stream—'mother tongue' would be taught as a third language.[68]
2. Phasing out the highly controversial monolingual stream by 1994 so that all students would be encouraged to sit for the modified PSLE[69] and complete secondary education.

At the secondary level, the educational structure included the following:
1. Gifted stream which remained intact.
2. Normal academic course where core subjects offered are English, Mathematics, and 'mother tongue'.
3. Normal technical course[70] where core subjects offered are English, Mathematics, and computer studies (*ST*, 10 July 1991).
4. Phasing out the three-year 'A' level course at centralized institutes and pre-university centres. Instead a fourth polytechnic would be established.

Changes at the post-secondary level included the following:
1. The Vocational Institute and Training Board (VITB) was renamed the Technical Institute (TI) and would only accept students with secondary education instead of primary school leavers (*ST WOE*, 2 March 1991).
2. Five new TIs were established.[71]
3. It would be easier for TI graduates to be upgraded to polytechnic education.[72]

The tertiary sector was also expanded:
1. A second university called the Nanyang Technological University (NTU) was established in 1992.

2. The Institute of Education (IE) and College of Physical Education were merged to form the National Institute of Education (NIE) and integrated with NTU.
3. A fourth polytechnic (National Polytechnic) was established in 1992.
4. It would become easier for polytechnic graduates to enrol at the universities (*ST*, 11 July 1991).

In addition, the Edusave Scheme was introduced. A concept borrowed from the neo-conservative educational discourse popular in the West, the Edusave Scheme is in effect a voucher scheme which grants an average annual allowance of between $40 and $50 from 1993.[73] The non-means tested grant, funded by the public purse, is to assist in paying the extracurricular and enrichment activities of students (*ST*, 15 September 1992). Unused Edusave funds will be transferred to the pupils' CPF account when they reach twenty-one years of age (*Sunday Times*, 1 November 1992).

The NES's rationale for delaying early streaming by one year (from Primary 3 to Primary 4) is based on the assumption that the one-year delay would help facilitate a more reliable assessment of academic ability. However, this assumption begs the question of whether streaming at Primary 4 is a more reliable assessment of academic ability than was the previous policy of streaming at Primary 3. Far from critically reappraising the concept of early streaming, the persistence of an early streaming policy by the NES demonstrates that the MOE is firmly committed to the eugenic ideological baggage of the NEP. Despite the plethora of academic research against early streaming discussed earlier, then Education Minister Tony Tan (*ST*, 15 March 1991) adamantly stated that the policy of streaming at Primary 4 would remain until the MOE received more convincing evidence to the contrary. Notwithstanding the minor adjustments and fine-tuning of the NEP by the NES, the NEP's ideological premises relating to early streaming remain sacrosanct and intact.

The abolition of the monolingual stream and its replacement with a policy which allowed the bottom 10 per cent of students to complete secondary education was an implicit admission of the ill-conceived nature of the monolingual stream in serving the economic and social requirements of the nation. However, its replacement with the EM3 stream represents more of a modification of the monolingual stream concept rather than a firm rejection of the fundamental principles governing the concept of early streaming. Instead of being channelled immediately to vocational/technical schools after a lengthy period of primary school, the NES allowed EM3 students to complete four years of secondary education in the normal technical stream before being rechannelled to vocational/technical institutes. Once in the EM3 stream, it is difficult to transfer to the academic stream because of the non-academic curriculum offered to students in the EM3 stream.

The recent efforts to expand the tertiary educational sector with the aim of enhancing its accessibility to 60 per cent of the annual cohort by 2001 has generally received popular support from the public because access to tertiary education in Singapore has long been stringently limited to a small minority.[74] The limited places in tertiary institutions in the past was a source of frustration (Sullivan and Gunasekaran, 1993) especially amongst those who could not afford to go abroad to attain tertiary qualifications.

However, does the expansion of the tertiary sector signify a shift towards an equalization of educational and socio-economic opportunities? Jencks et al. (1972) have argued that the expansion of the educational sector, particularly when the economy is not expanding sufficiently, does not necessarily lead to a more equal distribution of rewards and could even act as a diversion from this goal. Thus, education as a vehicle of social equality is severely limited if educational reform occurs without significant concomitant reform in the larger society. In Singapore, the expanded tertiary sector has witnessed the intake of relatively large numbers of foreign students, largely of Chinese ethnic origin, from Malaysia and Hong Kong who have been awarded scholarships (Lim and Pang, 1986: 21). The conspicuous presence of large numbers of foreign students at local tertiary institutions[75] when the applications of thousands of Singaporean students have been rejected has been a source of public disquiet. At a 1991 Feedback Unit dialogue session which included forty community leaders, concerns were expressed about foreign students depriving Singaporeans of local tertiary places (*ST WOE*, 8 June 1991).

The rapid expansion of the post-secondary sector, in particular the vocational or technical institutes from the 1980s, is poised to serve as the training ground for those considered as the 'less academically able'. As most TI students have largely come from lower-income families, with Malays constituting a disproportionately high number, the expansion of this sector will remain the most accessible avenue for post-secondary education by these groups.

With the expansion of the tertiary and post-secondary sectors, academic credentials will correspondingly inflate as there are more people with paper qualifications in the labour market. In an environment characterized by credential inflation, employers are likely to select employees with the highest qualifications in the expectation that they will become more productive workers. This phenomenon can already be discerned in Singapore, with good 'O' levels or 'A' level qualifications often being the minimal requirement to secure clerical jobs. Employers are now requiring higher educational qualifications for jobs which in the past required lesser qualifications as credentials have become increasingly devalued.[76] Instructively, the aggregate scores required to get into junior colleges, polytechnics, and the universities are becoming increasingly stringent despite the expansion of the post-secondary and tertiary education sectors.[77] Paradoxically, the expansion of the educational sector may well herald some reduction of educational inequality whilst maintaining the general structure of social inequality (Moore, 1989: 124). Thus the likelihood of a less élitist and rigidly competitive educational system, as a consequence of the NES reforms, may well be prematurely optimistic.

## THE IMPACT OF EDUCATIONAL ÉLITISM ON EQUAL EDUCATIONAL OPPORTUNITY

### The Rise of Parentocracy

Numerous studies (Mills, 1972; Domhoff, 1983; Useem, 1984) have found that élite schools tend to reproduce the privileged position of the social élite by preparing students for the most prestigious tertiary institutions[78] and in building a wide social network among the privileged scions for future use in the civil service,[79] politics, business,[80] and even matrimonial matters.[81] As with the educational experiences overseas, it would appear that the increasing congregation of the academically 'meritorious' in the élite GEP stream, independent schools, and SAP schools in Singapore since the 1980s is likely to exacerbate the importance of family background, and cultural and material capital in academic achievement.

Various foreign (Barker-Lunn, 1970; Mortimore and Mortimore, 1986; Oakes, 1988) and Singaporean studies (Yeo, 1982; Heng, 1985) have indicated that early streaming particularly disadvantages students with learning disabilities who are from dysfunctional families, lower socio-economic backgrounds, and ethnic minorities. The disparity in academic achievement among students is likely to intensify when students classified as the 'less able' are placed in less prestigious schools where educational facilities are poorer, teachers are less qualified, where there is a higher level of relief teachers, and classes are larger relative to the more prestigious schools.[82]

Yeo's (1982) and Heng's (1985) studies found that students from lower-income families tended to be overrepresented in the non-academic monolingual and normal streams. Their poor proficiency in English (cultural capital), due significantly to their non-English speaking home environments, contributed significantly to their poor performance in examinations which are primarily conducted in English.[83] Many start Primary 1 without having been to kindergarten and with little more than a smattering of English (*ST*, 29 August 1985). By contrast, students with English-educated parents are likely to speak fluent English, are acculturized to appreciate the value of intellectually stimulating books, and have been attuned to the challenges of schooling by their experiences at good kindergartens. This class/linguistic nexus was highlighted in the 1980 Census which revealed that English-speaking households were more likely to have an income of more than $3,000 per month whereas non-English speaking households tended to have incomes of less than $1,500 per month.[84]

The increasing importance of parental wealth and cultural capital (English language proficiency) in determining academic achievement and life chances has been conceptualized by Philip Brown (1990) in terms of the rise of parentocracy. Parentocracy is most prevalent when the quality of education a student receives conforms with the social origin of their parents and when educational attainment and achievement is increasingly reliant on wealth rather than effort (ibid.: 66). This enables the social élite to ensure that their offspring have acquired the educational credentials to effectively compete in the labour market. They are greatly assisted in achieving their aims by the arsenal of education policies such as early streaming, privatization of the better schools, and the escalation of educational costs.[85] Such policies have elevated the importance of education in maintaining the socio-economic divisions in society (Brown and Lauder, 1992: 26).

Research by Bowles (1972) and Brittain (1976) have found family background to have a profound influence on educational attainment and economic status. In particular, the socio-economic status of the family determines the extent of cultural capital attained which consequently allows easy access to the 'hidden curriculum'[86] in schools. Access to cultural capital and the 'hidden curriculum' is dependent upon factors such as the quality of reading material and intellectual environment at home, the linguistic skills of parents which are passed down to their children, and the educational attainment of the parents which also affects their ability to take an active interest in their children's progress. Children from socially privileged backgrounds are thus equipped with the cultural capital to have a head start in deciphering the 'hidden curriculum' and general demands of school life. By contrast, those from socially disadvantaged family backgrounds are not adequately equipped to compete in the educational race with others who have had an educational head start. They are disadvantaged by having parents who are less adequately equipped with the cultural capital and material resources required for high academic achievement. Schools can thus be metaphorically viewed as a race between teams of pupils and parents who compete for the limited prizes.

## Increasing Costs of Education

Prior to the introduction of independent schools in Singapore, school fees for government and government-aided schools were subsidized at $10 per month. Initially charging a modest fee increase of $25 per month in 1990, the monthly fee for independent schools like Raffles Institution and the Anglo-Chinese School had escalated to $200 in 1991 (*ST*, 6 December 1991) despite assurances made by the government, when the independent school concept was mooted, that fees at these schools would not escalate rapidly. As Table 7.2 indicates, the fee increase by independent schools since 1990 has made it twenty times more expensive and is even higher than some of the courses charged at tertiary institutions each year.[87]

In response to the strong public concern over the escalating fee rises in independent schools,[88] the MOE established a Financial Assistance Scheme (FAS) specifically for students whose families cannot afford to pay the fees at independent schools. However, only students from households with monthly incomes of up to $2,000 per month are eligible for the FAS subsidy[89](*ST*, 6 December 1991). Approximately 33 per cent

TABLE 7.2
Fee Increases in Independent Schools, 1990–1991 (S$ per month)

| School | 1990 | 1991 |
| --- | --- | --- |
| Raffles Institution | 100 | 200 |
| Anglo-Chinese School | 100 | 200 |
| Chinese High School | 100 | 100 |
| St Joseph's Institution | 50 | 150 |
| Methodist Girls School | 50 | 75 |
| Singapore Chinese Girls School | 50 | 70 |

*Source*: *ST*, 11 Sept 1990.

(one in three) of the students enrolled in premier schools were eligible for the FAS (*ST*, 11 September 1990) whilst only 25 per cent (one in four) of students from Raffles Institution and St Joseph's Institution were receiving the FAS in 1992 (M. Gasmier, *ST*, 9 April 1992).

The stringent FAS income eligibility cut-off ($2,000 monthly household income) has caused considerable hardship to students from families with a household income that is just above $2,000 per month but have a large number of dependents. Similarly, households with an income just over $2,000 per month but have to support more than one dependent in an independent school are caught in a financial bind. Thus, the high fees at independent schools may have deterred many students with the required academic qualifications from enrolling in these schools in an effort to preclude the likelihood of financial stress on their family even though the household income may be above the $2,000 per month cut-off.

Other than the stringently means tested FAS subsidy, there is a category of 'meritorious' students whose fees are subsidized without being subject to a means test. Raffles Institution, for example, offers a scholarship which covers monthly school fees and an annual allowance of $600 to those who excelled in the PSLE (*ST*, 4 December 1990). The government also offers Edusave[90] scholarships which cover the monthly fees of the top 25 per cent of PSLE students pursuing secondary studies at premier independent schools and 15 per cent of the top PSLE students at government schools. This 'merit' based scholarship sparked much public debate as the scholarship recipients, a disproportionate number of whom are likely to come from high-income families, are not means tested.[91] The lack of equity considerations in the Edusave scheme is evidenced by the fact that Edusave scholarship recipients from independent schools receive $2,400 a year whilst those from government and government-aided schools receive only $300 to $500 a year.[92] Defending the government's non-means tested Edusave scholarship in economic terms, Deputy Prime Minister Lee Hsien Loong (1992: 18–22) claimed that the scholarship was 'not charity but an investment ... because we have invested in the more able, all Singaporeans have progressed faster'. As a disproportionate number of Edusave scholarship holders are from socially privileged family backgrounds, the scholarship thus represents another institutional and financial advantage to those already equipped with an educational head start by their participation in élite programmes such as the GEP, the SAP, and the superior educational resources afforded to the scholarship holders in independent schools.

Responding to the public disquiet with the restrictive nature of the Edusave scholarship system, rising education costs, and the potentially damaging electoral repercussions it might incur, Prime Minister Goh Chok Tong (*ST*, 2 August 1995) announced in 1995 that an Edusave Merit Bursary would be established for students who rank among the top 25 per cent in the school and whose families earn less than $3,000 a month. A Constituency Top-Up Bursary Scheme has also been established to assist 'poor but hardworking students' who are not among the top 20 per cent in school (*ST WOE*, 2 September 1995). Despite Goh's assurances that these schemes would serve to uphold the supposed classlessness of Singaporean society, their efficacy in making a qualitative difference in relieving the financial costs to individual families has been criticized as the annual sums of $250, $200, and $150 offered per student are thought to be insufficient (ibid.).

The sharp rise in monthly fees has not just been restricted to independent schools but has permeated government schools, government-aided schools, and tertiary educational institutions. This can be largely attributed to the government's policy of allowing all schools from 1992 to raise their miscellaneous fees[93] which hitherto stood at $5 per month for primary students, $7 per month for secondary students, and $9 per month for pre-university students.[94] Fees for polytechnic students have risen from $840 per year in 1989 to $1,200 per year in 1992 (*ST*, 26 January 1990). At the university level (Table 7.3), 1991 saw a 35–50 per cent fee increase over the previous year, while 1992 heralded a further 5–7 per cent increase over 1991. The 1992 fee increase was the fourth since 1987 and generally reflected the government's long-term objective of slashing its

TABLE 7.3
University Fees, 1990–1992 (S$ per annum)

| *Courses* | *1990* | *1991* | *1992* |
|---|---|---|---|
| Non-laboratory-based | 2,600 | 3,500 | 3,750 |
| Laboratory-based | 3,100 | 4,350 | 4,550 |
| Medical/Dental | 7,200 | 10,800 | 11,450[a] |

*Sources*: *ST*, 21 April 1991; *ST*, 15 May 1992.
[a]The maximum loan for the tuition fee in 1992 was $1,320 for a non-laboratory based degree, $1,600 for a laboratory-based degree, and $4,010 for a medical/dental degree (*ST*, 15 May 1992).

subsidies to the two universities to 60–70 per cent of operating costs (*ST*, 22 April 1991). In 1997, fees for undergraduate students in all faculties except medicine and dentistry was scheduled at $5,500 a year (*ST*, 19 March 1997). University fees at the postgraduate level had been significantly increased in 1996. For example, a Master of Arts research student who used to pay $350 per year has been charged $1,300 per year from 1996 (*ST*, 21 June 1995).

The intense competition to attain the academic requirements for enrolment into the premier schools and the fear of being channelled into the slower streams has resulted in an increasing number of students resorting to private tuition.[95] The pervasive nature of this phenomenon, which has also been commonly referred to as the 'shadow education system', is evidenced by the fact that one third of all students, from kindergarten to university, resort to private tuition (*ST*, 11 April 1992). The tuition costs which generally range from $100 per month for primary school students to $180 per month for secondary school students (*ST*, 14 September 1987) has bolstered the aggregate cost of education. The relatively high private tuition cost has meant that tuition, other than the tuition offered by community self-help bodies, is more accessible to students from wealthier families. This was revealed by a *Straits Times* survey which indicated that whilst 45 per cent of students from families with a monthly household income greater than $4,000 per month received private tuition, only 27 per cent of students from families with a monthly household income below $2,000 per month received private tuition (*ST*, 11 April 1992). The survey also revealed that the majority of students that went without private tuition did so because their families could not afford it (C. George, *ST*, 4 April 1992). The higher than average private tuition participation of the supposedly academically 'talented' SAP and independent school (*ST*, 4 April 1992) students demonstates further the linkage between academic achievement and socio-economic background. With the head start afforded to them by their material and cultural capital, the superior educational facilities at independent and SAP schools, coupled with private tuition, it is thus hardly surprising that these educational 'props' have allowed them to surge further ahead in the educational race.

In addition to the growth of private tuition agencies, insurance agencies have capitalized on the insecurities stemming from the escalating school and university fees and bolstered education costs even further. For example, there has been a discernible rise in the number of Singaporeans taking up educational insurance policies with the American International Assurance tripling their policy sales from March to July 1987 (*ST*, 11 August 1987). After years of public pressure on the government, a CPF Education Scheme was introduced in 1991 to cover all full-time degree and diploma studies at local tertiary institutions. Tuition fees can be paid through withdrawals from a member's CPF account[96] (*ST*, 4 May 1991). However, CPF educational withdrawals impact differently on families depending on their occupational status. A tertiary student withdrawing from an already heavily depleted CPF fund may incur a substantial financial burden on the family until they are able to make their repayments.

## Competition for Entrance into the Élite Schools

The acute demand for places in the selective programmes and premier schools has witnessed the emergence of unscrupulous practices by administrators from some of the premier schools who have exploited the anxiousness of parents to place their children in élite schools. A *Straits Times* survey conducted to gauge the extent of such malpractices discovered that some SAP and premier schools were soliciting 'donations' ranging from $5,000 to $15,000 in return for a placement in these schools.[97] The MOE's response to such grave allegations of corruption was not to initiate a formal investigation but only to issue a mild warning to schools that they were not to accept or solicit donations in exchange for places.

In view of the educational environment that is increasingly oriented towards the free market ethos, it is perhaps not very surprising that some of the school administrators were tempted to use unscrupulous market-based methods in raising funds. After all, independent schools have been encouraged to use their discretionary creativity in raising funds to finance 10–20 per cent of their upgraded educational facilities.[98] It could be argued that the solicited 'donations' were but one form of 'creative' fund-raising by the enterprising school administrators. Indeed this commercial approach towards education is in congruence with the rationale underlying the privatization of élite schools. As a *Straits Times* editorial (11 September 1986) commenting on the legitimacy of this market-based approach to education aptly surmised, 'There is no good reason why education should not be run on business lines, provided those who run schools keep as much an eye on educational standards as the bottom line. If there are parents prepared to pay for the apparent advantages of certain schools, so be it. It is the old demand and supply equation, it is the private sector that best understands the workings of the equation.'

The other less controversial and more socially acceptable avenue to secure a placement at an élite school is through the MOE's priority entrance criterion. The nature of these MOE stipulated criteria has served to strengthen the salience of the parent's social status and educational background in the educational opportunities and attainment of a student. For example, the highest points in the priority criteria go to the child with a sibling in the same school, the second highest is accorded to children whose parents had prior links with the school, and finally to those who live within 2 kilometres of the preferred school's catchment area (*ST*, 17 March 1992).

This priority listing permits children whose parents are from élite schools such as Raffles Institution, the Anglo-Chinese School, St Joseph's Institution, and the Convent of the Holy Infant Jesus to begin the educational race with an inherited head start. The much coveted criteria of meritocracy as a governing principle of enrolment in these premier schools has thus been compromised by this priority scheme which rests strongly on the good luck and accident of birth of a student. The highly regarded professional expertise, social standing, and religious affiliation of some parents may help facilitate their linkages with élite schools through their active involvement in the community, school board, committees, or as staff members. This priority criteria which is ostensibly geared towards fostering a strong alumni support network for the school tends to disadvantage children whose parents are less educated and thus less likely to be teaching staff members, take an active interest in the administrative processes of the school, and afford the time to engage in community work. Students from non-Christian faiths are similarly disadvantaged by the priority given by the élite Christian schools to other Christians. Students who live in the exclusive residential 'Bukit Timah belt' of districts 10 and 11, where many of the independent and élite government primary and secondary schools are located[99] (W. Fernandez, *ST WOE*, 15 May 1993), or whose parents have the financial resources and are willing to move their residence within the vicinity of the premier school's catchment area, have also been advantaged.[100] The priority system thus favours wealthy families living in the exclusive residential suburbs where many of these premier schools are located. It is worth noting that these priority guidelines are not a new phenomenon and have been in place since the PAP assumed office in 1959. However, the priority scheme did not generate the same level of competition as it has in the last decade or so (Sunny Goh, *ST*, 1 February 1992). This can be largely attributed to the fact that the disparity in educational facilities offered by the various schools has been accentuated since the decade of the 1980s. Prior to that, the academically 'talented' students were more evenly spread in the various government and government-aided schools and more students were studying in the educational mainstream.

The conservative market-based educational reforms, which have been marked by a rise in the hierarchical differentiation of students and schools, have enhanced the importance of the socio-economic status and educational background of a student's parents, religious affinity, and other ascriptive factors in determining access into the highly sought after premier schools. When education is reduced to a commodity, like any other commodity, access to it relies heavily upon one's resources. The conservative educational discourse stresses the importance of choice. However, in reality, for many parents to make an effective educational choice in selecting a school for their children, they must be in a strong financial position and possess the required social and educational resources. For those without these resources, the educational choice for their children is severely restricted. The phenomenon of parentocracy thus exposes the contradictions of the conservative educational philosophy and its reliance on the meritocracy and equal opportunity rhetoric.

## An Escape Route for the 'Less Meritorious' with Financial Resources

Not all students are subservient to the dictates of the highly competitive education system in Singapore. For those who have been condemned to the slower streams, cannot meet the academic requirements of the prestigious junior college due to their weakness in the core subjects (English, 'mother tongue', and Mathematics) or fail to satisfy the stringent requirements for tertiary study, an expensive overseas education is a ready option. An overseas education thus affords the 'less meritorious' but financially secure the opportunity to attain the highly prized tertiary qualifications in the highly credential conscious society of Singapore. The widespread readiness to resort to this 'escape route' is demonstrated by the fact that approximately 2,000–3,000 Singaporeans go abroad for tertiary studies each year. They constituted approximately a third of the 34,257 students attending university in 1990.[101]

Educationally redeemed by their financial resources, these students have escaped the 'sentencing' of the Singaporean educational system which had labelled them 'unmeritorious', but return home triumphantly as 'meritorious' individuals armed with the credentials required for high-status and professional jobs.[102] However, most 'unmeritorious' students who did not 'make the grade' but are without the financial resources are not able to redeem themselves with an overseas education that can transform them into 'meritorious' individuals. With the increasingly expensive cost outlay of an overseas education as a result of the implementation of full-cost fees, in countries like Australia and the United Kingdom, an overseas education has become increasingly out of reach for many middle-class Singaporean families.[103] Other than for the wealthy, the educational escape route is now even less accessible to the bulk of Singaporeans.[104]

## Educational Opportunities for Special Education Students

In an educational system that is strongly oriented towards nurturing the academic potential of the 'talented', the educational well-being of ESN and other intellectually challenged students has been accorded a much lower priority rating by the PAP government. The educational needs of the physically impaired, academic 'failures', and ESN are catered to primarily by privately run special education schools that tend to be poorly funded, overcrowded, and offer poor educational facilities.

As there are only a handful of privately run schools for the ESN, despite the fact that ESN children constitute approximately 1 per cent of the school going population (*ST*, 28 March 1987), the demand for such schools far outpaces the supply of available places.[105] The Chao Yang Special School and Katong Special School are noted for being grossly overcrowded, understaffed, and offering poor educational facilities. At the School for the Deaf in 1983, there were twenty-two teachers but only four were qualified to teach deaf children (*ST*, 25 March

1983). Notwithstanding the fact that there are more than 500 autistic children under 12 years of age, there is only one private school, the Margaret Drive Special School, that offers a study programme for these children. Only able to accommodate approximately 292 students, with a waiting list of 153 in 1992 (*ST*, 1 October 1992), the educational needs of hundreds of autistic children are not being appropriately met. As a consequence of the overloading and lengthy waiting lists in these special education schools, many students with learning disabilities have been languishing in the slower streams at mainstream schools where they are not privy to the much needed special attention and teaching facilities which their academically 'gifted' peers in the SAP, GEP, and independent schools enjoy.

An academically viable means of alleviating the congestion at special education centres is the careful integration of ESN children into the mainstream schools. This has been successfully experimented in Scandinavian countries and Taiwan. In this way, ESN students and others with learning disabilities would then be afforded the opportunity to intermingle with 'normal' students. This approach provides immense benefit to the latter who are then likely to develop sensitivity and empathy for the difficulties of their less fortunate peers. Studies (Smith and Kennedy, 1967; Wang, 1982) suggest that the achievements of intellectually challenged students can be improved through participation in programmes that are well designed but incorporated into mainstream classes. Further, Slavin and Madden (1986) have postulated that the academically challenged attending regular classes are better adjusted, in social and emotional terms, than students attending special classes. Among others in the community, ex-PAP MP for Ulu Pandan Dixie Tan has since 1985 been unsuccessfully urging the government to integrate ESN children into mainstream schools (*ST*, 28 March 1987).

After years of punitive funding, the PAP government finally increased its grant in 1988 to each special education student by contributing half the cost of educating each pupil.[106] Even with this grant increase, parents of intellectually challenged children in special education schools pay almost three times as much in school fees as parents of children at mainstream schools (*ST*, 23 August 1988). The substantial fees of special education schools no doubt place a considerable strain on the families of these students particularly since a majority of them are from lower-income families and ethnic minority communities. At the Chao Yang Special School, for example, more than half come from poor families (*ST*, 15 January 1985). This has been corroborated by other studies (Levine et al., 1992) which indicate that socially disadvantaged ethnic minorities, in particular, are disproportionately categorized as ESN. Many who have been misclassified and are treated as such are prone to behave according to the label attached to them, thereby generating a self-fulfilling prophecy (Levine and Havighurst, 1992: 134).[107]

The government's parsimonious funding of special education schools stands in stark contrast to its generous funding of programmes for 'gifted' children as discussed earlier in the chapter. A disproportionate amount of public funds has been spent on the latter compared to those in the monolingual stream and ESN schools. The logic of this funding allocation can only be understood from the perspective of the PAP government's economic input-output approach which is premised on the logic that money spent on monolingual and ESN children does not constitute a profitable investment. This is founded on the belief that the latter will not be able to effectively contribute to the increasingly technological and complex demands of the economy.

The fact that students labelled as 'gifted' are largely from middle and upper-middle class backgrounds while the ESN are predominantly from lower-income families does in itself raise some questions about the propriety of this funding prioritization. It also raises questions about the fairness underpinning educational priorities which channel a disproportionate amount of public funds to the academic élite, most of whom also happen to be members of the social élite. This obvious discrepancy prompted the Executive Director for the Association for the Educationally Sub-Normal, June Tham, to publicly urge the government to give as much priority to the ESN children as it has accorded to gifted children in SAP and independent schools (*ST*, 28 March 1987). The equal educational opportunity principle also dictates that special education students be granted access to the kind of specialized educational attention which develops their intellectual potential to the fullest.

\* \* \*

Commonly criticized for being erratic, economic-oriented, motivated by political considerations, and premised on conservative and eugenics beliefs, the educational system has not engendered widespread public confidence. Because of its perceived shortcomings, education is one of the more vulnerable sites in the hegemony of the PAP government. Public discontent with the education system has contributed in no small measure to the high levels of 'brain drain' as manifested by the high levels of emigration by the well-educated (Sullivan and Gunasekaran, 1993) 'voting with their feet', the PAP's sharp electoral shortfall in the 1984 elections,[108] and as a source of social and ethnic discord.

The highly competitive, exam-oriented, and hierarchical education system, which is notable for its early streaming approach of nurturing the 'talented' minority whilst weeding out the 'less able' at an early age, has contributed to a high wastage of talent in human resources.[109] It has left little scope for the late developers, emotionally troubled, socially disadvantaged, and older re-entrants to participate in the educational mainstream. Instead of thinking about excellence in narrowly élitist terms, excellence of a collective nature, or the excellence, knowledge, and skill attainment of the whole society may be a more judicious approach if the ideals of equity, equal opportunity, and multiracialism are to be realized.

Singapore's exam-oriented education system has created the habit of rote learning and nurtured high levels of technical competence and conformity.[110] They are social ingredients which generate a hierarchical society dominated by conforming technocrats and bureaucrats. This runs counter to the view (Brown and Lauder, 1992: 7) that it is important to restructure society along less hierarchical lines in the international environment of the late twentieth century. A highly skilled, innovatively creative, analytical, and flexible work-force is contingent upon a less hierarchical and differentiated education system. Ensconced in an outmoded Fordist framework, the existing education system thus tends to stifle creativity, analytical and critical thinking, individual initiative, and risk taking, which are important for yielding innovative thinkers, scientists, social scientists, and business entrepreneurs (ibid.). A report by Singaporean small business entrepreneurs after the 1985 recession has criticized the educational system's 'pressure cooking' overemphasis on examinations, grades, and conformity for restricting innovation, creativity, and inculcating a risk averse ethos (cf. Clad, 1989: 129). Traits such as risk taking, creativity, innovation, and critical thinking are imperative for nurturing a sophisticated multiracial 'global' society that is increasingly based on a high-technology and service-based economy and is able to judiciously respond to the complex social and political currents of the fast approaching twenty-first century. Even though the NEP and NES policies were conceived with the aim of nurturing the island's scarce human resources, the existing education regime is not well prepared to meet the nation's long-term economic challenges and arguably less equipped to invigorate the delicate multiracial fabric of the society. The need to reappraise the education system was acknowledged by the then Education Minister Teo Chee Hean in early 1997 when he noted that the priorities of the education system would shift towards cultivating greater analytical and creative skills among students to ensure that Singapore remains economically vibrant (*ST*, 31 January 1997). It may be the case that if the cultivation of sharper analytical skills and creative thinking is to be realized, the system of early streaming and the exam-oriented approach of teaching and learning may be in dire need of reappraisal.

The education system in Singapore has enthusiastically embraced core components of the neo-conservative educational agenda as manifested by the implementation of the NEP's early streaming regime, the establishment of the SAP, GEP, and independent schools, and the (Edusave) Voucher Scheme. However, it appears that the myriad educational reforms have largely been geared towards catering to the academic élite who are also disproportionately from socially privileged family backgrounds. They have largely profited from these reforms which have presented greater opportunities for them to exercise educational choices. However, for the great majority of students, real educational choices appear to be little more than rhetoric. For the academically 'less able', educational choices have been limited by the process of streaming and curriculum orientation towards the non-academic streams.

The NEP and NES's educational reforms are likely to strengthen the importance of ethnicity and parentocracy in determining educational achievement. As schools have become increasingly differentiated, the élite schools have been able to offer smaller classes, better qualified teachers, and superior educational resources. Not surprisingly, they produce the best academic results[111] having attracted the 'best' students. In contrast, government schools are likely to fall further behind in the quality of teaching and educational facilities and accommodate an increasing proportion of the 'less talented' students in the community. Losing their 'better' students to the more prestigious independent and SAP schools, their overall academic performance is likely to lag further behind the more prestigious schools. In such an environment, schools will become increasingly stratified according to the 'abilities' of their students and their socio-economic background. The autonomous school concept represents a minor modification in the present educational dichotomy between the independent/SAP schools and the non-independent/non-SAP sector. Upgraded to semi-élite status on the basis of their students' academic performance, such schools appear to add on yet another layer in the pyramid-like educational hierarchy.

1. Educational intervention became a key strategy against poverty and educational disadvantage in the 1960s. In the United States, a Headstart Program was established with the aim of 'levelling up' socially disadvantaged children. In Britain, the Education Priority Areas was established.

2. Apple (1987) and Welch (1991) have explained the backlash against social democratic reforms, in particular educational reforms, in terms of it being made a scapegoat aimed at deflecting the deep-seated structural problems in the industrial economies of the West. As Apple (1987) aptly noted, 'by shifting the public's attention to the problems of education, the real sources of the current crisis of the political economy of capitalism is exported from the economy to the state. The state in turn exports the crisis downward into the school.'

3. Refer to educational reports such as the Goh Report (1979).

4. They took great issue with the fundamental contradiction of social democratic educational reforms, that is, it did not challenge the existing structures which create social inequality and instead concentrated on working within the existing structures.

5. At an address to Tanjong Pagar GRC residents in February 1992, Senior Minister Lee Kuan Yew criticized the liberal educational reforms in Britain for having undermined the economic health of the economy and educational standards. Lee claimed that after 'twenty years of liberal education in the West ... the result is a workforce that cannot compete'. Lee claimed that such policies had resulted in children not knowing their multiplication tables and having problems with English sentences (*ST WOE*, 15 February 1992).

6. Research by Myers (1976) indicates that a more balanced 'mixed' school will do little to penalize the 'more able' students while raising the academic achievements of the 'least able' thereby having a general levelling up effect. The conservative proposal of fostering differentiation between schools on the grounds that it leads to more variety and choice has serious social repercussions. With the expansion of educational differentiation, it is only the educational 'consumers' with significant financial resources that have the privilege of exercising more choice whilst others who are not so privileged cannot exercise this choice (Ball, 1986: 64).

7. As conservative ideologue Irving Kristol (1973) put it, 'There is practically no correlation between the physical plant of our schools and the academic achievement of our students.... What determines a child's academic achievement is his genetic endowment plus the values and motivation he acquires at home. Even class size turns out to have nothing to do with academic achievement.'

8. The government has acknowledged that the policy of rapid mass education in the 1960s sacrificed quality for quantity (Lim, 1989: 179).

9. Most schools in the colonial education system were privately financed and administered. There was limited government supervision and no standardized curriculum.

10. A minimum of six years of primary education and four years of secondary education with the option of an additional two years of secondary education for those intending to pursue tertiary studies.

11. An advisory committee on Curriculum Development was established in 1970 (Willmott, 1989: 588).

12. The policy of bilingualism was a means of cultural integration between the English and non-English educated, preserving distinct ethnic cultural values. English was a means of tapping into the major developments in science, technology, and the establishment of Singapore as a global village (Gopinathan, 1974: 63).

13. The impact of the streaming system was not extensive as a small minority of students were channelled to the vocational and technical stream and most students remained in the academic stream.

14. Refer to the Goh Report (1979) for a summary of the perceived weaknesses of the education system in Singapore.

15. Project teams from the Curriculum Development Institute of Singapore that have developed series of school textbooks including the ones on Confucianist ethics are often made up of 'experts' from overseas (Gopinathan and Gremli, 1988: 142).

16. Professor Taylor, 'Teacher Education in Singapore in 1980: The Role of the Institute of Education', 1980.

17. Between 1959 and 1980, the Ministry of Education has had as many as eight ministers (Gopinathan, 1991: 268).

18. The Goh Team uncritically endorsed the PAP leadership's assumptions of inborn intelligence.

19. The Goh Team uncritically endorsed the PAP leadership's belief in eugenics as manifested in its early streaming proposal.

20. One of the members from the Goh Team, Goh Kim Leong, was appointed to the post of Permanent Secretary and Director of Education (Gopinathan, 1991: 284).

21. A terminating eight-year primary education course for students who had performed poorly in the Primary 3 examinations.

22. Seventy-five per cent of those who completed skills training courses at the vocational institutes but only had primary school education did not end up in jobs they were trained for because employers preferred not to employ people with only primary education (*ST WOE*, 8 May 1993).

23. At a farewell dinner for Tony Tan as Minister of Education in January 1992, the latter admitted that the NES would give ten years of schooling for all students thereby cutting the wastage of the old system where one in five (20 per cent) primary school leavers did not make it to secondary school (S. Davie, *ST*, 27 January 1992).

24. The official reason given for this turn-around was that a government survey revealed that the proposed Science and Arts degrees offered by the Open University would not be popular. This begs the question of why such surveys were not conducted before the government revealed its intention to establish a publicly funded Open University.

25. The scheme's pilot programme was implemented at Pei Hwa, Rosyth, and St Michael's schools. Participation fell by half to only 10 per cent of the student population since its inception in January 1992 (*ST*, 2 June 1992).

26. The educational attrition rate at the primary level was 29 and 36 per cent at the secondary level. This compared unfavourably to that of the United Kingdom, France, Taiwan, and Japan (Goh Report, 1979).

27. A survey conducted by the Ministry of Defence in 1975 found that only 11 per cent of National Service recruits were able to competently deal with work/training situations when English was the sole means of communication (Goh Report, 1979: 3–4).

28. The Goh Report found the bilingual policy to be ineffective. More than 60 per cent of pupils who sat for the PSLE and General Certificate of Education examinations (GCE

or 'O' levels) failed in one or both languages. Only 19 per cent of each primary level cohort passed both languages at the 'O' levels (Soon, 1988: 10).

29. For those who performed well in Primary 1, 2, and 3.

30. For those who failed Primary 3 but performed reasonably well in Primary 1 and 2.

31. Students who have failed the Primary 3 examinations and performed poorly in Primary 1 and 2 are channelled into this stream. The curriculum largely concentrates on basic language and numeracy skills and does not prepare them for the PSLE which they do not sit for. Those from English, Malay, or Indian speaking home environments are taught mainly in English while others from Chinese-speaking home environments are taught in Chinese, in addition to some oral English. Pupils are tested on three subjects for the Primary School Proficiency Examination at the end of Primary 8 in order to qualify for a certificate. The subjects tested include the first language, second language (oral), and Mathematics (*ST*, 26 November 1986). After Primary 6, they are channelled to the VITB for training in a trade.

32. These students study English and Mandarin at the first language level but also have the option of studying Mandarin as a second language. The Mandarin bias of the system is exposed as students who are in the top 10 per cent but not studying Mandarin are not provided with the option of doing Malay or Tamil as a first language.

33. Express students only study English as a first language.

34. They take four years to prepare for the Certificate of Secondary Education exam (CSE). Those who pass English and two other subjects are promoted to Secondary 5. Approximately 30 per cent of 'N' course students sit for the GCE 'O' levels at Secondary 5.

35. The requirements for a lateral transfer from the normal to the express stream includes an overall performance of 70 per cent for Secondary 1 and 75 per cent for Secondary 2 students. If a student is weak in one or two subjects, then it is virtually impossible to attain the high averages required for a lateral transfer (*ST*, 24 September 1984).

36. Critical studies on intelligence testing (IQ tests) have shown that intelligence tests tend to favour children whose parents are of professional and middle-class status. Middle-class social environments provide better preparation for intelligence tests. The father of eugenics and intelligence testing, Cyril Burt, has been found to have fabricated data in his study of intelligence (Hearnshaw, 1979; Kamin, 1984).

37. Calhoun and Elliot (1977) found that Educationally Mentally Retarded and Emotionally Disturbed students assigned to regular classes held more positive self-concepts than those assigned to special classes.

38. A study by Associate Professor Kok Lee Peng and Professor Tsoi Wing Foo from the Psychological Medicine Department at the National University of Singapore found that since the 1960s, the teenage suicide rate has risen by 75 per cent. Relationship and school related problems were cited as the major contributors to the alarming increase in teenage suicide (S. Davie, *ST*, 28 July 1992).

39. Choo Wee Khiang (MP for Marine Parade GRC) has noted in a parliamentary debate that streaming at Primary 3 has caused tremendous problems for parents and pupils and has urged the MOE to consider reverting back to the pre-NEP policy of streaming at Primary 6 (*ST*, 17 March 1990).

40. This highly unpopular policy was initiated after a significant number of parents rejected the school's decision to channel their children to a particular stream.

41. To be eligible for admission to a SAP school, a pupil must obtain an aggregate score of at least 380 for the PSLE (*ST*, 20 January 1981).

42. Ironically the 'mother tongue' of most Singaporean Chinese is not the northern Chinese dialect of Mandarin but the southern Chinese dialects of Hokkien, Teochew, and Hakka. Before the advent of the Speak Mandarin campaign, Mandarin was not commonly spoken in Chinese homes and was incomprehensible especially to the older generation Chinese Singaporeans who were more familiar with the southern dialects.

43. The C6 mark will help to satisfy their language requirement for the prestigious junior colleges and eventually to university.

44. Prior to this, SAP students could only study EL1 and CL2 from Secondary 3 if they could not cope with studying both languages as their first language.

45. The government spends more money per head in recurring costs on pupils in SAP schools than other secondary pupils. It injects $4.85 cents in capitation grants per pupil to aid SAP schools compared to only $3.10 cents per head for other secondary pupils. In addition, SAP schools are given special grants on an ad hoc basis (*ST*, 16 May 1985).

46. The schools that offered the GEP include Anglo-Chinese Primary and Secondary, Raffles Girls Primary, Raffles Girls Secondary, Raffles Institution, and Rosyth Primary.

47. Four school principals from schools where the GEP was offered joined an MOE Gifted Children Project Team in Israel in 1984.

48. The statistical data made public showed that 38 per cent of fathers of gifted children were graduates compared to 5 per cent of Primary 4 normal stream students (*ST*, 22 January 1984). However, it could be inferred from this data that parents who are graduates are able to provide more cultural and financial capital to nurture the academic abilities of their children.

49. These teachers possess good academic qualifications and teaching records.

50. The Permanent Secretary (Education) R. Ong (*ST*, 7 April 1992) has justified the smaller classes for the GEP students on the grounds that 'the nature of the programme requires the pupils to engage in small group activities and project work requiring close supervision'. Despite the provision of smaller classes for GEP students, public requests for smaller classes for students in government schools (*ST*, 1 April 1992; *ST*, 2 April 1992) have been rejected on the grounds that it would 'entail a large increase in the number of teachers ... with our manpower constraints, it will be extremely difficult to recruit so many teachers' (ibid.).

51. In rationalizing this gender disparity of the GEP, Minister of State for Education, Tay Eng Soon noted that even at the 'O' and 'A' level examinations, males tended to do better than girls. The inference here was that the GEP gender imbalance was not too out of the ordinary (*ST*, 11 December 1983).

52. Thirteen schools were visited in the United Kingdom (twelve private and one state school) and twelve in the United States (six independent and six state schools).

53. In theory, more autonomy has been accorded to independent schools in a move to decentralize the educational system. School board members have powers of approval over the school budget, major financial decisions, changes in school policies, setting of fees, hiring and firing of teachers, expulsion of students, and appointment of principals. However, school board member appointments require the approval of the Minister of Education and the appointment of the principal requires the endorsement of the director of education (*ST*, 26 June 1987). In other important areas of decision making such as the core curriculum, power is still firmly retained by the MOE (Lim, *Commentary*, Vol. 8, September 1988).

54. The other recommendations for independent schools included single session days, teacher–pupil ratio to be reduced to 1:15, schools should have an executive officer, principal to be appointed by the school governing body, principal to select teachers and appoint them to positions of responsibility, admission be based on academic merit, and government financial assistance given to meritorious students who cannot pay tuition fees (*ST*, 9 February 1987).

55. The initial idea of the independent school concept was mooted by Goh Chok Tong at the 162nd Founders Day celebrations at Raffles Institution and Raffles Junior College in May 1985. He spoke of the need for schools to be given greater autonomy to encourage innovation, create traditions and cultures within schools, and encourage the pursuit of excellence (*ST*, 29 May 1985).

56. Raffles Girls Secondary and Nanyang Girls School attained independent school status in 1993.

57. Malays have always been underrepresented in the more academically prestigious and élite schools. In 1992, there were approximately 102 Malay/Muslim students in the premier independent schools.

58. Approximately 80 per cent of the budget of independent schools come from the government's capitation grant (*ST*, 21 September 1990).

59. Since 1986, students at the Raffles Institution have achieved a 100 per cent pass rate in the 'O' levels. Ninety-two per cent of each of this school's cohort qualify for uni-

versity education (*ST*, 19 August 1992). Eight out of the top ten schools with the best 'O' level results in 1992 were independent and SAP schools (ibid.).

60. Coleman and Hoffer (1987) found that the median income of parents from public schools in the United States was $18,700 whilst that of parents from private schools was $24,000. In another study of private boarding schools, Cookson (1985) found that 46 per cent of these students had families with incomes of over $100,000 a year.

61. The government provided $32 million of the $47 million required to renovate the Chinese High School in 1990. Another $32 million will be spent by the government to help build two new hostels at the Chinese High School and the Anglo Chinese School (*ST*, 3 September 1990). These hostels cater for the children of Singaporeans who are working overseas.

62. By contrast, most neighbourhood government schools and pre-university centres are noted for offering relatively mediocre educational facilities, high student–teacher ratio, large numbers of relief teachers, and a high teacher turnover rate. In particular, the morale of pre-university centre students tends to be low due to the stigma of being a mediocre student compared to students in the more prestigious junior colleges (*ST*, July 1984).

63. Each autonomous school will receive 10 per cent more funding or about $350 more per pupil per year. However, parents are expected to pay $3 more in miscellaneous fees (*ST WOE*, 24 July 1993).

64. Similar assurances were made to the public about the fees charged by independent schools. Initially charging $25 per month, some like Raffles Institution and the Anglo-Chinese School had by 1991 charged monthly fees of $200.

65. The streaming of Primary 4 pupils is based on their results in the core subjects which include English, mother tongue, and mathematics.

66. For those who passed all three subjects with marks of 85 per cent or more in all subjects.

67. For those who passed all three core subjects but attained less than 85 per cent passes in one or more subjects. In 1992, 75 per cent of students were streamed to EM2.

68. For those who failed English and/or 'mother tongue'. Approximately 10 per cent of students were channelled to this stream in 1992. The 1992 Chinese Language Review Committee's (CLRC) recommendation that the above Chinese students study all subjects in Mandarin and English as a second or third language has been accepted by the government and was implemented in 1993.

69. The PSLE is to be a placement examination with all students upgraded to Secondary 1. From 1993, the grading for the PSLE does not include 'fail' (*ST*, 2 August 1992).

70. EM3 students are expected to be channelled to this stream. The Normal (technical) course leads to the 'N' level examinations at Secondary 4 (*ST WOE*, 8 May 1993). A few are expected to be upgraded to Secondary 5, depending on their 'N' level examination results.

71. The changes at the vocational level were based on a report entitled 'Upgrading Vocational Training' by the review committee headed by Law Soon Beng, director of the then VITB. The expansion of the technical educational sector was based on the expectation that Singapore's economy will move towards a higher technological base in order to compete successfully in the world market (*ST*, 12 March 1991).

72. In 1991, 200 polytechnic places were made available to VITB graduates (*ST*, 11 July 1991).

73. It has been increased to $100 per student in 1994 to offset the rising costs of educational aides as a result of the GST being introduced from that year (*Sunday Times*, 31 October 1993).

74. In 1991, 35 per cent of each Primary 1 cohort attained tertiary qualifications (*ST*, 12 December 1991). However out of this, only 15 per cent make it to the university, and 20 per cent to the polytechnics (*ST*, 18 January 1992).

75. Ten per cent of the total student university population are from ASEAN countries (*ST*, 15 May 1992); in 1990, 17 per cent of students at the then Nanyang Technological Institute were foreigners. At the National University of Singapore (NUS), foreign students

comprise 14 per cent of the students in the Engineering Faculty and 4 per cent in the Arts and Social Sciences Faculty (*ST WOE*, 8 June 1991).

76. In the United States, more college graduates particularly from the 1980s were holding jobs that were in the past performed by high school graduates. In the United States, 1 million college graduates are working as sales clerks, 1.5 million as typists, file clerks, and telephone operators, whilst 1.3 million are labouring on assembly lines or construction sites (*ST*, 8 August 1992).

77. The number of students scoring at least 5 '0' level distinctions has increased nearly five times from 3.5 per cent in 1981 to 15.3 per cent in 1992 (*ST WOE*, 17 April 1993).

78. While only 7 per cent of the school population in Britain were from private schools, just under half of the students at Oxford and Cambridge were from private schools (Reid, 1986).

79. Reid found (1986) that more than 75 per cent of High Court judges and Appeal judges, 69 per cent of ambassadors, and 50 per cent of high-ranking civil servants in Britain were from private schools.

80. Useem and Karabel's (1984) study found that nearly half of the senior corporate managers in the United States had élite school backgrounds. There appears to be a collective social identity amongst the élite private school students.

81. They tended to join the same social clubs, marry other private school students, and are protective of the status quo (Cookson and Persell, 1985).

82. During the author's period as a relief teacher in the less prestigious government schools, the better educated teachers tended to be assigned to the express stream students whilst the non-graduate teachers were largely assigned to the normal stream students.

83. They tend to do better in subjects such as Mathematics and the 'mother tongue' (*ST*, 8 January 1984).

84. 'Languages Spoken at Home', Release 8, *Census of Population 1980*, Singapore: Department of Statistics, 1981.

85. A degree in the United States could cost as much as US $90,000. In the last three years (1989–92) at the twenty-five most selective private colleges in the United States, the percentage of students whose families earned at least US$100,000 a year jumped from 31 per cent to 37 per cent (*ST*, 28 April 1992).

86. Put simply, the 'hidden curriculum' includes the standards of social conduct, social skills, and interaction with peers and teachers. These social standards are that of the middle classes and alien to most students from socially disadvantaged backgrounds.

87. The reason put forward to justify the huge fee hikes is the high costs of the better educational and extracurricular facilities offered at these independent schools. They include smaller class size, drama centres, swimming pools, hostels, and extra courses such as environmental studies, aquatic biology, journalism, and photography (*ST*, 13 September 1990). Widespread public disquiet over the rapid increases in fees at independent schools has prompted Raffles Girls School and Nanyang Girls to assure the public that they will keep their fees low when they become independent in 1993. This would be attained by maintaining their existing class size, stepping up fund-raising activities, and keeping 'extras' to a minimum (S. Davie, *ST*, 13 August 1992).

88. PAP MP for Ayer Rajah and then chairperson of the Government Parliamentary Committee (GPC) for Education Tan Cheng Bok expressed concern that the high fees of independent schools were imposing a burden on many parents (*ST*, 4 October 1990). Many parents have revealed their fears that independent schools were increasingly priced beyond the reach of the average Singaporean (ibid.).

89. Full subsidy of school fees is given to pupils from families with a monthly household income of $800 or less or with a monthly household income/dependent child of $400 or less; 75 per cent subsidy is given to students from families with a monthly income of between $800 and $1,200 or a monthly household income/dependent child of between $400 and $600; and 50 per cent subsidy is given to families with a monthly household income of between $1,400 and $2,000 (*ST*, 6 September 1990).

90. The government has set aside $50 million for the Edusave scheme.

91. The opposition MPs have bitterly criticized this policy as grossly inequitable dur-

ing the 1992 parliamentary debate on the Presidential address. At least four PAP backbenchers have publicly urged those who can afford the fees to decline the scholarship offer and have the money transferred to a bursary fund for needy children (*ST*, 29 January 1992). This, in effect, is a roundabout way of revealing the weakness of the scholarship criteria at a time when the public is very concerned about the high costs of education.

92. Between 600 and 700 independent school students and 4,000 non-independent school students in each cohort are expected to receive the Edusave scholarship (Serene Lim, *ST*, 30 May 1992). In total, the government is expected to spend approximately $12 million a year on the Edusave scholarship. Out of this, $6 million will be distributed to independent school students and another $6 million to non-independent school students (*ST*, 30 May 1992).

93. Miscellaneous fees are collected to purchase teaching materials and equipment or for funding various educational projects in schools.

94. The miscellaneous fees however cannot exceed 30 per cent of the current fees (*Sunday Times*, 24 November 1991).

95. In 1982, only 19 per cent of students resorted to private tuition. By 1992, the figure jumped to a high 32 per cent (*ST*, 11 April 1992). The enormity of the private tuition industry is illustrated by the $260 million a year spent on tuition. This is equivalent to one-tenth of the total education budget (*ST*, 9 April 1992). More than two-thirds of the tuition market are handled by freelancers. Commercial schools handle 8 per cent while Mendaki, SINDA, and other community organizations handle 16 per cent of the total tuition market (*ST*, 4 April 1992).

96. The student will have to repay the full amount withdrawn plus interest after graduating.

97. The *Straits Times* found that in at least eleven cases, parents had donated large sums of money to obtain places for their children in SAP and government-aided schools in recent years. These parents admitted to giving 'donations' when officials from the school indicated that a place could be made for their child if a specific sum was forthcoming. These parents claimed that they had sought places for their children in these schools due to the higher quality of teaching (S. Davie, *ST*, 30 January 1992).

98. Approximately 80 per cent of the budget of independent schools come from the government's capitation grant (*ST*, 21 September 1990).

99. Seven out of the eight independent schools (the exception being Raffles Institution located in Bishan) are in the exclusive 'Bukit Timah belt' of districts 10 and 11. Other premier junior colleges such as Hwa Chong and the National Junior College are also found along Bukit Timah Road (*ST WOE*, 15 May 1993).

100. There have been numerous reported instances of parents who, in desperately wanting their children placed in the premier schools, went as far as to buy a house closer to the preferred school, join churches, and do community work (*ST*, 20 January 1992; M. Pereira, *ST*, 13 March 1992).

101. The 1990 National Census revealed that there were 15,371 Singaporeans studying overseas. Seventy-five per cent of the total were pursuing university degrees while a further 500 were reading postgraduate degrees. The rest were students in boarding schools (*ST*, 26 June 1992).

102. Despite being labelled as mediocre by the educational system in Singapore, many of these overseas students have flourished academically and turned into 'academic swans' in the educational institutions abroad. This in itself is an indictment of the educational system in Singapore.

103. The full-cost fee alone for undergraduate tertiary students in Australia ranges from about A$10,000 to $18,000 per annum. The fees in the United Kingdom and United States are generally higher.

104. The government has repeatedly rejected calls, the most notable advocate being the former Minister for Education Tony Tan, for the use of the CPF to finance overseas study (*ST*, 1 November 1992).

105. In 1988 there were 22,000 children in special education schools (*ST*, 23 August 1988).

106. From $1,500 per annum to $3,000 per annum (*ST*, 23 August 1988). It also seconds teachers to these special schools (*The Hammer*, No. 2, 1992).

107. In *Larry P* v. *Riles*, a California court ruled that African–American students could not be placed in Educationally Mentally Retarded classes on the basis of IQ tests and after hearing evidence that the family environment and linguistic skills of many African–American students caused them to attain misleadingly low scores in the tests (Levine et al., 1992: 135).

108. The highly controversial and unpopular graduate mothers scheme was a hotly debated issue exploited by the opposition parties in the 1984 elections where PAP electoral support declined and the opposition increased its electoral strength from 22.3 to 32.5 per cent. Chiam See Tong (SDP) and J. B. Jeyaratnam (Workers Party) were elected to Parliament.

109. Despite the dominance of the human capital perspective, Singapore's educational levels are far from impressive even when compared to comparable societies such as Hong Kong. Only 25 per cent of the work-force in Singapore have secondary and tertiary education compared with 40 per cent in Hong Kong (*ST WOE*, 24 January 1993). A high 40 per cent of the work-force below the age of forty have only primary education (*ST*, 16 October 1992). The government has pledged that education in the 'Next Lap' will constitute 5 per cent of GDP (Government of Singapore, 1991: 33). This is second to the public expenditure on defence.

110. In 1996, Singaporean students were rated number one world-wide in Mathematics and Science (*ST*, 5 February 1997).

111. In 1992, out of the top ten schools with the best 'O' level results, eight were the premier independent and SAP schools (*ST*, 19 August 1992). Since 1986, students at Raffles Institution have achieved 100 per cent pass rates in the 'O' level examinations.

# 8
# The Politicization of the Education System

THE education sector is an arena where the PAP government has actively engaged in maintaining its political hegemony and creating 'consent' by having young Singaporeans socialized into a world-view that is consistent with its own. Such a world-view is oriented towards promoting values that encourage competitive individualism and acceptance of authoritarian and hierarchical structures. Education policies are often implemented according to the political priorities and ideological preferences of the PAP leadership rather than educational considerations. This is demonstrated by the implementation of quotas in the tertiary sector and the promotion of Mandarin and Confucianism in schools. In particular, the promotion of Mandarin and Confucianism has contributed towards the weakening value of the Malay and Tamil languages as a form of economic and cultural capital. The contradictions in the PAP's rhetoric and practice of equal opportunity, meritocracy, and multi-racialism in the education sector are highlighted by examining the numerous policies which have disadvantaged women, children of the less educated, and ethnic minorities.

## Ideological and Political Socialization

The education system has commonly been used to promote the political interests, ideological preferences, and hegemony of the dominant groups in society. Because of their inherently political character, schools are as much political as they are educational agencies and commonly engage in forms of indoctrination,[1] socialization,[2] and political education[3] (Harber, 1991: 246). Indeed, some educationalists (Hess and Torney, 1967) have maintained that schools are the most important and effective instruments of political socialization. Despite the education system reflecting and mediating changes within the larger social and political spheres of society, it is commonly promoted as being ideologically neutral and independent of political considerations (Sharp, 1986). In this way, educational decision-making is easily detached from the arena of public debate. By upholding the image of schools as neutral and independent, Bordieu (1977: 178) has asserted that schools are better at 'concealing the social functions [they] perform and so perform them more effectively'.

The politicization of the educational system in Singapore has been acknowledged by Singaporean academics such as the late Ruth Wong (1974: 28), S. Gopinathan (1974), and Linda Lim (1989). Gopinathan (1974: 54) has observed that the education system operates not under the stewardship of educational specialists but under the political leadership who 'articulate and provide solutions to educational problems'. Lim (1989: 180) has also suggested that the education system has been used to inculcate conservative and traditional values favoured by the PAP leadership.

A discerning study of the moral education curriculum, education policies, and reports reveals the highly ideological and politicized orientation of these documents. They appear to complement the political, economic, and ideological priorities of the PAP government. Indeed, the importance of the education system as a vehicle for promoting the nation's 'Shared Values' was readily acknowledged by the PAP in its political manifesto, *Singapore: The Next Lap*.

In addition to the politicization of the education system, the more indirect and subliminal processes of socialization, often referred to as the 'hidden curriculum',[4] have been effective in presenting schools as neutral political and ideological agencies. The politicization of the education system thus operates at two levels. The first is direct and the second level is more subliminal and is dependent upon the covert processes of socialization (hidden curriculum) in schools for its efficacy. Importantly, its less obvious political and ideological orientation has subjected it to less public scrutiny and therefore renders it more ideologically penetrative. Educational processes operating at this indirect level are more likely to become reified and accepted as 'common sense'.

The process of ideological and political socialization is commonly operationalized through the covert or 'hidden curriculum' which instils values that are accepting of social hierarchy and uncritical deference to higher authority and establishes boundaries of legitimacy (Sarup, 1983: 2). In this way, attempts are made to mould students into compliant and depoliticized citizens who assume a political orientation that complements and promotes the dominant values. Contextualized in Gramscian terms, the process of manufacturing consent and establishing hegemony is generated in this way.

At a more tangible level, the deference to authority and acquiescence to social hierarchy is manifested in the appointment of selected students into commanding positions of authority such as class monitor and school prefect. As a reward for their conformity to the social rules and academic standards of the schools, they are bestowed with the powers to inform on and discipline the non-conformists. Rituals that instil patriotic fervour such as singing the national anthem and reciting the national pledge of allegiance[5] are faithfully performed at the start and the end of each school day. To forge stronger identification and support for the defence establishment, characterized by its authoritarian ethos and hierarchical structures, students have been encouraged to join uniformed and paramilitary bodies such as the National Cadet Corps and National Police

Corps as part of their extracurricular school activities. To ensure that these uniformed groups are accorded high priority in schools, principals have been informed by the educational and political authorities to regard National Service as an extension of schooling (Gopinathan, 1991: 277).

The myriad school rules and authoritarian rulings of teachers and principals are expected to be obeyed without question or prior consultation with students.[6] Corporal punishment in the form of public humiliation by caning students during school assembly is commonly practised in many schools. Coupled with that, the examination oriented teaching methods encourage passive and rote learning rather than lateral or critical forms of learning and thinking. Such practices tend to engender an uncritical acceptance of the dominant world-view, authoritarian values, and work practices in the larger society. The unmitigated deference to authority, existence of petty rules, and the uncritical acceptance of the 'knowledge' taught in school nurture authoritarian values and undermine the flowering of democratic values in the larger society.

With the implementation of the NEP in 1979, a more elaborate level of social differentiation was added to the already hierarchical education regime. The NEP's early streaming system has divided the student body into those in the normal, express, special, and gifted streams. The hierarchy between schools has been made more pronounced by their informal ranking on the basis of the academic results of their students in the major examinations. This informal ranking system of schools tends to correlate with the socio-economic standing of their students, with a disproportionately high number of students from socially privileged family backgrounds enrolled in the higher ranked schools (Domhoff, 1983; Useem, 1984; C. George, *ST*, 8 February 1992).

In legitimizing unequal educational outcomes, reifying hierarchical social divisions as 'common sense', and encouraging the ethos of ranking and competition over the spirit of collectivity, the education system socializes students to putatively accept that only a minority will attain high academic qualifications and prestigious jobs. In this way, the majority are expected to be satisfied with their lesser academic credentials and low-status jobs that are believed to be concomitant with their limited innate ability and/or lack of effort.

### The Construction of Morality

A subtle but exceedingly cogent form of political and ideological socialization can be generated through the formal school curriculum. The curriculum generally refers to 'knowledge' that has been carefully selected, constructed, institutionalized, and taught to students (Young, 1973). Schools therefore not only 'process' people but also 'process' knowledge (Apple, 1986: 63). Knowledge that is taught in the school curriculum is commonly projected as objective, non-ideological, and neutral (Sarup, 1983: 4).

An obvious illustration of the politicization of the school curriculum in Singapore is the inclusion of Religious Knowledge,[7] replacing Civics[8] as a compulsory Moral Education subject for Secondary 3 and 4 students from 1984. The rationale for introducing Religious Knowledge as a compulsory subject was that knowledge of religion would produce upright and virtuous citizens of high moral calibre. It was also assumed that religion would provide Singaporeans with the moral ballast to shield them from the supposedly decadent and morally corrosive values of the West.[9] However, the contradiction inherent in the compulsory study of Religious Knowledge, in an otherwise secular based society, fuelled public suspicions that it was another social engineering device to shore up the PAP government's political and electoral clout.

The political motives for introducing Religious Knowledge appeared to have been made more obvious when the government announced in 1987 that the subject would be phased out and replaced by a secular moral (civics) education programme[10] shortly after the detention without trial under the ISA of twenty-two people,[11] most notably Vincent Cheng and several Catholic social workers. Actively engaged in social welfare activities on behalf of Filipino maids and other socially disadvantaged groups, the detainees were accused by the PAP leadership of using religion to undermine the state in a Marxist style conspiracy.[12] In the aftermath of this episode, coupled with the institutionalized separation between the practice of religion and politics via the Maintenance of Religious Harmony Bill (1990), it became increasingly apparent that the PAP leadership was intent on thwarting the dissemination of radical religious doctrines which sanction political activism in furthering the cause of social justice. The 1987 arrests and the introduction of the Maintenance of Religious Harmony Bill (1990) can also be viewed as a means of reasserting the PAP leadership's policy of discouraging elements within civil society from actively engaging in political activity (Rodan, 1992). Consistent with these aims, the Christian Conference of Asia was swiftly dissolved and five Christian missionaries were expelled from Singapore for their involvement in domestic politics (M. Malik, *FEER*, 14 January 1988). Several foreign Islamic *ulama* (religious teachers) known for their highly politicized sermons were also denied visa permits into Singapore in 1987.

Having learnt from its misfired attempt at utilizing religion to instil 'desirable' moral values, a secular-oriented moral education syllabus was revived with the aim of inculcating selected aspects of 'Asian values' to students. However, the 'Asian values' that have been emphasized appear to possess a strong Confucianist orientation. They include values which instil unquestioning reverence for higher authority such as respect for elders, teachers, scholars, parents (filial piety), the state, and family. In unveiling the political agenda underpinning the revised 'secular' moral education programme, Gomez (1992: 57) noted that the programme breeds 'uncritical acceptance, on the part of its young citizens, of the government's standard of morality.... By extension, it can be suggested that this uncritical acceptance of morality can lead students to grow up to be uncritical of the government and a government subjected to less criticism would find it easier to perpetuate its stay in power.'

Inculcating students with conservative traditional values that legitimize paternalistic systems of government,[13] the Confucian-oriented moral education syllabus is expected to act as a buffer against the ostensibly 'negative' individualistic Western values and its adversarial political culture. It is also expected to strengthen the 'positive' communitarian and consensual (East) Asian values thought to be responsible for the political stability and economic success of Singapore and other Confucian societies such as the East Asian NICs and Japan. Importantly, the propagation of the family as the basic unit in society and the inculcation of 'positive' Asian values is also a means of encouraging adult children to care for their aged parents, relatives, and the disadvantaged, thereby unburdening the state from such a financial responsibility (Lim, 1989: 180; Khun, 1990: 379).

What is particularly instructive about the moral education syllabus is that the ideal of multiracialism and its related values such as racial harmony, tolerance, community living, and co-operation are only briefly mentioned in the 'Being and Becoming' and 'Good Citizen' syllabus (Gomez, 1992: 48). Indeed, values espousing ethnic harmony and tolerance do not even rate a mention in the 'Being and Becoming' moral education syllabus for secondary students whilst they appear only once in the 'Good Citizen' programme for primary students (ibid.: 52).

**The Construction of History**

The study of history in schools has had a chequered record due to the fact that for many years it was regarded as irrelevant[14] and therefore excluded from the primary school curriculum[15] so as to make way for subjects[16] regarded as more useful for the island's industrial and ecnomic development. However, by the mid-1970s it was reintroduced into the school curriculum albeit with an emphasis on the modern economic history of Singapore and as part of a wider subject called 'Education for Living'. It was then restructured in 1979 to 'Social Studies'. From 1984, a two-year history course for lower secondary students instructively entitled the 'Social and Economic History of Modern Singapore' was designed by the Lower Secondary History Project Team attached to the Curriculum Development Institute of Singapore.[17] In February 1997, the Ministry of Education revealed that a new history syllabus with an emphasis on post-independence Singapore would be taught to students. Importantly, emphasis on the modern economic history of the island allows prominent focus on the contributions of the immigrant communities in building the foundations of an economically dynamic society. It also serves to create a national identity that is closely identified with the immigrant communities rather than with indigenous Singaporeans.

The focus on the island's modern history at the expense of its pre-1819 Malay history was challenged by the Malay community when Singapore's pre-colonial Malay past was dismissed as mythology in a 1970/1 history school textbook entitled *Our Forefathers* [sic] *as Pioneers*. In denying the existence of the island's pre-colonial past as a trading centre, the establishment of Singapura by the Palembang Prince Sang

Nila Utama in the fourteenth century was dismissed in the 1971 history textbook as a legend despite the existence of a strong body of evidence confirming its authenticity.[18] Offended by what was perceived as an attempt to reconstruct the island's pre-colonial Malay history and denigrate the indigenous status of Malays, Malay historians, intellectuals, and cultural organizations successfully pressured the educational authorities to withdraw the history textbook from the school syllabus (Bedlington, 1974: 205). Many sensitivities were again aroused when a film entitled *Homeland*, produced for Singapore's twenty-fifth anniversary celebrations in 1990, depicted Singapore as an immigrant society and all Singaporeans, including Malays, as immigrants. Suffice to say, the film was offensive to many within the Malay community.

If placed within a broader global context, the historical amnesia and reconstruction of Singapore's history appear to be not much different from the tradition of historiography characteristic of colonial settler societies such as Australia and the United States. In these countries, history popularly begins with the arrival of the immigrants and imperial agents such as Singapore's Stamford Raffles in 1819, Australia's James Cook in 1770, and America's Christopher Columbus in 1492. In Singapore, Raffles has been elevated to a heroic and visionary founding father who engineered the rise of a commercially dynamic trading port from an insignificant barren and underpopulated fishing village devoid of a history and civilization worth mentioning.[19] This general portrayal stands in stark contrast to the generally less flattering Malay impressions of him as a conniving British imperialist who cheated Malays of Singapore.[20]

A distinct pattern in the mainstream historiography of these colonial settler societies is the propagation of the idea that before the arrival of the industrious immigrants, the land of the indigenous inhabitants was barren, empty or grossly underpopulated, unowned, and unclaimed.[21] In addition to this, the indigenous populace have often been portrayed as being somewhat backward, lazy, and unproductive, particularly when compared to the pioneering and industrious spirit of the immigrant community. Such a narrative no doubt serves to legitimize the settlement of the immigrants and serves as a moral basis for their continued domination of the power structures and the social marginalization of indigenous people (Berger, 1979: 8). The political agenda underpinning such historiographical omissions has generally not escaped the Malay community and other more discerning observers of Singapore. Connor (1987: 35) has, for example, interpreted the official histories of Singapore, which imply that the island was practically uninhabited and devoid of a memorable past prior to 1819, as motivated by 'an indirect, *ex post facto* effort to destroy the underlying rationale of Article 152 and, in so doing, to deny the validity of any future claims that might be raised at home or in neighbouring states, in the name of a primal Malay claim to homeland'.

The geopolitical ramifications of such a truncated construction of the island's history may in fact be detrimental to its long-term interests. It has clouded the understanding of non-Malay Singaporeans of the island's historically and culturally organic relationship with the surrounding 'Malay World'. This weak sense of regional consciousness and limited appreciation of the region's history, culture, and traditions has allowed the PAP government to marshal considerable public support in its periodic bouts of discord with neighbouring Malay nations. The PAP government's handling of the 1986 Hertzog Affair,[22] the inferences associated with the PAP leadership's exclusion of Singapore Malays from sensitive units in the SAF, the logic underpinning Singapore's garrison-like defence posture and sophisticated arms build-up (Huxley, 1991), and the ongoing territorial dispute with Malaysia over the ownership of Pedra Blanca island (referred to by Malays as Pulau Batu Putih),[23] are some examples of the PAP government's ability to generate considerable public support for its stance.

School history texts[24] have generally tended to downplay the positive contributions of the first popularly elected Labour Front government of the 1950s whilst promoting the image of it as a government unable to deal effectively with pro-communist and other left-wing elements of that period. In particular, the anti-colonial activities and aspirations of the pro-communist, radical Chinese-educated, and left-wing students in the 1950s and 1960s are generally interpreted in a threatening light. In contrast to the less than flattering depiction of the other political actors in the tumultuous decades of the 1950s, 1960s, and 1970s, the achievements of the 'old guard' PAP leadership, particularly Lee Kuan Yew, have been elevated to almost heroic proportions in school history textbooks. Triumphing over a series of arduous communal, political, and economic adversities, they have been credited with laying the foundations of the island's economic dynamism. Since the 1980s, the heroic portrayal of the first generation of PAP leadership during the tumultuous era of the 1950s and 1960s has been accorded much public coverage in an attempt to remind younger Singaporeans of the debt Singaporeans owe to the PAP leadership's vision and valour. This was particularly apparent during the island's twenty-fifth anniversary independence celebrations in 1990 when documentaries pertaining to the tumultuous political events in the 1950s and 1960s were regularly televised and extensively narrated in the local newspapers. Concerned that the historical events of the previous decades were not fully understood, particularly by younger generation Singaporeans,[25] during the controversy surrounding Lee Kuan Yew's remark in 1996 on the possibility of Singapore remerging with Malaysia, the Deputy Prime Minister Lee Hsien Loong stressed the importance of redressing this 'serious gap' in historical awareness (*ST*, 17 August 1996).

As discussed, it is not just the selective forms of knowledge that are taught but also the types of knowledge omitted from the school curriculum that offer instructive insights into the political agenda and socialization processes that are operating in the education system. Important areas of knowledge such as the workings of the political system, the vigilant preservation of democratic processes and multiracial harmony, the rule of law, the structural causes of poverty, and the nurturing of critical thinking are excluded from the school curriculum in

Singapore. Arguably, the inclusion of such a curriculum would provide young Singaporeans with the political tools for informed political participation. Armed with a discerning awareness of political knowledge, they are more likely to contribute effectively to democratic life and by doing so encourage the government to be more accountable and representative. However, such forms of knowledge are not deemed to be important areas of study despite their significance to the fast modernizing, industrializing and politically complex world that Singaporeans approaching the twenty-first century need to be well acquainted with. Instead, young Singaporeans have been instilled with values that emphasize deference to authority, citizen obligations to the state rather than state obligations to the citizen, and receptiveness of conservative Asian political values toward the state.

### Racial Quotas for Malays in Schools

Just as the 1989 ethnic residential quotas in public housing estates had the effect of diluting Malay numerical concentration in electoral constituencies (discussed in greater detail in Chapter 5),[26] the 1988 racial quotas for Malays in schools similarly served to dilute their numerical concentration in particular schools. The original idea for the Malay quota in schools can be traced back to Lee Kuan Yew's 1982 address at a Mendaki forum where he alleged that where there was a smaller percentage of Malay pupils in a school, the standards of English and science improved. Lee also noted that the large concentration of Malays in a particular school caused Malay students to neglect English as they tended to communicate with one another in Malay (*ST*, 29 May 1982).

Taking the cue from Lee Kuan Yew's statement about the consequences of Malay student concentrations in particular schools, the case for the Malay student quotas in each school was avidly championed by the PAP's Malay MPs.[27] In advocating that not more than 25 per cent of Malay students be enrolled in each school for the Primary 1 intake from 1988, they produced data which supported Lee's suggestion that there was a correlation between negative academic performance and the high concentration of Malays in particular schools. Muslim Affairs Minister Ahmad Mattar summoned MOE statistics which indicated that where Malays comprised 30 per cent or more of the student population, more than a third of them failed the PSLE. Conversely, when Malays comprised less than 10 per cent, the failure rate was less than 20 per cent (*ST*, 29 December 1986). Reminiscent of the cultural deficit discourse, Mattar suggested that the negative academic influences Malay students had on one another, in schools where Malay student representation was strong, included poor English proficiency and motivation to study. In lending credibility to this hypothesis, a survey which showed that Malay pupils spent 16 per cent to 24 per cent less time on homework than non-Malays was publicized (*ST*, 15 September 1986). Instructively, the nature, sample size, and social composition of students in this survey were not made accessible for public scrutiny.

The PAP government's purported correlation between poor academic performance and large Malay student concentration, when analysed closely, reveals significant anomalies and inconsistencies. In instituting the quota for Malays in schools, the PAP government and its Malay MPs ignored the pertinent linkages between poor academic performance and socio-economic factors, and the impact of education policies such as the school registration priority scheme and early streaming which have contributed to the concentration of Malay students in the less sought after neighbourhood government schools. As highlighted in Chapter 7, such schools generally have poorer educational facilities relative to the independent schools, fewer tertiary-educated teachers, a higher number of slower stream classes and relief teachers, and generally produce less salutary academic results. Immersed in their culturalist assumptions, the PAP leadership failed to appreciate the significance of the above-mentioned institutional factors in contributing to the weak educational performance of Malay students.[28]

In objecting to the 25 per cent national quota for Malay students in schools, opposition MP (Potong Pasir) Chiam See Tong (*ST*, 10 February 1986) pointed out that no study had been conducted to justify the implementation of the quota on Malay students. In suggesting that the root causes of educational underachievement be tackled, instead of arbitrarily setting quotas on Malay students, Chiam advised that more assistance should be given to pupils who were academically weaker and that the large class size in schools be reduced. Importantly, he cautioned that such a quota would only serve to make Malay pupils feel disoriented and insecure (*ST*, 1 September 1987).

Malay frustration with being unfairly singled out by the quota, which systematically breaks up concentrations of Malays in particular schools, has been further aggravated by the establishment of the monoethnic SAP schools in 1979. Public apprehensions (*BAKTI* [KGMS newsletter], December 1978; NCSMMP, 1990: 112; *ST*, 29 April 1990) that such monoethnic Chinese schools mitigate against the nurturing of a healthy multiethnic society have failed to motivate the PAP leadership towards making them multiethnic. That concentrations of Malays at the school level are not tolerated by the PAP government whilst all Chinese concentrations in schools are actively encouraged has served to fuel Malay insecurity against the perceived double standards by the PAP government.

At a comparative level, racial quotas for schools based on the rationale advanced by the PAP leadership would more than likely have been severely assailed on legal and ethical grounds in many liberal–democratic nations. For example, when the British government recommended in 1965 that the number of immigrants in any one school be kept to a maximum quota of one-third of the student population, on the grounds that it was important for immigrant children to assimilate into the British social milieu, the Race Relations Board intervened to remind the government that it was acting in breach of the Race Relations Act (Little, 1981: 66). The quota recommendation was also criticized on the basis that there was no clear and concrete evidence to justify its implementation on academic grounds (Mabey, 1974). That the student quota on Malays represents an infringement of the civil and democratic rights of the Malay student to be educated in whichever school they so desire appears not to have seriously alarmed the PAP government.

## Linguistic Bias towards Mandarin

The initiation of the 'Speak Mandarin Campaign' and the introduction of the SAP scheme in 1979 represented a watershed in the trajectory of language and cultural policy making in Singapore. The assiduous promotion of Mandarin as a 'mother tongue' was facilitated by the 1979 NEP which placed a high premium on 'mother tongue' proficiency in order to attain a good overall academic standing in the major examinations.[29]

Unlike the pre-NEP educational regime, which encouraged proficiency in the 'mother tongue'[30] but did not place tenuous educational barriers if proficiency was not attained, a pass in the 'mother tongue' was now crucial in gaining a place in the prestigious junior colleges and local universities. Whereas students could choose to study any second language prior to 1981, Mandarin was from that year made compulsory for all Chinese students primarily to ensure that Chinese students did not take up Malay as a second language.[31] While Chinese students were compelled to study their 'mother tongue', non-Chinese students were allowed the choice of studying their 'mother tongue' or Mandarin (*ST*, 22 July 1981).

The emphasis on Mandarin as a 'mother tongue' since the late 1970s has been largely attributed to the PAP leadership's belief that the 'mother tongue' is an effective transmitter of positive Asian/Confucianist cultural values which have been credited for Singapore's economic success and social discipline. As Lee Kuan Yew frankly stated in the Goh Report on education (1979: V), 'The greatest value in the teaching and learning of Chinese is in the transmission of the norms of social or moral behaviour. This means principally Confucianist beliefs and ideas, of man [*sic*], society and the state.' These Asian/Confucian values are perceived as a means of cushioning Singaporeans against the corrosive influence of Western values which if unmitigated, would reduce Singaporeans into a 'calypso-type' community who lack national and social responsibility and cultural ballast (Lee Kuan Yew, *ST*, 25 March 1979). Knowledge of Mandarin has also been cited as important in helping to tap into the fast expanding mainland Chinese economic market and facilitating *guanxi* (close connections) between Singaporean business people and mainland Chinese officials[32] (ST WOE, 1 May 1991). The social, economic, and political survival of Singapore is thus perceived to be strongly contingent upon the maintenance of Asian/Confucian values, of which the 'mother tongue', in particular Mandarin, is deemed to be an effective cultural transmitter.[33]

The promotion of Mandarin through the educational system has been greatly assisted by the nearly two decade-old 'Speak Mandarin

Campaign' which was initially launched in 1979. Having successfully attained its goal of getting more Singaporean Chinese to speak more Mandarin and less dialects,[34] the promotion of Mandarin has, since the early 1990s, focused on encouraging the English-educated Chinese to speak more Mandarin in both private and public domain.[35] From 1991, the new theme of the campaign appropriately entitled 'If you're Chinese, make a statement in Mandarin' aptly captured the trajectory of the Mandarin campaign which has incrementally expanded its original scope of getting Chinese Singaporeans to speak less dialects towards the more ambitious aim of promoting Mandarin as a primary language of social communication between all ethnic Chinese.[36]

The assiduous promotion of Mandarin and Confucian values in schools and the larger society has been interpreted by Huxley (1992: 292) as a means of strengthening the PAP's electoral support within the Chinese community, particularly the Chinese-educated and working classes. Having antagonized the Chinese-educated by abolishing and then integrating Nanyang University with the University of Singapore in 1980 and actively downgrading the use of dialects, the promotion of Mandarin is a politically expedient means of offering symbolic cultural goods to the numerically significant Chinese community. Such an approach is premised on the belief that a strong materialist neo-authoritarian and Confucianist oriented regime is likely to find a more receptive audience within the Chinese educated (ibid.).[37]

## The Revival of Monoethnic Schools

The establishment of the SAP scheme in 1979, as a means of preserving the Chinese stream schools from dwindling student enrolments and eventual extinction (Table 8.1), is another illustration of the favoured treatment rendered to Mandarin and Chinese stream schools. The main rationale for the preservation of the Chinese stream SAP schools, where Chinese and English are both taught as a first language, is that a strong proficiency in Mandarin would instil positive Chinese cultural values in

TABLE 8.1
Enrolments in Singapore Schools by Language Stream

| Year | Total | Language Streams ||||
| | | English | Chinese | Malay | Tamil |
| --- | --- | --- | --- | --- | --- |
| 1941 | 71,800 | 27,000 | 38,000 | 5,800 | 1,000 |
| 1949 | 115,544 | 38,302 | 68,065 | 7,862 | 1,315 |
| 1957 | 259,997 | 127,853 | 115,374 | 13,419 | 1,351 |
| 1968 | 384,392 | 232,376 | 122,368 | 27,980 | 1,668 |
| 1972 | 365,606 | 236,072 | 115,991 | 12,527 | 1,016 |
| 1978 | 311,510 | 249,676 | 60,123 | 1,581 | 130 |

*Source*: Inglis, 1983: 224.

SAP students, many of whom are expected to hold future leadership positions in society. In championing such assumptions, Senior Minister Lee Kuan Yew (*Petir*, October 1991: 15) has publicly complimented the Chinese-educated for their 'great contribution to our success because of their fighting qualities, stamina and hard work, which spring from their Chinese education with its emphasis on Confucian values'. In the face of such pronouncements, the demise of the Malay and the Tamil stream schools, after dwindling enrolments in the 1970s, whilst Chinese stream schools were revived and safeguarded, is illustrative of the PAP leadership's assumption that Malay (indigenous South-East Asian) and Indian (South Asian) cultural values are less crucial than the Confucianist East Asian cultural values for the economic and cultural ballast of the island.[38]

Even though Mandarin could be studied as a first language in the revived SAP schools from 1979, it was only after strident criticism, particularly from the minority communities, that the study of the 'mother tongue' as a first language was offered to Malay and Indian students in 1986. However, unlike their SAP counterparts, these students were not accorded the same opportunity of studying Malay or Tamil as a first language in their respective schools but had to travel to the MOE language centres after school hours. Despite vocal criticism by the ethnic minority communities against the SAP scheme for undermining the multiracial social fabric of society, embodying unequal treatment to the ethnic minorities (NCSMMP, 1990: 108), and contravening the principle of equal treatment for all four official languages (*ST*, 29 December 1978), the PAP leadership has remained firmly committed to the SAP scheme.

So committed was the PAP leadership with the promotion of Mandarin as a social, cultural, and value transmitter that Senior Minister Lee Kuan Yew offered clan groups the opportunity to take over and administer six to twelve government primary schools in October 1991.[39] In making the offer more attractive, Lee promised that these clan run schools could determine their own curriculum and examination standards (*ST*, 14 October 1991). In lending weight to the Senior Minister's 'suggestion', Goh Chok Tong purported that teaching Chinese as a first language and English as a second language to Chinese primary school students might be an effective way of preserving Asian (Chinese) values (*ST*, 20 October 1991).

When proposing the establishment of Chinese clan run schools, the social repercussions of ethnic based educational enclaves on the delicate multiracial fabric of society and its impact on ethnic minority sensitivities was not seriously considered. The salience of these considerations, however, did not escape the chairperson of the GPC (Education) and PAP MP (Ayer Rajah), Tan Cheng Bok, who hastened to remind the government of the social and political importance of English as an effective medium of interaction between the different ethnic communities and the socially retrogressive nature of clan run schools. Cautioned Tan (*ST*, 20 October 1991), 'If we want to have "One Nation, One People", we should not go back to schools where children start off speaking different languages.' The PAP leadership's lack of serious regard for the concerns expressed about monoethnic schools from various quarters within the community is all the more disturbing in view of the chauvinistic tendencies of the Chinese-educated particularly evident in the 1950s and 1960s. The latter's chauvinistic inclinations have been confirmed by Kay's (1971) research which found that the English stream students were the most communally tolerant whilst the Chinese stream students were the least communally tolerant.

Despite the Chinese Teachers Association and Middle School Chinese Teachers Association's support for the proposed Chinese language clan schools (*ST*, 29 September 1991), clan associations declined to take up the government's offer. In contrast to the PAP leadership's optimism with the long-term viability of clan schools, clan leaders were less sanguine, believing that children in such schools would be disadvantaged in a society and international community where English was an important medium of communication (Singh, 1992a: 145–6).

## Reviving Ethnic/Linguistic Based Language Review Committees

The establishment of the Chinese Language Review Committee (CLRC) in June 1991 is reminiscent of the colonial educational paradigm when ethnic/linguistic based educational review committees were the order of the day. Headed by the former Deputy Prime Minister Ong Teng Cheong, the high-profile[40] CLRC was initiated with the expressed objective of exploring ways to improve the quality of teaching and learning Mandarin so that Chinese students would continue to use the language after they left school. This would serve to nurture the growth and development of Mandarin in Singapore (*ST*, 9 May 1992; *Sunday Times*, 7 June 1992). Another aim of the CLRC was to investigate and find measures to help students who were weak in Mandarin.

The major recommendations that were implemented for PSLE students from 1993 include:
1. Allowing the use of Chinese dictionaries for essay writing papers.
2. Revising curriculum and examination format to reflect greater emphasis on reading and listening comprehension.[41]
3. Agreeing in principle to use Mandarin in Social Studies, Music, and Art.
4. Allowing pre-university students to sit the General Paper in Chinese as an optional examination paper.
5. Giving more Mandarin teachers opportunities to engage in further studies locally and overseas.

Without similar policies extended to the study of Malay and Tamil, the CLRC recommendations further augment the already strengthening 'mother tongue' foundations of the Chinese community. For example, in 1990, nearly 99 per cent of Chinese PSLE candidates passed Mandarin as a second language with 77 per cent awarded an 'A' or better grade. In the GCE 'O' levels, more than 93 per cent scored a C6 or better (*ST*, 12 May 1992). Despite these positive indicators and the persistence of the wide-reaching Mandarin campaigns, the government saw fit to establish a CLRC instead of a multiracially based Mother Tongue Language Committee which would address the 'mother tongue' deficiencies of all ethnic Singaporeans. A multiracial approach would be more in tandem with the multiracial social fabric of Singapore and effectively counteract accusations of linguistic and cultural favouritism against the government.

The case for a 'Speak Mother Tongue Campaign' supplanting the more than decade old 'Speak Mandarin Campaign' is made more germane in view of the fact that the ethnic minority communities have for some time suffered from a serious weakening in 'mother tongue' proficiency amongst their youth. For example, the Action Committee for Indian Education (ACIE) has expressed concern that the Indian pass rate for the 'O' levels in their 'mother tongue' was only 85 per cent. This fell short of the impressive Chinese pass rate of 94 per cent (ACIE, 1991: 11). Local Tamil teachers have expressed concerns that English was the predominant spoken home language for Indian families and that Tamil was only studied and spoken in school by most Indian students. Concerned with the state of Tamil in Singapore, calls were made by Tamil teachers to establish a committee parallel to the CLRC for Indians (*ST*, 16 June 1992). Noted Singaporean Malay educationist Suratman Markassan and the President of the Malay Language Teachers Association Ma'arof Salleh have also cautioned that the Malay language is in a state of decline and in jeopardy of eventual eclipse particularly amongst the youth (*ST*, 9 September 1988) and English-educated middle-class Malays (T. Sapawi, *ST*, 14 September 1992).

Unlike Chinese students who are compelled to study Mandarin, non-Chinese students have the option of studying Mandarin as the second language in school. This added option for non-Chinese students has encouraged many Indian and Malay students to study Mandarin instead of their 'mother tongue' for pragmatic purposes. The increasing prominence of Mandarin in Singapore affords far greater social and economic advantages to a proficiency in Mandarin rather than Malay or Tamil. As data on non-Chinese students studying Mandarin instead of their 'mother tongue' is politically sensitive and has not been made publicly available by the MOE, it is difficult to accurately gauge the extent of the phenomenon. However, during the author's field research in 1992, numerous Malay students studying Mandarin were encountered. When such students were questioned as to why they studied Mandarin instead of Malay as a second language, they invariably stated that their parents believed that it was more economically and socially expedient to study Mandarin. This pragmatism has been encouraged by PAP Malay MPs who urge Malays to study Mandarin in order to improve their future career opportunities.[42] Whereas many Chinese students studied Malay in the 1960s and 1970s, the PAP government's promotion of Mandarin since the 1980s has effectively reversed this phenomenon by increasing the number of non-Chinese studying Mandarin.

As noted earlier, there is evidence to suggest that the lack of 'mother tongue' proficiency by the English-educated middle class can be discerned across all ethnic communities in Singapore and thus cannot be genuinely said to be a uniquely Chinese, Malay, or Indian problem. The 1990 Population Census has indicated that the most commonly spoken language in wealthier families was English whilst English was not a commonly spoken language in lower income family households.[43] Because of this class based linguistic orientation, a national 'mother tongue' campaign could be profitably organized along the multiracial lines of a 'Speak Mother Tongue' campaign. It is of particular concern that while the promotion of Mandarin has been institutionalized by the more than decade old 'Speak Mandarin Campaign', SAP schools, and other educational policies, the Malay and Tamil languages have not been accorded the same treatment even though they, like Mandarin, are also the official languages of Singapore, with Malay holding the special position of the National Language.

Of the 350 or so PAP, People's Association (PA), and NTUC neighbourhood kindergartens in Singapore, only a few offer Malay and Tamil even though Mandarin is offered in all these kindergartens.[44] As a result of this, many Malay and Indian children enrolled in kindergartens not offering their 'mother tongue' have no choice but to study Mandarin (*Sunday Times*, 7 June 1992). Unlike Chinese students who continue to study Mandarin, most Malay and Indian students discontinue the study of Mandarin by taking up their 'mother tongue' in primary school. They have thus been deprived of a head start in the formal instruction of their 'mother tongue', a head start only guaranteed to Chinese students. As SINDA's Chief Executive put it (*Sunday Times*, 7 June 1992), 'We feel that children who don't have the exposure to the language when they are in pre-school are at a relative disadvantage once they start primary school.' Having been deprived of this linguistic head start, many non-Chinese students have had to spend much time catching up on their 'mother tongue' proficiency and therefore pay less attention to other subjects. This has been cited by SINDA as a major contributor to the educational underperformance of Indian students (ACIE, 1991: 18).[45]

## Population Policies and the Education System

The education system has long been used to further the PAP government's social engineering agenda and population policies. For example, when population growth was assiduously restricted in the 1960s and 1970s, special priority for primary school enrolment was awarded to children from small families and those with parents who were sterilized before the age of forty years. By offering such educational incentives, the government hoped that Singaporeans would be deterred from having large families.[46] The eugenics logic underpinning the promotion of population policies within the education system was initially acknowledged by Lee Kuan Yew (*ST*, 15 August 1983) in a 1983 National Day rally speech. Lee warned that if the poor reproductive patterns of tertiary educated women and higher reproductive patterns of less educated women persisted, the genetic talent pool would shrink. In foreboding terms, he warned that such a lopsided procreation trend would mean that 'levels of competence will decline. Our economy will falter, the administration will suffer and the society will decline.'

Only months after Lee's 1983 National Day rally speech, the Graduate Mothers Policy was implemented in an attempt to reverse the lopsided procreation trend[47] and by doing so ostensibly avert social and economic disaster. In justifying the policy, then Minister of State for Education, Tay Eng Soon (*ST*, 24 January 1984) stated that 'the government recognizes that if well-educated mothers .... produce three or more children, they are adding to the assets of the country'. According to this logic, graduate mothers with more children were performing a service to the nation and should therefore be generously rewarded for their patriotic endeavours. In encouraging graduate mothers to have more than two children, priority was extended to them when registering their children for the more prestigious schools in pre-primary and primary one classes. Other incentives offered included generous tax concessions and medical insurance privileges (Heng and Devan, 1992: 348).

Whilst graduate women were encouraged to have more children, the poorly educated were encouraged to have fewer or stop having children altogether. A cash incentive of $10,000 was offered to women who had no 'O' level passes and with a household monthly income of not more than $1,500 if they agreed to be sterilized.[48] In an effort to legitimize the government's eugenics inspired population policies, data which supported the eugenics thesis was widely disseminated through the media. A 1984 MOE study of 100 GEP students which suggested that highly educated parents tended to have more intellectually gifted children (*ST*, 28 January 1984) was held up as proof of the eminence of nature over nurture.[49] The MOE further revealed that where parents were both graduates, their offspring were three times more likely to attain at least five distinctions in their GCE 'O' level examinations (*ST*, 13 May 1984). Amidst the pro-eugenics media dissemination, the public was kept in the dark about the disassociation by the contemporary eugenics guru Hans Eysenck from the eugenics inspired policies in Singapore. In objecting to the logic of the Graduate Mothers Policy on the grounds that it places family background above IQ tests when determining a child's intelligence, Eysenck noted (cf. T. Selvan, 1990: 232): 'I see no justification for resting the case on the education of the parents.... Bright parents can have very dull children and very dull parents can have very bright children.'

With the establishment in the mid-1980s of the state matchmaking agency, referred to as the SDU, it became increasingly obvious that the Graduate Mothers Policy was not only geared towards encouraging graduate women to have more children but was also aimed at encouraging the relatively large number of unmarried graduate women to marry. Their unmarried status was viewed by the government as representing a waste of superior genes in the already limited 'talent pool'. Despite the

PAP government's efforts at rationalizing the Graduate Mothers Policy, it remained highly offensive to both the graduate and non-graduate populace from its inception to its demise in 1985. For example, in 1984 and 1985 there were dozens of dissenting letters in the English language daily, the *Straits Times*, criticizing the Graduate Mothers Policy. The policy was widely criticized for discriminating against the majority of children whose mothers were not tertiary educated and for contravening the principles of equal opportunity and meritocracy (NUSSU, 1984; Chua, 1989: 66).

In condemning the policy for discriminating against the vast majority of Singaporeans, the then Workers Party MP J. B. Jeyaratnam and ex-Deputy Prime Minister Toh Chin Chye asserted that the policy contravened Article 16(1) and 12(1) of the Singapore Constitution which guarantees that 'there shall be no discrimination against any citizens of Singapore on the grounds of religion, race, descent or place of birth ... in the administration of any educational institution maintained by public authority and, in particular, the admission of pupils or students or the payment of fees [and that] all persons are equal before the law and entitled to the equal protection of the law'.[50] On the defensive but unable to rebut the allegations convincingly, then Deputy Prime Minister Ong Teng Cheong purported that when the government gave preferential treatment to certain groups, it was not going against the letter and spirit of the Constitution as there was a 'rational reason' for treating a particular group differently from others (*ST*, 4 March 1984). As the only 'rational reason' given to justify the policy (that is, that graduate women beget intellectually superior children) is highly contentious on ethical grounds and scientifically inconclusive, the justification could not be readily accepted as either scientifically 'rational' or ethically 'reasonable' to the majority of Singaporeans who were discriminated against by the policy.

The eugenics premise of the policy was particularly offensive to the Malay community because of its racist inferences. As Malays have long been grossly underrepresented in the tertiary education sector, the Graduate Mothers Policy resulted in Malay school children being the most discriminated. Further, the eugenics logic, which infers that because Malays are the least represented at the tertiary level and therefore must be intellectually inferior relative to the other ethnic groups, was offensive to the community. The inference of Malay racial inferiority was affirmed by Lee Kuan Yew at a 1983 National Day Cultural Show when he noted that a study found that the Chinese in Malaysia had higher IQs by fifteen points relative to Malays (*Sunday Monitor*, 21 August 1983). Lee once again reaffirmed his belief in the intellectual inferiority of Malays *vis-à-vis* the Chinese, in an interview with the *International Herald Tribune* in June 1992, when he pronounced that Malays could never be as good as the Chinese in Mathematics and that there were inherent differences in learning aptitudes between the races (M. Richardson, *ST*, 26 June 1992).

The depth of public disapprobation towards the Graduate Mothers

Policy has been credited as a significant factor in contributing towards the sharp decline in electoral support[51] for the PAP government in the 1984 elections (Singh, 1992a). In the face of such strong public pressure, the policy was eventually abandoned in 1985. However, its official demise did not signify a retreat in translating the PAP leadership's eugenics beliefs into public policy. Other less conspicuous social engineering and eugenics inspired policies such as early streaming, the GEP, and ethnic based population and immigration policies have since emerged.

## The 'Meritocratic' Tertiary Education Sector

The entrance requirements for tertiary educational institutions have also been tailored in accordance to the social engineering priorities and political considerations of the PAP leadership. A glaring illustration of an education policy that is based on the PAP social engineering agenda is the quota limiting the female student intake to only one third of the total student enrolment in the Medical Faculty at the National University of Singapore. The quota appears to be premised on the supposition that upon marriage, women doctors cannot be assigned duties as freely as their male counterparts (*ST*, 27 June 1986). To date, no in-depth study has been forwarded to support the policy limiting women students into the Medical Faculty and preventing female applicants from competing with their male counterparts on meritocratic terms.

Concerned with the gender imbalance at the National University of Singapore, the government has deemed it appropriate to alter the entrance policy to facilitate the entry of more males with a view to 'correcting' the gender imbalance.[52] For the academic year 1986/7, the university admission criteria de-emphasized the language requirements in the hope that this would boost the number of male applicants. Coupled with that, the weightage accorded to the subject General Paper was reduced from twelve to eight points (Mannarlingham, 1989: 11). Like the quota on females in the Medical Faculty, the change in language requirements was premised on the assumption that women had an innate edge over men in language ability (*ST*, 11 November 1983) even though no concrete scientific evidence was ever cited to substantiate this proposition. Instructively, the argument advanced in support of the policy was that a gender balanced tertiary student population would help to curb the problem of unmarried women graduates (*ST*, 20 November 1983) and the depleting talent pool.

To assist children of 'talented' expatriate Singaporeans who have spent many years overseas enrol as students at the National University of Singapore, the second language entrance requirement has been waived (*ST WOE*, 3 July 1993). They have also been exempt from studying Mandarin in primary and secondary school (*ST WOE*, 2 December 1995). At a time when the study and proficiency in Mandarin is strongly encouraged for Chinese students, this waiver appears to be another means of providing a further inducement to the well educated and 'talented' Singaporean expatriate community to eventually return to

Singapore rather than emigrate because of their children's inability to cope with Mandarin.

The gender quota in the Medical Faculty has its parallel in the 12 per cent quota for Indian students enrolled each year into the Law Faculty at the National University of Singapore. However, unlike the quota in the Medical Faculty, the quotas for Indians in the Law Faculty is not a formal policy. In view of the PAP leadership's tumultuous relationship with the Indian chairperson of the Workers Party, J. B. Jeyaratnam, and Lee Kuan Yew's pejorative remarks about Indians being 'contentious' (cf. S. Selvan, 1990: 239), the official formalization of such a race based quota is bound to generate public speculation about the political motives underpinning the quota.[53]

Despite the government's vociferous meritocratic rhetoric that academic prerequisites were the only acceptable criteria for tertiary enrolment, some Singaporeans have been awarded with 'affirmative action' assistance in attaining tertiary enrolment. Numerous places have been reserved for SAF officers at the National University of Singapore whilst 200 places are set aside each year for 'mature aged' students, who have relevant work experience or vocational training, at the Singapore Polytechnic beginning in 1992 (*ST*, 2 August 1990). Ngee Ann Polytechnic has introduced a special admittance scheme for outstanding athletes under the auspices of the Singapore Sports Council Admission Scheme in 1991. Needing only minimum entry requirements, those who are award recipients or fall under the above categories are accorded the privilege of not having to compete with other school leavers for acceptance into the above mentioned tertiary institutions.

Quotas have also been reserved for ASEAN students who constitute a sizeable 17 per cent of the total student population at the NTU (*ST WOE*, 8 June 1991) and 14 per cent of the total student population at the National University of Singapore. The ASEAN student's programme was implemented as part of the PAP government's strategy of recruiting 'talent' to the island to make up for the island's relatively high emigration rate and low natural reproduction levels. The PAP leadership has also justified the programme in terms of the need to foster relations with the neighbouring ASEAN countries. As stated in *Singapore: The Next Lap* (Government of Singapore: 1991: 51): 'We must be conscious of the outside world, especially of our neighbours in ASEAN. We must get to know them, both as individuals as well as countries. We must build bridges between the peoples.' In view of the PAP government's population policy of maintaining Chinese numerical dominance, euphemistically referred to as 'maintaining the racial balance', the preponderance of ethnic Chinese amongst the ASEAN students (Mannarlingham, 1989) appears to have contributed to the PAP government's enthusiasm for the programme. In rationalizing the ASEAN students' programme, Minister of State for Education Tay Eng Soon (ibid., 1989: 14) stated that 'if we are able to attract to our shores, hopefully permanently, people who can make it to university and who are also culturally not too different from us, who are going to stay on with us and be part of the population and part of the economy, then it is to our gain to admit them to tertiary education.'[54]

In the face of strong public reservations with the large numbers of ASEAN students, who are perceived as appropriating tertiary places from Singaporeans,[55] the PAP leadership has contended that the benefits accrued from accommodating the ASEAN students were not only in the long-term economic interests of Singapore but also constituted an injection of cultural richness and diversity to local institutions (*ST*, 15 July 1991). However, the claim pertaining to the injection of cultural richness contradicts earlier statements made by the Minister of State for Education about the cultural compatibility of ASEAN students with Singaporeans, the vast majority of whom are ethnic Chinese and thus culturally similar to Chinese Singaporeans. This cultural congruence has been corroborated by Mannarlingham's study (1989: 88) which found that Singaporean students at the National University of Singapore did not generally notice the difference between the ASEAN students and themselves. He has suggested that if the government was genuinely committed towards injecting cultural diversity and richness into the tertiary institutions, an increase in the number of Singaporean ethnic minorities, who are at present disproportionately underrepresented in tertiary institutions, would be a more judicious approach. This could be accomplished by reducing the number of ASEAN students and adopting an already precedented, affirmative action measure[56] that ensures proportional ethnic minority representation at the tertiary education level (ibid.: 64).[57] Such a measure would not only enhance cultural diversity in tertiary institutions but would serve to diffuse the undercurrents of ethnic tension stemming from the underrepresentation of ethnic minorities at the tertiary level.

\* \* \*

There has emerged tangible signs of a trend towards the segregation of students from different ethnic communities, particularly at the pre-school level, in SAP schools, and mainstream schools.[58] This phenomenon is a direct consequence of the assiduous promotion of Mandarin in schools, often at the expense and demotion of the other 'mother tongues'.[59] If allowed to take root, this trend will increasingly resemble the characteristics of the segregated educational system of the colonial era which, according to Turnbull (1977: 121), served to widen the socio-economic distance between the various classes and ethnic communities and accentuated ethnic, cultural, and linguistic differences.

The education policies, curriculum, and values that are actively promoted within the education system tend to be competitively individualistic, hierarchical, authoritarian, and élitist. Such values serve to inculcate a greater tolerance of social hierarchy. They potentially represent a serious threat to the island's delicate multiracial social fabric and the promotion of a democratic ethos that is positively oriented towards the ideals of social justice and equity.

In a supposedly meritocratic educational system, numerous affirmative action based policies that are gender and linguistically biased have been initiated. Despite this precedent, affirmative action or compensatory programmes aimed at elevating the weak educational representation of ethnic minorities at the tertiary educational level might not have been seriously considered.

The educational bias towards particular groups has allowed for the emergence of cracks in the hegemony of the PAP. There are signs that these cracks and spaces are widening as more Singaporeans are becoming increasingly critical of the politicization of the educational system, the validity of élitist and eugenics initiatives such as early streaming, SAP schools, and their implications for the long-term interests of the nation as a multiethnic society.

  1. This refers to the intentional inculcation of values and beliefs as truths. It is often associated with authoritarian states where dissenting views have limited access.
  2. Refers to the learning of preferences based on the values which are accorded more prominence in schools. Values are transmitted as though they are facts particularly when they correspond with the dominant values in society. They commonly include the authoritarian relationship between teacher and student, unquestioned obedience to the teacher, and a school environment whereby the student has little power.
  3. Where political learning is overt and a range of political alternatives are discussed to create critical awareness of society and nurture democratic impulses by experiencing democracy in school. Students are encouraged to participate in school decision-making.
  4. The 'hidden curriculum' has been referred to as the non-academic but educationally significant aspect of schooling that occurs but is not made explicit (Vallance, 1983: 10). An example of this is the unequal power relations between teachers and students which reflects the institutionalized life of society. Children learn to relate and deal with authority based on their socialization in schools.
  5. The pledge is as follows: 'We the citizens of Singapore pledge ourselves as one united people, regardless of race, language, or religion, to build a democratic society based on justice and equality, so as to achieve happiness, prosperity, and progress for our nation.'
  6. Students in the elite schools are often provided with a broader curriculum and less authoritarian school environment which prepares them for undertaking future leadership positions in society. They tend to be afforded with wider opportunities to exercise authority, responsibility, and self-confidence (Harber, 1991: 251). This is evident in the more esoteric curriculum and activities offered to GEP, SAP, and independent school students in Singapore.
  7. Students had a choice of studying one of the major religions and philosophies such as Christianity, Islam, Buddhism, Hinduism, Sikhism, Confucian ethics, and a course on world religions.
  8. The Civics Moral Education programme was introduced in 1966 with the aim of instilling students with a sense of social and civic responsibility, loyalty and patriotism. In 1974, a Moral Education programme called 'Education for a Living' was introduced in primary schools and incorporated into the Civics, History, and Geography syllabus. In 1981, the 'Good Citizens' and 'Being and Becoming' Moral Education programmes were introduced for primary and secondary students.
  9. The theme of protecting Singaporeans from decadent Western values has long been a preoccupation of the government. The promotion of Asian values and Confucianism has also been justified on the grounds that it serves as a shield against negative Western influences.
  10. Muslim parents and leaders of the community made numerous overtures to the

government to retain the study of Islamic Religious Knowledge in the school system (*Berita Harian*, 19 April 1989; *ST*, 20 April 1989).

11. Some of whom were closely associated with the opposition Workers Party. In April 1987, four Malays were arrested under the ISA for allegedly creating unrest by spreading rumours of impending racial clashes on 13 May, the anniversary of the 1969 racial riots in Malaysia (*ST*, 4 June 1987).

12. The evidence to support the government's allegation of a Marxist conspiracy supposedly masterminded by exiled ex-student leader Tan Wah Piow lacked concrete substantiation other than the televised public confessions of the accused still detained under the ISA.

13. Confucianism promotes a concept of government by honourable men, who have a duty to do the right thing for the governed and who in turn receive their trust and respect. Lee Kuan Yew (*Sunday Times*, 12 January 1989) believes that this concept of government is more suitable for Singapore than the Western concept of government/people relations which accords the government with as 'limited power as possible and always treated with suspicion unless proven otherwise'.

14. S. Rajaratnam noted that at the time, the prevailing attitude promoted by the government was based on the belief that 'knowing where you are going is more important than knowing where you came from' (1983: 31). The PAP leadership also believed in those days that the search for Singapore's past could easily drift into socially divisive tendencies which would lead to a strengthening of ethnic identities and communal conflict (Rajaratnam, 1984: 5).

15. History was not offered to primary students from 1968 and was excluded as an examinable PSLE subject from 1972. From 1975, it became incorporated into a non-examinable subject called 'Education for a Living'. When this subject was abolished in 1979, History and Geography were taught under a new subject called 'Social Studies'.

16. Subjects perceived to be more 'relevant' and accorded higher status included Mathematics, Science, English, and technical-based subjects.

17. None of the numerous members of the Lower Secondary History Project Team was Malay.

18. When Raffles first set foot on the island, he wrote that 'the lines of the old city and its defences, can still be traced ...' and that the tombs of Malay kings were close to his residence (cited from Lim, 1991: 8). Writing in 1822, British Resident Crawfurd (1967: 44–5) noted that the greater part of the northern and western slopes of Forbidden Hill (now referred to as Fort Canning) were covered with the ruins of the foundations of buildings which were of good-quality brick. Crawfurd also noted the existence of an inscribed rock at the mouth of the Singapore River. The writing on the rock was a Majapahit script commemorating the capture and sacking of Temasek at the close of the fourteenth century. In 1928, workers excavating parts of Fort Canning found ancient ornaments such as a pair of large gold armlets, a gold ring, six rings set with eleven diamonds, and other items (Lim, 1991: 7). In 1984, archaeologist John Miksic found numerous precious ancient ornaments from the fifteenth century in Fort Canning.

19. Numerous non-Malays have even suggested that there be a national celebration and public holiday to commemorate the day S. Raffles landed in Singapore (*ST*, 13 January 1989; *ST*, 30 January 1989).

20. For an engaging insight into Raffles, please refer to S. H. Alatas's *Thomas Stamford Raffles: Reformer or Schemer*, 1971.

21. Then Foreign Minister S. Rajaratnam stated in a 1984 address to university students in Singapore that 'Singapore has no history to speak of. We can show the Raffles statue. I can tell people what we have achieved. Tomorrow? The MRT (Mass Rapid Transport System). Yesterday? Maybe, Lee Kuan Yew, that's all' (quoted in *FEER*, 18 October 1984: 51).

22. As discussed in Chapter 6, the Israeli President was invited on a state visit to Singapore in 1987 despite the vociferous objections of Malay Muslims in Singapore and the surrounding nations.

23. Pulau Batu Putih is situated on the eastern entrance to the Straits of Singapore. In 1979, the Malaysian government published a map placing the lighthouse within its waters (*ST*, 20 September 1991).

24. Refer to the Social and Economic History of Modern Singapore developed by the Curriculum Development Institute of Singapore for lower secondary students (Singapore: Longman, 1992).

25. A New Paper poll in 1996 revealed that many young Singaporeans did not know basic historical facts such as when the country became independent and why it separated from Malaysia (*ST WOE*, 27 July 1996).

26. The numerical quota for the Chinese community who form 76 per cent of the population is 80 per cent. Malays who make up 15 per cent of the total population have been served with a 22 per cent quota for all constituencies and a 25 per cent quota for each apartment block. A Chinese is not allowed to sell his flat to a Malay in districts where the Malay population has satisfied the quota. Before the passage of the racial quotas, Malays tended to be strongly congregated in constituencies such as Bedok which were located around the east coast of Singapore. The PAP has not done particularly well, in electoral terms, in constituencies where Malays are well represented.

27. They have been publicly credited with having recommended the racial quota for Malays in schools (*ST*, 30 December 1986).

28. The school registration priority scheme which accords priority to a child who has a parent or has a sibling in a particular school has contributed to the concentration of Malays in some schools. The weak historical links of Malays with the numerous Christian mission schools, who have always given enrolment priority to applicants with parental links to the school, coupled with the above-stated factors, has generally acted to strengthen Malay representation in the less prestigious government neighbourhood schools. For a number of years, the registration priority scheme was tied to the population policy of encouraging smaller families and favouring graduate mothers. Such policies placed Malays at a disadvantage as they tended to have larger families and were less-well educated compared to non-Malays. Malay children have also been excluded from entering many schools which only teach Mandarin and English in their pre-primary classes. Any possibility of entering the prestigious SAP schools was also ruled out as subjects were only taught in English and Mandarin (*ST*, 20 October 1986). The Malay student concentration in particular schools can also be explained in terms of the community's inclination towards sending their children to schools with a history of significant Malay student and teacher/principal representation and where the name of the school is in Malay or English rather than in Mandarin. For example, in the mid-1980s, 43 per cent of the student population in Bedok West Primary School and 50 per cent of the student population in Telok Kurau Primary School were Malays (*ST*, 1 September 1987). Malay students also tend to be well represented in schools which are located in or close to areas with a high Malay residential population.

29. In implementing the recommendations of the Goh Report, double weightage was given to languages in the PSLE. Marks for English and the 'mother tongue' were double those for Mathematics and Science (*ST*, January 1983). Thus pupils with an 'A' grade in Mathematics but 'D' in one of the languages would be placed in the Normal stream (*ST*, 6 March 1981). A pass in the 'mother tongue' was required for entry into secondary school. A minimum D7 grade in the 'mother tongue' was essential for enrolment into pre-university junior colleges from 1980. At the university level, students who had not attained a pass in Mandarin as a second language (CL2) for their 'A' levels had to attend a Chinese language programme on campus and had to pass a Chinese proficiency examination before they graduate (*ST*, 18 January 1984).

30. From 1966, all Secondary 1 pupils were required to learn a second language. It was offered as an examination subject at the GCE 'O' levels in 1969 (*ST*, 9 May 1992).

31. Many Chinese students studied Malay as a second language prior to the 1981 policy.

32. However, dialects such as Hokkein and Cantonese are widely used in the various southern provinces where Singaporeans are encouraged to invest.

33. English is thus perceived, in instrumental terms, as the language of modernization and technology whilst the 'mother tongue' is the language transmitting positive cultural values and morality.

34. The MOE announced that in 1991 66.7 per cent of all new entrants into primary school came from homes in which parents speak Mandarin to their children. This

compares favourably with 25.9 per cent at the start of the Mandarin campaign in 1979 (*ST*, 9 May 1992). On an average day, 33 per cent of Singapore's 2 million television viewers aged fifteen and above watch SBC's Mandarin news. This is more than double the viewership of 14 per cent for the English news (ibid.).

35. Lee Kuan Yew has called for Mandarin 'to be the Chinese in Singapore what Malay is to the Malays, which is widely spoken, understood and read' (*ST*, 18 May 1992).

36. This newer theme is offensive to minorities and Chinese who do not speak Mandarin. Its aggressive campaign strategy has also been criticized for being socially divisive for multiracial Singapore. These concerns have not made an impact on the PAP leadership as the 1992 Mandarin campaign has persisted with the theme 'If you're Chinese, make a statement in Mandarin'. As part of the 1992 Mandarin campaign, Telecom has provided a toll-free dial-a-lesson service in the month of September. A Miss Chinatown beauty contest kicked off the campaign. Obviously limited to Chinese contestants, finalists are expected to answer questions ranging from Chinese culture to Chinese social values in Mandarin (*ST*, 29 August 1990).

37. The English-educated middle classes are perceived by the PAP leadership as being too Westernized and preoccupied with demands for liberalization. They have been criticized for being pseudo-Westerners who have lost their Asian cultural roots.

38. Lee Kuan Yew (*Asia Magazine*, 30 November 1986) has asserted that Singapore could have achieved greater economic success if it was more ethnically homogeneous (that is, more Chinese).

39. Singh (1992a: 145–6) has, however, suggested that the offer to clan associations to run six to twelve schools may also be a means of placating the concerns of Chinese-educated élites about the decreasing opportunities for teaching Mandarin.

40. The CLRC also included a coterie of twenty-two Chinese- and English-educated academics, MPs, parents, and principals.

41. Similar changes for the GCE 'O' levels are expected to be introduced at a later date. This shift in emphasis from written tests is a means of reducing the extent of rote learning and represents an attempt to make examinations a less stressful experience. However, it is fair to say that this is a problem found in the study of all subjects.

42. Harun Abdul Ghani (MP, Hong Kah) has called on mosques to go beyond teaching compulsory religious knowledge and offer courses in Mandarin (*ST*, 21 May 1992).

43. In families where the combined monthly income was $10,000 and above, more than half used English. Conversely, those from families which took home $999 and below, only 8 per cent used English (*ST WOE*, 1 May 1993).

44. Only two of the neighbourhood PAP, PA, and NTUC kindergartens offer Tamil as a supplementary language of instruction (ACIE, 1991: 18).

45. The restricted availability of Tamil and the Malay language in neighbourhood kindergartens has instigated the Malay and Indian communities to establish kindergartens which offer their 'mother tongues'. The Ramakhrishna Mission, with the financial support of SINDA, will be opening a kindergarten where Tamil will be taught as a second language and English as a medium of instruction (*Sunday Times*, 7 June 1992). The Muslim-based Jamiyah kindergartens are also becoming increasingly popular with the Malay community as they offer the study of the Malay language.

46. However, by the late 1980s, the policy of penalizing students from large families and rewarding those from small families was reversed when the restrictive population policies were found to be so effective that the birth-rate began to fall below replacement levels. From 1988, children from more than three sibling families were given priority when applying for school entrance into Primary 1 (*ST*, 4 July 1987). After much criticism from the public for the capricious social engineering nature of population policies, the linkage between awarding school priority to the number of children in a family was downgraded in 1992.

47. At his 1983 National Day rally speech, Lee Kuan Yew expressed concern over the low fertility rate amongst graduate women. He claimed that if this trend persisted the national talent pool would shrink. This would then result in a deterioration of the nation's economic health (*ST*, 15 August 1983).

48. The money would be credited to their CPF account and could be withdrawn when they turned fifty-five years of age (*ST*, 3 June 1984).

49. The 'scientific' evidence forwarded by proponents of the eugenics discourse such as Cyril Burt and Arthur Jensen has been discredited for being fraudulent (Lewontin et al., 1984).

50. The *Catholic News* also joined in the public attack of the policy whilst 500 undergraduates from Nanyang Technical Institute signed a petition condemning the policy (Gopinathan, 1991: 286).

51. The PAP lost a further 12.6 per cent of the votes to the opposition and another opposition member, Chiam See Tong (SDP) was swept to office.

52. From 1983, there were more female students enrolled relative to male students (Mannarlingham, 1989).

53. In 1985, Lee described the Chinese in Parliament as 'a practical people whose culture tells them that contention for the sake of contention leads to disaster. I have said it on many a previous occasion that had the mix in Singapore been different, had it been 75 per cent Indians, 15 per cent Malays, and the rest Chinese, it would not have worked. Because they believe in the politics of contention, of opposition' (cf. Selvan, 1990: 239).

54. Another educational initiative overtly geared towards attracting 'talent' from the region to Singapore is the Goh Keng Swee Undergraduate Scholarship. Initiated in 1994, one or two scholarships are offered to students from the region to study in Singapore. Upon graduation, they are required to work in Singapore for a period of time. If they decide to return to their country of origin after serving their bond, their stay in Singapore is expected to place them in a good position to conduct future business relationships between Singapore and their country of origin (*ST WOE*, 26 June 1993).

55. These concerns were voiced by community leaders at a Feedback session in July 1991 (*ST WOE*, 15 July 1991).

56. As elaborated above, the PAP government has on numerous occasions compromised the merit principle in the education sector to accommodate its larger political priorities.

57. So as not to compromise academic standards, ethnic minority applicants who have not attained the aggregate points for a particular year should be made to satisfy minimal academic entrance requirements. Mannarlingham (1989: 64) has suggested that a minimal drop of one aggregate point in the tertiary entrance requirement be instituted for ethnic minorities as a means of safeguarding academic standards.

58. Ethnic minority students not studying Mandarin are commonly placed in separate classes from students studying Mandarin supposedly for administration reasons. All Chinese classes are a common phenomenon in schools.

59. Even in the PAP kindergartens which offer Malay and Tamil, Malay and Indian children are often placed in separate classes supposedly for administrative reasons.

# 9
# Understanding the Malay Educational Marginality

THE Malay community's educational marginality has strongly contributed to its marginal socio-economic standing. The linkage between the community's socio-economic status (class), English language proficiency (cultural capital), and educational achievement is investigated in this chapter. Malay student responses and resistance to the education system, teacher attitudes towards Malay students, and the impact of education policies, in particular the NEP, on Malay educational progress are examined. The question of whether the educational marginality of the Malay community is a racial manifestation of a distinct class pattern is also a focus of analysis. It is argued that a serious consideration of historical, class, ethnic, and institutional factors is imperative if the Malay educational malaise is to be clearly understood and effectively addressed.

## The Educational Marginality of Ethnic Minority Communities

Biological determinist explanations have long been utilized by eugenicists to explain the educational marginality of ethnic minority communities. Eugenicists (Terman, 1924; Eysenck, 1973) have postulated that the innate intellectual deficiencies of certain classes, ethnic communities, and individuals are the major factors which contribute to their socio-economic and educational malaise. Similarly, the subordinate status of women in the work-force was also rationalized in terms of their 'inadequate' mental ability and 'innate maternal instinct'. Such ideas found expression in the discourse on IQ testing, early streaming in schools, population and immigration restriction policies.[1]

By the post-Second World War era, biological determinist explanations were systematically challenged by social psychological research (Myrdall, 1944; Allport, 1954). Instead of focusing on the cultural shortcomings of the ethnic minority community, this research approach drew attention to the attitudes and beliefs of the dominant ethnic community in circumscribing the socio-economic life chances of minorities. Building on Myrdall and Allport's researches, sociologists such as Jencks (1972) drew linkages between unequal school performance and unequal social context and questioned the credibility of IQ tests. The structural linkages between race, class, and gender based 'under-achievement' directly contradicted the conservative perspective which saw them as separate phenomena. Many educationists (Bowles and Gintis, 1977; Apple, 1979; Dale, 1989) have continued to challenge the notion that academic (under)achievement rests largely on innate talent, coming on the side of nurture in the nature versus nurture debate. They have critically examined and pointed to institutional factors such as early streaming, resource allocation of different schools, minority representation in special schools, higher education and the school curriculum, teacher attention, stereotyping, and expectations to explain the educational marginality of ethnic minorities and other socially disadvantaged students.

Having expediently abandoned the discredited biological determinist perspective of the earlier era, many conservatives (Moynihan, 1965) appear to have since relied on the cultural deficit thesis to explain the poor educational and economic attainment of ethnic minorities. By adopting this perspective, they have expediently replaced the more controversial biological determinist discourse in favour of culture as an explanatory tool (Baker, 1983). Importantly, such a perspective allows them to disregard the dynamics of class, gender, and racism in schools, particularly the salience of a gender and ethnically biased curriculum, on educational achievement. In societies such as the United States, the impressive educational achievements of Asians have often been compared with those of other ethnic minority communities such as African–Americans in order to legitimize the cultural deficit thesis (Sowell, 1981; Nee and Sanders, 1985). In Singapore, the cultural deficit thesis has been commonly relied upon to explain the educational marginality of the Malays relative to the non-Malay communities.

**Explaining the Malay Educational Malaise**

Numerous academic studies (Djamour, 1965; Bedlington, 1974; Betts, 1975; Syed H. Alatas, 1977) have cited the deficiencies of colonial educational policies for the poor educational and socio-economic standing of the Malay community during the colonial and post-colonial period. The neglect of colonial authorities in providing educational facilities in Singapore appeared to be influenced by social Darwinist thinking. In advising the East India Company against the need to establish educational facilities for Malays in Singapore, Resident Crawfurd (cf. Turnbull, 1977: 146) revealed a distinctly racialist countenance: 'The native inhabitants of Singapore have not attained the state of civilization and knowledge which would qualify them to derive advantage from the enlarged system of education.' When free educational services[2] were eventually provided for the Malay community,[3] it was only Malay-medium education of a rudimentary kind. This was justified according to the rationale that the traditional cultural lifestyle of Malays had to be preserved. Guided by this logic, the study of English was deemed to be irrelevant and excluded from the curriculum whilst non-academic subjects of a rural orientation were given particular emphasis. The blanket implementation of colonial educational policy for the largely rural based Malay masses failed to equip the urban based Singapore Malay community with the resources to effectively participate in the highly competitive island society.

The establishment of the Singapore Free School as the first Malay-medium secular school in 1834 was short-lived and closed down a decade later largely due to a lack of support from the Malay community. In 1956, two Malay-medium schools financed by the Sultan of Johore and the colonial authorities were established but suffered the fate of their predecessors as a result of poor student attendance (Zahoor Ahmad, 1969: 3–5). Many Malays tended to avoid Malay- and English-medium schools as they were generally of poor quality and did not hold good job prospects (Roff, 1980). By contrast, those who were educated in the *pondok* or religious schools were accorded respect and high status within the community (Zahoor Ahmad, 1969: 5).

In marked contrast to the low standard of education offered to the Malay masses, the scions of the Malay feudal élite were generously provided with schools of a high educational calibre such as the Malay College in Kuala Kangsar, Perak. These élite schools were primarily geared towards educating Malays for administrative positions in the colonial civil service. To ensure that these students were able to carry out their future responsibilities, the educational curriculum offered to them was of a higher and more comprehensive standard relative to the one for the Malay masses (Bedlington, 1974: 297).

The élitist and socially hierarchical nature of the colonial educational regime handicapped Singapore Malays from keeping pace with the fast urbanizing and competitive society that was unfolding on the island. Other factors such as the general poverty of the Malays, the poor educational and teaching facilities of village and religious schools, the avoidance of the good educational facilities at secular[4] and Christian missionary schools due to the fear of conversion, have all contributed in varying degrees towards laying the weak educational foundations of the Malay community.[5]

The marginal educational standing of the Malay community in post-1965 Singapore has been explained by the PAP government, its Malay representatives and sections of the Malay middle classes, primarily from the cultural deficit perspective. The focus on the cultural deficiencies of Malays served to deflect attention from the weaknesses of the education system and their marginal socio-economic status. By diagnosing the 'problem' as culturally based and primarily lying within the Malay community, the onus was thus easily removed from the government and firmly placed on the Malay community to provide solutions for their ostensible internally generated deficiencies. This allowed the PAP government, ironically in the tradition of the colonial British authorities, to adopt a minimalist policy of neglect towards the educational problems confronting the community in the post-independence decades of the 1960s and 1970s.

The PAP leadership has consistently promoted the cultural deficit thesis, and to a lesser extent the biological determinist thesis, to explain the weak educational achievements of the Malay community. Comparing the educational progress of Malays with that of the dominant Chinese community, Lee Kuan Yew (*ST*, 29 May 1982) proudly proclaimed that the importance accorded to success in examinations was an integral part of Chinese culture. In more recent times, Lee (*ST*, June 1992) has publicly asserted that educational practices should be based on the innate differences in learning aptitudes between the different racial groups. By extending the cultural deficit thesis into the even more controversial realms of biological determinism, Lee (ibid.) frankly announced that the Singapore government was resigned to the fact that Malays could not score as well as the Chinese in Mathematics.

Poor parental supervision of Malay parents towards their children has long been cited by PAP leaders to explain the educational malaise of the community. Malay parents were blamed for not giving their children enough encouragement in their studies (Ahmad Mattar, *ST*, 27 December 1982). Similarly, Abdullah Tarmugi (*ST*, 4 March 1984), current Minister for Community Development (MP, Siglap GRC) has blamed Malay parents for not placing enough emphasis on the education of their children. When the author asked Tarmugi to provide concrete evidence to substantiate his cultural deficit view during a 1990 interview, Tarmugi was only able to present anecdotal evidence. In a similar vein, the evidence cited by Yatiman Yusof (*ST* WOE, 2 March 1991) for alleging that Malays placed more value on material comforts rather than their children's education was limited to his 'observations' during the flat to flat constituency visits.

The large number of children in Malay families has also been commonly cited as an important causal factor contributing to the poor performance of Malay students. At a dinner to celebrate the twentieth anniversary of the Prophet Muhammad Birthday Scholarship Fund Board in 1985, Goh Chok Tong (*ST*, 25 August 1985), armed with an impressive array of statistical data showing the correlation between large families, poverty, and academic performance, urged Malays to have smaller families in order to improve their educational standing. However, the argument that large families cause poverty contradicts the empirical evidence which suggests that larger families are often a symptom of poverty and poor education. The relevance of this social phenomenon to the Singapore context has been verified by the 1990 census which indicated that the mean number of children among parents with university education was 1.36 compared to 1.58 for those with secondary education, 2.37 for the primary school educated and 4.60 for those without education (*ST*, 26 June 1992). As a disproportionate number of Malays relative to the Chinese are overrepresented in the lower socio-economic categories and have educational levels below the national average, it is then hardly surprising that they tend to have larger families. The symptoms and manifestations of economic deprivation rather than its root causes appear to be the PAP leadership's focus of attention.

The PAP government's consistent promotion of the cultural deficit thesis has been uncritically endorsed by segments of the teaching profession within the Malay and non-Malay community. Their regular affirmations of the cultural deficit thesis has been unfailingly given media coverage. Malay teachers interviewed by the *Straits Times* (23 June 1986), Li (1989: 176), and the author in 1990 and 1992 have strongly endorsed the dominant cultural deficit thesis when explaining the Malay educational malaise. In interviews with the author, they commonly attributed the problem to poor supervision by Malay parents and the lack of academic interest by Malay youth.

The unshakeable commitment by PAP leaders and segments of the Malay political and educated élite to the cultural deficit thesis has persisted despite the existence of numerous studies (Leong, 1978; Salaff, 1988; Ow Report, 1992) which suggest that socio-economic background strongly affects educational attainment and that the more socially privileged are enjoined with attitudes which are more conducive to high educational attainment irrespective of ethnicity. Salaff's (1988: 89–95) study found that lowly educated and poorer Chinese parents did not closely monitor their children's schoolwork or keep abreast of the latest educational policies. They largely depended on the schools to assist their children pass examinations and generally exhibited weak educational support for their children. Confirming Salaff's study, the Ow Report (1992) found that 80 per cent of the 'underachieving' Chinese students were from households with average monthly incomes of S$780. Much like their 'underachieving' Malay counterparts, many could not afford private tuition, spoke their 'mother tongue' at home, were not proficient in English, and had poor role models. Coupled with that, their parents also tended to have low expectations of their academic abilities, were not able to actively assist them in their studies, were preoccupied with earning a living, and had limited leisure time to spend with their children. Similarly, Ganapathy (1988: 1–5) has noted that many Indian parents were not aware of the details of the NEP and could not provide sufficient attention to their children's education as both parents were engaged in full-time employment. The similar problems and profiles of low-income households regardless of ethnicity has been acknowledged by the chief statistician, Paul Cheung, in his analysis of the 1990 National census (*ST*, 28 July 1991).[6]

### The Promotion and Subsequent Demotion of Malay-medium Education

In the pre-merger and merger years of 1959 to 1965, the PAP government found it politically expedient to adopt numerous measures to strengthen the educational standing of the Malay community. While maintaining the policy of free education for Malays, the community was promised bursaries and scholarships to improve their representation in tertiary institutions. Also assiduously promoted were Malay stream education and the Malay language which was not only the National Language of Singapore and the dominant language in Malaysia but also widely spoken in the region. In an attempt to further social integration with the mainland and the region, all Singaporean students were required to study Malay as a second language. From 1959, all teachers had to pass at least Standard 1 Malay before being confirmed as a teacher.

Demonstrating further its commitment to promote the Malay language, the Malay Education Advisory Committee was established to advise the Minister of Education on matters relating to Malay education (Gopinathan, 1974: 35). The first Malay secondary school (Sang Nila Utama) was established in 1961, and by 1965 there were thirteen Malay secondary schools on the island.[7] For the first time in the island's history, there was continuity in Malay-medium education from primary to pre-university level.

The PAP government's assiduous expansion of Malay education precipitated a marked increase in the number of Malays educated in the Malay language stream. Unfortunately for Malay stream students, the PAP government's efforts at promoting Malay-medium education were not matched by a corresponding commitment to provide a satisfactory institutional and infrastructural support base so as to ensure a high standard of teaching in Malay schools. Important considerations such as facilitating a smooth transition for the Malay educated GCE 'A' level students to university and ensuring a reasonable source of employment opportunities for the thousands of Malay-medium secondary school leavers, commensurate with their Chinese- and English-educated counterparts, appeared not to have been accorded serious consideration.

As the newly established Malay secondary schools suffered from an acute shortage of qualified teachers, they had to rely on teachers that were only qualified to teach at the primary level. There was also a lack of good quality Malay language texts on subjects like Mathematics and Science. It was thus hardly surprising then that the poor quality of education in Malay-medium schools was reflected in the poor results of students completing their secondary and pre-secondary education. For example, only half of these students passed the Malaysian Certificate of Education (MCE) examinations between 1963 and 1969. At the Higher School Certificate (HSC) level, less than a quarter of students were successful in 1969 (Sharom Ahmad and Wong, 1974: 18–19). For those who triumphed over the odds and qualified for a place at the local university, other formidable hurdles awaited them.

Unlike the Chinese stream students who had the option of continuing tertiary studies in Mandarin at the Nanyang University[8] and Ngee Ann Technical College, there was no Malay-medium tertiary institution in Singapore for the Malay educated. To further their studies, they were required to make the radical linguistic transition to English at the University of Singapore, where the language of instruction has always been English. The language impediment proved to be too arduous for many Malay undergraduate students as was reflected in their higher than average attrition rate (Yang R. Kassim, 1979: 68).

The hurdles encountered by Malay stream students were made more burdensome by their poor employment prospects. Despite the government's efforts to upgrade the importance of Malay, English reigned supreme as the language of administration and commerce in the fast industrializing island. The negligible use of Malay in both the private and public sector rendered the educational credentials and cultural capital of Malay stream students of limited economic value (Sharom Ahmad and Wong, 1974). Whilst the Chinese-educated had the opportunity of attaining employment in Chinese firms,[9] the marginal participation of Malays in the commercial sector meant that this avenue was virtually negligible. At best, many who completed their secondary studies ended up in the teaching profession, distinguishing it as the highest level of professional and social attainment for Singapore Malays (Hashimah Johari, 1984: 5).

In view of the economic and social realities discussed, it was not altogether surprising that Malay education endured a debilitating demise as Malay parents recognized the futility of sending their children to Malay stream schools. This phenomenon was exemplified in a survey by Gordon and Gunn (1968) who found that 82 per cent of their Malay educated respondents wished that they had been English-educated. As there was little incentive in attaining Malay education after 1965, enrolments began dwindling and by the late 1970s, its continued existence was not viable (Table 9.1).

Malay-medium education suffered a further setback after separation in 1965 when the PAP government's promotion of Malay education and assistance to Malays in the educational sector was abruptly downgraded. Bursaries which were hitherto granted to Malays students, as part of the government's policy of improving the educational standing of the indigenous community, were drastically cut back in 1968 (Table 9.2). Further, the amount of university scholarships for Malays was reduced from S$2,500 to S$750 per annum and restricted only to those in the technical and science related disciplines. As their Malay stream education did not qualify most Malay students for enrolment into these disciplines, the stringent scholarship requirements meant that they were

TABLE 9.1
Enrolment Decline in Malay Schools, 1968–1980

| Year | Primary 1 | All Levels |
| --- | --- | --- |
| 1968 | 3,025 | 36,086 |
| 1970 | 1,479 | 28,340 |
| 1972 | 589 | 20,946 |
| 1974 | 281 | 14,369 |
| 1976 | 125 | 8,361 |
| 1978 | 109 | 4,267 |
| 1980 | 32 | 1,788 |

Source: *Singapore Statistical Bulletin*, 1965–80.

TABLE 9.2
Special Malay Bursaries Awarded, 1966–1970

| Year | 1966 | 1967 | 1968 | 1969 | 1970 | Total |
|---|---|---|---|---|---|---|
| Number of Awards | 15 | 15 | 40 | 9 | 4 | 83 |

Source: Bedlington, 1974: 342.

offered to only a handful (Abu Bakar bin Alias, 1969; Betts, 1975: 196). Whereas forty Malays were awarded bursaries in 1968, only four were awarded bursaries in 1970 (Sharom Ahmad and Wong, 1974: 11).

The post-merger period also witnessed more stringent criteria for Muslim students to be recognized by the educational authorities as Malay and thus entitled to free education. For example, those of Indonesian origin but born in Singapore, or whose father had died before taking up Singapore citizenship, or who were not born in Singapore even though both parents were Singaporeans, and step-children of Singaporeans born in Malaysia were now not entitled to the fee waiver. So stringently defined were the eligibility criteria that nearly half of the Malay student population was denied free education (Betts, 1975: 197).

The PAP government's policy of actively promoting Malay education in the pre-merger and merger era and swiftly demoting Malay education in the post-merger era thus left thousands of Malays with educational credentials that were economically unmarketable other than for the more menial jobs. The Malay community thus incurred a heavy economic burden as a consequence of the politicking in the pre-merger and merger era where Malay education appeared to be a pawn in the PAP government's political machinations with the Malay dominated federal government.

### Educational (Under)achievement, Socio-economic Status, and Cultural Capital

The relative socio-economic and educational standing of the Malay community has weakened since the PAP came into office in 1959. In 1957, there was a similar proportion of Malays and Chinese in the unskilled and semi-skilled category of the work-force. However, by 1980, there were 10 per cent more Malays in that category. The gap between the percentage of Malays and Chinese in the two highest status occupational categories (professional and technical, administrative and managerial) in 1957 was only 2.3 per cent in favour of the Chinese. By 1970, it widened to 4.1 per cent and in 1980 rose to 9.6 per cent (Li, 1989: 102). There is also an overrepresentation of Malays in the lower socio-economic levels and households living in poverty[10] (*ST*, 14 May 1989; Chiew, 1991: 156).

The impact of poverty on the educational achievement of Malay students was highlighted by a 1971 Ministry of Education study of three

Malay schools which found that Malay school children were undernourished and suffered from severe vitamin deficiencies leading to poor concentration in the classroom (*Berita Minggu*, 11 July 1971). A 1977/8 survey of students at the Malay-medium Tun Seri Lanang Secondary School found that 64 per cent of the students lived in small one- or two-room flats while 32 per cent had nine or more persons living in their homes (*ST*, 1 June 1978). Living in home environments which are not particularly conducive to academic study, it is not surprising that only 20 per cent of the students surveyed obtained three or more passes in the 'O' levels (ibid.).

The socio-economic and educational position of Malays relative to other ethnic communities did not show incipient signs of improvement by the start of the 1980s and in some instances appeared to have degenerated. As discussed in greater detail in Chapter 2, nearly every socio-economic indicator in both the 1980 and 1990 National Census revealed the Malays to be clearly lagging behind the other ethnic communities. They revealed that there were disproportionately fewer Malays earning more than $1,000 per month and more earning less than $600 per month compared to other ethnic communities (Jesudason, 1993: 17) (Table 9.3). The gap in occupational terms has also widened since the 1980s (ibid.).

The high levels of one-parent Malay families, which according to a study of the Malay underclass by Myrna Blake (1991) are more vulnerable to falling into poverty,[11] has had an adverse impact on the economic security and educational progress of Malay youth. The plight of one-parent Malay families living in poverty is aggravated further by the high drug addiction and divorce rates[12] within the community and the generally deficient nature of financial assistance rendered to the poor by the public and private welfare agencies (ibid.). As the mother is more often than not the 'breadwinner' in the single parent Malay family (ibid.: 4), many who are in paid work often have to work long and irregular hours to support the family and thus are not able to spend much time with their children. Many children from families where both parents or a single parent engage in paid work but cannot afford a child-minder, end up as latchkey children with minimal parental supervision over their studies and the company they keep. The generally low educational attainment of most Malays has made it very difficult for them to fully

TABLE 9.3
Average Monthly Household Income by Ethnic Group

| Ethnicity | 1973/4 | 1987/8 |
|---|---|---|
| Malay | 741 | 1,529 |
| Chinese | 1,271 | 2,313 |
| Indian | 1,291 | 2,129 |
| Others | 3,142 | 3,906 |

*Source*: Household Expenditure Surveys; cf. *ST WOE*, 3 August 1991.

comprehend the complex and frequent modifications in education policies. As a large number of Malay adults, particularly those born before 1945, were only educated in Malay-medium schools, (Sharom Ahmad and Wong, 1974: 8) they have difficulty in fully comprehending the English language based curriculum and taking an active role in assisting and supervising their children's studies.

Due to their lack of cultural capital (English proficiency) and material resources, limited academic assistance, and intellectual stimulation from their parents, many Malay students, like others from socially disadvantaged backgrounds, commence primary school with a distinct handicap. If not given special assistance to catch up in the early years of school life, they are likely to lag further behind in the competitive educational race. As a primary school teacher has perceptively observed (*ST*, 29 May 1982), Primary 1 Malay students generally begin school with the same level of enthusiasm as the other children. However, by Primary 3 their academic performance degenerates as they appear to have lost the enthusiasm, interest, and self-confidence in their studies (ibid.), and become disheartened with the highly competitive and examination oriented school system.

As discussed earlier in the chapter, the educational ramifications arising from poor English proficiency were acutely felt by the Malay community particularly in the immediate decade following independence when many Malay students made the arduous switch from the Malay to the English stream. Malays from the Malay language stream tended to do better than those who switched to the English language stream as the latter were disadvantaged by their poor English language skills. For example, only 6 per cent of the Malay stream students who switched to the English stream National Junior College passed their 'A' levels in 1979. By comparison, the success rate for 'A' level students from the Malay-medium Sang Nila Utama was 45 per cent (*Sunday Times*, 9 March 1980). A high 33 per cent of primary and secondary English school students who repeated their subjects at least once was a Malay. An alarming 35 per cent of those who repeated the school year in the primary and secondary levels were also Malay (*ST*, 20 September 1979).

In the 1984 PSLE, the failure rate of Malays in English was 18.7 per cent compared to the national average of 13 per cent (*ST*, 30 May 1986). By 1991, the PSLE failure rate for Malays in English was reduced to 11.6 per cent. However, this failure reduction was not particularly impressive when compared with the national average of 5.7 per cent (*Sunday Times*, 31 May 1992). More alarmingly, the gap in PSLE English passes between Malays and the national average widened by 0.2 per cent in the period 1984 to 1991 (ibid.). Their relative performance at the 'O' levels was less promising with 64 per cent failing English compared to the national average of 47 per cent in 1984 (*ST*, 30 May 1986).

This weak English language proficiency of Malay students can be strongly attributed to their limited home exposure to English. For example, in 1980, only 2.3 per cent of Malay households spoke English at home compared to 10.2 per cent for Chinese and 24.3 per cent for Indian households (Table 9.4). By 1990, the proportion of Malay households speaking English had increased to 5.7 per cent. However, this still fell far short of the 21.4 per cent of Chinese and 34.3 per cent of Indian households speaking English (*ST WOE*, 1 May 1993).

The limited usage of the English language in Malay households is generally reflective of the community's relatively marginal socio-economic standing and the general tendency for the less educated Singaporeans to speak more of their 'mother tongue' rather than English at home (*ST WOE*, 1 May 1993). This phenomenon was verified by the 1990 Population Census which revealed that the most common language used in wealthier families was English. In families where the combined monthly income was $10,000 and above, more than half (about 57 per cent) used English. Conversely, in families which took home $999 or less per month, only 8 per cent used English (ibid.). Strong home usage of the 'mother-tongue' by Malay students, particularly those from lower socio-economic backgrounds, appears not to be a unique characteristic of Malays. For example, Ow Chin Hock in his 1992 Report noted that most underachieving Chinese students were from lower-income families that predominantly spoke dialects and Mandarin at home (*ST*, 28 October 1992).[13] The author's 1992 survey of 291 Malay students revealed that 68 per cent spoke only Malay at home. A further 13.4 per cent spoke a combination of English and Malay whilst only 18.2 per cent spoke only English (Table 9.5). The class/cultural capital nexus was exemplified by the fact that a minority of the students who spoke English at home tended to be from middle-class families with parents holding largely professional and white collar jobs.

In sharp contrast to the higher PSLE failure rate of Malay students in English compared to Chinese and Indian students (Table 9.6), their PSLE pass rates in the 'mother tongue' (Malay language) in 1991 was

TABLE 9.4
Language Spoken at Home (percentage)

|  | 1980 | 1990 |
| --- | --- | --- |
| Chinese |  |  |
| Dialects | 76.2 | 48.2 |
| Mandarin | 13.1 | 30.0 |
| English | 10.2 | 21.4 |
| Malays |  |  |
| Malay | 76.7 | 94.1 |
| English | 2.3 | 5.7 |
| Indians |  |  |
| Tamil | 52.2 | 43.5 |
| Malay | 8.6 | 14.1 |
| English | 24.3 | 34.1 |

*Source*: *ST WOE*, 1 May 1993.

TABLE 9.5
Languages Predominantly Spoken by
Malay/Muslim Students at Home

| Languages | Number of Students | % of Students |
|---|---|---|
| Malay | 198 | 68.0 |
| Malay and English | 39 | 13.4 |
| English | 53 | 18.2 |
| Tamil/Arabic/Others | 1 | 0.2 |
| Total | 291 | 100.0 |

Source: Ow, 1992.
Note: Out of the 291 respondents surveyed, 126 were MEP students, 133 were neighbourhood school students, and 32 were S1 Project students.

99.8 per cent. This was higher than the national average which stood at 98.7 per cent (*Sunday Times*, 31 May 1992). However, the strong Malay language skills that most Malays possess is not as effective and potent a cultural and educational asset in the present educational system which is weighted towards proficiency in the English language.

The weak Malay performance in Mathematics[14] can be attributed to their poor grasp of the English language and subsequent weak understanding and familiarity of often abstract terminology and complicated concepts which are conveyed in the English language. This problem is likely to be compounded in later years when teachers introduce more advanced terminologies and concepts which are reliant upon an earlier understanding of basic ideas which were not properly understood (Adams, 1990: 199). Studies (Husen, 1967; Oakes, 1988) have found that a weak foundation in English and poor performance in Mathematics are strongly linked to the socio-economic background of the student. This has been corroborated by the 1992 Ow Chin Hock Report on Chinese educational underachievers which found that the socially disadvantaged Chinese

TABLE 9.6
PSLE Passes in English and Mathematics,
1984 and 1991 (percentage)

| Subject | National Average | Chinese | Malay | Indian | Others |
|---|---|---|---|---|---|
| English | | | | | |
| 1984 | 85.5 | 87.7 | 74.3 | 84.9 | 94.9 |
| 1991 | 94.3 | 95.4 | 88.4 | 92.7 | 97.4 |
| Mathematics | | | | | |
| 1984 | 74.6 | 83.3 | 37.4 | 51.8 | 68.0 |
| 1991 | 78.0 | 84.9 | 46.6 | 55.9 | 71.0 |

Source: *Sunday Times*, 31 May 1992.

students tended to be weak in English, Mathematics, and Science. The salient linkage between class and academic performance in subjects like Mathematics serves to dispel the assumption promoted by the PAP leadership that Malays are inherently weak in Mathematics.

The constellation of weak English proficiency, poor academic performance in Mathematics and Science, and its link with class based factors was supported by a *Straits Times* survey which revealed that students from the more modest one to three bedroom flats were taking more tuition in subjects like English, Mathematics, and Science (*ST*, 4 April 1992). In contrast, the weakness of the middle and upper middle class students in their 'mother tongue' (who constitute less than 20 per cent of the population, who live in prestigious private flats and houses) is evidenced by their tendency to resort to private tuition in the Chinese language rather than the English language (*ST*, 4 April 1992; Table 9.7). The empirical evidence thus suggests that weakness in English, Mathematics, and Science should not, as PAP leaders such as Lee Kuan Yew (cf. Richardson, *ST*, 26 June 1992) have done, be reduced to an inherent racial trait.

The nexus between cultural capital, class, and academic performance has been acknowledged in numerous academic studies (Hess and Shipman, 1965; Zigler, 1970; Snow et al., 1982). For example, Hess and Shipman's study (1965) found that teaching techniques used by mothers vary according to their educational attainment. Middle-class mothers, relative to working-class mothers, were found to be more intellectually stimulating and talked almost twice as much to their children when teaching them. They also used more abstract words, adjectives, complex grammar, and longer sentences. Early socialization, particularly from the mother, impacts significantly on how children respond to the demands of school life (Bernstein, 1977). The child-rearing practices of the middle class thus tend to favour a rapid development of cognitive skills (Zigler, 1970). The above-mentioned foreign studies have been corroborated by local data (ACIE, 1991: 15) which reveal a correlation

TABLE 9.7
Correlation between Housing Type and Tuition Subjects Chosen (percentage)

| Tuition Subjects | HDB Flat (1–3 rooms) | HDB Flat (4–5 rooms) | Private House/Flat |
| --- | --- | --- | --- |
| English | 89 | 73 | 47 |
| Chinese | 32 | 50 | 64 |
| Malay | 4 | 4 | 8 |
| Tamil | – | 2 | 1 |
| Mathematics | 86 | 84 | 59 |
| Science | 57 | 49 | 34 |

*Source*: *ST*, 4 April 1992.

between the educational standing of Singaporean mothers and the educational achievement of their children, lending further credence to the potency of cultural capital and class on academic achievement. As the data from Table 9.8 indicates, regardless of ethnicity, mothers with no schooling tended to have more children in the slow track extended and monolingual streams. In contrast, only a small percentage of mothers with more than upper secondary education had children in the slower track streams.

Like Malays, the weak aggregate educational performance of the Indian community corresponds with their weak aggregate socio-economic standing within the larger society. For example, in 1991, their median monthly household income was $1,891. This was far short of the average national figure of $2,114 (*ST*, 28 March 1992). Only 85 per cent of Indians own their homes compared with 94 per cent of Malays and 90 per cent of Chinese (*ST*, 22 June 1991). The significant number of poor Indians within the Indian community who cannot provide the cultural/material capital and home environment that is conducive to sustaining an interest in schooling is reflected by the fact that 9 per cent of Indian children do not attend school compared to 6 per cent for Malays and 2 per cent for Chinese (*ST*, 22 June 1991). Like Malays, Indian children are overrepresented in the slower streams. For example, in 1986, 14 per cent of Indian children were channelled into the monolingual and extended streams. In contrast, only 5 per cent of Chinese children were in those streams (*ST*, 5 June 1988). Indians are also, like

TABLE 9.8
Educational Standing of Mothers and the Streaming of Their Children in the Extended and Monolingual Streams

| Mothers' Education | % of Children in Extended and Monolingual Streams |
|---|---|
| Malay | |
| No schooling | 35.0 |
| Primary | 27.5 |
| Secondary/vocational | 11.0 |
| Upper secondary and above | 5.0 |
| Indian | |
| No schooling | 40.0 |
| Primary | 25.0 |
| Secondary/vocational | 10.0 |
| Upper secondary and above | 3.0 |
| Chinese | |
| No schooling | 20.0 |
| Primary | 12.5 |
| Secondary/vocational | 4.0 |
| Upper secondary and above | 2.0 |

*Source*: ACIE, 1991: 15.

Malays, underrepresented at the National University of Singapore and constitute 4.3 per cent of the total student population there even though they make up 6.5 per cent of the population (*ST*, 28 March 1992).

Despite the strong linkage between a student's socio-economic background, English language proficiency, and educational achievement, this phenomenon has been disregarded by the education policy makers and the PAP government. The acknowledgement of such a linkage would entail a critical reappraisal of the educational system and the initiation of educational programmes for 'underachieving' students.

### The NEP and Malay Educational Progress in the 1980s and Early 1990s

Studies (Townsend and Brittain, 1972; Figueroa and Swartz, 1982; Oakes, 1988: 115) have demonstrated that where a rigorous system of streaming is introduced in schools, particularly in the lower grades, ethnic minorities and other socially disadvantaged students tend to be clustered in the slower track streams. Having been classified as 'weak' students and relegated to the slower stream classes early in their school life, they are less likely to have access to learning experiences that prepare them for studies in secondary school (Oakes, 1988: 115).

Stationed in the margins of the educational race prior to the NEP, the Malay community's academic performance appeared to lag even further behind under the rigid streaming regime of the NEP. For example, for most of the 1980s, the percentage of Malay passes, relative to the Chinese, at the PSLE and GCE 'O' levels widened by 3 to 5 per cent (NCSMMP, 1990: 104). Whereas only 4 per cent of non-Malay students were channelled to the monolingual stream in 1985, the figure for Malays was an alarming 10.4 per cent (*ST*, 27 March 1986). In 1988, 71 per cent of Malay students passed the PSLE compared to 89 per cent of Chinese and 70 per cent of Indian students (*ST*, 20 May 1989). Only 25 per cent of Malay students from each cohort made it to the express stream at secondary school (NCSMMP, 1990: 105).

Just as Malays were poorly represented in the faster track streams, élite programmes, and tertiary institutions, they were overrepresented at the non-academic technical institutes which largely prepared them for semi-professional and low-status jobs in the work-force. The majority (75 per cent) of Malay students were thus channelled to the slower track monolingual, extended, and normal streams and eventually redirected to the technical (vocational) institutes (NCSMMP, 1990: 107). In 1980, Malays constituted a high 25 per cent of the student body at technical institutes. However, with the expansion of the technical institutes in the 1980s, their participation there has dropped to 19 per cent in 1989 (*ST*, 28 November 1989).[15]

Despite the expansion of the tertiary sector, as manifested by the establishment of more polytechnics, Nanyang Technological Institute, and the larger enrolment intakes at the National University of Singapore in the 1980s, the percentage of Malays enrolled at these institutions during that decade failed to improve and in fact decreased in percentage terms away from the national average. From a mere 3.3 per cent of the total intake at the National University of Singapore in 1983, the proportion of Malay intake slipped to 3.0 per cent in 1986 (Table 9.9). At the Nanyang Technological Institute, the Malay intake increased marginally from 0.7 per cent in 1983 to a less negligible 1.6 per cent in 1986 (Mattar, 1986: 12) (Table 9.10). In 1990, only 1 per cent of Malays were university graduates compared to 4.6 per cent for the Chinese community and 3.1 per cent for the Indian community (*ST WOE*, 1 May 1992). Of the total number of Malay university students, 55 per cent were also enrolled in the Arts Faculty in 1990 compared to 25.5 per cent for Chinese and 35.5 per cent for Indian university students. By contrast, only 2.4 per cent of Malay students were enrolled in the Medical Faculty compared to 6.0 per cent for Chinese and 8.12 per cent for Indian university students (*ST WOE*, 1 May 1993).

The decline in the proportion of Malay student enrolment at the National University of Singapore in the 1980s (see Table 9.9) has been further aggravated by the implementation of stringent entry requirements for pre-university students in 1989. A pass in Mathematics and Science was now a mandatory requirement for entry to pre-university/junior colleges and centres.[16] As Malay performance in these subjects tends to be weaker, their access to the pre-university level became more restricted. Alarmed by the potentially adverse impact of the new entrance requirement on Malay educational participation at the tertiary level, Malay MPs Yatiman Yusof and Sidek Saniff (*New Straits Times*, 8 September 1986) urged the MOE to reassess the new entry requirements. Their calls were not favourably heeded by the education authorities despite the drop in the number of Malays enrolled at the pre-university level (*ST*, 21 March 1989) to less than 50 per cent of the national average (Mannarlingham, 1989: 50). It is worth noting that the new stringent pre-university entry requirements was a policy response to the higher levels of 'O' level passes which significantly increased the number of applicants for the limited places at the junior colleges. The phenomenon of credential inflation in the 1980s thus acted as another obstacle in hindering the educational progress of the Malay community.

The elimination of Religious Knowledge[17] as an examinable subject in

TABLE 9.9
Malay Student Enrolment at the National University of Singapore

| Year | Number of Students | % of Total Student Intake |
|------|--------------------|---------------------------|
| 1983 | 165 | 3.3 |
| 1984 | 192 | 4.1 |
| 1985 | 215 | 3.9 |
| 1986 | 427 | 3.0 |

*Source*: Ahmad Mattar, 1986: 12.

TABLE 9.10
Malay Student Enrolment at the Nanyang Technological University

| Year | Number of Students | % of Total Student Intake |
| --- | --- | --- |
| 1983 | 5 | 0.7 |
| 1984 | 11 | 1.6 |
| 1985 | 8 | 1.1 |
| 1986 | 13 | 1.6 |

Source: As for Table 9.9.

1991 denied Malay/Muslim students the opportunity of having the subject accredited to their overall aggregate for the GCE 'O' levels. As Malay students tended to perform well in Religious Knowledge examinations, this change in policy has served to undermine the educational standing of Malay/Muslim students (*Berita Harian*, 19 April 1990). For example, an impressive 86 per cent of those who took Religious Knowledge in the GCE 'O' levels passed the subject (*ST*, 27 April 1986). This no doubt helped to bolster the aggregate marks of Malay/Muslim students in the GCE 'O' level examinations. Strong calls by Muslim parents and community leaders for the reinstatement of the subject within the school system went unheeded.[18]

Many of the NEP policies such as early streaming have thus served to further weaken the educational standing of the Malay community and strongly limit their educational opportunities other than the path towards technical education. The class bias of the educational regime has made it particularly tenuous for those without a strong foundation in material resources and cultural capital to make a lateral transfer to the educational mainstream from the slower track streams. It is particularly instructive that like the Malays, there has also been a regression in educational standing, relative to the national average, of the Indian community since the implementation of the NEP (ACIE, 1991: 15).

### Has the Educational Gap Narrowed?

In the early 1990s, there was a considerable amount of media coverage on the supposed relative educational gains of the Malay community (*ST*, 14 May 1991; *ST WOE*, 17 July 1993; *Sunday Times*, 25 July 1993). However, the only evidence advanced to substantiate the optimistic claim was the 6.5 per cent increase in the Malay PSLE pass rate from 1991 to 1992. In contrast, the Chinese and Indian PSLE pass rate increase for the same period was 0.4 per cent and 5 per cent respectively (Table 9.11). While highlighting the PSLE gains by Malays, insufficient attention had been accorded to the fact that Malays still remained 11.5 per cent points behind the Chinese, 4.5 per cent points behind the Indians, and a high 10.1 per cent points behind the national average in the PSLE in 1992 (ibid.). Further, the data on the 6.5 per cent Malay

TABLE 9.11
PSLE Examination Results (percentage)

|  | 1988 | 1989 | 1990 | 1991 | 1992 |
|---|---|---|---|---|---|
| National average | 86.5 | 88.4 | 88.2 | 89.8 | 91.2 |
| Ethnic Group |  |  |  |  |  |
| Chinese | 89.4 | 91.3 | 91.1 | 92.9 | 93.3 |
| Malay | 70.5 | 74.3 | 74.1 | 75.3 | 81.8 |
| Indian | 79.4 | 81.5 | 80.2 | 81.3 | 86.3 |
| Others | 85.4 | 88.9 | 84.9 | 84.4 | 91.9 |

Source: ST WOE, 17 July 1993.

pass increase at the PSLE in 1992 did not correspondingly highlight Malay PSLE passes in subjects such as Mathematics which stood at 50.6 per cent, compared with 85.2 per cent for Chinese and 56.3 per cent for Indians (*Sunday Star*, 15 August 1993). In 1991 the Malay PSLE pass rate in Mathematics was 46.6 per cent compared with 84.9 per cent for Chinese, and 55.9 per cent for Indians (Table 9.12).

The Malay pass rate of 81.8 per cent at the GCE 'O' level in 1992 (Table 9.13) has been less notable compared to the Chinese pass rate of 93.0 per cent and the Indian pass rate of 86.3 per cent that year (*ST WOE*, 17 July 1993). Alarmingly, the rate of Malay students obtaining at least 5 'O' levels in 1992 dropped marginally as did that of Chinese students (ibid.). In contrast, the Indian pass rate increased by 2 per cent points that year (ibid.).[19] As only 24 per cent of Malay students received at least 5 'O' levels in 1990, compared to 60 per cent for Chinese and 35 per cent for Indians (*ST*, 14 May 1991), the lack of progress by Malays at this level will circumscribe Malay participation in the tertiary sector where at least 5 'O' level passes are required. Thus, in the opening years of the 1990s, the educational pattern that has long dogged the Malay community has persisted, that is, the higher up the educational ladder, the weaker Malay representation is. For example, only 1.4 per cent of Malays have tertiary education compared to 9.6 per cent for Chinese

TABLE 9.12
PSLE Passes in Mathematics (percentage)

|  | 1991 | 1992 |
|---|---|---|
| National average | 78.0 | – |
| Ethnic Group |  |  |
| Chinese | 84.9 | 85.2 |
| Malay | 46.6 | 50.6 |
| Indian | 55.9 | 71.0 |
| Others | 56.3 | – |

Sources: *Sunday Times*, 31 May 1992; *Sunday Star*, 15 August 1993.

TABLE 9.13
Students Obtaining a Minimum of 3 'O' Levels
by Ethnic Group (percentage)

|  | 1980 | 1985 | 1988 | 1990 | 1992 |
|---|---|---|---|---|---|
| Chinese | 72.0 | 91.0 | 91.0 | 90.0 | 93.0 |
| Indian | 62.0 | 84.0 | 81.0 | 82.0 | 86.3 |
| Malay | 48.0 | 75.0 | 78.0 | 78.0 | 81.8 |

Sources: Petir, April/May 1989; ST, 14 May 1991; Sunday Star, 15 August 1993.

and 6.4 per cent for Indians in 1992 (Sunday Star, 15 August 1993). Thus, to assert that the educational gap between the Malays and non-Malays was narrowing, just on the basis of the PSLE pass rates of Malays in the last few years, is a misrepresentation of the generally weak overall educational performance of Malays relative to non-Malays. Malay gains at the PSLE need to be similarly replicated at least at the 'O' level examinations (particularly 5 'O' level passes) and 'A' level examinations before incipient signs of a narrowing in the educational gap are to have any qualitative meaning.

It is worth noting at this juncture that the educational reforms of the 1991/2 NES, which have softened some of the more rigid policies implemented by the 1979 NEP, have gone some way towards creating a more conducive educational infrastructure for educational 'underachievers'. The abolition of the monolingual stream in 1994 makes secondary education accessible to more students and thus improve their career opportunities and life chances. Similarly, the deferment of early streaming from Primary 3 to Primary 4 is a measure that is welcomed by many students, particularly those from socially disadvantaged backgrounds, who tend to do poorly in examinations at an early age. The expansion in the number of polytechnics to four in 1992 and the elevation of Nanyang Technological Institute to university status in the same year have widened tertiary opportunities for Singaporeans.

## Student Responses to School

Ethnographic and cultural studies (Willis, 1977; McRobbie, 1978; Ogbu, 1978; Troyna, 1978; Everhart, 1979; Weis, 1985; Brown, 1987) have highlighted the shortcomings of the orthodox Marxist correspondence theory which generally depicts working class students as being passively drilled into appropriate work habits required by the economy. Sensitive to the internal cultural dynamics of class, ethnicity, and gender, the former posit that working class and other socially disadvantaged minorities strongly exhibit cultural forms of resistance within the educational system. The resistance theory holds that working class and socially disadvantaged ethnic youth consciously or subconsciously reject the knowledge taught in schools and instead turn to working class adults who represent a more achievable role model for emulation. This culture of resistance may be further strengthened by educational systems which stigmatize them as academic failures in the early years of primary school. They are also likely to assume that all schoolwork and forms of mental labour are tedious and that their future career as semi-skilled workers does not require the high status academic qualifications that entail a serious approach towards schoolwork.

Encumbered by the double burden of class and ethnicity, socially disadvantaged minority youth often become alienated and disillusioned with the education system when their self esteem has been dented by their placement in the slower streams. Additionally, the pervasiveness of negative stereotyping and discriminatory employment practices by employers from the dominant ethnic group (Nurliza Yusuf, 1986; Li, 1989; NCSMMP, 1990) has contributed to the belief that even if high academic credentials were attained, their future employment opportunities are limited. The rising prominence of Mandarin as a job requirement (Nurliza Yusuf, 1986: 29) is also perceived as yet another hurdle for ethnic minorities in the work-force. Writing about his experiences with Malay students, former Singaporean teacher Tan Tarn How (*ST*, 10 July 1992) recalled how his Malay students tended to have a more pessimistic view of their future career possibilities and 'just did not think it was worthwhile slogging it out' in school.

Stigmatized as a 'failure', many ethnic minority students have responded by acting out their label and like a self-fulfilling prophecy ensured their 'failure'. Frustrated with school, many Malay youths, particularly in the slower streams and technical institutes, wage cultural forms of resistance by resorting to various forms of disruptive behaviour as a means of striking back against the school system. They include refusing to pay attention in class, neglecting their homework, not studying for tests and examinations, being verbally abusive, playing truant, joining cliques and gangs, fighting in school, dressing unconventionally, taking drugs, smoking, and dropping out of school altogether. Their acts of defiance and resistance provide them with a feeling of empowerment and identity in an education system that has stripped them of their self-worth. The disproportionately high number of Malay youth labelled as delinquent students is indicative of the depth of their resistance and alienation with the education system. Twenty per cent of 'problem' students referred to the Ministry of Community Development in the mid-1980s were Malay (*ST*, 29 June 1986). By the early 1990s, Malays constituted 80 per cent of school drop-outs (*ST*, 5 October 1993).

It is worth noting that the above-mentioned manifestations of student resistance are generally characteristic of those from socially deprived family backgrounds. For example, a 1988 survey conducted by the Committee on Destitute Families cited four likely consequences for children from economically deprived backgrounds. They included poor academic performance, early school drop outs, truancy, drug abuse, juvenile delinquency, and emotional disturbance (*ST*, 14 May 1989). The disproportionately high level of Malay students exhibiting resistance to school can also be attributed to the promotion of the cultural deficit and biological determinist theses by the PAP leadership. Both perspectives serve to further dampen the confidence and ability of Malay students to succeed educationally. This is compounded further by the cultural and social environment in school which generally does not positively affirm nor highly value the attributes and contributions of ethnic minorities.[20]

Myrna Blake's (1991) insightful study of the Malay underclass highlighted the link between socio-economic deprivation and the higher than national average Malay school drop out rates. She found that many Malay children who have dropped out of school sought paid employment or engaged in assisting their parent/s in rearing the younger siblings (ibid.: 5). Noted Blake (ibid.: 8): 'It is not uncommon for families to stop children's schooling—either to save the expenses or in order to send the children to work.... Since children from such families are often not doing well in school, due to the lack of stimulation and encouragement in the home, leaving school makes sense to the family.' The ability to effectively cope with the demands of the highly competitive educational system is hampered further by the significantly large numbers of Malay children who are from emotionally and financially unstable home environments.[21]

In addition to the above-mentioned forms of student resistance to school, other subtle forms of psycho-social coping mechanisms have been discerned. Philip Brown (1987) has termed the three major frames of reference of 'being' in school as 'getting in', 'getting on', and 'getting out'. Like the culture of resistance, students who are 'getting in' will attempt to leave school and find employment in low-status jobs at the earliest opportunity to earn income and be relieved of the alienation of school life. Those who are 'getting out' view school and academic success a passport out of the working class and a means of attaining social mobility.[22] Like others who are 'getting in', those who adopt a 'getting on' approach are alienated from school. However, the major difference between the two groups is that the 'getting on' group see school as providing some social advancement within their class. Their aspirations tend not be very high and they are likely to aim for the minimal academic requirements or credentials required to attain a relatively secure and stable job (Brown, 1987: 106). Their pragmatic attitude towards school is a compromise between rejecting the school outright, which they recognize as eventually undermining their long-term interest, and aspiring towards high academic achievement, which they believe to be unattainable.

The author's 1992 survey of 133 Malay students from government schools indicates that Malay students, under the impact of socio-economic, parental, and peer influence, more commonly adopt a 'getting in' and 'getting on' frame of reference. The high percentage (82.7 per cent) of Malay students surveyed who indicated that they enjoyed going to school,[23] albeit primarily to socialize with friends, does provide further contextual insights into the complexities of Malay student culture, beyond the confines of the 'getting in' culture of resistance, within the 'getting on' frame of reference (Table 9.14).

TABLE 9.14
Students' Response to Survey Question: Do You Enjoy School?

| Response | Number of Students | % of Total |
|---|---|---|
| Yes | 110 | 82.7 |
| Sometimes | 9 | 6.8 |
| No | 14 | 10.5 |
| Total | 133 | 100.0 |

**Perceptions of Bias**

There is an extensive body of research which purports that many teachers are inclined to operate on the basis of negative ethnic stereotyping (Haynes, 1971; Bagley, 1975; Brittain, 1976; Dorn, 1985). In particular, teachers are likely to view ethnic minority students as disruptive and underrate their academic potential[24] (Bagley, 1975; Brittain, 1976). Some have also been found to hold racist frames of reference particularly towards ethnic minority students who are disproportionately found in the lower socio-economic rungs of society (Mabey, 1981). When teacher attention is accorded to minority students, it often manifests itself in the form of discipline, punishment (Williams, 1987: 343), and chidings for their disruptive behaviour and poor academic progress. Ethnic minority students are also more likely than non-minority students to receive harsher punishments particularly in cases of suspension and expulsion (Sedlak et al., 1986).

Prejudicial attitudes and low teacher expectations adversely impact on the self-esteem and confidence of ethnic minority students and socialize them into accepting lower levels of academic performance (Rist, 1970; Haynes, 1971). The prejudicial attitudes of teachers, repeated failure in examinations, and the stigmatization caused by being placed in the slower track classes have all contributed towards minority students rebelling against the education system by resisting school rules and engaging in other forms of disruptive behaviour (Troyna, 1989: 109–26). Invidious ethnic stereotyping is often left unchecked and allowed to proliferate due in part to the relatively small number of ethnic minority teachers, principals, vice-principals, and others holding influential positions in schools. A stronger representation of such role models and authority figures in the educational sector could well assist in tempering negative ethnic stereotyping in schools and the larger society. They are also more likely to hasten the facilitation and implementation of policies that are more sensitive to ethnic minority communities.

To date, there has been an absence of substantive academic research on teacher attitudes towards ethnic minority students in Singapore. However, the author's 1992 survey of 291 Malay secondary students from government and independent schools indicates that there is a discernible perception, particularly amongst those at the upper secondary levels,[25] that some teachers have treated them in a prejudicial fashion because of their ethnicity. Some of the survey responses of Malay students to the question of whether their teachers treated them differently because of their ethnicity are as follows:

'Some teachers are quite biased because we are Malays but I don't really care about them.'
'The teachers ill-treat by saying things that hurt our feelings.' 'One particular teacher. She treats all the Malay students coldly, finding fault whenever there's a chance.'
'Yes, because my teacher has something wrong with her brain.'
'They think that we Malays had [sic] bad behaviour.'
'Some teachers think that Malays always give trouble.'
'Yes. They treat us badly and never give us a chance.'
'Yes, definitely—they pay little attention to me unless it is for scolding.'
'Yes, cos' she's Malay and she is trying not to show that she is favouring the Malays, so she favours the Chinese and I lose out in the end.'
'Yes, my Science teacher is very biased against the Malays.'
'Teachers are very biased towards the Chinese.'
'Sometimes they look down on me and I would feel quite inferior.'
'Yes, sometimes they prefer Chinese students for leaders in class activities.'
'In primary school they think I'm inferior and the Chinese received [sic] more special attention.'
'Yes, my history teacher praised the Chinese and looked down upon the Malays when some Malays failed the tests.'
'They are sometimes biased and unreasonable and refrain from answering our questions.'
'Yes, because some of them really, really, really look down at Malays.'

Perceptions of teacher bias by Malay students, whether real or imagined, tends to dampen their self-esteem and self-worth. For many, low self-esteem becomes a self-fulfilling prophecy when they act out the perceived prejudicial attitudes of teachers. It is worth noting that the negative stereotyping of Malay students is not just limited to non-Malay teachers. During the author's discussions with Malay teachers, it was apparent that many had resorted to the dominant stereotypical notions of Malays and the cultural deficit thesis to explain the poor academic success of Malay students relative to Chinese and Indian students.

When contextualized in institutional terms, teacher bias and ethnic stereotyping can be explained in terms of the generally stressful nature of the profession, particularly those teaching in neighbourhood government schools.[26] The relatively poor working conditions, heavy workload, and poor promotion prospects associated with the feminization of the teaching profession,[27] have contributed to the generally low morale of teachers (Goh Report, 1979: 3–7).[28] They often teach under tenuous conditions, such as large classes of up to forty students[29] and have to contend with the traffic noise and sweltering heat when conducting lessons. Functioning under such trying conditions, students who do not conform to class rules or are disruptive are often severely reprimanded instead of being counselled.[30] The regular changes in education policies, often formulated with minimal consultation with teachers even though they may be required to teach a new curriculum, may well have had the effect of compounding teacher frustration and ruffling their confidence in the education system.

In particular, the packing of approximately forty students per class in most government schools, particularly when the class is made up of 'underachieving' students from the normal stream, has made it very difficult for teachers to render the kind of special attention and individualized attention which these 'underachievers' and others with learning problems require. Large classes have also been found to hamper the mastering of reading, comprehension, problem solving, critical thinking, and other higher order skills which require attentive assistance from teachers[31] (Levine and Havighurst, 1992: 263).

The prevalence of cultural deficit perspectives and negative ethnic stereotyping against ethnic minorities is likely to adversely influence the attitude of students from the dominant ethnic community towards minority students. The tendency to group Malay and Indian students in the same classes[32] (ACIE, 1991: 20), their overrepresentation in the slower streams, poor numerical representation in prestigious independent schools such as Raffles Institution, Anglo-Chinese School, and Singapore Chinese Girls School[33] and their absence from the prestigious SAP schools serve to minimize forms of meaningful social contact and shared experiences between ethnic minority and majority students thereby strengthening the impact of pernicious ethnic stereotyping. In such an environment, negative communal attitudes are easily perpetuated.

The salience of negative stereotyping towards ethnic minorities by students from the dominant ethnic community was noted by Figuero and Swart's (1982) study. They found that 'white' British pupils in comprehensive schools tended to believe that their West Indian peers primarily possessed non-academic attributes such as being fun-loving and having a good sense of humour. From the author's discussions with Malay students about their relations with non-Malay students in school, there appeared to be a perception by many Malay students that Chinese students held prejudicial attitudes against them. The author has personally observed on several occasions, in the course of her duties as a relief teacher in government schools in 1992, derogatory jokes and racist comments made by students in the monoethnic classes about ethnic minorities. Students in monoethnic Chinese classes were also more inclined to communicate in Chinese dialects compared to those in the multiethnic classes who tended to speak more in English and less in the dialects. The nurturing of healthy ethnic relations would be better facilitated by the abandonment of monoethnic classes in favour of classes and a schooling environment which reflected the multiethnic social composition of the larger society.

\* \* \*

Competing in the 'educational race' with a distinct handicap as a consequence of colonial education policies, the weak educational standing of the Malay community has been hampered further by the capricious policy of promoting and then demoting Malay-medium education. The educational marginality of Malays was made even more tenuous by the implementation of the 1979 NEP which has made the education system more hierarchical and elevated the importance of parentocracy in educational attainment. The weak socio-economic standing of the community has served to reinforce their weak educational standing, which further reinforces their weak socio-economic standing. This cumulative cycle of socio-economic and educational disadvantage helps to explain the inability of the Malay community to narrow the gap with the non-Malay community and the persistence of the Malay community on the margins of society.

The Malay educational marginality cannot be adequately explained and resolved simply from within the cultural deficit paradigm. A holistic perspective which seriously considers the constellation of historical, class, ethnic, and institutional factors is imperative if the Malay educational malaise is to be properly understood. A holistic understanding of the community's educational malaise dictates the implementation of educational programmes which address the root causes, rather than the symptoms, of educational underachievement. The élitist and eugenics based premises of educational policies need to be reappraised to make way for an education system which nurtures the self-esteem of young Singaporeans and firmly operates on the principles of equal educational opportunity and multiracialism.

1. Eugenicists were concerned with the different birth-rates of the races and the threat of genetic pollution. Terman (1924) advocated immigration restriction, sterilization measures, and the massive testing of children so that the 'gifted' could be identified and specially educated. Eugenicists also advocated discriminatory American immigration restrictions against Chinese and South Europeans early in the twentieth century in order to maintain the genetic superiority of the Anglo-Saxon community.

2. By 1990, the PAP government terminated the principle of unconditional free education for Malays which it had hitherto inherited from the British. Malays in independent schools and those from household incomes of more than $2,000 per month have since been required to pay tertiary fees.

3. The colonial authorities neglected to provide similar educational services to the Chinese and Indian community. As a result, they established their own vernacular schools funded by the wealthier members of the community and clan organizations. Poor quality schools in rubber estates were established by the rubber companies. A minority of the more socially privileged non-Malay students attended Christian missionary schools.

4. English-medium schools were established mainly in urban areas where the Malay population was underrepresented. These English-medium schools were largely attended by non-Malays (Watson, 1984: 15).

5. In contrast, the Peranakan Chinese were able to sustain their economic head start by sending their children to English secular and missionary schools without much hesitation since the nineteenth century (Roff, 1967).

6. Only on very rare occasions has Goh Chok Tong (*ST*, 25 August 1985) stepped out of the cultural deficit paradigm by acknowledging the correlation between class and academic achievement. Citing statistical data from the MOE, Goh noted that Malay students who did poorly in examinations and were placed in the monolingual stream came

largely from poor and large families. He then proceeded to acknowledge that the correlation between low-income and poor academic achievement was not unique to Malays but 'true of all races whether they were Chinese, Indian or Malays' (ibid.).

7. *Singapore Statistical Bulletin*, Singapore: Ministry of Education, 1965.

8. Concerned that Chinese stream students were handicapped in qualifying for entrance to the English-medium University of Singapore, the Chinese Chamber of Commerce, aided by donations from the Chinese business community, established Nanyang University in May 1953 (Seah and Partoatmodjo, 1974: 6). Nanyang University was also established not only to meet the needs of the Chinese-educated, but also to preserve Chinese culture and to keep Chinese-medium education independent (Gopinathan, 1989: 211).

9. However, compared to the English-educated, even the Chinese-educated were badly off. For example, in 1976, 60 per cent of Nanyang graduates were still found to be unemployed six months after graduation. This compared unfavourably with the negligible levels of unemployment amongst English-educated graduates (*FEER*, 19 November 1976).

10. Malay families constitute 21 per cent of households in Singapore (approximately 8000 households) who are living in poverty with per capita income that is less than the MHE or minimum financial requirement for subsistence (*ST*, 14 May 1989).

11. Blake's study found that a significant number of the Malay underclass are single mothers such as widows and divorcees. Most of these single mothers have primary education or none at all. She found that most brought home an income of only $400 a month. This is below the poverty line of $468 per month for a household of four as set in 1988 by the Committee on Destitute Families.

12. In 1960, the divorce rate for Muslim women was 36 per cent, whilst the average for non-Muslim women was only 5 per cent. In 1990, the divorce rate was 20 per cent for Muslim women compared with 14 per cent for non-Muslim women (*ST WOE*, 1993). About half of the 4,000 drug addicts in Singapore are Malay (*Sunday Star*, 15 August 1993).

13. In 1980, only 10.2 per cent of Chinese households spoke English (Census, 1980: VIII: 106).

14. In 1984, only 37.4 per cent of Malay pupils who sat for Mathematics in the PSLE passed the subject compared to the national average of 74.6 per cent. By 1991, the Mathematics pass rate for Malays at the PSLE was 46.6 per cent compared to the national average of 78 per cent (*Sunday Times*, 31 May 1992).

15. However, 23 per cent of Malays enrolled in the full-time courses dropped out before completing their programme. For the other ethnic communities, the figure was 15 per cent (*ST*, 28 November 1989).

16. The entrance requirement for junior colleges in the early 1990s include: (a) an aggregate of 20 points or less for six subjects including English, (b) one humanities subject, (c) one Science subject, (d) Mathematics, (e) two other subjects. They must also have at least a C6 in English, D5 in the 'mother tongue', and D7 in mathematics. The requirement for the three-year courses at the less prestigious pre-university centres where most Malay candidates were enrolled included an aggregate of not more that 20 points in five subjects which include English, two humanities subjects, Science, and Mathematics. They also required at least a C6 in English, D7 in 'mother tongue', and D7 in Mathematics (*ST*, 21 March 1989).

17. The study of Religious Knowledge as an examination subject was first offered in 1982.

18. A significant proportion of Malays have demonstrated their resistance and lack of confidence in the educational regime providing fair educational opportunities to their children by enrolling them into privately run religious schools or *madrasah*. Between 1990 and 1992, student enrolments at the five *madrasah* increased by 42 per cent, that is from 1,612 to 2,780 students (*ST*, 5 October 1992). However, the economic prospects of *madrasah* graduates and the quality of education in the *madrasah* remain poor. They suffer from a lack of standardization in the syllabus and inadequate educational facilities, and they also have difficulty in recruiting qualified teachers (Hussin Mutalib, 1989).

19. Unfortunately, more specific figures have not yet been released.

20. The relatively weaker culture of resistance by Chinese 'underachieving' students can be attributed to their wider pool of role models, feeling psychologically confident with being part of a numerically, economically, and politically dominant ethnic community, and the wider accessibility to generous forms of educational and welfare assistance from Chinese welfare organizations.

21. As noted earlier, the Malay community has the highest divorce and drug addiction rates in Singapore.

22. Based on the author's study of Mendaki Enrichment Programme (MEP) students (for the top 10 per cent of Malay students in the PSLE examinations), it appears that the MEP students from lower socio-economic family backgrounds have adopted and are encouraged to adopt this 'getting out' mentality.

23. The Ow Chin Hock Report to the Chinese Development Assistance Council (CDAC) (1992) and Quah Mayling's study (1988: 111) of predominantly Chinese students in the monolingual stream also found that 'underachieving' students enjoyed school. However, one suspects that the primary reason for enjoying school is the same for Malay students, i.e. school serves as an avenue for socializing.

24. Similarly, studies have also shown that teachers tend to expect better academic performance from middle-class children compared to those from socially disadvantaged family backgrounds (Harvey and Slatin, 1974: 140–59).

25. The lower secondary Malay pupils tended to have a more sanguine and optimistic outlook of their future career prospects, teachers, and the education system in general.

26. In contrast, teachers in independent schools such as Raffles Institution are burdened with less administrative work, teach smaller groups of about 30–35 students per class, and often get to go on overseas field trips with their students ('Friday Background' Programme, SBC, 17 June 1992).

27. The promotion prospects for teachers without tertiary qualifications is generally lower than non-graduates in other sectors of the civil service. Despite the fact that the majority of teachers are women, most vice-principals and principals are men. For example, in 1980, only 26 per cent of primary and secondary principals were women whilst only 31 per cent of vice-principals were women (Inglis, 1983: 219).

28. The teaching profession has suffered a decline in terms of its job attractiveness. This is manifested by the relatively high level of teacher vacancies in schools. At any one time, there is on average at least two vacancies in each school. There has also been a drop in the number of people wanting to teach. For example, in 1992, out of the 1,000 places in the NIE, only 800 places were filled. In 1992, forty teachers left the profession ('Friday Background' Programme, SBC, 17 June 1992).

29. The PAP government has stated that it intends to reduce the class size in the PAP manifesto *Singapore: The Next Lap* (1991: 38). However, dates specifying when this promise will be fulfilled have not been revealed.

30. The tight teaching, marking, and administrative schedule of teachers often makes it difficult for them to find the time to counsel their more problematic students.

31. Research by Finn and Archilles (1990) has found that students in small classes scored well in Reading and Mathematics in kindergarten and the first grade. They also maintained their advantage in the second and third grades.

32. In many schools, Malay and Indian students are grouped together in classes ostensibly for the administrative convenience of time-tabling second-language periods.

33. In the early 1990s, there were less than a dozen Malay students in the élite Anglo-Chinese School and Singapore Chinese Girls School.

# 10
# The Inherent Limitations of Mendaki

THIS chapter examines the efficacy of Mendaki in improving the relative educational standing of the Malay community. Towards this end, the efficacy and ideological premises underpinning Mendaki's programmes such as the Enrichment Programme for the 'high achievers' and the S1 Programme for 'underachieving' students are examined. A quantitative survey of the parental occupational background, career aspirations, and cultural capital of Malay/Muslim students in both programmes has been administered to determine the linkage between academic achievement, cultural capital, and socio-economic background. It is suggested that Mendaki's commitment towards working within the ideological parameters established by the PAP government has tempered its ability to effectively represent and address the educational challenges confronting the Malay community.

### The Political and Ideological Underpinnings of Mendaki

The establishment of the Malay/Muslim self-help body Yayasan Mendaki[1] (Council on Education of Muslim Children) in May 1982 represented a marked shift in the PAP government's management of the intractable socio-economic and educational malaise confronting the Malay community. In the decades preceding independence and prior to the birth of Mendaki, the PAP leadership, like the British colonial authorities before them, adopted a minimalist approach towards the weak socio-economic and educational standing of the Malays.[2] This minimalist stance was largely predicated on the PAP leadership's cultural deficit and biological determinist understanding of the Malay marginality.

Mendaki's formation was precipitated by the 1980 national census which starkly revealed that the minimalist approach had failed to improve the relative socio-economic and educational position of Malays. The PAP leadership recognized that the minimalist stance had to make way for a more interventionist approach if the acute sense of relative deprivation and frustration felt by Malays were to be attenuated and the delicate nature of ethnic relations maintained at an even keel. An interventionist approach promised an improvement in the PAP government's long standing tenuous relationship with the Malay community. The PAP leadership was also cognizant of the fact that if the restructuring of the island's economy towards a higher technological base was to be successful, its limited labour resource needed to be utilized to the fullest potential.

As education has long been promoted as the most effective vehicle of social mobility, Mendaki's primary mission was to improve the community's socio-economic standing through education. Instructively, no doubts were at any time raised about the efficacy of the educational system in elevating the relative standing of the socially marginal community. Clearly, the onus was firmly placed on the Malays to adapt, adjust, and change their supposedly deficient cultural values and attitudes. Although Mendaki represented a marked shift from the PAP government's minimalist approach towards Malays, the body was consistent with the corporatist nature of the state which has a history of establishing institutional channels for the various interest groups to articulate their demands. Like other state sponsored bodies such as the NTUC, the internal leadership and ideological orientation of Mendaki are closely linked to and consistent with that of the PAP government.[3]

In reaffirming the maintenance of the ideological parameters and ground rules established by the PAP leadership, the Malay community has been consistently reminded by PAP Malay leaders that its success was contingent upon changing their attitudes and resolve. At the inaugural Mendaki Congress in May 1982, Mendaki's then chairperson and Minister of Malay/Muslim Affairs Ahmad Mattar reminded the Malay community not to develop a 'crutch mentality' when requesting assistance and co-operation from the government and the private sector. Mattar reaffirmed the importance of working within the meritocratic framework despite the founding of Mendaki. The main thrust of Mattar's message was to emphasize the point that Mendaki was not to be considered an affirmative action based organization which would set in motion structural reforms within the educational system but an ethnic based self-help welfare body set out primarily to reform the attitudes of the community.

The belief in the limited intellectual capabilities of the masses and the importance of nurturing the inherent capabilities of the 'talented' few have been steadfastly maintained by the Mendaki bureaucrats and their advisers from the MOE. Indicative of Mendaki's endorsement of the NEP's élitism is the special focus rendered to its enrichment programme for Malay/Muslim students who were among the top 10 per cent of PSLE students. At a Mendaki dialogue session with community leaders, Mattar firmly reiterated the sanctity of the PAP's ideological and educational ground rules. As he put it, Mendaki's 'goal is to ensure that every child is given the right education commensurate with his [sic] ability' (ST, 27 June 1988).

Mendaki's blueprint entitled *Collection of Mendaki Papers* (Mansour Sukaimi, 1982: 44) affirmed the 'importance of making correct analysis of the reasons for the poor performance of Malay students'. Despite this caveat, the diagnosis and prescription of the Malay educational malaise in the *Mendaki Papers* have been restricted to the cultural deficit paradigm. Faithfully traversing the ideological parameters of the colonial and more contemporary discourse on the socio-economic and educational marginality of the Malay community, the *Mendaki Papers* purport that there remains an 'absence of a long-standing tradition of excellence and high achievement in the community ... [that there is] ... a relative weakness of the Malay family in rendering the motivational and control function in Malay children [and there exists a] ... low level of health and mental vigour of most Malay children' (ibid.: 164). Guided by this *ubah sikap* premise, Mendaki entrusted itself with the mission of creating 'many more young Malay/Muslim parents who are not only committed and willing to provide proper care and guidance to their children but also capable in rendering proper care and guidance [and that] the lifestyles and value systems of Malay/Muslim families must be made to be consistent with the objective of preparing the Malay/Muslim children to excel in education and life' (ibid.: 32–44).

Working within the dominant cultural deficit paradigm, Mendaki programmes were geared towards reforming Malays to better cope with the system. Put simply, the problem lay with the cultural deficiency of Malays and not with their socio-economic marginality, the educational system, or institutions in the larger society. Flowing from this perspective, programmes such as the home and community tutorial programmes for PSLE and 'A' levels students, family counselling and parenting courses, granting bursaries and scholarships to the top Malay students at the PSLE, 'O' and 'A' levels, and the VITB (Manzoun Sukaimi, 1982: 47–70) were essentially premised on reforming the Malays and nurturing the 'talented' few. More than fifteen years after its establishment, Mendaki's commitment towards reforming the perceived cultural deficits of Malays remains intact.

## The Restructuring of Mendaki

Mendaki's educational initiatives, costing the community approximately $3.4 million between 1981 and 1989 (NCSMMP, 1990: 06), have been roundly applauded by the PAP government and its Malay MPs as responsible for the educational achievements of the Malay community (*ST*, 6 October 1992). Prima facie, its record of catering to more than 45,000 students attending its weekend tuition classes between 1982 and 1992 is impressive.[4] Mendaki has provided data which indicate that on average, students attending Mendaki's weekend tuition classes attained better grades compared with those that did not attend the classes in 1991.[5] The MOE has also cited data which indicate that the average pass rates for English, Mathematics, and Science subjects at the PSLE for those attending Mendaki's weekend tuition scheme was 11–12 per cent higher than the average score of non-attending Malay students (*Sunday Times*, 18 October 1992).

Without doubt, the community has made educational progress in terms of the higher aggregate levels of passes at the critical examinations since Mendaki's establishment.[6] However, Malays have, in relative terms, remained intractably behind the Indian and Chinese communities. In terms of its lack of success in narrowing the educational gap with the non-Malay community, Mendaki has failed to live up to this central concern of the community. Furthermore, its programmes and initiatives are generally perceived not to be effectively catering to the Malay masses but instead largely benefiting Malays and other Muslims from the middle classes (Mannarlingham, 1989). This perception was regularly voiced by the author's informants and participants of the 1989 Mendaki Congress. They expressed the concern that it was largely the well educated middle-class Malays who had the financial resources to send their children to Mendaki's tuition classes and that Mendaki bursaries and awards accorded to the 'meritorious' were largely given to the latter leaving the Malay masses relatively unaffected by Mendaki's initiatives.

Confronted by public criticism with Mendaki's limited success at narrowing the educational gap between Malays and the larger community, Malay MPs and Mendaki bureaucrats in the late 1980s initiated ambitious plans to restructure and widen Mendaki's areas of focus in an attempt to improve its effectiveness. These initiatives rested on the premise that a broadening of Mendaki's functions would more effectively tackle the intractably marginal socio-economic and educational standing of the Malay community. Mendaki's existing focus on education was thought to be too narrow in scope to effectively tackle the complex socio-economic problems plaguing the community. Additionally, its existing financial base was too weak for it to make a substantive impact.[7] An enlarged Mendaki encompassing wider functions and responsibilities was believed to improve Mendaki's performance.[8]

This period of Mendaki's restructuring presented an opportunity to reflectively analyse the factors contributing to its hitherto limited achievements and critically reappraise the relevance of the ideological premises underlying Mendaki's programmes. Instead, Mendaki's administrators persisted in remaining ideologically locked in the cultural deficit thesis. Narrowly confined within this ideological paradigm, an opportunity to critically re-examine the educational system and its impact on the Malays and other socially disadvantaged groups was forfeited.

Why was this opportunity allowed to pass? It has remained the firm conviction of the PAP Malay leaders and other prominent leaders in the community that the survival of Mendaki necessitated the political and financial support of the PAP leadership (Wan Hussein Zoohri, 1990: 82). Because of this conviction, the ideological preferences of the PAP leadership were not challenged. Instead, a symbiotic relationship between the community, Mendaki, and the PAP government was sought (ibid.) in the belief that such an arrangement was in the interest of the community.

Thus far, Mendaki 2 has not been able to significantly narrow the educational gap between the Malay and the non-Malay communities. Its commercial undertakings have run into difficulties. Established in August 1992 primarily to offer quality haj pilgrimage packages to Muslims, Mendaki Travels incurred a financial loss of $197,637 in 1993 even before its major business venture was clinched (*ST WOE*, 22 May 1993).[9] Further, the $35 million equity base of Mendaki Amanah Saham (MAS or Growth Fund) failed to return any dividends to its 13,000 Malay/Muslim investors in 1992 (*ST*, 5 October 1992). These commercial failures fuelled wide speculation of incompetence by Mendaki's administrators. Concerned with the adverse ramifications of Mendaki's lacklustre commercial undertakings, Goh Chok Tong has advised Mendaki not to be 'side-tracked' by its commercial ventures and urged Mendaki to refocus its energies on education (*ST*, 13 October 1992).

## The Perceived Politicization of Mendaki

An unexpected bombshell was dropped on the Malay community when the then Deputy Prime Minister Goh Chok Tong, at an address to the Mendaki Congress on 19 May 1989, 'proposed' that the policy of free tertiary education for Malays be abolished.[10] In return for the community giving up its education fee waiver, the newly revamped Mendaki would, in addition to continued financial support from the government, receive the fees that would be paid by Malay tertiary students.[11] Goh's 'proposal' was initially greeted with shock and disbelief by Congress participants and the general Malay community. As free education was one of the few remaining tangible symbols of the community's indigenous status and a manifestation of the government's constitutional responsibility towards the socially marginal community, Malays found the government's quid pro quo approach (the abolition of free education in return for continued support for Mendaki from the government) difficult to countenance.[12] Many Malays supported the 'proposal' in principle but believed that it was not the right time to terminate the free education policy given the intractably weak socio-economic and educational standing of the community relative to the other ethnic communities.

The quid pro quo nature of the 'proposal' had the added effect of aggravating long-held Malay suspicions with the PAP government's genuine empathy towards the community's socio-economic and educational malaise. Malay suspicions were aroused only a year earlier when Goh threatened to terminate the government's support for Mendaki after accusing the Malay community of not supporting the PAP during the 1988 elections.[13] Shaken by Goh's quid pro quo countenance, Mendaki began to be increasingly viewed by the Malay community as a political football used by the PAP government primarily to promote its ideological and political interests. Furthermore, the pivotal role of PAP Malay MPs in facilitating the realization of Goh's 'proposal' likened them to PAP 'hatchet men' who helped 'sell out' the last remaining historic[14] and symbolic vestiges of constitutional trust accorded to Malays as indigenous Singaporeans.

Despite much cajoling and persuasion from Mendaki bureaucrats and PAP Malay MPs, most Congress delegates did not endorse Goh's tertiary fee 'proposal'. Recognizing that if a vote was taken at the Congress, Goh's 'proposal' would very likely be lost, a final decision was expediently deferred to an unspecified future date. Clearly demonstrating that Mendaki's bureaucrats and PAP Malay MPs were not going to concede to the general mood of the Congress participants, the 'proposal' was none the less adopted a year or so later.[15] For all intents and purposes, the issue had been resolved and was not open for debate.

The handling of the fee 'proposal' and the politicization of Mendaki have generated immense unhappiness within the Malay community (NCSMMP, 1990). These events run counter to the community's strong preference for Mendaki to remain politically non-partisan, motivated principally by the concern for the socio-economic and educational elevation of the community, accountable to the community, and democratically administered in accordance with the aspirations of the community.

Energized by the controversial events centred on the fee 'proposal' at the 1989 Mendaki Congress, the strong undercurrent of frustration and dissent within the community towards the politicization of Mendaki and the nature of its leadership was coherently externalized at the AMP Inaugural Congress in October 1990. Explicit calls were made by the AMP leadership to depoliticize Mendaki and other community based organizations such as Majlis Pusat by excluding politicians from holding executive positions in community bodies (NCSMMP, 1990).[16] They alleged that the overtly political role played by PAP Malay MPs in steering the direction of the reconstituted Mendaki had alienated the Malay community from the body, thereby undermining its independence as well as credibility and circumscribing its efficacy.[17] These assertions by the AMP appeared to be substantiated by a *Straits Times* survey of 284 randomly sampled Malays (*ST*, 31 October 1990) which confirmed that a depoliticized Mendaki was popularly preferred by the community.

Caught on the defensive but unwilling to relinquish Mendaki's links with the PAP leadership and its Malay MPs, Prime Minister Goh called on the AMP to translate its ideas of a depoliticized self-help organization into substance by establishing its own version of Mendaki (*ST*, 9 October 1990). Adding further inducement to the suggestion, Goh offered to give the proposed AMP self-help body 'the same support which it gives Mendaki'.[18] This was an ingenious move on the part of the PAP leadership as it served to deflect the spotlight away from community grievances against Mendaki's credibility, administrative competency, and politicized leadership structure towards a focus on whether an alternative depoliticized Mendaki administered by the AMP should be established.

Goh's 'proposal' was seriously considered by the AMP leadership despite expressions by many community members about the practicality of establishing another self-help body during its consultative meetings with activists and prominent members within the community.[19] In less than twelve months, the AMP agreed to take up Goh's 'proposal' of establishing its own self-help community body.[20] The issue of the politicization of Mendaki was now safely out of the public agenda thereby allowing Mendaki to proceed with its 'politicized' association with PAP Malay MPs.[21]

## Awarding the 'Meritorious' Malay/Muslim Student

In addition to financial grants and loans,[22] Mendaki has encouraged and nurtured the academic achievements of 'meritorious' Malay/Muslim students by awarding them scholarships and prizes.[23] Since 1982 the Anugerah Mendaki Awards have been given to Malay/Muslim students who have topped their cohorts at the critical examinations from the PSLE to the tertiary level (Yayasan Mendaki, *Annual Report*, 1990: 15). From 1990, Temasek and Merit Scholarships were awarded to Malay/Muslim students with the best overall results at the PSLE and other examinations (ibid.: 14). Each year approximately ten scholarships are awarded to 'talented' Malays in independent schools to help pay for their monthly fees. To qualify for the scholarship, the student must obtain at least As (distinction) in the PSLE and be among the nation's top 10 per cent of PSLE students (*ST*, 26 November 1989).

The exclusivity of these Mendaki awards, which are limited to rewarding the 'talented' few within the Malay/Muslim community, has even prompted Deputy Prime Minister Lee Hsien Loong in 1992 to recommend that Mendaki widen its award scheme to include more students from government schools.[24] Concern with the exclusivity of Mendaki's awards has been made more germane by the tendency for a substantial proportion of the more socially privileged Malay students to be recipients of the awards. For example, a *Straits Times* (15 June 1986) interview of twenty of the seventy-five Mendaki prize winners in 1985 revealed that most had fathers who held professional and white-collar jobs such as teachers, middle to upper-level civil servants, and businessmen. As is generally characteristic of those from higher income families, almost all came from small families of no larger than four children (*ST*, 15 June 1986).

Ever mindful of downplaying the link between the socio-economic background and high academic achievement of many of these 'talented' Mendaki scholars, and by doing so preserving the meritocratic image of Singapore, profiles of academically successful Malays from socially disadvantaged family backgrounds have been accorded high media profile. This serves to remind the public of the notion that the educational system provided equal opportunities for all to succeed and that the meritocratic ideal was attainable.

## Nurturing the 'Meritorious' Malay/Muslim Student

Of the numerous educational programmes initiated by Mendaki,[25] one of the most controversial is the Mendaki Enrichment Programme (MEP) specifically established for Malay/Muslim students in the national top 10 per cent of the PSLE. Why has the enrichment programme generated much controversy within the Malay/Muslim community and why is the programme considered important to the Malays and to the national community? When analysing the MEP, one will be struck by its similarities with the élite GEP and SAP programmes. Like the GEP and SAP, the ideological premises of the MEP are rooted in the eugenics notion that only a small élite within the community are well-endowed with innate intellectual abilities. It is believed that this innate intellectual prowess can be detected at an early age and thus should be nurtured to maximize intellectual potential. Firmly endorsing the importance of nurturing the 'talented' few, Mendaki's Director of Education, Suparman Adam, metaphorically likened the students in the MEP to a precious and valuable 'plant that needs to be carefully nourished and fertilized'.[26]

The close resemblance of the MEP with the GEP and SAP programmes can be better appreciated when one is aware that the MEP is 'advised' by the 'educational experts' from the MOE, the NIE, and the GEP (IQRA, 1992: 4) who generally support the eugenics premises of such programmes. Indeed, the prior establishment of other élitist and eugenics based educational programmes has helped to pave the philosophical foundations and provided the ideological, political, and economic rationale for the MEP.

Educational 'experts' from the MOE and GEP have consistently promoted the cultural deficit perspective to explain the poor educational progress of Malays at Mendaki forums and other educational seminars. At a Mendaki workshop for tutors and mentors in June 1992,[27] the adviser to the GEP and MEP programmes, Agnes Chan, suggested that Malay educational underachievement was primarily due to the low academic expectations of Malay parents and motivation of Malay students. In contrast, she claimed that Chinese parents were highly achievement motivated and inculcated this ethos in their children. The clear inference was that Malay parents and students were culturally deficient relative to their Chinese counterparts.

Just as the SAP is primarily geared towards nurturing the intellectual 'talents' of the young Chinese academic élite who are groomed to hold future leadership positions within the Chinese and the national communities, the MEP is similarly fashioned to nurture the intellectual 'talents' of the young Malay academic élite in preparation for their future leadership positions within the Malay and the national communities. As the MEP's newsletter *IQRA* (1992: 2) put it, the primary objective of the MEP is to ensure that the top 10 per cent of Malay/Muslim PSLE students[28] 'continue to do well in their studies in secondary school, move on to tertiary institutions and become role models and future leaders of the community and the nation in the Next Lap'.

The overtly instrumentalist character of the MEP is further magnified by its heavy emphasis on the mastery of English, Mathematics, and Science subjects. This is in line with the view of the PAP leadership that the mastery of these subjects is crucial for Singapore's economic and technological progress. MEP seminars have thus largely focused on these disciplines with the aim of steering the top 10 per cent into the science stream where the 'talents' of these students are thought to be best resourced. At the MEP Science Fair address on 17 June 1992 and at the Careers Guidance Seminar in September 1992, the chairperson of the MEP, Associate Professor Aziz Nather, reminded the MEP

Secondary 2 students of the importance of being channelled into the science stream.[29]

In addition to regular one-day seminars,[30] leadership training camps have been held for the top 10 per cent. At these camps, the students are inculcated with the skills, moral values (*Aspire*, March/April 1992, No.1), and other 'qualities of a good leader'.[31] Writing of her training in the art of leadership, MEP student Nazrifah Mohammad (*IQRA*, 1992: 8) recalled how 'during a classroom session, we learnt about how to become a forceful and effective leader and were given booklets on Jonathan Livingston Seagull ... we had a game based on leadership skills and strategy. Each group of 10 had to cross two rivers full of piranhas with the help of only three and a half tiles. This game involved everyone's co-operation and thinking.' The success of the MEP in inculcating and strengthening the confidence of MEP students could be clearly discerned in the author's interview and survey of 126 MEP students in 1992. A significant number stated that their sense of self-confidence had been enhanced since their enrolment into the programme. The boost in confidence felt by MEP students was of immense gratification to the MEP co-ordinators who proudly divulged to the media (*ST*, 10 September 1992) the socio-psychological fruits of their endeavours. The confidence of MEP students appeared to have been further elevated by the comments of a resounding majority of the MEP students interviewed by the author in 1992 that the numerous MEP seminars and camps had widened their circle of friends and generally improved their social life. In contrast, the MEP's initiatives aimed at enhancing their study skills was not as widely credited compared to the MEP's efficacy as a kind of social club.

The confidence of the MEP students has been buttressed by the assignment of a tertiary educated role model or mentor to each student. The latter represents a kind of older sister/brother figure who acts as an additional human resource available to the pupils other than their peers, siblings, parents, and teachers.[32] These mentors are also meant to 'provide the pupils with exemplary role models ... (and) motivate the pupils to pursue academic excellence' (*IQRA*, 1992: 2). In justifying the considerable amount of publicly funded resources these 'talented' Muslim students were receiving, Mendaki claimed that the needs of these 'able' students were not met in the mainstream curriculum of the school (ibid.). This logic stems from the PAP eugenics belief that these innately talented students need to be nurtured with special care and attention as the talent pool within the community is limited.

Efforts directed at holistically addressing the underlying causes of low academic achievement, the complex needs of the majority of students, and interrogating the institutional and structural factors contributing to poor Malay academic progress constitutes a politically tenuous course for Mendaki to adopt. As the adoption of such a strategy would require intrusions into politically sensitive territory, the option of nurturing the top 10 per cent, who have been likened to a 'streamlined high capacity vehicle [that only needs] a bit of touching up or a little fine tuning' (*ST*, 26 May 1991), has been given priority.

It is anticipated that out of the students participating in the MEP, President Scholars and others who have excelled academically will emerge as prominent frontline victors in the national competitive educational race. Just as these top 10 per cent of Malay/Muslim students have been allotted mentors as a source of inspiration, they are also expected to expand the relatively small pool of Malay professionals and serve as future role models to Malay youth.

If the Malay/Muslims as a community, and not a small conglomeration of middle-class professional individuals, are to surge ahead and narrow the educational gap with the other communities, it is highly unlikely that the preoccupation with élitist based educational initiatives, which focus on a selected minority, will provide an equitable and satisfactory long-term resolution to the Malay educational marginality.

### The Salience of Parental/Class Background and Cultural Capital in the Educational Achievement of MEP Students

The author's 1992 survey of 126 MEP students (50.8 per cent of the total number of 248 MEP students)[33] reveals a distinct correlation between socio-economic background and academic achievement. Of the MEP students interviewed from independent schools, 81.3 per cent were from white-collar and professional family backgrounds (Table 10.1).[34]

The correlation between parental occupational status, cultural capital (English proficiency), and academic achievement is demonstrated in the results of the survey of the MEP students shown in Table 10.2:

TABLE 10.1
Occupational Status of Parents of MEP Students Surveyed

| Occupational Status of Parents[a] | Number of Students | % of Students |
|---|---|---|
| Unskilled and semi-skilled[b] | 41 | 32.5 |
| White collar and semi-professional[c] | 26 | 20.6 |
| Professional[d] | 59 | 46.8 |
| Total | 126 | 100.0 |

*Note*: Of the total number of 248 MEP students, 126 or 50.8 per cent were surveyed. Of the number surveyed, 51 were male and 75 female while 54 were in Secondary 1 and 72 in Secondary 2.

[a]The survey has used the occupational status of the student's parents as an indicator of their social status. This is because occupations often carry with them connotations of income, patterns of consumption, lifestyles, values, and attitudes (Payne, 1987: 20).

[b]This occupational category generally refers to menial jobs requiring less than 3 GCE 'O' levels.

[c]Jobs which require at least 3 GCE 'O' level passes, diploma, certificate or post-secondary qualifications.

[d]Jobs requiring a diploma or other tertiary qualifications.

TABLE 10.2
Language Use of MEP Students Surveyed

| Language Used at Home | Number of Students | % of Students |
|---|---|---|
| Malay | 74 | 58.7 |
| Malay/English | 13 | 10.3 |
| English | 38 | 30.2 |
| Tamil | 1 | 0.8 |
| Total | 126 | 100.0 |

30.2 per cent spoke English and 10.3 per cent spoke English/Malay at home. The relatively strong usage of English and English/Malay (compared to the 'underachievers' from the S1 Project (see Table 10.5) corresponds with the relatively strong professional occupational background of their parents. The correlation between strong English usage in the home environment and socio-economic family status of the MEP students surveyed appears to mirror the class/linguistic nexus of the larger society as indicated in the 1990 population census. According to the census findings, in Singaporean families with a combined monthly income of $10,000 and above, more than half, or about 57 per cent, used English. Conversely, in families which took home $999 and below a month, only 8 per cent used English at home (*ST WOE*, 1 May 1993).

The survey findings lend support to the importance of material resources and cultural capital (English language proficiency) in contributing towards high educational attainment. The significance of parental occupational background thus further highlights the propriety of diverting limited community resources to MEP students, many of whom are already well endowed with the cultural and material capital which strongly assists in attaining good academic results.

### Career Aspirations of MEP Students

The cultural and material capital possessed by the majority of MEP students, compounded by the boost in self-confidence from their close access to role models via the MEP's mentor programme, has provided the MEP students with the added confidence to have high career aspirations (Table 10.3). Of MEP students surveyed, 76.2 per cent cited aspirations towards professional careers requiring tertiary qualifications. The most commonly chosen professions included medicine, law, accountancy, engineering, and teaching. Many also volunteered the possibility of either doctor/lawyer, engineer/pilot, accountant/doctor as potential career paths; 17.5 per cent of the respondents did not volunteer their preferred career paths claiming that they had not yet decided on one. It is of particular interest that despite the career guidance and confidence enhancement programmes of the MEP, 6.3 per cent cited professions such as artist, musician, stewardess, footballer, and technician,

## TABLE 10.3
### Career Aspirations of MEP Students Surveyed

| Career Aspirations | Number of Students | % of Students |
|---|---|---|
| Professional[a] | 96 | 76.2 |
| Non-professional | 8 | 6.3 |
| Did not know/vague/blank | 22 | 17.5 |
| Total | 126 | 100.0 |

[a] Jobs requiring a diploma or other tertiary qualifications.

which do not require tertiary qualifications. These low career aspirations may reflect their identification with the majority of Malays who hold non-professional jobs.

### Mendaki's S1 Project for Normal Stream Students

It was a decade after Mendaki's establishment and two years after the inception of the MEP that Mendaki finally initiated a programme specifically tailored for Malay/Muslim secondary students who have been channelled into the normal stream. The relatively timely delay in initiating a specific programme for normal stream students, where most Malays are streamed, is generally reflective of Mendaki's priorities. An experimental programme referred to as the S1 Pilot Project was initiated in 1992 at the Bedok Town Secondary School where forty normal stream students participated. The central objectives of the S1 Project include:

1. transferring as many normal stream students as possible to the express stream;
2. encouraging those still in the normal stream to complete the GCE 'O' levels (*ST*, April 20 1992); and
3. instilling students in the normal stream with a sense of self-confidence and aspirations of studying at a polytechnic or university.

The facilitators (tutors) of the S1 Project were NIE undergraduate trainee teachers who took on the tasks of teacher and counsellor to students in their assigned group.[35] As the classes consisted of approximately ten to seventeen students, the trainee teacher facilitators were able to get to know individual students better and provide the kind of personalized academic attention to each student which is generally not accessible to them in the larger classes in school. Like their MEP counterparts, camps and seminars were organized for the S1 students.

The salience of socio-economic background and English language proficiency (cultural capital) in affecting academic performance is clearly demonstrated in the author's survey of normal stream students from the S1 Project (Tables 10.4 and 10.5). A majority of 65.6 per cent of the S1 Project students had parents who held unskilled and semi-skilled occupations whilst 28.1 per cent were from white-collar and only 6.3 per cent

TABLE 10.4
Occupational Status of Parents of S1 Project Students Surveyed

| Occupational Status | Number of Students | % of Students |
|---|---|---|
| Unskilled and semi-skilled | 21 | 65.6 |
| White collar and semi-professional | 9 | 28.1 |
| Professional | 2 | 6.3 |
| Total | 32 | 100.0 |

Note: Of the total number of forty normal stream students in the S1 Project, thirty-two or 80 per cent were surveyed. Of the number surveyed, twenty-two were male and ten female.

[a]While there were more female students participating in the MEP seminars attended by the author, conversely, there were more male students in the S1 Pilot Project. The over-representation of females surveyed in the MEP programme generally mirrors the under-representation of Malay males in the tertiary education sector.

from professional backgrounds. This data is particularly telling when it is compared with the parental occupational status of students from the MEP (see Table 10.1) where a minority of 32.5 per cent were from unskilled and semi-skilled, 20.6 per cent from white-collar, and a majority of 46.8 per cent were from professional occupational backgrounds.

The disproportionately low occupational and educational parental status of S1 students (see Table 10.4) has meant that most of their parents are not able to effectively supervise and directly assist them with their studies. More often than not, these parents do not actively participate in school activities and do not fully understand the complexities of the educational system, educational policies, and the significance of the normal stream placement of their children. Typical of parents with low educational attainments and incomes (Salaff, 1988; Blake, 1991), they tend to be preoccupied with making ends meet and place greater reliance on the teachers and the school in monitoring their children's educational well-being.

A factor which could have contributed significantly to the poor academic progress of many of the S1 Project students, indeed many 'underachieving' students, is the fact that 18.7 per cent of those surveyed are

TABLE 10.5
Usage of English at Home of S1 Project Students Surveyed

| Language | Number of Students | % of Students |
|---|---|---|
| Malay | 23 | 71.9 |
| Malay/English | 6 | 18.7 |
| English | 3 | 9.4 |
| Total | 32 | 100.0 |

from single parent families where financial and emotional stability tends to be more tenuous. This factor was considered to be pertinent by the S1 Project facilitators when explaining the students' poor academic progress to the author. In contrast to the significant number of S1 students from single parent families or living with relatives, less than 5 per cent of MEP students surveyed were from single parent families.

Indicative of the proficiency in the English language as a form of cultural capital is the relatively weak level of English language use in the family households of S1 Project students. For example, only 9.4 per cent of S1 respondents primarily spoke English at home compared with a high 71.9 per cent that largely spoke Malay and 18.7 per cent who spoke a combination of Malay/English (see Table 10.2). In the course of the author's observations of the S1 tutorial classes, students appeared to have difficulty in expressing themselves in English and often resorted to the Malay language to make themselves better understood. As confirmed by the tutorial facilitators, the poor English proficiency of the S1 students has caused many of them not to fully understand scientific and mathematical concepts, and the often abstract terminology. Thus they have difficulty in comprehending Mathematics and Science exercise questions that are in English. This problem is likely to be compounded in later years when teachers introduce more advanced terminologies and concepts that are reliant upon an earlier understanding of the basic ideas not properly understood. Their weak usage and proficiency in English stands in stark contrast with MEP students, particularly in independent schools, where usage (and proficiency) of the English language has assisted their academic performance.

## Career Aspirations of S1 Project Students

A majority (56.3 per cent) of the S1 Project students surveyed aspired to non-professional careers that did not require tertiary qualifications whilst only 28.1 per cent noted professional career aspirations (Table 10.6). Conversely, only 6.3 per cent of MEP students surveyed aspired to non-professional careers whilst a high 76.2 per cent aspired towards professional careers (see Table 10.3).

The most commonly cited non-professional career aspiration was that of a police officer followed by air steward/stewardess, soldier, technician,

TABLE 10.6
Career Aspirations of S1 Project Students Surveyed

| Career Aspirations | Number of Students | % of Students |
| --- | --- | --- |
| Professional | 9 | 28.1 |
| Non-professional | 18 | 56.3 |
| Did not know/vague blank | 5 | 15.6 |
| Total | 32 | 100.0 |

chef, and diver. Most of these occupations are commonly represented within the Malay community and thus reflect the nature of occupational role models strongly available to Malay youth. It may also reflect the generally low sense of self-confidence of normal stream students in their academic potential and ability and a sense of realism of their likely future careers based on their poor academic achievements. In view of these factors, it may in fact be as, or even more, crucial for normal stream students, rather than MEP students, to be accorded mentors to regain their self-confidence and enhance their aspirational goals.

Notwithstanding Mendaki's and the AMP's inability to work in synergy on the high-profile MEP for the 'top 10 per cent', they launched their first joint educational project named the Lower Primary Foundation Programme to assist 'underachieving' Malay/Muslim students in four primary schools in 1993 (*Aspire*, September–October 1992: 6). Commonly dubbed as the P1 Programme, at least thirty Primary 1 and 2 students[36] from Tampines Primary, Eunos Primary, Clementi Town Primary, and Si Ling Primary[37] participated in the pilot programme. P1 students attended two classes per week of specialized instruction to improve their skills in English and Mathematics. Although somewhat of a delayed response to the deep-seated educational malaise of the Malay/Muslim community, the greater attempts made by Mendaki and the AMP to assist the 'underachievers' represents a move that is welcomed by the community. Importantly, such programmes are likely to assist in exposing the myriad institutional and structural limitations of the educational system. In this way, the dominant perspective which denotes that the Malay community's educational malaise is rooted in its myriad cultural deficits will be subject to critical investigation.

Notwithstanding certain weaknesses in the S1 Project,[38] it appears to have provided a window of understanding of the institutional weaknesses of the educational system, the salience of socio-economic factors and cultural capital, the importance of confidence building particularly amongst students in the normal stream, and the efficacy of adopting a more congenial relationship between teacher and student that is based on mutual respect, friendship, and empathy. Such a relationship appears to have inspired and restored some faith in the S1 students to believe in themselves and motivated them to view their studies in a less formidable light.

The informal pedagogical styles or teaching methods of S1 facilitators which sought to continually capture the interest of students by patiently relating everyday examples to relatively complex concepts, that demystifies the formidability of subjects such as Mathematics and Science, provides excellent teaching guidelines for teachers in the mainstream. This personal rapport and individualized attention to students cannot be effectively attained in large classrooms of thirty-eight to forty students commonly found in government schools. Indeed, there is a good case to be made for students from a less intellectually stimulating home environment that offers limited material and cultural capital to be placed in smaller classes so that they are able to receive personalized attention in order to catch up with other students.

Crucially important is the obvious dedication of the S1 facilitators towards the educational well-being of their students. They strongly believed in the academic abilities of their normal stream students to achieve high standards. They empathetically viewed the S1 student's limited academic success in terms of their disadvantaged socio-economic background, weak cultural capital, unstable family environments, and poor self-confidence. As a facilitator remarked to the author, 'I am convinced that they are as intelligent as any student from the express stream, it's just that they haven't been given the right guidance and intellectual stimulus to bring out the best in them.'

\* \* \*

The original premise and spirit of Mendaki's self-help philosophy of assisting the socially disadvantaged appears to have been somewhat compromised by programmes such as the MEP which disproportionately benefits a social minority within the community. This is evidenced by the author's survey of the parental occupational background of MEP students. The Malay community's response to such initiatives has generally been characterized by an undercurrent of disquiet and apprehension. In the Malay television current affairs programme 'Tinjuan', telecast on 28 September 1992, Malays interviewed on their attitudes towards Mendaki clearly registered their disapproval of the MEP. They generally expressed the opinion that more assistance and resources should be spent on those who are struggling in the educational system rather than the academic élite in the MEP.[39]

Recognizing the Malay community's disquiet with the enrichment programme, Prime Minister Goh Chok Tong urged Mendaki to strike a balance between assisting the high achievers and the underachievers (*ST*, 31 December 1992). In addition to the initiation of the S1 Pilot Project in 1992, Mendaki has begun responding to community preferences by actively reaching out to Malay/Muslim 'underachievers' who are not participating in its tuition programmes by establishing educational centres in housing estates (ibid.). There are also plans for Mendaki to implement tuition programmes for the academically weak Malay students in schools where there is a high proportion of Malay student drop-outs (*ST*, 23 August 1993). Partly in reaction to the elaborate initiatives unveiled by the Chinese Development Assistance Council (CDAC) to assist socially disadvantaged Chinese, Mendaki has, after a decade since its inception, indicated that it is in the process of drawing up a coherent plan to assist the poor in the community.[40] Despite its delayed focus on implementing specific programmes catering to the 'underachievers', such initiatives are a welcome and encouraging sign for the community.

Ideologically committed to the cultural deficit perspective, Mendaki has censored itself from critically examining the impact of the élitist and hierarchical educational system on the Malay community. Indeed, its educational premises and initiatives such as the MEP appear to mirror the ideologically élitist and eugenics orientation of the educational system. Mendaki's inability or lack of will to critically challenge the dominant ideological perspective is indicative of its essence as a constituent entity of the corporatist state that is symbiotically linked to the PAP government. Its ideological and political attachment to the PAP government has been sustained despite its status as a holding company that is primarily dependent on the financial support of the Malay community.

In the face of CDAC's focus on the Chinese underclass and the AMP's (NCSMMP, 1990) and SINDA's critique of the 'institutional impediments' (ACIE,1991)[41] confronting Malay and Indian students in the educational system, Mendaki's reluctance to critically reappraise fundamental weaknesses in the educational system is particularly instructive. Instead, it has adopted the politically circumspect option of attempting to change and reform the perceived deficient Malay cultural attitudes and values rather than the institutional weaknesses of the educational system. Unlike SINDA, which has specific plans to elevate the Indian community's educational performance to the national average by the year 2010 (ACIE, 1991), Mendaki has yet to set such targets. Malays are expected to be content with their educational gains in comparison to the community's past performance despite the fact that they have remained educationally marginal more than a decade after the establishment of Mendaki. It is of particular concern that its strict adherence to work within the ideological and political parameters set by the PAP leadership may have tempered its will to directly challenge existing anomalies and inequities in the educational system. This lack of will has tempered its ability to effectively represent the educational interests of the Malay community.

Has Mendaki made a difference? Since Mendaki's establishment there has been greater public discussion about the socio-economic and educational position of the Malay community. The S1 Pilot Programme for 'underachieving' Malay students has raised public consciousness about the salience of institutional and class-related factors in contributing to educational underachievement and exposed the contradictions of the cultural deficit thesis. In political terms, Mendaki has made a difference for the PAP government in that it has contributed to the public perception that the PAP government is actively fulfilling its constitutional responsibility in assisting the economically and educationally marginal indigenous community. In all but name, Mendaki has become a *de facto* Ministry for Malay/Muslim Affairs[42] with its agenda and leadership strongly guided by the PAP government but without the financial responsibilities and political sensitivities of such a ministry in the PAP government. As an entity within the state corporatist structure that is operating within the acceptable ideological and political structures, it has accorded legitimacy to the ideology of meritocracy and multiracialism.

It has to be acknowledged that the Malay community has improved its educational standing relative to its position a decade ago. However, despite the existence of Mendaki, the educational gap between the Malay and the non-Malay communities has not appreciably narrowed.

Malays were educationally marginal prior to the establishment of Mendaki and have remained marginal for more than a decade after the establishment of Mendaki. If Mendaki's performance is to be assessed along such terms, than clearly Mendaki's achievements are limited. As this chapter has attempted to demonstrate, Mendaki can only help facilitate minimal educational gains (that is, improve gross educational performance but not the relative educational performance) for the Malay/Muslims unless it directly challenges the ideological premises of the cultural deficit thesis, existing institutional impediments, and the educational structures which have circumscribed the educational progress of the Malays and other socially disadvantaged groups. Indeed, Mendaki's educational programmes such as the MEP, and scholarship and awards schemes may well contribute towards widening the class disparity within the Malay community as the Malay middle classes have benefited most from its educational programmes.

The social and political ramifications of Mendaki as an ethnic based self-help organization within a multiethnic society and the efficacy of the ethnic based self-help paradigm in bringing about greater social equity is the subject of the next chapter.

1. In Malay, *mendaki* means 'to ascend'.
2. The only form of assistance rendered to Malays by the PAP government was the policy of free education for all Malay students. This policy was essentially an administrative continuation of the colonial policy towards Malays. Partly in response to the minimalist approach of the government, the period after independence witnessed a mushrooming of community-oriented welfare organizations within the Malay community (Bedlington, 1974: 61).
3. Mendaki's founding chairperson was the Minister of Environment and Malay/Muslim Affairs, Ahmad Mattar. With Mattar's resignation in June 1993, PAP MP Abdullah Tarmugi took over as Mendaki's chairperson. Several other PAP Malay MPs have held executive positions in Mendaki.
4. The weekend tuition classes are held at fourteen tuition centres. Classes cater to students from Primary 3 to GCE 'O' levels. Subjects taught include Mathematics, English, and Science. A home tuition scheme was introduced in 1987 to cater for those who prefer more personalized tuition (Yayasan Mendaki, *Annual Report*, 1990: 11). More Malay students (39 per cent) attend the public tuition services offered by community organizations compared to 17 per cent Indians and 13 per cent Chinese (*ST*, 4 April 1992). Conversely, only 25 per cent of Malay students take on private tuition compared with 43 per cent of Indian and 32 per cent of Chinese students (Ibrahim, *ST*, 18 October 1992).
5. For students not attending the weekend tuition classes, 88 per cent passed English, 46.6 per cent passed Mathematics, and 77.3 per cent passed Science. In contrast, for those attending the classes, 99.5 per cent passed English, 68.9 per cent passed Mathematics, and 99 per cent passed Science (*Aspire*, June–August 1992: 1).
6. For example, in 1980 only 16 per cent of Malays attained 5 'O' levels. In 1990, the figure had increased to 45 per cent (*Sunday Times*, 18 Octobet 1992). In 1992, 75 per cent of Malays passed the PSLE compared to 67 per cent in 1982 (*ST*, 6 October 1992).
7. Up till then, Mendaki's financial resources were largely derived from the Malay community's CPF contributions of 50 cents per person to the body and an annual financial grant from the government totalling about $250,000.
8. None the less, the educational initiatives of the newly reconstituted Mendaki have

remained a dominant priority, as evidenced in the prominence of education in Mendaki's 1991 budget allocations.

| Expenditure Item | Percentage of the Budget |
|---|---|
| Education | 63 |
| Administration, corporate services, and public relations | 8 |
| Research and development | 9 |
| Finance and economic development | 6 |
| Socio-cultural affairs | 4 |
| Total | 100 |

*Source*: 'Aspiring to a Better Community', Yayasan Mendaki Pamphlet, 1992.

The Chief Executive Officer of Mendaki, Zainul Abidin Rasheed, confirmed in 1992 that education would continue to be Mendaki's main focus (*ST*, 13 April 1992).

9. Mendaki Travels is the reconstituted Mendaki Travel and Tours which ran into financial difficulties and partnership problems with Smailing Tours.

10. In the debate that followed Goh's 'proposal', little publicity was given to the fact that the principle of free education for Malays had already been violated as Malays in independent schools were paying school fees from 1988 (*ST*, 23 June 1987).

11. Free tertiary education, for the small number of Malay students enrolled in tertiary institutions, cost the government $1.5 million a year in 1988. In contrast, the subsidization of tertiary fees for the approximately 20 per cent of ASEAN students at tertiary institutions in Singapore has not come under critical scrutiny by the government.

12. In opposition to the tertiary fee 'proposal', former PAP Minister of State (Prime Minister's Office) Haji Ya'acob Mohammed maintained that the free education policy for Malays should remain as the relative socio-economic position of the Malay community was still weak and thus the original rationale for the policy stands (*ST*, 30 June 1989).

13. Just as the PAP government had threatened to cut off its support for Mendaki in the 1988 elections, in the months just prior to the 1991 elections, it offered the Malay community $10 million over a period of five years to be administered by Mendaki. Many of the author's informants cynically viewed the PAP's generous offer as an electoral bribe in view of the PAP's past actions during elections.

14. Free education for Malays was initiated by the British colonial administration in recognition of the indigenous status of the community.

15. From the academic year 1990/1, all Malay students studying at tertiary institutions were not automatically exempted from paying fees. Mendaki was given the responsibility for processing the application for the tertiary fee subsidy which was subject to a means test. Full subsidy was given to applicants whose family income was below $1,200 a month whilst those with a monthly family income of $2,000–$3,000 received a 70 per cent subsidy.

16. The chairpersonship of Mendaki was held by Ahmad Mattar from 1982 until his resignation as Minister of Environment and Malay/Muslim Affairs in 1993. Minister of State for Environment and Malay/Muslim Affairs Abdullah Tarmugi has since taken over the chairpersonship of Mendaki.

17. The matter was complicated further as no consensus was reached at the convention on the depoliticization of Mendaki and other community-based organizations. In view of the close links between the PAP government and organizations such as the trade union movement and the instrumental role of PAP MPs in the establishment of Mendaki in 1982, AMP's call for the depoliticization of Mendaki could be perceived to be a politically naive move as its fruition was highly improbable. Like Mendaki, SINDA and the CDAC could also be said to be politicized as PAP MPs are closely associated with these ethnic based self-help bodies in a formal and informal sense.

18. The PAP government has since provided the AMP with the use of the premises of the ex-Haig Boys School for a nominal annual rent of $12 (*ST*, 28 June 1992).

19. The author was present at one such consultative meeting held in November 1990.

20. However, the AMP cautioned that it would only accept the PAP government's assistance as long as it retained its independence (*ST*, 14 April 1991).

21. Mendaki's board of directors in 1992 included PAP MPs such as Ahmad Mattar, Zulkifli Mohammed, and Abdullah Tarmugi. In 1992, Mendaki's Board of Directors included Prime Minister Goh Chok Tong and Minister for Information and the Arts, Brigadier General George Yeo.

22. From 1982 to 1988, Mendaki awarded $1.3 million in study loans and $258,000 in postgraduate grants.

23. From 1982 to 1988, Mendaki disbursed merit awards totalling $93,700 (*Suara Mendaki*, 10 March 1989). Mendaki also administers scholarships sponsored by MUIS (Majlis Ugama Islam Singapura), LBKM (Prophet Muhammad Memorial Fund Board), Jamiyah (Muslim Missionary Society), MSE Angullia, British Council, Institute of Certified Public Accountants of Singapore, Hotel Properties Pte Ltd, Institution of Engineers of Singapore, Marketing Institute of Singapore, Regional Applied Computing Centre, Singapore Institute of Management, and the Western Australian College of Advanced Education.

24. He also suggested that the awards should not be limited to the top performers in the national examinations and should include the best students in English, Mathematics, and Science, the best students in individual schools, and students with the biggest improvements (*ST*, 21 July 1991).

25. The educational initiatives include the weekend tuition scheme, home tuition scheme, revision classes and clinics, Mathematics workshop for tutors, computer-based learning in Mathematic courses for Primary 3 and 4, Mendaki scholarships, buddy scheme, English language courses, interest-free loan for tertiary students, computer appreciation courses, certificate in computer operations courses, diploma in computing and information technology, and child and family development talks/workshops.

26. Address to participants at the Mendaki 'Seminar for Tutors and Mentors' on 30 May 1992, Anderson Junior College.

27. Attended by the author.

28. In 1990, 134 Malay/Muslim students who were in the top 10 per cent of the PSLE were invited to participate in the enrichment programme. In 1991, 113 Malay/Muslim students participated in the programme (*Aspire*, March/April 1992, No. 1, p. 11).

29. Held at the Science Centre, the one-day Science Fair included interesting lectures and demonstrations by scientists attached to the Science Centre on topics such as 'Creating Magic with Science', a chemistry laboratory where the students were shown how to make soap and a physics laboratory entitled 'Potpourri of Flower Petals'. The seminar was attended by the author.

30. On 25 May 1991, a seminar at the National University of Singapore was organized by Mendaki to 'meet the parents and students' of the prized top 10 per cent. The rampant élitism of the MEP's seminar was clearly demonstrated by the title of the different proceedings such as 'Raising Superstars'.

31. Norazlina Abdul Wahab, 'Growing Together—The Path to Leadership', *IQRA*, (1992: 10).

32. A study of the list of mentors in *IQRA* (1992: 12) reveals the tertiary qualifications and professional occupations held by most if not all mentors. They include an impressive list of Malay/Muslim lawyers, doctors, academics, and teachers.

33. The MEP students randomly surveyed included those who attended Mendaki's 1992 Science, English, and Mathematics seminars attended by the author.

34. Only 10 per cent of Malay workers held professional and technical jobs in 1990 (*ST*, 10 October 1992). The figure would drop significantly, if those holding technical jobs were not included under the professional category.

35. From the author's observations and discussions with S1 administrators, a close rapport or friendship has been established between the group facilitators and students. Social outings such as picnics, sports, reading sessions, and other activities are often organized by the group facilitator about once a month.

36. The students selected will undergo diagnostic tests to determine their learning ability. They will also be assessed on their classroom performance.

37. These schools were primarily chosen because of their relatively high concentration of Malay students.

38. Some of the facilitators complained that at the beginning of the programme they were provided with worksheets of high quality. Gradually the quality declined and by the end of the year they were not provided with any worksheets to assist them in their teaching during tutorials.

39. At Mendaki's 10th anniversary celebration dinner, Mendaki's Chief Executive Officer, Zainul Abidin Rasheed (*ST,* 9 December 1992), defended the MEP against community criticism by using the equity argument. He claimed that the 'high fliers', like other students, should not 'be deprived of support simply because he or she did well'. At the same function, Prime Minister Goh Chok Tong (ibid.) lent weight to Rasheed's defence of the MEP by arguing that the 'high achievers' were instrumental in elevating the community to new peaks and that if their potential were not maximized 'the community as a whole will be worse off because there will be less resources within the community to help the underachievers'.

40. Up to the early 1990s, there was no body or organization that co-ordinated the assistance rendered to the Malay underclass by the various Malay community welfare organizations. This was one of the recommendations by M. Blake (1991).

41. The institutional impediments cited include the lack of availability of Tamil as a second language in nearly all kindergartens. Tamil is often taught out of the curriculum time in many schools and is an impingement on the limited study time of students who have to travel from school to the language centre to study Tamil (ACIE, 1991: 20). There is also a dearth of books and materials as well as computer-aided learning material in Tamil for kindergarten students (ibid.). S. K. Bhattacharya, a Tamil representative council member, has cited education policies such as the lumping together of the academically weak Indian pupils in schools which lacked good teachers and adequate facilities (*ST,* 4 July 1991).

42. Mendaki is responsible for overseeing the five-year plans of Malay/Muslim organizations and of distributing finances to these organizations (*ST,* 7 March 1991).

# 11
# The Ethnic Based Self-help Paradigm

THIS chapter examines the efficacy of the ethnic based self-help approach in effectively addressing the socio-economic and educational marginality of the Malay community. The extent to which the ethnic based self-help approach reinforces cultural and biological determinist stereotypes, downgrades the significance of historical, class, and institutional factors in contributing towards social disadvantage and enhances inter- and intra-ethnic socio-economic cleavages is considered. While the ethnic based self-help paradigm complements the PAP government's minimalist approach towards social welfare, the contradictions inherent in the ethnic based self-help approach in a multiracial society are highlighted.

## Motivations and Premises Guiding the Ethnic Based Self-help Paradigm

The PAP government's minimal assistance towards redressing the socio-economic and educational marginality confronting the Malay community in the immediate decades after independence precipitated Malay/Muslim welfare organizations into mobilizing their resources to ameliorate the position of the Malay community.[1] The initiatives of the self-help bodies were encouraged by the PAP leadership as it was consistent with their belief that as the root causes of the Malay marginality stemmed from the deficient attitudes and values within the community, the onus was thus largely on the community to resolve their problem.

The PAP government's preference for private charitable and community based self-help initiatives largely reflects its philosophical opposition towards the state playing a prominent role in financing social welfare programmes for the needy. State welfare services have been vigilantly kept to a minimum in the belief that a widening of state welfare services would spell economic and social disaster for the nation (Rodan, 1989: 185). Indeed, recent policy trends indicate that the PAP government is not only minimizing but systematically privatizing the state's social welfare services. In its place, the family, national community, ethnic community, and market (Ramesh, 1992: 1) have been encouraged to take on the responsibility of addressing the needs of the poor. In an address to

PAP activists in June 1992, Prime Minister Goh Chok Tong (Editorial, *ST*, 25 June 1992) reiterated that the central thrust of the government's programme would continue to be its strong opposition against pressures to expand its social welfare commitment. The importance attached to this theme was reiterated in his 1992 and 1993 National Day speeches.[2]

As discussed in Chapter 10, the findings of the 1980 census alerted the PAP leadership and its Malay MPs of the inability in the uncoordinated and piecemeal nature of ethnic/religious based welfare organizations to qualitatively improve the socio-economic status of Malays. More alarming was the census revelation that the gap between the Malay and the non-Malay communities was not narrowing but may have in fact widened.[3] In responding to this alarming trend, a social assistance programme was mooted by PAP Malay MPs in the early 1980s in an attempt to address the Malay marginality. The programme's ingenuity lay in the fact that it did not significantly compromise the PAP government's minimalist stance towards social welfare. Instead it was centred on harnessing the resources of the Malay community and its numerous grass roots welfare organizations under a centralized body focused on addressing the educational malaise of the community. Education was selected as the focus of attention on the premise that it was the most effective vehicle of social mobility in ameliorating the community's weak socio-economic standing. To ensure the financial viability of the proposed ethnic/religious based body, monthly donations from each working Malay/Muslim were to be harnessed by utilizing a CPF check-off system.[4]

Having established the ethnic self-help paradigm with Mendaki's formation, it was only a matter of time before the socio-economic and educational problems of other ethnic communities were addressed along Mendaki's ethnic based self-help paradigm. In 1990, not long after concerns were expressed (ACIE, 1991) by members of the Indian community about the alarming educational and socio-economic malaise of a deprived segment within the community, the Singapore Indian Development Association (SINDA) was formed. Two years later, the CDAC was inaugurated after strong encouragement and inducement from the PAP leadership about the necessity of such a welfare body for the Chinese.[5] Concerned that the Eurasian community would be left behind by the self-help initiatives of the major ethnic communities, the Eurasian Association formed an Endowment Fund in July 1992. The Fund would provide educational and welfare assistance to the 13,000 strong community[6] (*ST*, 9 July 1991). With the establishment of the various ethnic based self-help bodies, the PAP government was thus able to ensure that state welfarism continued to be kept to a minimum.

Articulated concerns with the sectarian ethnic based self-help trend (*Sunday Times*, 5 May 1991; *ST*, 20 July 1991; *Sunday Times*, 3 May 1992: Rahim, *ST*, 26 September 1992) have been countered by the PAP leadership in terms of the effectiveness of the ethnic based approach in procuring financial and human resource support within the respective ethnic communities. In the tradition of the sociobiology school of thought, they purported that the ethnic based self-help approach effectively harnessed primordial 'kin altruism' towards the less socially privileged within the ethnic community. This sociobiologist logic assumes that humans are naturally selfish to one another and are only inclined to assist the needy within their own community rather than to others in a similarly disadvantaged position.[7] Using this logic, Senior Minister Lee Kuan Yew (*ST WOE*, 18 January 1992) claimed that people were more willing to 'share their last bag of rice ... [with] those whom they instinctively and culturally feel an obligation because they are members of one's clan, so to speak'. Adding further weight to the merit of the ethnic based self-help approach, Lee (*ST*, 26 June 1992) declared that a committed leadership amongst the social élite in each ethnic community working within a communally oriented welfare paradigm held the 'key' to resolving the problems of socially disadvantaged ethnic minority communities such as Singapore Malays.[8]

Leaving aside the contentious moral and empirical validity of such claims, arguments which putatively accept the sociobiological notion that primordial ethnic bias is 'natural' and thus should be encouraged tend to promote insecurity and vulnerability particularly amongst ethnic minorities. Ethnic minorities may well fear that in times of political, social, or economic instability, political leaders in government from the ethnic majority community will fall prey to this primordial ethnic bias and orient policies accordingly. In a social milieu that is marked by ethnic insecurity, a combination of class and ethnic based grievances is likely to manifest itself solely in ethnic terms as the class dimension is effectively attenuated.

History is replete with examples of politicians and political parties in government, or in opposition, resorting to forms of communal and other sectarian political posturing for political gain particularly in periods of national crisis or when their political power is tenuously held. A society that is organized and mobilized on the basis of race can thus be easily divided on the basis of race, making it easier for the various racial communities to be manipulated against one another (Clammer, 1982: 127–30). The PAP government's institutionalization of communal oriented politics through the GRC, ethnic housing quotas, the continued exclusion of Malays from sensitive units in the SAF, its active promotion of Mandarin and Confucianism for the exclusive benefit of the Chinese community, its policy of maintaining the Chinese numerical dominance in Singapore, the repeated statements by PAP leaders that the economic success and political stability of Singapore is largely attributed to the dynamic cultural attributes of the Chinese (Goh Keng Swee, *ST*, 4 February 1982; Lee Kuan Yew, *ST WOE*, 2 November 1991), and the belief that Singapore could have attained higher rates of economic development if it was more culturally homogeneous (Lee Kuan Yew, *Asia Magazine*, 30 November 1986) have contributed towards intensifying ethnic minority insecurity in Singapore.

Moreover, the contradictions inherent in the ethnic based self-help paradigm, which accepts and exploits primordial ethnic affinities over other forms of affinity, contradicts the larger multiracial ideals upon which the island republic was founded.[9] This contradiction has been defended by Prime Minister Goh Chok Tong on the grounds that the ethnic self-help approach represented a judicious synthesis of communalism and multiracialism (*BT*, 8 February 1991). Another line of argument intended to counter public appeals for the establishment of a multiracial self-help body and allay minority apprehension was Goh's (*ST*, 30 October 1992) claim at a SINDA function in October 1992 that a national body to help underachievers of all races would not be effective as the ethnic minorities would perceive the body as being dominated by the majority Chinese community.[10] Goh Chok Tong (*ST*, 30 October 1992), Deputy Prime Minister Lee Hsien Loong (*ST*, 31 August 1992), and Minister of Law S. Jayakumar (*ST*, 12 October 1992) have also alleged that ethnic based bodies are more effective than a multiracially based self-help body as they are better equipped to cater to the 'specific needs' and 'different problems' of their own ethnic communities. What actually constitutes the 'specific needs', 'different problems', and 'different value systems' (BG Yeo, *Sunday Times*, 4 October 1992) of each ethnic community has never been clearly articulated by the PAP leadership.

In an attempt at relieving the PAP government from its contradictory interpretation, rationale, and justification for the ethnic based self-help paradigm, a *Straits Times* editorial (*ST*, July 1991) asserted that ethnic based welfare bodies were 'only an interim arrangement along the way to building a truly national community of compassionate and self-reliant Singaporeans'. That the PAP government should be adopting this 'interim' communal arrangement, after nearly thirty years of political independence could be read as an admission of the limitations of its multiracial social experiment. It may also be indicative of the PAP leadership's politically expedient shift from its original multiracial ideal that was so avidly championed during the merger years towards institutionalizing communal approaches.

### Inter-ethnic and Intra-ethnic Social Divisions

The existence of Mendaki for nearly ten years prior to the formation of SINDA and CDAC may have generated some tension and insecurity particularly within the less educated and lower income sections of the non-Malay community who were not accorded the same social and educational assistance which Mendaki extended to the Malay/Muslim community. Mendaki represented not only a threat to their already insecure economic position but also the potential of restricting their future life chances. Particularly during periods of economic recession when jobs are scarce and general economic security is vulnerable, the advances and set-backs of the numerous self-help bodies is likely to engender inter-ethnic envy, rivalry, and resentment. This has been noted by Wilson (1989: 120) who has argued that a non-ethnic based social welfare approach is likely to enjoy greater public support and thus able to sustain itself through periods of economic downturn and political instability. As he (ibid.) put it, 'The hidden agenda is to improve the life chances of groups such as the underclass by emphasizing programmes in which the more advantaged groups of all races can positively relate.'

Accusations of unfairness and favouritism towards the assisted ethnic minority community over the other ethnic communities are given currency when there is a substantial number of socially disadvantaged individuals from the majority ethnic communities. Concerned that they are not getting their share of government assistance and attention, an environment of insecurity and communal competitiveness is fostered. As is often the case, the heightening of insecurity and resentment between the different ethnic communities is reinforced by the heightening of ethnic consciousness.

Undercurrents of tension within segments of the non-Malay communities towards Mendaki could be discerned in the earlier years of its formation and prior to the eventual formation of SINDA and CDAC in the 1990s. At the PAP's Biennial Conference in January 1989, Goh Chok Tong (*ST*, 9 January 1989) admitted that the PAP government's assistance to the Malay community via Mendaki brought with it the risk of a drop in non-Malay support for the PAP. This point was reiterated by the Deputy Prime Minister Lee Hsien Loong (*Sunday Times*, 9 June 1991) who noted that the PAP government's assistance to minority groups was constrained by the electoral preferences of the majority Chinese community towards the PAP. In other words, a government whose political survival is dependent on a particular ethnic community, cannot afford to be perceived to be according too much assistance and attention to a minority community.

The potential for ethnic antagonisms arising from the ethnic based welfare approach is likely to materialize not just between ethnic communities but also between groups within the assisted community. Manifestations of an intra-community schism have already occurred between Mendaki's Muslim constituents. For example, representatives from the Indian Muslim community have complained that Mendaki has not paid sufficient attention to the needs of the Indian Muslim community and have criticized the body for mainly catering to the concerns and interests of Malay Muslims rather than all Muslims. Aggrieved by the absence of Indian Muslim representation in Mendaki's Board of Directors and Board of Advisers,[11] six Indian Muslim organizations in 1991 mooted the idea of forming a federation to improve the living and educational standards of Indian Muslim children (*Sunday Times*, 27 August 1991). The formation of the Federation of Indian Muslims in March 1992 could thus be perceived as a vote of no-confidence by the Indian Muslim community in Mendaki's ability to fairly represent the interests of all Muslims.

Tension within the Chinese community between those who are opposed to CDAC's ethnic based approach towards assisting the needy and have declined to contribute to CDAC's CPF check-off scheme[12] and others who have assented to CDAC's approach emerged even before the inauguration of the body in September 1992. The 8.7 per cent of the 760,000 working Chinese (*ST*, 1 January 1993) who have opted out of the CDAC CPF check-off scheme have been identified by Goh Chok Tong as belonging to the English-educated Chinese community (*ST*, 21 September 1992). Instructively, the major reason cited by the English-educated Chinese for withholding financial support from CDAC[13] was their philosophical aversion to the ethnic based self-help approach of CDAC (*Sunday Times*, 3 May 1992; *ST*, 22 September 1992; G. Lee *ST*, 26 September 1992). Many have urged for the establishment of a multiracial self-help body which would help all Singaporeans in need so as to safeguard the multiracial Singaporean ideal (ibid.).

**The Unequal Engines of Assistance**

As the long-term financial security of these ethnic based self-help bodies is primarily contingent upon the CPF contribution and other forms of financial donations from the respective ethnic communities, the numerically and economically dominant Chinese community would have access to a disproportionately larger financial reservoir to draw on. In the early 1990s, an estimated 550,000 Chinese who earned less than $2,000 per month contributed 50 cents a month to CDAC through their CPF while the 200,000 Chinese who earned more than $2,000 per month contributed $1 per month (*ST*, 28 April 1992). With 800,000 working Chinese contributing to CDAC, it received $5.7 million a year just on the CPF contributions alone (*Sunday Times*, 2 August 1992). In contrast, Mendaki received $870,000 from the monthly flat rate CPF contributions of $1 per month from working Malay Muslims in 1991 while the numerically smaller Indian constituency is expected to raise $1.5 million through the CPF check-off system in 1992.[14] The significance of the strong financial base of CDAC is particularly pertinent when it is viewed in the context of the deeper socio-economic and educational problems confronting the Malay and the Indian communities, relative to the Chinese community.

Even before the official inauguration of CDAC in September 1992, its endowment fund had collected an impressive $5.5 million in pledges and donations from clan associations, business guilds, community groups, and individuals (*ST*, 5 September 1992). Wealthy clan bodies such as the Hokkien Huay Kuan and Ngee Ann Kongsi have pledged $1 million to be paid over ten years while the Nanyang Khek Community Guild pledged $100,000 over a period of five years. Millionaire banker Wee Cho Yaw became the biggest individual donor when he donated $1 million in August 1992.[15] The Singapore Chinese Chamber of Commerce and Industry (SCCCI) had made a pledge of $250,000 whilst the Chinese Press had raised $1.7 million (*ST*, 5 September 1992) and $400,000 was raised from CDAC's inaugural dinner in September 1992 (*ST*, 14 August 1992). In addition to financial donations from Chinese-based organizations, CDAC had been offered premises for its tuition centres by thirteen members of the Singapore Federation of Chinese Clan Associations (SFCCCA) (*ST*, 20 July 1992).

Spurred on by the generous donations from these wealthy clan, guild, and business organizations, CDAC planned to raise $50 million in ten years for its endowment fund to help finance its educational and community projects (*ST*, 11 July 1992; *Sunday Times*, 2 August 1992). The ambitious target of $50 million is more than likely to be realized as multimillionaire business tycoons such as Wee Cho Yaw (chairperson of the United Overseas Bank), Lien Ying Chow (chairperson of the Overseas Union Bank), Ong Beng Seng (chairperson of Kuo International), and Shaw Vee Meng (Director of the Shaw Brothers Organization) have been appointed to spearhead CDAC's drive to build up its endowment fund (*ST*, 14 August 1992). A cursory glance at the list of CDAC's Board of Directors and Trustees reveals names of socially prominent multimillionaires such as Ong Lay Khiam of the Tay Lee Bank, Wee Cho Yaw of the United Overseas Bank, Lien Ying Chow of the Overseas Union Bank, Shaw Vee Meng of the Shaw Brothers Organization, and Tan Eng Joo from Haw Par Brothers (*ST*, 28 April 1992). Furthermore, CDAC has the strong backing of the economically powerful and politically influential SCCCI and the SFCCA. In stark contrast to CDAC's impressive list of multimillionaires, Mendaki's, and to a lesser extent SINDA's, Board of Directors and Trustees consists largely of civil servants, activists from grass roots bodies and organizations whose wealth are limited to that of their community-based experiences, and business executives largely from the non-Malay communities.[16]

With its stronger demographic, financial, and political base, CDAC will not only be able to effectively sustain the already relatively advantaged educational position of the Chinese community but is also well poised to widen the community's socio-educational position relative to the other ethnic communities. It is in a better position to raise funds and outperform the other ethnic based community self-help bodies in terms of the quality of assistance, educational facilities, and resources offered.[17] Even before its official inauguration in September 1992, CDAC's solid financial base has allowed it to offer handsome inducements to the less skilled and weaker academic achievers within the ethnic community to enrol for educational and occupational self-improvement programmes. From 1993, its tuition programme was launched in more than thirty clan associations and community centres across the island. An estimated 4,500 students (*ST*, 19 September 1992) attending CDAC's weekly tuition classes will only have to pay a nominal fee of a few dollars for these classes.[18] A counselling and pastoral programme was implemented in June 1993 (*ST*, 4 November 1992).

In encouraging less skilled members of the Chinese community to attend evening and weekend skills upgrading courses as part of the Skills Upgrading Programme, CDAC awarded cash incentives to those who have successfully completed each module of a course (*ST*, 5 September 1992). Such generous financial incentives have not been offered to unskilled Indian and Malay workers by SINDA and Mendaki simply because of financial constraints. Under this scheme, the Chinese unskilled worker is more likely to attain higher qualifications and greater possibilities of social mobility compared to the non-Chinese worker. For those encountering a period of family crisis and emergency, a Hardship Assistance Fund will render financial assistance to families in need to ensure that the education of children in these families will not be effected as a result of sudden hardship (*ST*, 2 November 1992).

The generous financial incentives, rewards, and assistance by CDAC clearly exemplify the unequal engines of support that are differentially accorded to the underachievers of each community via the ethnic based self-help approach. This begs the question of whether all the unskilled and 'underachievers' in a multiracial society should be assisted equally regardless of their race, language, or religion and whether it is fair that some are accorded a head start and are likely to emerge in front as a result of the quality of support accorded to them. Concerned with the unequal access and competition for resources between the ethnic based self-help bodies, educationalist S. Gopinathan (*ST*, 30 December 1991), in an address to the Tamil Youth Conference in December 1991, lamented, 'It is worrying that all the groups are competing. As the smallest minority, the Indians now have to fight even harder.'[19] Indeed, the problem of resource procurement by smaller ethnic minorities such as the Eurasians would even be more tenuous.

Instead of the various self-help bodies duplicating each other's educational and skills improvement programmes, there is a strong case to be made for the self-help bodies and their ethnic constituents in a spirit of *gotong-royong*[20] co-operation, goodwill, and plain economic logic, to collectively harness their resources under one multiethnic self-help umbrella. Such inter-ethnic initiatives will not only help to break down pernicious ethnic stereotyping but also highlight the similar educational problems and social symptoms which beset the socially disadvantaged from all ethnic communities. Collaborative inter-ethnic initiatives also serve to foster a sense of empathy, common destiny, and national identity among all Singaporean contributors and recipients of the self-help initiatives.

## Obfuscating the Structural and Institutional Sources of Underachievement

As discussed in greater detail in Chapter 4, cultural determinist perspectives and ethnic stereotypes of the different ethnic communities were initially perpetuated by the policies of the colonial authorities. Such policies were tangible manifestations of the ethnic stereotyping held by British colonial administrators who more often than not possessed a superficial understanding of their colonial subjects. Malays, like indigenous subjects in other colonized territories,[21] were characterized as lazy and lacking in industry, whilst the immigrant Chinese were perceived as being diligent but money-hungry and opportunistic. The persisting status of the Malay community on the socio-economic and educational margins of society close to three decades after Singapore's political independence has only served to reinforce and strengthen the existing negative cultural stereotypes. Similarly, the economically privileged position of a substantial number of Chinese relative to Malays in Malaysia and Singapore has assisted in lending weight to the cultural determinist perspective that the Chinese are an innately industrious community.

Significantly, the potency in the stereotypical notion of the industrious Chinese as culturally armed to overcome the hurdles standing in the way of upward socio-mobility has, according to Muzaffar (1989a), become a convenient excuse for socially privileged Malaysian Chinese to do little for the socially depressed Chinese. Their 'failure' has commonly been individualized whilst the 'failure' of the Malays has been culturalized. The prevalence of the Chinese cultural stereotype within the Chinese community explains the initial reticence by the more privileged members of the Singapore Chinese community to initiate a Chinese Mendaki. Indeed, the pervasive nature of the Chinese cultural stereotype was illustrated in a *Straits Times* editorial (16 July 1991) which argued against the establishment of a Chinese-style Mendaki: 'Poor Chinese do often pull themselves out of poverty through education, of themselves or their children, or by sheer dogged enterprise. Not many lapse into hopelessness and remain poor generation after generation as other less striving, materialistic, and success-oriented peoples might do.'

The promotion of this cultural stereotyping of Malays and Chinese is exemplified in the regular advice by PAP leaders such as Lee Kuan Yew (*ST*, 7 July 1987; *ST*, 26 June 1992) to Malays against the 'psychological trap' of measuring their socio-economic and educational position against other ethnic communities and that hopes of a narrowing in the socio-economic gap between ethnic communities were not likely to materialize but would only ferment further disillusionment. In comparing the educational progress of Malays with the Chinese, Lee Kuan Yew (*ST*, 29 May 1982; *ST*, 26 June 1992) has asserted that the better educational performance of the Chinese community was due to their cultural and intellectual capacities. As Lee (*ST*, 26 June 1992) put it, 'If you pretend that the problem does not exist, and that in fact [the Malays] can score as well as the Chinese in Mathematics, then you have created yourself an enormous myth which you will be stuck with. And there will be such great disillusionment.'

Collaborative efforts and joint programmes between the various ethnic self-help bodies and ethnic communities are important as they help to generate greater public awareness of the similar educational problems and social symptoms which beset the socially disadvantaged across all ethnic groups. Local studies conducted by Leong (1978), Salaff (1988), Li (1989), and the 1992 Ow Chin Hock Report (*ST*, 28 October 1992) on 'underperforming' Chinese students have revealed that the underclass and academic underachievers across all ethnic communities tend to share a low sense of self-esteem and often give up trying to persevere particularly after repeated failures in school. Their lack of role models, limited cultural (English language proficiency) and material capital, and a disruptive and less than academically stimulating family environment contribute significantly to their poor academic progress. They have difficulty in keeping up with students who are fortuitous enough to be well equipped with these sources of capital and compete with a head start in the educational race. Multiethnic educational programmes are likely to erode cultural stereotypes by highlighting the existence of many Chinese students who are weak in Mathematics and Science for generally the same reasons as non-Chinese students who perform poorly in these subjects.[22] Poor motivation, disruptive behaviour in classrooms, lack of self-esteem, and poor English proficiency can be discerned particularly amongst students of all ethnic groups in the slower track normal stream. Many of the academic 'underachievers' and 'problem' students are from lower-income families, single parent, and emotionally dysfunctional family environments where there is minimal academic supervision and where English is barely spoken. Lacking in cultural and material capital, coupled with poor motivation and confidence required to do well in school, such students are more likely to leave school at the earliest opportunity and take on low-status jobs which at least offers them the satisfaction of earning an income. The significance of class based factors over cultural deficit explanations for educational underachievement has also been verified by the overrepresentation of middle class and upper middle class students at the prestigious independent schools and tertiary institutions (*ST*, 26 September 1990; *ST*, 9 April 1992).

## Communal Welfarism

Contextualized within a historical perspective, the ethnic based welfare paradigm is one of the monumental policy reversals in contemporary Singapore. During the pre-merger and merger period, the PAP leadership vociferously criticized ethnic based policy approaches on the grounds that they undermined the process of nation-building. At a time when the PAP was split between the left and right factions and the PAP leadership needed the support of the English-educated, Malays, and Indians, the multiracial banner served to strengthen their vulnerable political standing.[23] By championing the multiracial 'Malaysian Malaysia', where all citizens would be treated equally regardless of race, language, religion, and other ascriptive factors, the credibility of the PAP as a socially moderate but politically progressive party was enhanced.[24] Minority/majority dichotomies, *bumiputra*/non-*bumiputra* dichotomies, and the special rights and programmes singularly catering to any ethnic community were rejected on the grounds that it fostered national disunity.[25] It was thus ironic that despite the PAP government's fierce disapproval of communal based social initiatives during its first two decades in office, it has reformulated its original philosophical commitment to the 'Singaporean Singapore' multiracial ideal by sponsoring the establishment of the ethnic based self-help bodies Mendaki, SINDA, and CDAC which bear conspicuous resemblance to UMNO, MCA (Malaysian Chinese Association), and MIC's (Malaysian Indian Congress) ethnic based assistance initiatives.[26]

Much like UMNO's comprehensive initiatives to elevate the position of the indigenous Malaysians, Mendaki has, through the years, extended its initial focus on educational matters to social–cultural and commercial ventures. Its wide-ranging functions liken it to a *de facto* Ministry of Malay/Muslim Affairs. Mirroring UMNO's priorities and programmes,[27] Mendaki's educational and commercial priorities appear to be geared towards bolstering the number of Malay middle-class professionals and business people. Mendaki's investment arm, Mendaki Holdings Pte. Ltd.[28] aimed at enhancing the Malay community's corporate investment and ownership,[29] is reminiscent of Malaysia's NEP goals of increasing the capital/corporate ownership of the *bumiputra* community in Malaysia. Mendaki's proposed Tabung Haji (Pilgrimage) Fund and Islamic Insurance scheme (Takaful)[30] are similarly modelled on existing schemes in Malaysia (*ST*, 3 August 1992). However, unlike the Malaysian investment schemes which are fully backed by administrative/professional expertise and resources from the National Front government to ensure its financial viability, Mendaki's nascent investment schemes such as the MAS have not been conferred a similar degree of support. Partly because of this lack of government support, the MAS Growth Fund which was inaugurated amidst much optimism and support within the community in 1991, with 13,000 Malay/Muslims investing some $35 million in the scheme,[31] failed to even meet its obligation of returning dividends to its investors a year later.[32]

Even if ASM and other Mendaki commercial ventures had been more successful, it is doubtful whether such forms of communal oriented commercial initiatives will effectively ameliorate the general socio-economic and educational position of the Malay community. In the case of Malaysia (Muzaffar, 1989a: 75) and the United States (Wilson, 1989; Grove, 1993; Marable, 1993), these sectarian ethnic based initiatives have disproportionately benefited the middle and upper middle classes. The latter have benefited disproportionately from the various forms of educational assistance such as educational scholarships which have been largely granted on the basis of ethnicity rather than need. Mirroring this phenomenon, Mendaki's Enrichment Programmes, educational scholarships, bursaries, and tuition schemes have disproportionately benefited the children of middle-class Malays rather than the bulk of Malays from lower socio-economic backgrounds.[33]

The goal of increasing the number of middle-class professionals relative to the other ethnic communities discounts the impact of such ethnic based initiatives on intra-ethnic socio-economic inequality. The focus on ethnic rather than class-based assistance may well pave the way for the emergence of élite professional Malays whose socio-economic distance from the majority of Malay masses may eventually be as great as the current socio-economic disparity between the Malay and non-Malay communities. Put simply, ethnic-based initiatives enhance the opportunities of the more socially advantaged within the community without addressing the more complex problems of the 'truly disadvantaged' that are systemically embedded within the institutions and structures of society (Wilson, 1989; Marable, 1993). The phenomenon where the more socially privileged members in the community, who have a greater command of economic, educational, social, and cultural resources, are best able to capitalize on the ethnic based assistance programmes can be discerned within the African–American community. Notwithstanding the existence of such ethnic based initiatives, the socio-economic standing of the more socially disadvantaged members in the community did not appreciably improve and in some instances worsened (Hochschild, 1988: 177; Wilson, 1989; Grove, 1993; Marable, 1993). The widening intra-ethnic disparity in the United States has resulted in the social complexion of the ethnic minority communities increasingly resembling that of the dominant ethnic community. Evidence of some decline in inter-ethnic socio-economic inequality may well be supplanted by the ominous trend towards intra-ethnic socio-economic inequality (Hout, 1984: 311–14; Hochschild, 1988: 177–9; Marable, 1993: 117).

The emergence of a distinct group of middle-class ethnic minority professionals who have 'made it' acts as a legitimizing and stabilizing force for the preservation of the existing institutions and dominant ideological beliefs in society.[34] Their co-optation is manifested by an uncritical acceptance of the dominant world-view and a receptiveness to the cultural deficit thesis which stems from the belief that if they can make it then others should be able to do so as well. Their well-being is commonly equated with the well-being of the general ethnic community even though their socio-economic status is far from representative of most members in the ethnic community (Muzaffar, 1984: 379). Their newfound social status and material well-being has provided them with a vested interest in preserving the *status quo* and to act as 'watchdogs' against the more radical members within the community who challenge the established ideological, social, and political ground rules (Bonacich, 1987: 109).

\* \* \*

As each ethnic community is encouraged by the PAP government to focus inwardly on the problems of their respective ethnic underclass, the similar class based problems confronting the various ethnic communities have been obfuscated. This obfuscation reinforces negative ethnic stereotypes and fosters cultural deficit interpretations to explain the weak socio-economic status of the marginal ethnic communities whilst individualizing the socio-economic problems of the underclass within the ethnic majority community. This inward focus obfuscates the complex miltiplicity of historical, institutional, structural, and political factors which have worked to the advantage of some socio-economic, linguistic, and ethnic communities. Ethnic based programmes also tend to disproportionately benefit those from socially privileged backgrounds and are likely to enhance intra-ethnic social cleavages. This is attributed to the ability of the privileged middle and upper middle-class members from the ethnic minority community to fully exploit the social assistance programmes for their community.

The PAP leadership's sociobiologist assumption that ethnic based self-help approaches are the most natural and effective means of assisting the disadvantaged appears highly questionable particularly when it is placed within the context of fostering harmonious inter-ethnic societies and strengthening the multiethnic social fabric of society. An over-reliance on sectarian ethnic based solutions in multiethnic entities may well undermine social cohesion whilst instilling a sense of group separateness, competitiveness, and the rise of communal politics.

Due recognition needs to be afforded to the adage that the means of attaining a goal be as important as the desired ends. This is because the means used inevitably impacts heavily on the nature of the ends. The symbiotic linkage between means and ends and the potentially volatile long-term ramifications of 'using the wrong means to achieve the right end' (Muzaffar, 1989a: 36) are important considerations that can only be ignored at the risk of weakening the social fabric of multiethnic societies.

1. Some of which include community organizations such as Majlis Pusat, Young Muslim Women's Association, and the LBKM.

2. Refer to the *Singapore Bulletin*, 9 September 1993, Vol. 21, No. 9, p. 1. The Prime Minister's National Day rally speeches are notable for forewarning and cautioning Singaporeans against the major economic, social, and political difficulties confronting the nation.

3. The educational, income, and occupational gap between the Malays and Chinese was widening (Singapore, Ministry of Labour, *Report on the Labour Force Survey of Singapore*, 1980; Ahmad Mattar, 1984: 121; *FEER*, 28 June 1984; Li, 1989*).*

4. Initially, 50 cents was deducted from the monthly salary of all Malay Muslim workers. In the early 1990s, it was $1 a month.

5. At a community dialogue session in Tanah Merah in July 1991, Goh Chok Tong called on Chinese community leaders, clan associations, and Chinese groups to take the lead in establishing a 'Chinese Mendaki' to assist the Chinese underclass (*ST*, 8 July 1991). He promptly appointed Ker Sin Tze (former Minister of State for Education, Information and the Arts) and Tan Guan Seng (Political Secretary in the Prime Minister's Office) to lay the groundwork for the body (*ST WOE*, 16 November 1991).

6. Eurasians make up less than 0.5 per cent of Singapore's total population.

7. Noted sociobiologists include Pierre van den Berg (1978) and Edward Wilson (1976). They assert that over a long period of time, humans have developed a genetic closeness and closedness to 'powerful sentiments'. Racism and ethnocentrism are thus rooted in the genes.

8. Lee asserted that the reason for the failure of programmes to assist the urban African–Americans in the United States was because it was not run by African–Americans but liberal whites (*ST*, 26 June 1992).

9. The national anthem stresses that Singaporeans are 'one united people regardless of race, language, or religion'.

10. This logic appears to be somewhat fatuous as ethnic minorities numerically dominated by the Chinese community have had to accept the numerical dominance of the Chinese community in most sectors of society. However, if operated within a multiracial social context based on equal and fair opportunity, this numerical dominance should not pose a problem for the ethnic minorities.

11. This matter of representation was brought up as a complaint to the Prime Minister Goh Chok Tong, who is a patron of Mendaki.

12. Under this scheme, CDAC deducts 50 cents from the salaries of those earning less than $2,000 a month and $1 from others earning more (*ST*, September 1992).

13. They have also criticized the CPF check-off scheme for being undemocratic and an infringement on human rights (*ST*, 21 September 1992).

14. Indians earning less than $600 per month contribute $1 per month to SINDA. Those earning between $600 and $1,500 per month pay $2 per month, whilst those earning between $1,500 and $2,500 per month contribute $4 per month. A sum of $6 per month is donated by others who earn more than $2,500 per month (*Sunday Times*, 15 March 1992).

15. He had also magnanimously donated $100,000 each to Mendaki and SINDA. This represents the biggest individual donation to both organizations (*ST*, 18 August 1992). Businessman and poet Poon Kit Foo donated $150,000 to CDAC earlier in the month. Poon is the founder of *Shin Min Daily News* and Kwong Wai Shui Hospital (*ST*, 13 August 1992).

16. The board of directors elected in 1992 include ex-Member of Parliament Rohan Khamis, Zainul Abidin Rasheed (Mendaki CEO), Abdul Aziz Hussain (Pia Corporation), George Thia (Managing Director of Lum Chang Holdings), and H. M. Sathawalla (General Manager of ACMA Electrical Industries) (*ST*, 14 August 1992). In June 1992, Indian Muslim property developer Amir Jumabhoy was appointed chairperson of Mendaki Holdings' board of directors replacing senior civil servant and diplomat Ridzwan Dzafir (*ST*, 14 August 1992).

17. A lack of funds and too much time spent on fund-raising has always been an obstacle for the implementation of programmes by Mendaki, AMP, and SINDA. It has no doubt circumscribed their ability to primarily focus on the efficient implementation of educational and other social programmes. Energy dissipated on fund raising is not likely to be a problem for CDAC. Indeed, the problem may well be how to spend their large financial coffers. Recognizing this fact, Goh has suggested that CDAC help Mendaki and SINDA raise funds after it has reached its $50 million target for its endowment fund.

18. Initially, there was a debate within the community about whether these tuition students should pay any money at all. Finally, it was decided that for each subject (English, Mathematics, and Mandarin), a primary school pupil will be charged $18 a month whilst a secondary student will be charged at $12 a month. This fee is a quarter of the total cost. Fees are to be waived in hardship cases. Each tuition class is limited to fifteen students (*ST*, 19 September 1992).

19. In attempting to raise $2.5 million to finance its activities, SINDA spearheaded a fund-raising drive by organizing a donation draw in 1992 (*Sunday Times*, 9 August 1992).

20. *Gotong royong* in Malay means to work together as a community.

21. They included the New Zealand Maori, the American Indian, and the Australian Aborigine. Their lack of consuming interest in pecuniary material accumulation and emphasis on the more spiritual aspects of life were perceived as indicative of their cultural deficiency.

22. The unimaginative and staid manner by which Mathematics is being taught has been found to be a significant factor in contributing to the poor achievement of students who have previously performed badly in this subject. Tobias's (1978) investigation of the failure of many girls to succeed in high-level maths found them to have developed a fear of Mathematics and feelings of incompetence in the subject. Fox (1970) found that when girls who fear Mathematics were taught upper-level Mathematics by teachers who used individualized learning techniques and when co-operative (as opposed to competitive) learning techniques were incorporated with a social content in Mathematics problems, their achievement levels improved markedly.

23. During this period the leftists left the PAP to establish the Barisan Socialis. Many Chinese-educated Singaporeans supported the Barisan Socialis and other left-wing parties.

24. For a detailed account of the PAP leadership's championing for a multiracial 'Malaysian Malaysia' during the merger years, refer to Fletcher (1969), Sopiee (1974), and Betts (1975).

25. As late as 1982, Lee Kuan Yew (cf. SFCCA and SCCCI, 1991: 15) advised Singaporeans, in an address to the Residents Committee, that 'the more able and successful

must help cater for the needs of the less able, when they are of different races, not just clans, when they speak different languages and practise different religions.... Leadership in Singapore requires us to transcend the natural pulls of kinship and sentiment. We must get around our old biases to leave out those who do not share our ethnic and cultural inheritance.'

26. Since the racial riots of 1969, the National Front government dominated by UMNO has initiated a series of New Economic Policy to improve the socio-economic and educational standing of the indigenous *bumiputra* communities. The body PERNAS was established to promote Malay participation in insurance, construction, trading, properties, engineering, and securities. The Urban Development Authority (UDA) was formed to look after the commercial and property development of Malays. MARA and Bank Bumiputra were similarly established to encourage the development of Malay tertiary education and businesses through financial assistance. Working within the communal social assistance paradigm set by UMNO, the MCA, and the MIC have similarly established their own ethnic based commercial and educational initiatives. The MCA's Multi-Purpose Holdings and the MIC's Maika Holdings are geared towards upgrading the commercial and educational position of their respective ethnic constituents.

27. The Malaysian National Front's solution to the socio-economic disparity between the *bumiputra* and non-*bumiputra* communities has been to focus on the creation of a larger group of Malay middle-class professionals and capitalist entrepreneurs. The New Economic Policy has made it easier for the urban based Malay middle classes to utilize their social, economic, and cultural capital to exploit the educational and commercial opportunities available.

28. Established in 1990.

29. It was a means of providing the Malay/Muslim community with the opportunity to invest in businesses which do not contravene Islamic laws.

30. Established in 1993, Takaful is a joint project between Mendaki and the Singapore Malay Teachers Cooperative Society. As an insurance scheme managed along Islamic principles, Takaful's funds will be used to invest in areas permitted under *syariah* law. It will offer life insurance policies, endowment policies, and other forms of coverage such as fines, thefts, vehicles, and travel.

31. When it was launched in May 1990, it was the fourth largest trust fund in Singapore (*Aspire*, September–October 1992: 5).

32. Managed by Development Bank of Singapore (DBS) Asset Management, MAS only attained a pre-audit profit of $590,000 in 1992 from its capital base of $35 million. This represented a minuscule return of 1.5 per cent which is much lower than the interest rates offered by the banks. MAS's DBS Asset Management advised that dividends would not be paid in 1992 as the pre-audit profit was to small to be shared out as dividends (*ST*, 13 October 1992).

33. It is acknowledged that such ethnic based programmes do 'trickle down' and create some opportunities for the less advantaged ethnic minority members. However, they are underrepresented amongst those who benefit from such programmes (Wilson, 1989: 115). This phenomenon has been corroborated by the author's survey of MEP students.

34. The existence of a small élite of Malay professionals with tertiary education has prompted PAP leaders such as Lee Kuan Yew (*ST*, 19 February 1990) to pronounce that the Malays have made considerable progress in the meritocratic society of Singapore.

# Conclusion

THE study has attempted to demonstrate the salience of historical, ideological, and institutional factors in contributing towards the socio-economic, political, and educational marginality of the Malay community and other socially marginal Singaporeans who experience difficulty in attaining social mobility and keeping apace with the highly competitive Singaporean society. The common problems and impediments shared by the poorly educated and socially marginal across all ethnic communities suggest that the socio-economic and educational marginality of Malays cannot be simplistically explained away as a 'Malay problem' requiring Malay solutions. Such an explanation has engendered a truncated and fragmented understanding of a complex phenomenon that is strongly rooted in the historical, ideological, and institutional processes of Singaporean society.

The élitist and eugenics-oriented nature of the education system since the implementation of the NEP has enhanced the importance of material and cultural capital in educational attainment. Policies such as early streaming, the privatization of premier schools, and the rising costs of education have rendered the education system a more tenuous vehicle for social mobility particularly for lower income Singaporeans. Indeed, the élitist nature of education policies and the ethnic based educational programmes are likely to exacerbate class and ethnic socio-economic disparities. In particular, educational initiatives such as the MEP have disproportionately benefited the more socially privileged within the Malay community. The ethnic based self-help paradigm is also likely to maintain the inter-ethnic socio-economic disparity due to the unequal material and political resources available to the different ethnic communities. Premised within the cultural deficit perspective, the ethnic based self-help paradigm has failed to address the institutional weaknesses of the élitist education system.

Just as the structure of opportunity provided by ethnic based initiatives such as Mendaki is different for the different social classes within the ethnic community, the effect of class is not uniform across the various ethnic communities. For example, Malay middle-class students and professionals generally do not experience the same level of opportunities as their counterparts from the dominant ethnic Chinese community due in part to the persistence of negative stereotyping nurtured by the cultural deficit thesis. Ethnicity, class, and even gender based factors are thus important considerations in understanding the 'Malay dilemma' and the structure of opportunities in the highly competitive and élitist society.

The higher than average school drop out, divorce, and drug addiction rates in the Malay community can be profitably contextualized as symptoms of a wider web of socio-economic problems that have been compounded by institutional impediments such as early streaming in schools, a lack of satisfactory welfare support for the poor, unequal opportunities in the work-force, and discriminatory attitudes against minorities. Linked to the importance of a critical appraisal of the cultural deficit thesis is the need for a critical examination of the contradictions and inconsistencies in the practice of multiracialism, meritocracy, and equal opportunity in Singapore. The erroneous premises of the cultural deficit thesis and the contradictions between the ideal of multiracialism and equal opportunity and the reality of ethnic bias and unequal opportunities have contributed towards the persisting socio-economic and educational marginality of the Malay community. However, the significance of this linkage has been somewhat obfuscated by Singapore's impressive economic record and the absence of an outbreak of ethnic unrest since the mid-1960s. This has allowed the PAP government a level of success in upholding Singapore's image as a multiracial and meritocratic society.

Associated with a critical reappraisal of the cultural deficit thesis and the imperative for a broader conceptual framework in understanding the Malay marginality is the importance of understanding the multiracial ideal beyond a tolerance for difference and the cultural trappings of physical appearance, food, song, and dance. While the cultural dimension of multiracialism is more easily facilitated and invites the appreciation and celebration of cultural diversity, the more complex and less obvious structural dimension of multiracialism is often neglected. A more holistic understanding of multiracialism requires that the principle of equal opportunity and access to all sectors in society is adhered to and that all ethnic groups not only participate fully in society and the economy but are equitably represented in all levels of government and management. Further, multiracialism requires that there be equitable treatment and fair political representation of all ethnic communities and that the procedures determining the allocation of political, economic, and social resources do not discriminate against any ethnic community.

While multiracialism at the cultural level is encouraged in Singapore, the empirical evidence presented in the study does suggest that multiracialism and equal opportunity, particularly at the institutional level, are far from satisfactory. Government policies such as the ethnic residential quotas, population/immigration policies based on 'maintaining the racial balance', education policies which appear to favour students from socially privileged families, educational policies which promote Mandarin, educational programmes such as the SAP, the exclusion of Malays from 'sensitive' units in the SAF, the spectre of disloyalty cast on the Malay community, and the 'cultural favouritism' of the PAP government in terms of its greater willingness to actively assist the linguistic and cultural inadequacies of the Chinese community but not the socio-economic deficit of the Malay community are clear illustrations of the dereliction of the multiracial and equal opportunity ideal in Singapore. Contextualized within a broader conception of multiracialism, the socio-economic and educational marginality of the Malay community appears to be reflective of the general dereliction of multiracialism, equal opportunity, and democracy in Singapore.

The Malay community has not been particularly effective in encouraging the PAP government to adopt a more interventionist approach towards addressing the Malay marginality and in safeguarding the ideals of multiracialism and equal opportunity due to their weak political clout. The efficacy of the Malay community and the PAP Malay politicians in representing the concerns and aspirations of the community has been tempered by the political, electoral, and population engineering initiatives of the PAP government which have ensured that the Malay community remain a numerical minority that is electorally weak in every electoral constituency. The weak electoral clout of the Malay community has allowed the PAP government to be less sensitive to Malay concerns without incurring substantial electoral consequences. In contrast, the numerical and electoral dominance of the Chinese community and the rising economic importance of China have allowed the PAP government to be more sensitive to the concerns of the Chinese community. As elaborated in greater detail in Chapters 5 and 6, the conflicting demands and roles of the PAP Malay politician have prevented them from assertively representing and articulating the concerns and aspirations of the Malay community. As a result, Malay concerns tend to be compromised in favour of the larger political agenda of the PAP government. In accordance with the corporatist approach of the PAP government, the positioning of PAP Malay MPs and PAP activists in leadership positions in many community grass roots organizations has placed limitations on the autonomy of these organizations to assertively represent and articulate Malay concerns.

The persistence of the Malay community on the socio-economic and educational fringes of society constitutes an unhealthy obstacle towards improving relations between Malays and non-Malays and Singapore's Malay neighbours. As the various ethnic communities benefit unevenly from the nation's economic development, ethnic relations are likely to be characterized by suspicions, jealousies, and disparate perceptions of 'group-worth' (Jesudason, 1989). Furthermore, as the socio-economic disparities between ethnic communities remain or widen, the various ethnic communities are likely to be more receptive to communal appeals and political élites are more inclined to make communal appeals for their short-term political gain. It is thus unrealistic to expect the undercurrents of ethnic tension to be attenuated merely through a tolerance and understanding of different cultures without addressing the challenges of multiracialism at the structural level and ensuring that equal opportunity for all Singaporeans is safeguarded at the institutional level. The narrowing of socio-economic and political disparities between the different ethnic communities is imperative so that they can all relate and communicate with one another as social equals rather than as the dominant and subordinate community in the social, economic or political realms of life.

The importance of narrowing the socio-economic disparities between ethnic communities in order to foster healthy inter-ethnic relations is not fully appreciated by the PAP leadership. Ethnic tension has been simplistically reduced to racial, linguistic, and religious differences. Cultural deficit, biological determinist, and sociobiologist explanations have all been relied upon by the PAP leadership to justify inter-ethnic socio-economic and educational disparities and the establishment of state-sponsored ethnic based self-help organizations. Enunciating the PAP government's view of the sources affecting inter-ethnic relations in Singapore at the African Leadership Forum in 1993, Minister for Information George Yeo (*ST*, 12 November 1993) stated: 'There are three areas affecting inter-tribal relations in Singapore which obsess us. They are race, language, and religious difference.' The political and socio-economic dimension affecting ethnic discord has not been seriously considered.

The Malay insecurity stemming from their socio-economic and political marginality and the Chinese insecurity stemming from their numerical minority status in the Malay region have reinforced and augmented one another. This vicious cycle of insecurity and vulnerability can be effectively attenuated by reappraising policies that appear to be culturally biased towards the Chinese community and by seriously addressing the socio-economic and political marginality of the Malay community. In this way, regional perceptions of the PAP government and Singapore as a Chinese-dominated island that has relegated its Malay/Muslim community to the margins of society and compromised its multiracial ideal are dispelled. The attenuation of such perceptions is imperative in view of the island's position as a regional centre for financial capital, its economic triangle of growth initiatives, and significant economic investments, and linkages with its immediate neighbours. The PAP government's management of the Malay marginality thus has important domestic as well as geopolitical implications.

On a more optimistic note, Singapore's maturing economy, coupled with an increasingly sophisticated and educated populace, has facilitated greater public pressure on the PAP government for a more equitable distribution of resources, a less élitist educational system, more state assistance to the socially marginal, and greater democratic space. In such a political climate, more possibilities are potentially available to the Malay community, and others within a civil society, to creatively challenge the relevance of the cultural deficit thesis and highlight the institutional, structural, and ideological factors that have contributed towards sustaining the socio-economic and educational marginality of the Malay community and other socially disadvantaged Singaporeans.

Public pressure on the PAP government has also been fuelled by the growing public consciousness of the contradictions in the government's practice of meritocracy, equal opportunity, multiracialism, and democracy. Lower income Singaporeans are increasingly disgruntled with the élitist educational system and the rising costs for basic essentials such as education and health as a consequence of the government's privatization initiatives. The poor performance of the PAP in many working-class constituencies during the 1991 and 1997 elections is but one manifestation of this level of public disgruntlement. The lack of political openness, the highly competitive and exam-oriented education system, and the authoritarian style of the PAP leadership have ruffled many within the middle classes. Malays on the other hand continue to be alienated and increasingly cynical of the practice of meritocracy, equal opportunity, and multiracialism. However, counterbalancing this groundswell of public disquiet is the depoliticization and pragmatic acquiescence of many in the community who have diverted their attention towards 'earning a living'. The fear of detention without trial under the ISA, the media and the education system's propagation of a 'social reality' which complements that of the PAP, and the compartmentalization of society along ethnic lines have in no small measure contributed towards diffusing the undercurrents of alienation and frustration. All these factors have contributed towards the PAP government maintaining its hegemony and authoritarian top-down approach of governance. However, such a form of governance has resulted in the PAP leadership becoming increasingly out of touch with the lived culture and aspirations of the masses. They have become so righteously assured with the correctness of their diagnosis and solution to the socio-economic and educational marginality of Malays that their intransigent reliance on the cultural deficit thesis has become an ideological cul-de-sac.

The steady decline in the electoral popularity of the PAP particularly in the 1980s has precipitated further moves by the PAP leadership towards 'changing the rules' of the system through institutional means (Huxley, 1991; Rahim, 1993). Attempts to regain greater electoral support from the numerically dominant Chinese community have been undertaken, particularly by offering symbolic cultural goods (Mandarin) to the Chinese community and the revival of philosophies such as Confucianism to legitimize the persistence of its paternalistic and authoritarian style of governance. Suffice it to say, the resolution of the Singapore Malay marginality within an increasingly Sinicized polity is problematic in domestic and geopolitical terms.

The Malay marginality, which is inextricably linked to the fundamental questions of multiracialism and social justice, exposes the institutional and structural bases of social disadvantage in Singapore and is an important factor in the island's relations with its immediate neighbours. It raises the question of whether the multiracialism that currently exists in Singapore is based on the ideals of equal opportunity for all, regardless of ethnicity, language, and religion. It encompasses issues of power, democracy, and equity and highlights the question of whether the political engineering processes that have served to maintain Chinese numerical and electoral dominance in all constituencies whilst undermining the electoral clout and numerical position of the Malay community contravene the democratic and multiracial ideal. The dominant perception and prescription of the Malay marginality reveals the élitist and eugenics biases of the PAP government. The PAP's intractable commitment to the cultural deficit thesis to explain the Malay marginality reveals more of its political, economic, and social agenda than any satisfactory explanation of the root causes of the phenomenon. Like a hologram, the Singapore Malay dilemma is intrinsically connected to and embodies a web of questions, issues, aspirations, contradictions, struggles, fears, and vulnerabilities that in its essence is a national dilemma that cannot be satisfactorily resolved without seriously addressing the myriad interlocking dilemmas extant in contemporary Singapore.

# Appendices

## APPENDIX 1
Interview with Ahmad Mattar, Minister of Environment and Malay/Muslim Affairs, Chairperson of Mendaki, 26 October 1990

**Author**: What were the major factors that precipitated your entry into politics?
**Mattar**: In 1965, after I joined the Singapore Polytechnic as Assistant Lecturer in the Engineering Department, I was introduced to the Siglap CCC (Citizens Consultative Constituency) by Dr Lee Chiaw Meng (former Minister for Education) who was then my colleague at the Polytechnic. I was approached by Mr Wee Ghim Siong (PAP grass roots activist) to join the party (PAP), thought it over and decided to join.... After involving myself in grass roots activities and party work, I felt that I could get more things done from 'within' rather than the 'outside'. In 1969, I left for my study leave in the UK. I came back after two years and rejoined the Siglap CCC.... I was introduced to Majlis Pusat by its President, Enche Yusof Ahmad. Majlis Pusat was starting a tuition scheme in Mathematics and since I'm basically Mathematics-based, I volunteered my services.

In my first CCC meeting after I returned from the UK, Mr Rahim Ishak (MP for Siglap) told me that he had put up my name for the 1972 elections. At that time, I was not really prepared (for politics). He told me that 'the PM [Prime Minister Lee Kuan Yew] would like to see you'. The appointment to see the PM was at 3 p.m. When I arrived at the Istana, I was made to wait for a short while and then I was brought into the Cabinet office and made to face the whole CEC (Central Executive Committee). It was Chua Sian Chin (former Minister for Home Affairs) who asked me in the CEC meeting whether I had thought of making politics a career and I replied 'No, not immediately.' I said that I have a Colombo Plan scholarship undertaking and also wanted to consolidate my expertise in Applied Acoustics. Chua asked me how much time I needed to consolidate my expertise. My reply was 'It depends on the number of projects I can get myself involved in.'

At that time, there was a spate of resignations by graduate Malays in the civil service. Many of them crossed over to Malaysia. So, I was posed this question: Would I consider migrating to Malaysia?.... As I opened the door to leave, the PM said, 'Thank you for being very honest.' That's basically how my political career started.
**Author**: Would you like to elaborate on the 'behind closed doors' approach of Malay MPs?
**Mattar**: As far as Malay MPs are concerned, we have been working 'behind closed doors' simply because Malay issues are more sensitive. We talk about

Malays in the SAF (Singapore Armed Forces) and mosques. The issue of Malays in the SAF would not have surfaced (publicly) had it not been for Lee Hsien Loong's way of answering it. This question of Malays in the SAF was posed to him when he was on a ministerial walkabout. That was a turning point as far as the Malays were concerned. Malay problems and issues have since been discussed more openly.

The PM would have answered it another way.... The way the younger Ministers have commented on this situation (the Iraqi invasion of Kuwait) caused our neighbours to be upset. It looked as though we had compared ourselves with Kuwait, that we drew a parallel between Iraq and Indonesia and Malaysia.... The PM answered it in a better way (when interviewed by reporters). [He said], 'Singapore is not like Kuwait, we don't have oil for loot. Our success is due to our own efforts, skill, interactions with the rest of the world.' The PM's answer did not cause a stir with our neighbours.

**Author**: When will the issue of the exclusion of Malays in 'sensitive' units of the SAF be resolved?

**Mattar**: To be fair to Goh Chok Tong, when he became Minister of Defence, he looked upon the issue of Malays in the SAF with an open mind. He was not prejudiced by what he had heard before, [that is] separation with Malaysia and so on. He tried to put Malays in certain sensitive areas. He did it slowly and with caution. He discussed it with me and other Malay MPs. We were pleased with this.

Then the Hertzog visit came along. It was perfectly legitimate for Muslims to be against the visit of a Zionist leader, to feel unhappy about it. What was unfortunate was that Muslims began to treat the visit in an aggressive manner. After they saw Muslim groups in KL staging demonstrations, burning effigies of the PM, the Singapore flag, this is when the [Singapore] Muslims should have drawn the line by coming out to say [to the Malaysian demonstrators], 'Look, we agree with you as Muslims, we don't like Hertzog to visit Singapore, but we end there.' This is an oversight or maybe the Muslims here are not politically sensitive. The leadership then formed certain conclusions. They asked themselves, 'Are the Muslims in Singapore taking cues from the Muslims in Malaysia?' The Muslims in Singapore began to be more vocal after the Muslims in Malaysia staged demonstrations. Because of that, things (Goh's steady inclusion of Malays into sensitive units in the SAF) were slowed down a little. I believe that Goh will still give it a try but at a much slower pace.

**Author**: So Malay loyalty is still very much in question?

**Mattar**: There are specific instances which cast doubt in the minds of the leadership.... The question of loyalty is still a question mark in the minds of the leadership.

**Author**: What can the Malay community do to erase the question mark in the minds of the PAP leadership?

**Mattar**: They could have seized the opportunity during the Hertzog visit by stating their disapproval of Malaysian actions against Singapore. Spontaneous responses by Malay organizations not closely linked to the PAP would have been profitable.

**Author**: The PAP leadership's doubts about Malay loyalty appears to contradict many surveys and studies which have indicated that Malays have the highest level of national loyalty relative to the other ethnic communities.

**Mattar**: I have also maintained in my discussions with Chok Tong that in situations like Konfrontation, Malays fought against Malays. This proves that Malay soldiers will fight for Singapore when the crunch comes. But the leadership is not particularly worried about going to war with Malaysia. What they are most concerned with is the possibility of Malaysia being run by a fundamentalist group. If for some reason we are in a war with them and they shout *Allahuakhbar*, I have been asked how would they, Malay Muslims, then respond. I have said that I cannot answer this (question) with certainty.

**Author**: You initially toyed with the idea of Mendaki becoming a statutory body. However, it has since become a registered society. How did this come about?

**Mattar**: We weighed the pros and cons and came to the conclusion that it would be better for Mendaki not to be a statutory board but to be a society registered under the Societies Act and at the same time enjoying the government's backing in terms of moral support and professional expertise. Mendaki is now enjoying the best of both worlds. Mendaki is the only registered society in Singapore where the government allows the CPF (Central Provident Fund) machinery to be used for contributions to Mendaki. In that sense, we are at par with MUIS (Majlis Ugama Islam Singapore) which is a statutory body. We have a free hand to do whatever we want to do with our money, with projects. Mendaki is getting some financial help from the government. Every year it receives a grant of $250,000 for the purposes of research and development. The main source of income comes from financial contributions from CPF contributions of Malay/Muslim workers.... We are getting a grant from the government, yet we are a society.... It took me two years to convince the Cabinet to allow the CPF machinery to deduct the financial contribution for Mendaki. The PM wanted to see how well the organization could run before he agreed to use the CPF check-off.

**Author**: Many Malays feel uneasy about the fact that a large number of students that attend Mendaki's tuition classes particularly those who are recipients of Mendaki scholarships and prizes are from socially privileged family backgrounds. Should Mendaki's educational programmes not be more focused on targeting 'underachieving' students from socially disadvantaged backgrounds?

**Mattar**: It's a chicken and egg situation. We want to highlight the successes. Success can be obtained from this group of people, those with four A stars in the PSLE, with seven, eight, nine distinctions. Psychologically it will be a boost to the community ... people like to hear about them.

You are right, the people that attend Mendaki's tuition classes are the motivated people, from motivated backgrounds. We still have not resolved this yet. The children in the target group are just not coming. The purpose of the tuition classes should be for these target students. The people in the lowest income group are not responding at all. Their parents are not motivated. Based on my observation, whenever I go for my Sunday morning (public housing) block visit, they don't have newspapers at home, not even *Berita Harian*. When they watch TV, they don't listen to the news. They prefer to watch entertainment programmes. What (information) we release to the mass media doesn't reach them. If they don't come forward, the next step for us is to go to them. This means that we need more money because we have to rent HDB spaces in the void decks. When we have dialogue sessions with parents, those that come are the more committed. The parents that are working as labourers and daily rated employees are just not coming. This is the problem.

**Author**: Perhaps one of the reasons why some people do not utilize the facilities offered by Mendaki is because they see the body as being closely associated with the PAP government.

**Mattar**: This (point) was raised by J. B. Jeyaratnam (in Parliament) when he was a Member of Parliament. My answer to his suggestion was that Mendaki was not initiated by the PAP *per se*. It was conceived and initiated by the Malay MPs who happen to be PAP.... After we saw the report of the 1980 census, Malay MPs and I found to our horror that after all these years, there were only slightly over 600 Malay graduates. Then if you minus the PRs (Permanent Residents), you only have over 400 Malay graduates. That set us thinking. We discussed the issue amongst ourselves and then invited the leading Malay organizations actively involved with education.... When we started this, we were not sure how the government would look upon all this because all these years PAP Malay MPs were supposed to have a national outlook. My group in 1981 was bold enough to say, 'Let's do something for the Malays.' Fortunately, our efforts were welcomed by the PM. At the Mendaki Congress, the PM even stated that the problems of the Malays were not Malay problems, they were actually a national problem. This statement by the PM allowed us to get tremendous support from non-Muslim organizations. The government did not look at our efforts as chauvinistic.... As I said to Jeyaratnam, if Mendaki was initiated by the government and it is going to benefit the Malays, then why not? Why should the fact that Mendaki is supported by the PAP government be a hindrance?

In the early years of Mendaki, there was a predominance of Malay MPs in Mendaki's Council. I was sensitive to this and since then, there are fewer MPs in the Council. At present, they include Abdullah Tarmugi, Zulkifli Mohammed, and myself in a Council of fifteen members. In fact Zulkifli was not nominated by me but by Majlis Pusat. Ali Redha, who is an UMNO member, is also a Mendaki Council member. We made no attempt to exclude Ali Redha.

**Author**: Would you like to comment on the Association of Malay/Muslim Professionals (AMP)'s call for the depoliticization of Mendaki and other Malay community organizations.

**Mattar**: The PM has issued a statement stating that Mendaki was initiated by Malay MPs. He saw no reason why Malay MPs should withdraw (from Mendaki). Those organizations who have worked with us (Malay MPs) realize the benefits. They can get things done. All these things are done 'behind the scene'. We do not like to 'blow our trumpets'. A lot of issues are resolve 'behind the scenes'. This may give rise to the perception that Malay MPs are not doing anything. Pertapis's halfway house, Perintis, was able to get a building which was a former school. I wrote a strong recommendation to the Land Office for Pertapis and they got it. The Muslim Women's Organizations (PPIS) ... I helped them to get their second premises in Jurong. Those organizations who have worked with us see the benefits. That is why we have been appointed as patrons and advisers of organizations. We are accessible to the (PAP) leadership. The Prophet Mohammad Memorial Fund (LBKM) recently had the PM as their guest of honour for their 25th anniversary celebrations. I put up a note to the PM recommending that he attend LBKM's function and he accepted.

**Author**: How do you respond to the view of some Malays who feel that the government should be rendering greater direct assistance to the Malay community?

**Mattar**: In the Singapore context where the majority of voters are Chinese and where the government is seen to be helping the Malays, there will be complaints from the other communities. Chok Tong is already receiving a lot of complaints.

**Author**: How successful have you been in recruiting Malays into the PAP?

**Mattar**: In the first round, general issues are discussed. When we spot a person (that) we think makes the grade, we invite them [*sic*] for a second round. The moment we pose 'the question' (becoming an MP), they say, 'No, thank you.' They give all kinds of excuses such as wanting to concentrate on their family or career. The problem of recruitment I am facing is worse than the problem faced by Goh Chok Tong and Lee Hsien Loong as they have a bigger base to contend with. In our case, we have a smaller base. Many of them don't perform as well as they did with me when they are interviewed by Goh Chok Tong. They have strict criteria. Qualifications are not the only criteria. They are interested in the character of the person, honesty, integrity. There is a lot of checking and counter-checking of people who know the candidate. They are asked to put two character referees and then asked to write about themselves. The selection is very thorough, very rigorous. There are always people who volunteer to be considered. Normally, if they are too enthusiastic, then there is a question mark.

I feel that many Malay professionals are not willing to come forward and serve the government because of the kind of dilemmas faced by Malay MPs.... Malay MPs cannot be playing to the gallery. Certain sensitive issues, we do not bring out into the open. We are more guarded in our approach whereas others have no constraints and play to the gallery.... Malay MPs are really walking on a tightrope in the sense that we cannot appear to be too Malay in our approach because we have to go back to our electorate once every three to four years and they are predominantly non-Malay. If we appear to be very Malay in our thinking and our approaches and only interested in the Malays, then we are bound to get some reactions from our electorate. On the other hand, if we appear to be too nationalistic, then the Malays may not like you. It's a catch-22 situation.

**Author**: The very fact Malay MPs are expected to deal with Malay issues, that you are a Minister of Malay/Muslim Affairs may have further compounded the dilemma confronting Malay MPs. How instrumental were the Malay MPs in coming up with the Mendaki 'Swasta' proposal mooted by Goh Chok Tong at the recent AMP (Association of Malay/Muslim Professionals) Congress?

**Mattar**: The idea was mooted by Goh Chok Tong and the 'inner circle'. I was in the UK at the time. There are ten Malay MPs, only two were consulted. Some Malay MPs had reservations about the proposal. The Malay ground is generally not happy with it. I am opposed to it.

## APPENDIX 2
### Interview with Abdullah Tarmugi, Deputy Speaker of Parliament, MP for Siglap and Deputy Chairperson of Mendaki,*
### 25 August 1990

**Author**: Could you please tell me a little bit about your personal background?
**Tarmugi**: I was born in Jalan Sultan from poor, illiterate parents. My mother is an Indonesian Chinese and my father is Javanese. I went to a Malay primary school (Kota Raja Primary) for one year, then went to Monks Hill Primary School and Raffles Secondary. I graduated from the University of Singapore and majored in sociology. I was sent to the United Kingdom on a Merit Scholarship to do a Postgraduate Diploma in Urban Planning and Urban Sociology. I joined the Ministry of National Development in 1980, then went to the *Straits Times* first as a feature writer, then as an associate editor. I am now in the research section. I entered politics in 1984.
**Author**: What community activities were you involved in before your entry into party politics?
**Tarmugi**: I was in Majlis Pusat and counselled drug addicts at SANA (Singapore Anti-Narcotics Association). My involvement at the grass roots level

was minimal before entering politics. I was more or less absorbed into politics. When I joined the press, I became more interested in politics both at the domestic and international level. I was called up to one of those tea parties and was asked by Goh to run for public office. I took some days to decide. I saw it as an extension of what I was doing in the press. There were only a few Malays with tertiary qualifications in those days. Those that were tertiary educated were generally noticed by government ministers.

**Author**: How would describe the general political approach of PAP Malay MPs?

**Tarmugi**: Malay MPs realize that we operate in a multiracial environment dominated by the Chinese. At the same time, we also realize that we also have a duty and responsibility to our own people. I feel we are trying to balance two roles. We try to be a national leader in a constituency where the majority of the electorate is non-Malay. Another constituency is the Malay community. Sometimes the demands and interests of these two constituencies may conflict so we find ourselves trying to find a middle way, not to get into extreme positions where either side will either accept or reject you. Up till now, we have been accused of not trying hard enough to push for Malay interests. We do realize the need to argue for the interests of Malays but we do also have to be cognizant of the feedback and response of the non-Malay electorate. In a sense, the Malay community sees this moderation as a kind of compromise of their interests. Its a question of looking at the role of the Malay MPs from the viewpoint of the Malay community. From that perspective, we are not doing enough. When there are policies effecting the Malays, we do as much as we can. On some occasions, we push to modify policies which we think Malays will be sensitive to. We have been criticized for not being transparent in our work. Our actions are often not transparent and for that reason, the Malay community does not really know what we actually contribute. We don't really shout about what we do.

If we seem to be strongly pushing Malay interests, we will given an image that we are communal, something which I am personally not happy with. I am colour-blind in the sense that I don't deal with people in terms of their race and colour. Although I come from a conservative family background, when it comes to mixing with others, my parents were colour-blind. I don't believe in communal politics. That's my world-view.

**Author**: What are your views of government policies such as the promotion of Mandarin and the stress on maintaining one's separate ethnic identity, cultural mores, and values?

**Tarmugi**: I see nothing wrong with a person keeping his [sic] identity. I teach my kids about Malay culture. I have more non-Malay friends than I have Malay friends. My Malay is not as good as my English. I also know many Chinese who don't know how to speak Mandarin. They are more internationalized and Westernized. It's a drift which I see as something gaining momentum. The government is trying to slow the process of cultural drift. I see many things good and bad about Western culture. There is good and bad in every culture. I am not too concerned about the debate about finding one's roots. The more seriously you get into it, then you begin to take sides. That is when the problem starts.

**Author**: How would you explain the persisting socio-economic and educational marginality of the Malay community?

**Tarmugi**: Malay MPs hold the view that there is something in Malay culture, Malay attitudes, that keeps them from doing as well as the non-Malays. I personally think that there are some attitudes that have become obstacles. But to what extent these attitudes are responsible for the Malay community's socio-economic position is difficult to know. Some Malays, because of their attitudes, do not want to strive as hard, to risk as much.

**Author**: I have noticed that many, if not most, of the Mendaki prize and scholarship holders are from middle-class family backgrounds. Could not the Malay educational underachievement be plausibly explained as a strongly class-based phenomenon?

**Tarmugi**: The Ministry of Education has done studies which show that the higher academic achievers are from more comfortable family backgrounds.

**Author**: Would not policies such as early streaming disadvantage the 'late developers' and other students from socially disadvantaged backgrounds?

**Tarmugi**: I know a high proportion of mono [lingual stream] students are Malays. If the argument is class, how does one explain the higher than national average of Malays [in the monolingual stream]? ... I believe in the possibility of late development. A person who appears as a low achiever can improve as he/she grows older. To what extent should we put resources into the 'non-achievers' rather than the 'achievers'? It is a philosophical problem and a moral problem as well.

**Author**: Many educationalists work on the premise that most people, given encouragement, support, and an intellectually stimulating environment, can achieve high academic attainments. This premise then purports that as many of the academic 'underachievers' come from socially disadvantaged family backgrounds, they should be accorded more resources and support in a levelling up initiative. At present, the education system appears to be skewed the other way, with the 'underachievers', a disproportionate number of whom are Malays, relegated to the slower streams and the 'high achievers' in the GEP and SAP getting the best educational facilities and considerable resources.

**Tarmugi**: It is a complex issue. It has to do with philosophy, with the likely response of non-Malays. When you talk about assistance (of Malays) by non-Malays, then you have to tackle the issue of: to what extent, how much and how? Although most people will agree that the Malays need help, but when it comes to the nitty-gritty, of how to go about it, then it becomes difficult.

**Author**: Perhaps a way out of this difficulty is to adopt a non-ethnic based approach. In this way, no ethnic group will feel disadvantaged as the socially disadvantaged from all ethnic communities are assisted under a non-ethnic based assistance umbrella body.

**Tarmugi**: A class-based approach has been considered by many people. It then becomes a question of: at what level to pitch your assistance to—the lower 5 per cent, 10 per cent or 25 per cent? Some of the fund-raising efforts of the 25th Anniversary Charity Fund are geared towards helping the poor across ethnic lines.

**Author**: But charity only goes so far. It does not really address the root causes of poverty.

**Tarmugi**: There are some leaders who take the view that you help people who can succeed so that they can help the rest. I think that that philosophy is held by many people. Presently, the argument based on helping those who can help the others is strong. The policy of early streaming (in school), for example, is softening. The system will not be totally overturned but there will be other supplementary or complementary systems that will help those who are unable (to compete). There is a change of emphasis rather than a change of philosophy; a softening and modification will occur.

**Author**: Can you explain the rationale behind Mendaki's status as a registered society rather than a statutory board?

**Tarmugi**: There is a love–hate relationship between the (Malay) community and the (PAP) government. They want the government to help but at the same time they try to avoid having anything to do with the government. If Mendaki was a statutory board, there would be assumptions that it is under government control.

**Author**: What is the government's interpretation of Article 152 of the Constitution?

**Tarmugi**: Well, the official interpretation is that it is a provision which enables the government to help the Malays but should not be construed as the government having to place Malays in a privileged position. The free education provision for Malays is not so much a constitutional provision but something that the government of the day has extended to the Malay community. It was able to do that because the Constitution allowed them to do that. Well, of course, there are others that dispute that interpretation, saying that it is in fact the government's duty and responsibility, whether they like it or not. Some people believe that Article 152 gives Malays special privilege. They will never veer away from that. There are quite a few Malays who subscribe to that view. The government's position is that the Constitution does not describe how the government should do it (assist the Malay community).

*Abdullah Tarmugi was promoted to Minister of State for Environment and Malay/Muslim Affairs with the resignation of Ahmad Mattar in July 1993.

# Bibliography

### Official Publications and Ministerial Speeches

Ahmad Mattar (1986), 'Challenges Facing the Malay/Muslim Community in Singapore', Keynote Address at the Seminar 'Challenges Facing the Malay/Muslim community', September, Singapore.

Colony of Singapore (1966), *Annual Report*, Singapore: Government Printing Office.

Curriculum Development Institute of Singapore (CDIS) (1984), Lower Secondary History Project Team, *Social and Economic History of Modern Singapore*, Singapore: Educational Publishers.

―――― (1986), *Confucian Ethics*, Textbook for Secondary 3 and 4, Singapore: Educational Publishers.

Federation of Malaya (1958a), *Report of the Committee on Malay Education*, Kuala Lumpur: Government Printers. Usually referred to as the Barnes Report.

―――― (1958b), *Report of the Education Committee, 1956*, Kuala Lumpur: Government Printers. Usually referred to as the Razak Report.

Goh, Chok Tong (1986), *A Nation of Excellence*, Address to the Alumni International Singapore, 1 December 1986, Singapore: Ministry of Communication and Information.

Goh, Keng Swee and the Education Study Team (1979), *Report on the Ministry of Education, 1978*, Singapore. Cited as Goh Report in text references.

Lee, Hsien Loong (1992), *Core Principles of Government*, Singapore: Ministry of Information and the Arts.

Lee, Khoon Choy (1967), *National Culture in a Multiracial Society*, Singapore: Ministry of Culture.

Lee, Kuan Yew (1966), *New Bearings in Our Education System*, Singapore: Government Printing Office.

Majlis Ugama Islam Singapura (MUIS) (1988), *Annual Report, 1988*, Singapore.

Ow, Chin Hock (1992), *Self-help Tradition at Work*, Singapore: Chinese Development Assistance Council (CDAC).

Rajaratnam, S. (1983), 'Future Oriented and Nationalistic Leadership', in *Speeches*, Singapore: Ministry of Communications and Information, Vol. 7, No. 1 (January–June).

―――― (1984), 'The Uses and Abuses of the Past', in *Speeches*, Singapore: Ministry of Communications and Information, Vol. 8, No. 2 (March–April).

The Education Study Team (1987), *Towards Excellence in Schools: A Report to the Minister of Education*, Singapore.

The Education Study Team to Japan and Taiwan (1990) *Building a Firm Foundation: A Report to the Minister of Education*, Singapore.

Singapore (1980), *The Constitution of the Republic of Singapore*, Singapore: Government Printers.
_____ (1991), *Shared Values*, White Paper, Singapore: Singapore National Printers.
Singapore (1991), *Singapore: The Next Lap*, Singapore: Times.
_____ (various years), *Parliamentary Debates*.
_____ (relevant years), *Yearbook of Statistics*, Singapore.
Singapore, Department of Statistics (relevant years), *Report on the Census of Population*, Singapore.
Singapore, Ministry of Community Development (1988), *Report of the Committee on Destitute Families*, Singapore.
Singapore, Ministry of Education (1959), *First Education Triennial Survey (1955–1957)*, Singapore: Government Office.
_____ (1979), *Report on Moral Education*, Singapore.
Singapore, Ministry of Education and the History Department (University of Singapore) (1970), *Our Fathers as Pioneers*, Singapore.
Singapore, Ministry of Labour (relevant years), *Report on the Labour Force Survey of Singapore*, Singapore: Research and Statistics Department.
Singapore, Ministry of Trade and Industry (1991), *Economic Survey of Singapore, 1990*, Singapore: Singapore National Printers.
Singapore Council of Social Services (1989), *Annual Report, 1989*, Singapore.
Singapore Economic Committee (1986), *The Singapore Economy: New Directions*, Singapore: Ministry of Trade and Industry.
Singapore Teachers Union (STU) (1980), *Perception and Practice in Education*, Singapore.
Wee, Kim Wee (1989), 'A Meaningful Life for All', Address to Parliament, 9 January 1989, Singapore: Ministry of Communications and Information.
Yeo, George (1989), 'Evolving a National Identity in a Changing World', in *Speeches*, Singapore: Ministry of Communications and Information, Vol. 10, No. 4 (May–June).
_____ (1990), 'Principles That Guide Inter-tribal Ties in Singapore', Address to the African Leadership Forum, 10 November (excerpts published in *Straits Times*, 12 November 1993).

## Interviews

Abdullah Tarmugi (then Deputy Speaker, Member of Parliament, Deputy Chairperson of Mendaki), interviewed on 25 August 1990.
Ahmad Mattar (then Minister of Environment and Malay/Muslim Affairs, Member of Parliament, Chairperson of Mendaki), interviewed on 26 October 1990.
Alami Musa (Executive Member, Association of Malay/Muslim Professionals), interviewed on 18 June 1992.
Chiam See Tong (then Secretary-General, Singapore Democratic Party), interviewed on 2 April 1990.
Gopinathan, S. (Lecturer, National Institute of Education), interviewed on 28 November 1992.
Halijah Rahmat (Lecturer, National Institute of Education), interviewed on 14 July 1990.
Hussin Mutalib (Lecturer, National University of Singapore, then Chairperson, Association of Malay/Muslim Professionals), interviewed on 8 March 1990.
Juffrie Mahmood (then Executive Member, Singapore Democratic Party), interviewed on 4 April 1990.

Sahid Sahoorman (then President, Pertubohan Kebangsaan Melayu Singapura), interviewed on 3 March 1990.
Said Zahari (former *Utusan Melayu* Editor, detained under the ISA from 1963–79), interviewed on 31 May 1990.
Sidek Saniff (then Parliamentary Secretary, Ministry of Education, Member of Parliament), interviewed on 31 August 1990.
Sopiee Haji Kassiman (then Vice-President, Malay Teachers Union of Singapore), interviewed on 21 September 1990.
Sumardi Ali (then Assistant Director, Mendaki), interviewed on 29 June 1990.
Suratnam Markassan (educationist, poet, and community activist), interviewed on 3 May 1989.
Vasoo (PAP Member of Parliament, Head of Social Work and Psychology Department, National University of Singapore), interviewed on 14 November 1990.

## Books and Articles

Abaza, Mona (1991), 'The D Discourse on Islamic Fundamentalism in the Middle East and Southeast Asia: A Critical Perspective', *Sojourn*, 6(2).
Abdullah bin Abdul Kadir Munshi (1974), *Hikayat Abdullah*, 2 vols., Kuala Lumpur: Pustaka Antara.
Abdullah bin Haji Ahmad Badawi (1990), *Malaysia–Singapore Relations*, Institute of Policy Studies, Regional Speakers Lecture Series, Lecture No. 21, Singapore: Times Academic Press.
Abdul Maulud Yusuf (1989), 'Culture and Change in Malay Society: From Peasantry to Entreprenuership', *Crossroads*, 3(2).
Abercrombie, N. (1980), *Class, Structure and Knowledge*, Oxford: Basil Blackwell.
Abercrombie, N. and Turner, B. (1989), 'The Dominant Ideology Thesis', *British Journal of Sociology*, 29(2).
Abercrombie, N. et al. (1990), *Dominant Ideologies*, London: Unwin & Hyman.
Abraham, Colin (1986), 'Manipulation and Management of Racial and Ethnic Groups in Colonial Malaya: A Case Study of Ideological Domination and Control', in Raymond Lee (ed.), *Ethnicity and Ethnic Relations in Malaysia*, Centre for Southeast Asian Studies, Occasional Paper No. 12, Singapore: Singapore University Press.
Abu Bakar bin Hashim (1985), 'Shariah and Social Order: The Singapore Experience', *Shariah Law Journal*, November.
Action Committee for Indian Education (ACIE) (1991), *At the Crossroads*, Singapore.
Ahmad Mattar (1980), 'The Singapore Malays: Their Education and Role in National Development', *PAP 25th Anniversay Issue, 1954–1979*, Singapore: Central Executive Committee of the People's Action Party.
_____ (1984), 'Changes in the Social and Economic Status of Malays', *Petir: 30th Anniversary Issue*, 21, Singapore: Central Executive Committee of the People's Action Party.
Akerman, Susan and Lee, Raymond (1988), 'Theory, National Policy and the Management of Minority Cultures', *Southeast Asian Journal of Social Science*, 16(2).
Alatas, Syed Hussein (1971), *Thomas Stamford Raffles: Reformer or Schemer?*, Sydney: Angus and Robertson.
_____ (1977), *The Myth of the Lazy Native*, London: Frank Cass.

Alexander, K; Cook, M.; and McDill, E. (1978), 'Curriculum Tracking and Educational Stratification: Some Further Evidence', *American Sociological Review*, 4(3).
Aljuneid, S. (1978–80), 'A General Outlook of Malay Participation in the Singapore Economy', *Sedar (Journal of the National University of Singapore Muslim Society)*.
Allport, G. (1954), *The Nature of Prejudice*, Cambridge: Addison-Wesley.
Altbach, P. and Selvaratnam, V. (1989), *From Dependence to Autonomy*, Dordrecht: Kluwer Academic Publishers.
Althusser, Lois (1971), 'Ideology and the Ideological State Apparatuses', in L. Althusser (ed.), *Lenin and Philosophy*, London: New Left Books.
_____ (1984), *Essays on Ideology*, London: Verso.
Amir,Yehuda; Ben-Ari, R.; and Bizman, A. (1986), 'Prospects of Intergroup Relations in an Intense Conflict Situation: Jews and Arabs in Israel', in Anand C. Paranjpe (ed.), *Ethnic Identities and Prejudices: Perspectives from the Third World*, Leiden: E. J. Brill.
Andaya, B. and Andaya, L. (1982), *A History of Malaysia*, London: Macmillan Press.
Anderson, Ben (1983), *Imagined Communities: Reflections on the Origins and Spread of Nationalism*, London: Verso.
Anthias, F. (1992), 'Connecting Race and Ethnic Phenomenon', *Sociology*, 26(3).
Anyon, Jean (1983), 'Workers, Labor and Economic History and Textbook Content', in M. Apple and L. Weiss (eds.), *Ideology and Practice in Schooling*, Philadelphia: Temple University Press.
Apple, Michael (1979), *Ideology and Curriculum*, Boston: Routledge & Kegan Paul.
_____ (1982), *Education and Power*, Boston: Routledge & Kegan Paul.
_____ (1986), 'Ideology and Educational Reform', in P. Altbach and G. Kelly (eds.), *New Approaches to Comparative Education*, Chicago: University of Chicago Press.
_____ (1987), 'Foreword', in C. Lankshear and M. Lawler, *Literacy, Schooling and Revolution*, London: Falmer Press.
Apple, M. and Weiss, L. (eds.), *Ideology and Practice in Schooling: A Political and Conceptual Introduction*, Philadelphia: Temple University Press.
Apter, David (ed.) (1964), *Ideology and Discontent*, New York: Free Press.
Aronowitz, Stanley and Giroux, Henry (1985), *Education under Siege*, Massachusetts: Bergin & Garvey.
Asher, Mukul (1991), *Social Adequacy and Equity of Social Security Arrangements in Singapore*, Occasional Paper, Centre for Advanced Studies, Singapore: National University of Singapore.
Ashraf, Ahmad (1977), *The Social Scientist and the Challenges of Development in Asian Rethinking in Development*, New Dehli: Abhinov Publishers.
Asian Perspectives Project (1985), *Transnationalization, the State, and the People: The Singapore Case, Part 2*, Tokyo: Working Papers of the United Nations University.
Asiawatch (1990), *Silencing All Critics: Human Rights Violations in Singapore*, New York: Asiawatch Committee.
Astin, A. (1992), 'Educational "Choice": Its Appeal May Be Illusory', *Sociology of Education*, 65(4).
Auletta, Ken (1983), *The Underclass*, New York: Random House.
Bachrach, Peter (1967), *The Theory of Democratic Élitism*, Boston: Little Brown.

Bachrach, P. and Baratz, M. (1974), *Power and Poverty: Theory and Practice*, New York: Oxford University Press.
Bagley, C. (1975), 'The Background of Deviance in Black Children in London', in G. Verma and C. Bagley (eds.), *Race and Education Across Cultures*, London: Heinemann.
Baker, Donald (1983), *Race, Ethnicity and Power*, London: Routledge & Kegan Paul.
Baker, John (1987), *Arguing for Equality*, London: Verso.
Balakrishnan, N. (1991), 'Mandarin Virtues', *Far Eastern Economic Review*, 10 October.
Ball, Stephen (1986), 'The Sociology of the School: Streaming and Mixed Ability and Social Class', in R. Rogers (ed.), *Education and Social Class*, London: Falmer Press.
Banfield, Edward (1970), *The Unheavenly City*, Boston: Little, Brown.
Banton, Michael (1972), *Racial Minorities*, London: Fontana.
_____ (1983), *Racial and Ethnic Competition*, Cambridge: Cambridge University Press.
_____ (1988), *Racial Consciousness*, London: Longman.
Barker, Martin (1981), *The New Racism*, London: Junction Books.
Barker-Lunn, J. (1970), *Streaming in the Primary School*, Windsor: National Foundation for Educational Research.
Barlay, W.; Kumar, K.; and Sims, R. (eds.) (1976), *Racial Conflict, Discrimination and Power*, London: AMS Press.
Barlow, Robin; Brazer, H.; and Morgan, J. (1966), *Economic Behaviour of the Affluent*, Washington, DC: Brookings Institute.
Barton, Len and Walker, Stephen (eds.) (1983), *Race, Class and Education*, London: Croom Helm.
Bayard, Rustin (1988), 'From Protest to Politics: The Future of the Civil Rights Movement', *Commentary*, 39(3).
Beck, E.; Horan, P.; and Tolbert, C. (1980), 'Industrial Segmentation and Labor Market Discrimination', *Social Problems*, 28(5).
Becker, Gary (1957), *The Economics of Discrimination*, Chicago: University of Chicago Press.
Bedlington, Stanley (1971), 'The Malays of Singapore: Values in Conflict?', *Sedar (Journal of the National University of Singapore Muslim Society)*, 4(2).
Bell, Daniel (1960), *The End of Ideology*, Cambridge: Harvard University Press.
_____ (1973), *The Coming of the Post-Industrial Society: A Venture in Social Forecasting*, New York: Basic Books.
_____ (1976), *The Cultural Contradiction of Capitalism*, New York: Basic Books.
Bell, Roger (ed.) (1987), *Multicultural Societies: A Comparative Reader*, Sydney: Sable Publishers.
Bello, W. and Rosenfeld, S. (1992), *Dragons in Distress: Asia's Miracle Economies in Crisis*, Harmondsworth: Penguin.
Bellows, Thomas (1990), 'Singapore in 1989: Progress in Search of Roots', *Asian Survey*, 30(2).
Bellwood, Peter (1985), *The Pre-History of the Indo-Malaysian Archipelago*, Sydney: Academic Press.
Benjamin, Geoffrey (1976), 'The Cultural Logic of Singapore's Multiracialism', in Riaz Hassan (ed.), *Singapore: Society in Transition*, Kuala Lumpur: Oxford University Press.
Berg, Elias (1988), 'The Meaning of Legitimacy', in D. Anckar, H. Nurmi, and

M. Wilberg, *Rationality and Legitimacy: Essays on Political Theory*, Helsinki: Finnish Political Science Association.
Berger, Julian (1979), *Report from the Frontier: The State of the World's Indigenous Peoples*, London: Zed Books.
Bernstein, B. (1977), 'Class and Pedagogies: Visible and Invisible', in J. Karable and A. Halsley (eds.), *Power and Ideology in Education*, Oxford: Oxford University Press.
Beteille, Andre (1981), 'The Idea of Natural Inequality', in Gerald Berreman (ed.), *Social Inequality*, New York: Academic Press.
'The Biggest Secret of Race Relations: The New White Minority', Editorial, *Ebony Magazine*, April 1989.
Birch, A. (1971), *Representation*, London: Pall Mall Press.
Birch, David (1993), *Singapore Media*, Melbourne: Longman Cheshire.
Bizman, A. and Amir, Y. (1984), 'Integration and Attitudes', in Y. Amir and S. Sharon, *School Desegregation*, Hillsdale: Lawrence Erlbaum.
Blake, Myrna (1991), *The Underclass in the Malay/Muslim Community*, Report of Research and Action Project, 1990-1, Conducted jointly by Mendaki and the Department of Social Work and Psychology, National University of Singapore.
Blalock, Hubert (1967), *Towards a Theory of Minority Group Relations*, New York: Wiley.
Blau, P. and Duncan, O. (1967), *The American Occupational Structure*, New York: Wiley.
Bloom, Allan (1987), *Closing of the American Mind*, New York: Simon & Schuster.
Bobo, Lawrence (1988), *Race in the Minds of Black and White Americans*, Paper prepared for the Committee on the Status of Black Americans, Washington, DC: National Research Council.
Bock, J. (1982), 'Education and Development: A Conflict of Meaning', in P. Altbach (ed.), *Comparative Education*, New York: Macmillan.
Bonacich, Edna (1980), 'Class Approaches to Ethnicity and Race', *Insurgent Sociologist*, 10(2).
_____ (1987), 'The Limited Social Philosophy of Affirmative Action', *Insurgent Sociologist*, 14(1).
Bordieu, Pierre and Passeron, J. (1977), *Reproduction*, London: Sage Publications.
_____ (1990), *Reproduction in Education, Society and Culture*, London: Sage Publications.
Boston, Thomas (1988), *Race, Class and Conservatism*, Boston: Unwin & Hyman.
Boucher, J.; Landis, D.; and Clard, K. (eds.) (1987), *Ethnic Conflict: International Perspectives*, Newbury Park: Sage Publications.
Boudon, Raymond (1973), *Education, Opportunity and Social Inequality*, New York: John Wiley.
_____ (1977), 'Education and Mobility: A Structural Model', in J. Karabel and A. Halsey (eds.), *Power and Ideology in Education*, New York: Oxford University Press.
Bowles, Samuel (1972), 'Schooling and Inequality from Generation to Generation', *Journal of Political Economy*, 80(6).
Bowles, Samuel and Gintis, H. (1976), *Schooling in Capitalist America*, New York: Basic Books.
_____ (1977), 'I.Q. in the U.S. Class Structure', in J. Karabel and A. Halsey (eds.), *Power and Ideology in Education*, New York: Oxford University Press.

―― (1988), 'The Correspondence Principle', in Michael Cole (ed.), *Bowles and Gintis Revisited*, London: Falmer Press.
Break, George (1957), 'Income Taxes and Incentive to Work', *American Economic Review*, 47(8).
Brennan, John and McGeevor, P. (1990), *Ethnic Minorities and the Graduate Labour Market*, London: Commission for Racial Equality.
Brennan, T. (1981), *Political Education and Democracy*, Cambridge: Cambridge University Press.
Brittain, E. (1976), 'Multiracial Education: Teacher Opinions on Aspects of School Life', *Educational Research*, 18(3).
Brown, David (1985), 'Crisis and Ethnicity: Legitimacy in Plural Societies', *Third World Quarterly*, 7(4).
―― (1988), *The Legitimacy of Governments in Plural Societies*, Centre for Advanced Studies, Occasional Paper No. 43, Singapore: Singapore University Press.
―― (1989a), 'The State of Ethnicity and the Ethnicity of the State: Ethnic Politics in Southeast Asia', *Ethnic and Racial Studies*, 12(1).
―― (1989b), 'Does Ideology Have Any Place in Modern Democracy?' in Cedric Pan (ed.), *Thinking about Democracy*, Singapore: Political Association, National University of Singapore.
―― (1993), *The State and Ethnic Politics in Southeast Asia*, London: Routledge.
Brown, P. (1987), *Schooling Ordinary Kids*, London: Tavistock Publications.
―― (1990), 'The Third Wave: Education and the Ideology of Parentocracy', *British Journal of Sociology of Education*, 2(6).
Brown, P. and Lauder, H. (eds.) (1992), *Education for Economic Survival*, London: Routledge.
Buci-Gluckman, Christine (1982), 'Hegemony and Consent: A Political Strategy', in A. Sasson (ed.), *Approaches to Gramsci*, London: Writers and Readers Publishing Cooperative Society Ltd.
Bunce, Valerie (1981), *Do New Leaders Make a Difference?*, New Jersey: Princeton University Press.
Burtonwood, Neil (1986), *The Culture Concept in Educational Studies*, Windsor: NFER–NELSON Publishing.
Calhoun, G. and Elliot, R. (1977), 'Self Concept and Academic Achievement of Educable Retarded and Emotionally Disturbed Pupils', *Exceptional Children*, 46(8).
Capra, Fritjof (1987), *The Turning Point: Science, Society and the Rising Culture*, London: Fontana.
Carnoy, Martin (1974), *Education as Cultural Imperialism*, New York: David Mckay.
―― (1984), *The State and Political Theory*, Princeton: Princeton University Press.
Carnoy, Martin, and Levin, Henry (1986), 'Educational Reform and Class Conflict', *Journal of Education*, 1(68).
Central Advisory Council for Education (1967), *Children in Primary Schools: A Report of the Central Advisory Council for Education*, London.
Chai, Hon Chan (1977), *Education and Nation-Building in Plural Schools*, Canberra: Australian National University Press.
Chan, Heng Chee (1971), *The Politics of Survival*, Singapore: Oxford University Press.
―― (1976a), *The Dynamics of One Party Dominance: The PAP at the Grassroots*, Singapore: Singapore University Press.

_____ (1976b), 'The Role of Parliamentary Politicians in Singapore', *Legislative Studies Quarterly*, August.
_____ (1983), 'Singapore in 1982: Gradual Transition to a New Order', *Asian Survey*, 23(2).
_____ (1991), 'Political Developments, 1965-1979', in E. Chew and E. Lee (eds.), *A History of Singapore*, Singapore: Oxford University Press.
Chan, Heng Chee and Hans Dieter Evers (1978), 'National Identity and Nation Building in Singapore', in Peter Chen and Hans Dieter Evers (eds.), *Studies in ASEAN Sociology: Urban Society and Social Change*, Singapore: Chopmen.
Charvet, John (1969), 'The Idea of Equality as a Substantive Principle of Society', *Political Studies*, 27(14).
Cheah, Boon Keng, *Red Star over Malaya*, Singapore: Singapore University Press, 1983.
Che Man, Wan Kadir (1990), *Muslim Separatism: The Moros of Southern Philippines and the Malays of Southern Thailand*, Singapore: Oxford University Press.
Chen, Peter (ed.) (1977), *Élites and National Development in Singapore*, Tokyo: Institute of Developing Economies.
_____ (ed.) (1984), *Social Development Policies and Trends*, Singapore: Oxford University Press.
Chen, Peter and Evers, Hans Dieter (1978), *Studies in ASEAN Sociology: Urban Society and Social Change*, Singapore: Chopmen.
Chester, M. (1976), 'Contemporary Sociological Theories of Racism', in P. Katz (ed.), *Towards the Elimination of Racism*, New York: Pergamon.
Cheung, Paul (1990), 'Summary of Census Findings', in Yap Mui Teng (ed.), *Forum on the Census of Population 1990*, Institute of Policy Studies, Report No. 4, Singapore.
Chew, Sock Foon (1987), *Ethnicity and Nationality in Singapore*, Athens: Ohio University Centre for International Studies.
Chew, Soo Beng (1982), *Fishermen in Flats*, Monash Papers on Southeast Asia, No. 9, Centre for Southeast Asian Studies, Melbourne: Monash University.
Chiew, Seen Kong (1978), 'National Integration: The Case of Singapore', in Peter Chen and Hans Dieter Evers (eds.), *Studies in ASEAN Sociology: Urban Society and Social Change*, Singapore: Chopmen.
_____ (1990), 'National Identity, Ethnicity and National Issues', in Jon Quah (ed.), *In Search of Singapore's National Values*, Singapore: Institute of Policy Studies.
_____ (1991), 'Ethnic Stratification', in Stella Quah et al. (eds.), *Social Class in Singapore*, Singapore: Times Academic Press.
Chomsky, Noam (1984), 'I.Q. Tests: Building Blocks for the New Class System', in Chan Chee Khoon and Chee Heng Leng (eds.), *Designer Genes: I.Q., Ideology and Biology*, Petaling Jaya: INSAN.
Choo, Carolyn (1986), *Singapore: The PAP and the Problem of Political Succession*, Kuala Lumpur: Pelanduk Publications.
Chua Beng Huat (1983), 'Re-Opening the Ideological Discussion in Singapore: A New Theoretical Discussion', *Southeast Asian Journal of Social Science*, 2(2).
_____ (1985), 'Pragmatism of the PAP Government in Singapore: A Critical Assessment', *Journal of Southeast Asian Studies*, 13(2).
_____ (1988), 'Public Housing Policies Compared: U.S., Socialist Countries and Singapore', Working Paper No. 94, Sociology Department, Singapore: National University of Singapore.
_____ (1989), 'Doing Comparative Social Science in Singapore', *Commentary*, 8(1 & 2).

# BIBLIOGRAPHY

Chubb, J. and Moe, T. (1986), 'No School is An Island: Politics, Markets and Education', *Brookings Review*, 5(1).

———— (1990), *Politics, Markets and America's Schools*, Washington, DC: The Brookings Institute.

Clad, James (1989), *Behind the Myth: Business, Money and Power in Southeast Asia*, Sydney: Allen & Unwin.

Clammer, John (1982), 'The Institutionalization of Ethnicity: The Culture of Ethnicity in Singapore', *Ethnic and Racial Studies*, 5(2).

———— (1987), 'Peripheral Capitalism and Urban Order: Informal Sector Theories in the Light of Singapore's Experience', in John Clammer (ed.), *Beyond the New Economic Anthropology*, New York: St. Martins Press.

Clapham, Christopher (1985), *Third World Politics*, London: Croom Helm.

Clark, Kenneth (1965), *Dark Ghetto: Dilemmas of Social Power*, New York: Harper & Row.

Cole, Michael (ed.) (1988), *Bowles and Gintis Revisited*, London: Falmer Press.

Coleman, J. and Hoffer, S. (1987), *Public and Private High Schools: The Impact of Communities*, New York: Basic Books.

Collier, D. and Collier, D. (1979), 'Who Does What, To Whom and How?', in James Malloy (ed.), *Authoritarianism and Corporatism in Latin America*, Pittsburg: University of Pittsburg Press.

Collins, Randall (1979), *The Credential Society: An Historical Sociology of Education and Stratification*, New York: Academic Press.

Connell, R. W. (1989), 'Curriculum Politics, Hegemony and Strategies of Social Change', in H. Giroux and R. Simon (eds.), *Popular Culture, Schooling and Everyday Life*, New York: Bergin & Garvey.

———— (1993), *Schools and Social Justice*, Sydney: Pluto Press.

Connell, R. W.; White, V.; and Johnston, K. (1990), 'Poverty and Education: Changing Conceptions', *Discourse*, 11(1).

Connor, Walker (1978), 'A Nation Is a Nation, Is a State, Is An Ethnic Group Is a ...', *Ethnic and Racial Studies*,1(4).

———— (1987), 'Prospects for Stability in Southeast Asia: The Ethnic Barrier', in K. Snitwongse and S. Paribatra (eds.), *Durable Stability in Southeast Asia*, Singapore: Institute of Southeast Asian Studies.

———— (1992), 'The Nation and Its Myth', *International Journal of Comparative Sociology*, 33(1 & 2).

Converse, Philip (1980), *American Social Attitudes Data Sourcebook, 1947–1978*, Cambridge: Harvard University Press.

Cookson, P. M. and Persell, C. H. (1985), *Preparing for Power: America's Élite Boarding Schools*, New York: Basic Books.

Cox, Oliver Cromwell (1970), *Caste, Class and Race: A Study in Social Dynamics*, New York: Penguin.

Crawfurd, John (1828), *Journal of an Embassy to the Courts of Siam and Cochin China*, reprinted Singapore: Oxford University Press, 1967.

Cruz, Leonardo de la (1989), 'Education and Development', *Innotech Journal*, July–December.

Dahl, Robert (1961), *Who Governs? Democracy and Power in an American City*, New Haven: Yale University Press.

Dale, Roger (ed.) (1976), *Schooling and Capitalism: A Sociological Reader*, London: Routledge & Kegan Paul.

———— (1989), *The State and Education Policy*, London: Open University Press.

Dar, Y. and Resh N. (1986), 'Classroom and Intellectual Composition and Academic Achievement', *American Educational Research Journal*, 23(3).

Darling-Hammond, Linda (1985), *Equality and Excellence*, New York: College Entrance Examination Board.
Darmaputera, Eka (1988), *Pancasila and the Search for Identity and Modernity in Indonesian Society*, Leiden: E. J. Brill.
Davidson, Alistair (1990), 'Antonio Gramsci', in P. Beilharz (ed.), *Social Theory*, Sydney: Allen & Unwin.
Davidson, Chandler (1972), *Biracial Politics*, Baton Rouge: Louisiana State University Press.
_____ (ed.) (1984), *Minority Vote Dilution*, Washington, DC: Howard University Press.
Davidson, Chandler and Fraga L. (1984), 'Non-Partisan Slating Groups in At-Large Setting', in C. Davidson (ed.), *Minority Vote Dilution*, Washington, DC: Howard University Press.
Davis, Kingsley and Moore, Wilbert (1945), 'Some Principles of Stratification', *American Sociological Review*, 10(2).
_____ (1966), 'Some Principles of Stratification', in R. Bendix and S. Lipset (eds.), *Class, Status, and Power: Social Stratification in Comparative Perspective*, New York: Free Press.
Dench, Geoff (1986), *Minorities in the Open Society: Prisoners of Ambivalence*, London: Routledge & Kegan Paul.
Deutsch, A. and Zowell H. (1988), *Compulsory Savings and Taxes in Singapore*, Research Notes and Discussion Paper No. 65, Singapore: Institute of Southeast Asian Studies.
Deutsch, Morton (1985), *Distributive Justice—A Social/Psychological Perspective*, New Haven: Yale University Press.
Deyo, Frederic (1981), *Dependent Development and the Industrial Order: An Asian Case Study*, New York: Praeger.
Dillingham, Gerald L. (1981), 'The Emerging Black Middle Class: Class Conscious or Race Conscious?', *Ethnic and Racial Studies*, 4(4).
Di Stefano, Christine (1991), 'Masculine Marx', in M. Shanley and C. Pateman (eds.), *Feminist Interpretations and Political Theory*, London: Polity Press.
Djamour, Judith (1965), *Malay Kinship and Marriage in Singapore*, London: Athlone Press.
Doise, W. and Sinclair, A. (1973), 'The Categorization Process in Intergroup Relations', *European Journal of Social Psychology*, 3(5).
Domhoff, G. (1983), *Who Rules America Now?*, Englewood Cliffs: Prentice-Hall.
Dore, Ronald (1980), 'The Future of Formal Education in Developing Countries', in John Simmons (ed.), *The Education Dilemma: Issues for Developing Countries in 1980s*, Oxford: Pergamon.
Dorn, Andrew (1985), 'Education and the Race Relations Act', in Madeline Arnot (ed.), *Race and Gender*, London: Pergamon.
Drysdale, John (1984), *Singapore: Struggle for Success*, Singapore: Times Books.
Duberman, Martin (1968), 'Black Power and the American Radical Tradition', in Alfred Young (ed.), *Dissent: Explorations in the History of American Radicalism*, Illinois: Illinois University Press.
Du Bois, W. E. B. (1969), *The Souls of Black Folks*, New York: Signet.
Durkheim, Emile (1960), *The Division of Labor in Society*, New York: Free Press.
_____ (1972), 'Essays on Morals and Education', in W. S. F. Pickering (ed.), *Durkheim: Essays on Morals and Education*, London: Routledge & Kegan Paul.
Dworkin, Anthony and Dworkin, Rosalind (1976), *The Minority Report*, New York: Holt, Rinehart & Winston.

Ecceleshall, Robert (1984), 'Introduction: The World of Ideology', in R. Eccleshall et al., *Political Ideologies*, London: Hutchinson.
Edwards, John and Batley, Richard (1978), *The Politics of Positive Discrimination*, London: Tavistock.
Eells, K. et al. (1951), *Intelligence and Cultural Differences*, Chicago: University of Chicago Press.
Eller, J. and Coughlan, R. (1993), 'The Poverty of Primordialism: The Demystification of Ethnic Attachments', *Ethnic and Racial Studies*, 16(2).
Emerson, R. (1964), *Malaysia: A Study in Direct and Indirect Rule*, Kuala Lumpur: University of Malaya Press.
Enloe, Cynthia (1973), *Ethnic Conflict and Political Development*, Boston: Little, Brown.
―――― (1978), 'Ethnicity, Bureaucracy and State Building in Africa and Latin America', *Ethnic and Racial Studies*, 1(3).
―――― (1980), *Police, Military and Ethnicity: Foundations of State Power*, New Jersey: Transaction Books.
Epstein, A. L. (1978), *Ethos and Identity*, London: Tavistock.
Esman, Milton, J. (1985), 'Two Dimensions of Ethnic Politics: Defence of Homelands, Immigrants Rights', *Ethnic and Racial Studies*, 8(3).
Everhart, Robert (1979), *The In-Between Years: Student Life in a Junior High School*, Santa Barbara: University of California.
Eysenck, Hans (1973), *The Inequality of Man*, London: Temple Smith.
―――― (1979), *The Structure and Measurement of Intelligence*, New York: Springer-Verlag.
Fanon, Frantz (1963), *The Wretched of the Earth*, London: Penguin.
―――― (1967), *Towards the African Revolution*, New York: Grove Press.
Fatimi, S. Q. (1963), *Islam Comes to Malaysia*, Singapore: Malaysian Sociological Research Institute.
Fay, Brian (1975), *Social Theory and Political Practice*, London: George Allen & Unwin.
―――― (1987), *Critical Social Science: Liberation and Its Limits*, London: Polity Press.
Femia, Joseph (1981), *Gramsci's Political Thought*, Oxford: Clarendon Press.
Figueroa, I. and Swartz, L. (1982), 'Poor Achievers and High Achievers among Ethnic Minority Pupils', Report to the Commission for Racial Equality, London.
Finn, J. D. and Archilles, C. M. (1990), 'Answers and Questions About Class Size: A State Wide Experiment', *American Educational Research Journal*, 27(3).
Fiori, Guiseppe (1970), *Antonio Gramsci: Life of a Revolutionary*, London: New Left Books.
Fischer, Claude (1976), *The Urban Experiment*, New York: Harcourt Brace & Jovanovich.
Fishkin, James (1988), 'Do We Need a Systematic Theory of Equal Opportunity?', in N. Bowie (ed.), *Equal Opportunity*, London: Westview Press.
Fisk, E. K. (1964), *Studies in the Rural Economy in Southeast Asia*, Singapore: Eastern University Press.
Fletcher, M. (1969), *The Separation of Singapore from Malaysia*, Cornell University Paper No. 73, Ithaca: Cornell University Press.
Foucault, Michel (1986), 'Disciplinary Power and Subjection', in Stephen Lukes (ed.), *Power*, Oxford: Basil Blackwell.
Fox, Lynn (1970), 'Sex Differences in Mathematical Precocity', in D. F. Keating (ed.), *Intellectual Talent*, Baltimore: Johns Hopkins University Press.

Freire, Paolo (1972), *Pedagogy of the Oppressed*, Harmondsworth: Penguin.
Fried, C. (1983), *Minorities: Communities and Identity*, Berlin: Springer-Verlag.
Friedman, Milton and Friedman, Rose (1980), *Free to Choose*, New York: Harcourt, Brace & Jovanovich.
Furnival, J. S. (1948), *Colonial Policy and Practice*, Cambridge: Cambridge University Press.
Gallie, D. (1983), *Social Inequality and Class Radicalism in France and Britain*, Cambridge: Cambridge University Press.
Galton, Francis (1959), *Hereditary Genius*, London: Watts.
Gamer, Robert (1972), *The Politics of Urban Development in Singapore*, Ithaca: Cornell University Press.
_____ (1976), *The Developing Nations*, Boston: Allyn & Bacon.
Gamoran A. (1986), 'Instructional and Institutional Effects of Ability Grouping', *Sociology of Education*, 59(5).
_____ (1990), 'Instructional Organizational Practices That Effect Equity', in H. Baptiste Jr., et al. (eds.), *Leadership, Equity and School Effectiveness*, Newbury: Sage.
Gane, M. (1991), *Baudrillard's Bestiary*, London: Routledge.
Ganes, Herbert (1968), 'Culture and Class in the Study of Poverty: An Approach to Anti-Poverty Research', in D. Moynihan (ed.), *An Understanding of Poverty*, New York: Basic Books.
_____ (1973), *More Inequality*, New York: Pantheon Books.
Ganesan, Nara (1988), 'Islamic Responses within ASEAN to Singapore's Foreign Policy', *Asian Thought and Society*, 13(38).
_____ (1991), 'Factors Effecting Singapore's Foreign Policy towards Malaysia', *Australian Journal of International Affairs*, 45(2).
Gardiner, D. et al. (1983), 'A Nation At Risk: The Imperative for Educational Reform; An Open Letter to the American People', New York.
Geertz, Clifford (1963), *Old Societies and New States*, New York: Free Press.
George, T. S. (1974), *Lee Kuan Yew's Singapore*, London: Andre Deutsch.
George, Vic and Wilding, Paul (1985), *Ideology and Social Welfare*, London: Routledge & Kegan Paul.
Giddens, Anthony (1979), *Central Problems in Social Theory*, London: Macmillan.
Gillian Jr., Reginald Earl (1975), *Black Political Development*, New York: Dunellen Publications.
Girling, John (1981), *The Bureaucratic Polity in Modernizing Societies: Similarities, Differences and Prospects in the ASEAN Region*, Singapore: Institute of Southeast Asian Studies.
Giroux, Henry (1981), *Ideology, Culture and the Process of Schooling*, Philadelphia: Temple University Press.
_____ (1984), 'Ideology, Agency and the Process of Schooling', in Len Barton and Stephen Walker (eds.), *Social Crisis and Educational Research*, London: Croom Helm.
_____ (1992a), *Border Crossings*, New York: Routledge.
_____ (1992b), 'Rewriting the Politics of Identity and Difference', *Review of Education*, 14(7).
Glass, D. V. (ed.) (1954), *Social Mobility in Britain*, London: Routledge & Kegan Paul.
Glazer, Nathan (1975), *Affirmative Discrimination, Ethnic Inequality and Public Policy*, New York: Basic Books.
Glazer, Nathan and Moynihan, Patrick (1970), *Beyond the Melting Pot*, Cambridge: Massachusetts Institute of Technology Press.

Glesne, C. and Peshkin, A. (1992), *Becoming Qualitative Researchers*, New York: Longman.
Goh, Keng Swee (1972), *The Economics of Modernization and Other Essays*, Singapore: Asia Pacific Press.
Goldman, M.; Stockbaeur, J.; and McAlcliffe, T. (1977), 'Intergroup and Intragroup Competition and Cooperation', *Journal of Experimental Social Psychology*, 13(10).
Gonzalez, Gilbert (1986), *Progressive Education: A Marxist Interpretation*, Minneapolis: Marxist Education Press.
Good, Leslie (1989), 'Power, Hegemony and Communication Theory', in I. Angus, and S. Jhally (eds.), *Cultural Politics in Contemporary America*, New York: Routledge.
Gook, Aik Suan (1981), 'Singapore: A Third World Fascist State', *Journal of Contemporary Asia*, 11(7).
Gopinathan, S. (1974), *Towards a National System of Education in Singapore, 1945–1973*, Singapore: Oxford University Press.
—— (1989a), 'Being and Becoming: Education for Values in Singapore', in W. Cummings; S. Gopinathan; and Y. Tomoda (eds.), *The Revival of Values Education in Asia and the West*, Oxford: Pergamon Press.
—— (1989b), 'University Education in Singapore: The Making of a National University', in P. Altbach and V. Selvaratnam (eds.), *From Dependence to Autonomy*, Kluwer Academic Press.
—— (1991), 'Education', in F. Chew and E. Lee (eds.), *A History of Singapore*, Singapore: Oxford University Press.
Gopinathan, S. and Gremli, M. S. (1988), 'The Educational and Research Environment in Singapore', in S. Gopinathan and H. D. Nielsen, *Educational Research Environments in Southeast Asia*, Singapore: Chopmen.
Gopinathan, S.; Yap, J.; and Chua Toh Chai (1990), *A Review of Values, Education Policies and Practices in Israel, Japan and Taiwan*, Singapore: Institute of Education.
Gordon, Milton (1964), *Assimilation in American Life: The Role of Race, Religion and National Origins*, New York: Oxford University Press.
Gordon, S. and Gunn. T. (1968), 'Problems of Malay School Leavers', *Intisari*, 2(7).
Gouldbourne, Harry (1989), 'The Offence of the West Indian: Political Leadership and the Communal Option', in P. Werbner and M. Anwar (eds.), *Black and Ethnic Leadership in Britain*, London: Routledge.
Gramsci, Antonio (1971), *Selections from Prison Notebooks*, edited and translated by Q. Hoare and G. Smith, New York: International Publications.
Green, Philip. (1981), *The Pursuit of Inequality*, Oxford: Martin Robertson.
Grofman, B. and Lyphart, A. (1986), *Electoral Laws and Political Consequences*, New York: Agathon Press.
Grove, D. (1993), 'Have the Post-Reform Ethnic Gains Eroded?', *Ethnic and Racial Studies*, 16(4).
Gunasekaran, Subbiah and Sullivan, Gerard. (1990), 'Push or Pull? Emigration from the ASEAN Countries', *Pacific Newsletter*, 4(5).
Habermas, Jurgen (1971), *Towards a Rational Society*, Boston: Beacon Press.
Hall, D. G. E. (1968), *A History of Southeast Asia*, New York: Macmillan.
Hall, Stuart. (1977), 'Culture, the Media and the Ideological Effect', in J. Curran; M. Gurevitch; and J. Woollacott (eds.), *Mass Communication Society*, London: Arnold.

_____ (1989), 'Gramsci's Relevance for the Study of Race and Ethnicity', *Journal of Communication Inquiry*, 10(10).

_____ (1991), 'Ethnicity: Identity and Difference', *Radical America*, 23(4).

Harber, Clive (1991), 'International Contexts for Political Education', *Educational Review*, 43(3).

Harding, Vincent (1968), 'Black Radicalism: The Road from Montgomery', in Alfred Young (ed.), *Dissent: Explorations in the History of American Radicalism*, Dekalb, Illinois: Northern Illinois University Press.

Hargreaves, D. H. (1967), *Social Relations in Secondary Schools*, London: Routledge & Kegan Paul.

Harris, Keith. (1979), *Education and Knowledge: The Structured Misrepresentation of Reality*, London: Routledge & Kegan Paul.

Harris, Nigel. (1986), *The End of the Third World*, London: Penguin.

Harvey, D. G. and Slatin, G. T. (1974), 'The Relationship between a Child's Socio-Economic Status and Teacher Expectations', *Social Forces*, 54(8).

Hassan, Riaz (1971), 'Occupational and Class Structure of the Singapore Malays', *Suara University*, 2(1).

_____ (1976), *Singapore: Society in Transition*, Kuala Lumpur: Oxford University Press.

_____ (1977), *Families in Flats: A Study of Low Income Families in Public Housing*, Singapore: Singapore University Press.

Hawkesworth, M. E. (1988), *Theoretical Issues in Policy Analysis*, New York: State University Press.

Hayek, F. C. (1960), *The Constitution of Liberty*, London: Routledge & Kegan Paul.

_____ (1976), *Law, Legislation and Liberty: The Mirage of Social Justice*, London: Routledge & Kegan Paul.

Haynes, J. M. (1971), *Educational Assessment of Immigrant Pupils*, London: National Foundation for Educational Research.

Hearnshaw, L. (1979), *Cyril Burt: Psychologist*, Ithaca: Cornell University Press.

Heath, A. (1981), *Social Mobility*, London: Fontana.

Hechter, Michael (1972), *Internal Colonialism*, London: Routledge & Kegan Paul.

Heng, Geraldine and Devan, Janadas (1992), 'State Fatherhood: The Politics of Nationalism, Sexuality and Race in Singapore', in A. Parker et al. (eds.), *Nationalisms and Sexualities*, New York: Routledge.

Hess, R. and Torney, J. (1967), *The Development of Political Attitudes in Children*, Chicago: Aldine Press.

Hess, R. D. and Shipman, V. C. (1965), 'Early Experience and the Socialization of Cognitive Modes in Children', *Child Development*, 36(9).

Hewison, Kevin; Robinson, Richard; and Rodan, Gary (eds.) (1993), *Southeast Asia in the 1990s*, Sydney: Allen and Unwin.

Hewstone, M. and Jaspers, J. (1982), 'Explanations for Racial Discrimination: The Effect of Group Discussion and Inter-Group Attributions', *European Journal of Social Psychology*, 12(7).

Hewstone, M. and Ward, C. (1985), 'Ethnocentricism and Casual Attribution in Southeast Asia', *Journal of Personality and Social Psychology*, 48(12).

Hill, Stephen (1990), *Britain: The Dominant Ideology Thesis After a Decade*, London: Unwin & Hyman.

Hillsgate Group (1986), *Whose Schools? A Radical Manifesto*, London: Claridge Press.

_____ (1987), *The Reform of British Education: From Principles to Practice*, London: Claridge Press.

Hirschman, Charles (1987), 'The Meaning and Measurement of Ethnicity in Malaysia: An Analysis of Census Classifications', *Journal of Asian Studies*, 46(3).
Hirst, Paul (1979), *On Law and Ideology*, London: Macmillan Press.
Ho, Wing Meng (1989), 'Value Premises Underlying the Transformation of Singapore', in Kernial Sandhu and Paul Wheatley (eds.), *Management of Success*, Singapore: Institute of Southeast Asian Studies.
Hochschild, Jennifer (1988), 'The Double Edged Sword of Equal Opportunity', in Ian Shapiro and Grant Reeher (eds.), *Power, Inequality and Democratic Politics*, Boulder: Westview Press.
Holt, John (1964), *How Children Fail*, New York: Pitman Publications.
Honerich, Ted (1990), *Conservatism*, London: Hamish Hamilton.
Horowitz, Donald (1985), *Ethnic Groups in Conflict*, Berkeley: University of California Press.
Hout, M. (1984), 'Occupational Mobility of Black Men: 1962-1973', *American Sociological Review*, 49(12).
Hua, Wu Yin (1983), *Class and Communalism in Malaysia: Politics in a Dependent Capitalistic State*, London: Zed Press.
Huber, Joan and Form, William (1973), *Income and Ideology: An Analysis of the American Political Formula*, New York: Free Press.
Husen, T. (ed.) (1967), *International Study of Achievement in Maths*, New York: Wiley.
Hussain, Ashfaq (1970), 'The Post-Separation Effects on the Malays and Their Response, 1965-1966', *Journal of the Historical Society*, 7(8).
Hussin Mutalib (1989a), 'Challenges and Prospects of Singaporean Malays', *Mirror*, 25(17).
_____ (1989b), 'Education and Singapore Muslims: An Overview of the Issues, Parameters and Prospects', *Fajar Islam (Journal of Muslim Issues in Singapore)*, 2.
_____ (1990), *Islam and Ethnicity in Malay Politics*, Singapore: Oxford University Press.
Huxley, Tim (1991), 'Singapore and Malaysia: A Precarious Balance', *Pacific Review*, 4(3).
_____ (1992), 'Singapore's Politics in the 1980s and 1990s', *Asian Affairs*, 23(6).
Hyung, Baeg Im (1991), 'Hegemony and Counter Hegemony in Gramsci', *Asian Perspective*, 15(1).
Ibrahim Hassan (1978/80), 'The NUS Muslim Society—Challenges Ahead', *Sedar (Journal of the National University of Singapore Muslim Society)*.
Inglis, Christine (1983), 'The Feminization of the Teaching Profession in Singapore', in Lenore Manderson (ed.), *Women's Work and Women's Roles: Economics and Everyday Life in Indonesia, Malaysia and Singapore*, Developmental Studies Centre, Monograph No. 32, Canberra: Australian National University.
International Monetary Fund (1990 and 1991), *Government Finance Statistics*, Washington.
Islam, Iyanatul and Kirkpatrick, Colin (1986), 'Export Led Development, Labour Market Conditions and the Distribution of Income: The Case of Singapore', *Cambridge Journal of Economics*, 10(7).
Ismail Kassim (1974), *Problems of Élite Cohesion: A Perspective from a Minority Community*, Singapore: Singapore University Press.
James, W. (1993), 'Migration, Racism and Identity: Caribbean Experience in Britain', *New Left Review*, 193(24).

Jameson, F. (1984), 'Postmodernism or the Cultural Logic of Late Capitalism', *New Left Review*, 146(17).
Jarvis, Helen (1991), *Tan Malaka: From Jail to Jail*, Athens: Ohio University Press.
Jayasuriya, Kanishka (1994), 'Singapore: The Politics of Regional Definition', *Pacific Review*, 7(4).
Jaynes, G. D. and Williams, R. M. (eds.) (1989), *A Common Destiny, Blacks and American Society*, Washington DC: National Academy Press.
Jeffers, Sydney (1989), 'Black Sections in the Labour Party: The End of Ethnicity and Godfather Politics', in P. Werbner and M. Anwar (eds.), *Black and Ethnic Leadership in Britain*, London: Routledge.
Jencks, Christopher. (1988), 'What Must Be Equal for Equal Opportunity to be Equal?', in N. Bowie (ed.), *Equal Opportunity*, Boulder: Westview Press.
Jencks, Christopher et al. (1972), *Inequality: A Reassessment of the Effects of Family and Schooling in America*, New York: Basic Books.
Jensen, Arthur (1969), 'How Much We Can Boost I.Q. and Scholastic Achievement', *Harvard Educational Review*, 23(7).
Jesudason, James (1989), *Ethnicity and the Economy: The State, Chinese Business and Multinationals in Malaysia*, Singapore: Oxford University Press.
Jiobu, Robert (1988), *Ethnicity and Assimilation*, Albany: State University of New York Press.
Johari, Hashimah (1978–80), 'Islam and Economic Actions among the Muslims in Southeast Asia', *Sedar (Journal of the National University of Singapore Muslim Society)*.
Johnson, Dale (1976), 'Marginal Classes, Internal Colonies and Social Change', in W. Barclay; K. Kumar; R. Sims (eds.), *Racial Conflict, Discrimination and Power*, New York: AMS Press.
Johnson, David and Anderson, D. (1976), 'Effects of Cooperative Versus Individualized Instruction on Student Social Behaviour, Attitudes toward Learning and Achievement', *Journal of Educational Psychology*, 68(12).
Jones, J. (1981), 'The Concept of Racism and its Changing Reality', in B. Bowser and R. Hunt (eds.), *Impacts of Racism on White Americans*, Beverly Hills: Sage.
Jones, Ken (1989), *Right Turn*, London: Hutchinson Radius.
Josey, Alex (1968), *Lee Kuan Yew*, Singapore: Donald Moore Press.
Kamin, Leon (1984), 'The Cyril Burt Affair', in Chan Chee Khoon and Chee Heng Leng (eds.), *Designer Genes: I.Q., Ideology and Biology*, Kuala Lumpur: INSAN.
Kapur, Basant (ed.) (1986), *Singapore Studies: Critical Surveys of the Humanities and Social Sciences*, Singapore: Singapore University Press.
Karabel, J. and Halsy, A. H. (eds.) (1977), *Power and Ideology in Education*, New York: Oxford University Press.
Kassim Yang Razali (1990), 'Why There is Still a Malay Problem', in a *Straits Times* Special, 'Singapore 25 Years', 9 August.
KEMAS (1985), *Buku Kongres Ekonomic Masyarakat Melayu Islam*, Singapore.
Khoo, Hagen (1985), 'Transformation of the Class Structure: The Impact of Dependent Development', *Research in Social Stratification and Mobility*, 4(2).
Khoo, Kay Kim (1988), 'Chinese Economic Activities in Malaya: A Historical Perspective', in Manning Nash (ed.), *Economic Performance in Malaysia*, New York: Paragon.
Khun, Eng Kuah (1990), 'Confucian Ideology and Social Engineering in Singapore', *Journal of Contemporary Asia*, 20(3).

King Jr., Martin Luther (1964), *Why We Can't Wait*, New York: Harper and Row.
Kluegel, James and Smith, Elliot (1986), *Beliefs about Inequality*, New York: Aldine de Gruyter.
Kohn, Alfie (1986), *No Contest*, Boston: Houghton Mifflin.
Krause, L., et al. (ed.) (1987), *The Singapore Economy Reconsidered*, Singapore: Institute of Southeast Asian Studies.
Kristol, Irving (1973), *On the Democratic Idea in America*, New York: Harper and Row.
―――― (1978), *Two Cheers for Capitalism*, New York: Basic Books.
Kuhn, T. (1973), *The Structure of Scientific Revolutions*, Chicago: Chicago University Press.
Kunio, Yoshihara (1988), *The Rise of Ersatz Capitalism in Southeast Asia*, Singapore: Oxford University Press.
Kwen, Fee Lian (1982), 'Identity in Minority Group Relations', *Ethnic and Racial Studies*, 5(1).
Laclau, E. and Mouffe, C. (1985), *Hegemony and Socialist Strategy: Towards a Radical Democratic Politics*, London: Verso.
Laderriere, Pierre (1984), 'Is Failure at School Inevitable?', *Prospects*, 14(3).
Lai, Ah Eng (1995), *Meanings of Multiethnicity: A Case Study of Ethnicity and Ethnic Relations in Singapore*, Kuala Lumpur: Oxford University Press.
Lal, B. (1983), 'Perspectives on Ethnicity: Old Wine in New Bottle', *Ethnic and Racial Studies*, 6(2).
Larrain, Jorge (1984), *The Concept of Ideology*, London: Hutchinson.
Lash, Scott (1990), 'Coercion as Ideology: The German Case', in Nicholas Abercrombie et al., *Dominant Ideologies*, London: Unwin & Hyman.
Lauder, Hugh (1992), 'Education Policy Impairs Democracy', *News VUW*, 25.
Lee, Kuan Yew (1965), *The Battle for a Malaysian Malaysia*, Singapore: Ministry of Culture Publications.
Lee, Tsao Yuan (1987), 'The Government in the Labour Market', in L. Krause et al. *The Singapore Economy Reconsidered*, Singapore: Institute of Southeast Asian Studies.
Leong, Choon Cheong (1978), *Youth in the Army*, Singapore: Federal Publications.
Levine, D. and Havighurst, R. (1992), *Society and Education*, Boston: Allyn & Bacon.
Lew, Eng Fee (1989), 'Singapore in 1988—Uncertainties of a Maturing Polity', *Southeast Asian Affairs*, Singapore: Institute of Southeast Asian Studies.
Lewis, Lionel and Warner, Richard (1979), 'Private Schooling and Status Attainment Process', *Sociology of Education*, 52(12).
Lewis, Oscar (1961), *The Children of Sanchez*, New York: Random House.
―――― (1968), 'The Culture of Poverty', in Daniel Moynihan, *On Understanding Poverty: Perspectives from the Social Sciences*, New York: Basic Books.
―――― (1970), *Anthropological Essays*, New York: Random House.
Lewontin, R. et al. (1984), 'Bourgeois Ideology and the Origins of Biological Determinism', in Chan Chee Khoon and Chee Heng Leng (eds.), *Designer Genes: I.Q., Ideology and Biology*, Petaling Jaya: INSAN.
Li, Tania (1989), *Malays in Singapore: Culture, Economy and Ideology*, Singapore: Oxford University Press.
Lim, Chong Yah and Associates (1986), *Report of the CPF Group*, Singapore.
Lim, Joo-Jock, Arthur (1991), 'Geographical Setting', in Ernest Chew and Edwin Lee (eds.), *A History of Singapore*, Singapore: Oxford University Press.

Lim, Linda (1983), 'Singapore's Success: The Myth of the Free-Market Economy', *Asian Survey*, 23(6).

―――― (1989), 'Social Welfare', in Kernial Singh Sandhu and Paul Wheatley (eds.), *Management of Success*, Singapore: Institute of Southeast Asian Studies.

Lim, Linda and Pang Eng Fong (1986), *Trade Employment and Industrialisation in Singapore*, Geneva: International Labor Organisation.

Lim, Teck Ghee (1977), *Peasants and Their Agricultural Economy in Colonial Malaya*, Kuala Lumpur: Oxford University Press.

Lin, Vivian (1984), 'Productivity First', *Bulletin of Concerned Asian Scholars*, 16(4).

Lind, Andrew (1971), *Nanyang Perspective: Chinese Students in Multiracial Singapore*, Hawaii: University of Hawaii Press.

Linville, P. and Jones, E. (1980), 'Polarized Appraisals of Out-Group Members', *Journal of Personality and Social Psychology*, 38(15).

Lipset, S. (1960), *Political Man*, London: Heinemann Publications.

Little, Alan (1981), 'Educational Policies for a Multiracial Britain', in B. Simon and W. Taylor (eds.), *Education in the Eighties*, London: Batsford Academic and Educational Limited.

Loh, Kok Wah and Joel Kahn (eds.) (1992), *Fragmented Vision: Culture and Politics in Contemporary Malaysia*, Sydney: Allen & Unwin.

Long, Litt Woon (1989), 'Zero as Communication: The Chinese Muslim Dilemma in Malaysia', in M. Gravers et al. (eds.), *South-East Asia: Between Autocracy and Democracy*, Denmark: Aarhus University.

Lopez, D. and Espiritu, Y. (1990), 'Pan-ethnicity in the United States: A Theoretical Framework', *Ethnic and Racial Studies*, 13(2).

Lowe, V. (1987), *Dependency Within Bounds: Media and Information Technology Policies within the ASEAN Region*, Bangkok: Institute of Asian Studies.

Lukes, Stephen (ed.) (1978), *Power and Authority*, New York: Basic Books.

―――― (ed.) (1986), *Power*, Oxford: Basil Blackwell.

Lyotard, J. (1986), *The Postmodern Condition: A Report on Knowledge*, Manchester: Manchester University Press.

Ma'arof Salleh (1975-7), 'Aspects of Dakwah in Singapore', *Sedar (Journal of the National University of Singapore Muslim Society)*.

Mabey, C. (1974), *Social and Ethnic Mix in Schools and the Relationship with Attainment of Children Aged Eight and Eleven*, London: Centre for Environmental Studies.

―――― (1981), 'Black British Literacy: A Study of Reading Attainment of London Black Children from Eight to Fifteen Years', *Educational Research*, 23(2).

Macarov, David (1970), *Incentive to Work*, San Francisco: Jossey-Bass.

Mack, Raymond (1963), *Race, Class and Power*, New York: American Book.

Mah, Hui Lim (1985), 'Affirmative Action, Ethnicity and Integration: The Case of Malaysia', *Ethnic and Racial Studies*, 8(2).

Mahathir Mohamad (1970), *The Malay Dilemma*, reprinted Petaling Jaya: Federal Publications.

Malcolm X (1965), *An Autobiography*, New York: Penguin.

Malik, M. (1988), 'No Politics Please', *Far Eastern Economic Review*, 14 January.

Mannheim, Karl (1940), *Ideology and Utopia*, London: Kegan Paul.

Mansur Sukaimi (1982), *Collection of Mendaki Papers*, Singapore: Mendaki.

Marable, Manning (1985), *Black American Politics: From the Washington Marches to Jesse Jackson*, London: Verso.

―――― (1992), *Black America: Multiracial Democracy in the Age of Clarence Thomas, David Duke and the L.A. Uprisings*, Open Magazine Pamphlet Series.

―――― (1993), 'Beyond Racial Identity Politics: Towards a Liberation Theory for Multicultural Democracy', *Race and Class*, 35(1).
Marginson, S. (1993), *Education and Public Policy in Australia*, Cambridge: Cambridge University Press.
Martin, J. (1981), 'Relative Deprivation: A Theory of Distributive Injustice for an Era of Shrinking Resources', *Research in Organizational Behaviour*, 3(4).
Marx, Karl (1958), *The 18th Brumaire of Lois Bonaparte, Selected Works*, Moscow: Foreign Language Publishing House, Vol. 1.
―――― (1959), *Capital*, Moscow: Foreign Languages Publishing House, Vol. 3.
Marx, Karl and Engels, F. (1965), *The German Ideology*, London: Lawrence & Wishart.
Mason, D. (1986), 'Introduction: Controversies and Continuities in Race and Ethnic Relations Theory', in John Rex and D. Mason, *Theories of Race and Ethnic Relations*, Cambridge: Cambridge University Press.
McRobbie, A. (1978), 'Working Class Girls and the Culture of Femininity', in Womens Studies Group (ed.), *Women Take Issue*, London: Hutchinson.
Melson, Robert and Wolpe, Howard (1970), 'Modernization and the Politics of Communalism: A Theoretical Perspective', *American Political Science Review*, 34(4).
Mendaki (1990), *Yayasan Mendaki Annual Report*, Singapore.
Mercer, J. R. (1988), *Labelling the Mentally Retarded*, Berkeley: University of California Press.
Meszaros, Istavan (1989), *The Power of Ideology*, New York: Harvester Wheatsheaf.
Miksic, John (1985), *Archaeological Research on the Forbidden Hill: Excavations at Fort Canning 1984*, Singapore: National Museum.
Miller, S. M. and Roby, P. (1980), 'Poverty: Changing Social Stratification', in P. Townsend (ed.), *The Concept of Poverty*, London: Heinemann.
Mills, C. Wright (1943), 'The Professional Ideology of Social Pathologists', *American Journal of Sociology*, 49(2).
―――― (1972), *The Power Élite*, London: Oxford University Press.
Milne, R. S. (1981), *Politics in Ethnically Bipolar States*, Vancouver: University of British Columbia Press.
Milne, R. S. and Mauzy, D. (1990), *Singapore: The Legacy of Lee Kuan Yew*, Boulder: Westview Press.
Minchin, James (1986), *No Man is an Island*, Sydney: Allen & Unwin.
Mohd. Aris Haji Othman (1983), *The Dynamics of Malay Identity*, Kuala Lumpur: Universiti Kebangsaan Malaysia Press.
Mohamed Suffian bin Hashim (1988), *An Introduction to the Constitution of Malaysia*, Kuala Lumpur: Government Printing Office.
Mokhtar, Abdullah (1975), 'The Value of Malay Education', *Intisari*, 3(3).
Moore, R. (1989), 'Education, Employment and Recruitment', in R. Dale (ed.), *Framework for Teaching*, London: Edward Arnold.
Moorehouse, H. F. (1973), 'The Political Incorporation of the British Working Class: An Interpretation', *Sociology*, 7(3).
Mortimore, J. and Blackstone, T. (1982), *The Disadvantaged and Education*, London: Heinemann.
Mortimore, J. and Mortimore, P. (1986), 'Education and Social Class', in Rick Rogers (ed.), *Education and Social Class*, London: Falmer Press.
Mouffe, Chantel (ed.) (1979), *Gramsci and Marxist Theory*, London: Routledge & Kegan Paul.
―――― (1988), 'Radical Democracy: Modern or Postmodern?', in A. Ross (ed.),

*Universal Abandon? The Politics of Postmodernism*, Minneapolis: University of Minnesota Press.

Moynihan, Daniel (1965), *The Negro Family: The Case for National Action*, Washington DC: Government Printing Office.

―――― (ed.) (1968), *An Understanding of Poverty*, New York: Basic Books.

Muhammad Ikmal Said (1992), 'Ethnic Perspectives of the Left in Malaysia', in Loh Kok Wah and Joel Kahn (eds.), *Fragmented Vision: Culture and Politics in Contemporary Malaysia*, Sydney: Allen & Unwin.

Murray, Charles (1984), *Losing Ground: American Social Policy, 1950–1980*, New York: Basic Books.

Musgrove, F. (1977), *Margins of the Mind*, London: Metheun.

Muzaffar, Chandra (1984), 'Has the Communal Situation Worsened over the Last Decade', in Syed Hussein Ali (ed.), *Ethnicity, Class and Development*, Kuala Lumpur: Persatuan Sains Social Malaysia.

―――― (1986), 'Islamic Resurgence: A Global View', in Bruce Gale (ed.), *Readings in Malaysian Politics*, Kuala Lumpur: Pelanduk Publications.

―――― (1988), *Nation on Trial*, Penang: Aliran.

―――― (1989a), *The NEP: Development and Alternative Consciousness*, Penang: Aliran.

―――― (1989b), *Challenges and Choices in Malaysian Politics and Society*, Penang: Aliran.

Myrdal, Gunnar (1944), *An American Dilemma: The Negro Problem in Modern Democracy*, New York: Harper.

―――― (1968), *Asian Drama: An Inquiry into the Poverty of Nations*, London: Allen Lane.

Nagata, Judith (1974), 'What Is a Malay? Situational Selection of Ethnic Identity in a Plural Society', *American Ethnology*, 1(2).

―――― (1979), *Malaysian Mosaic: Perspectives from a Poly-ethnic Society*, Vancouver: University of British Columbia.

Nair, Devan (ed.) (1976), *Socialism That Works: The Singapore Way*, Singapore; Federal Publications.

Naronha, Llewellyn (1981), 'Educational Reality in Singapore: Manipulation or Management?', *Forum of Education*, 40(3).

Nash, Manning (1989), *The Cauldron of Ethnicity in the Modern World*, Chicago: University of Chicago Press.

National Convention of Singapore Malay/Muslim Professionals (NCSMMP) (1990), *Malay/Muslims in 21st Century Singapore: Prospects, Challenges and Directions*, Singapore: Stamford Press.

Nee, Victor and Sanders, J. (1985), 'The Road to Parity: Determinants of the Socio-economic Achievements of Asian Americans', *Ethnic and Racial Studies*, 8(6).

Neilson, Kai (1985), *Equality and Liberty: A Defence of Radical Egalitarianism*, New Jersey: Rowman & Allanhead.

Norman, Richard (1982), 'Does Equality Destroy Liberty?', in Keith Graham (ed.), *Contemporary Political Philosophy*, Cambridge: Cambridge University Press.

Oakes, J. (1988), 'Tracking in Maths and Science Education: A Structural Contribution to Unequal Schooling', in Linda Weiss (ed.), *Class, Race and Gender in American Education*, New York: State University of New York Press.

Ogbu, J. U. (1978), *Minority Education: The American in Cross-Culture Perspectives*, New York: Academic Press.

Owens, Craig (1983), 'The Discourse of Others: Feminists and Postmodernism', in Craig Owens (ed.), *Postmodern Culture*, London: Pluto Press.

Pang, Cheng Lian (1971), *Singapore's People's Action Party*, Kuala Lumpur: Oxford University Press.
Pang, Eng Fong and Lim, Linda (1977), *The Electronics Industry in Singapore*, Singapore: Chopmen.
Panitch, Leo (1979), 'The Development of Corporatism in Liberal Democracies', in P. Smitter and G. Lehmbruch (eds.), *Trends Toward Corporatist Intermediation*, London: Sage.
⎯⎯⎯ (1980), 'Recent Theorization of Corporatism: Reflections on a Growth Industry', *British Journal of Sociology*, 12(8).
Parker, Frank (1984), 'Racial Gerrymandering and Legislative Reapportionment', in Chandler Davidson (ed.), *Minority Vote Dilution*, Washington DC: Howard University Press.
Parkinson, B. (1975), 'Non-Economic Factors in the Economic Retardation of the Rural Malays', *Modern Asian Studies*, 1(1).
Pascall, Anthony H. (ed.) (1972), *Racial Discrimination in Economic Life*, n.p.: Heath.
Patterson, C. H. (1973), *Humanistic Education*, Englewood Cliffs: Prentice-Hall.
Patterson, Orlando (1977), *Ethnic Chauvanism: The Reactionary Impulse*, New York: Stein & Day.
Paul, Erick (1993), 'Prospects for Liberalization in Singapore', *Journal of Contemporary Asia*, 23(3).
Payne, Geoff (1987), *Mobility and Change in Modern Society*, London: Macmillan Press.
People's Action Party (1959), *The Tasks Ahead: The PAP's Five-Year Plan, 1959-1964*, Singapore: People's Action Party Central Executive Committee.
Pereira, Desmond (ed.) (1986), *Being and Becoming*, Singapore: Longman Publications.
Pettigrew, Thomas (1981), 'The Mental Health Impact', in B. Browser and R. Hunt (eds.), *Impact of Racism on White Americans*, Beverly Hills: Sage.
Phua, Kai Hong (1990), *Privatization and Restructuring of Health Services in Singapore*, Singapore: Institute of Policy Studies.
Pitkin, Hanna (1967), *The Concept of Representation*, Berkeley: University of California Press.
Pitsuwan, Surin (1990), *Islam amd Malay Nationalism: A Case Study of the Malay Muslims of Southern Thailand*, Cambridge: Harvard University Press.
Policy Options Study Group (1988), *Policy Options for the Singapore Economy*, Singapore: McGraw Hill.
Polsby, Nelson (1980), *Community Power and Political Theory: A Further Look at Problems of Evidence and Inference*, New Haven: Yale University Press.
Poulantzas, Nicos (1973), *Political Power and Social Classes*, London: New Left Books.
Preston, M.; Henderson, L.; and Puryear, P. (1987), *The New Black Politics*, New York: Longman.
Quah, Jon S. T. (1988), *Religion and Religious Conversion in Singapore: A Review of the Literature*, Report prepared for the Ministry of Community Development, Singapore.
⎯⎯⎯ (ed.) (1990), *In Search of Singapore's National Values*, Singapore: Institute of Policy Studies.
Quah, Jon S. T.; Chan Heng Chee; and Seah Chee Meow (eds.) (1985), *Government and Politics of Singapore*, Singapore: Oxford University Press.
Quah, Stella et al. (1991), *Social Class in Singapore*, Singapore: Times Academic Press.

Rabushka, Alvin (1971), 'Integration in Urban Malaya: Ethnic Attitudes Among Malays and Chinese', *Journal of Asian and African Studies*, 6(2).
Rahim, Lily Z. (1994a), 'Consent, Coercion and Constitutional Engineering in Singapore', *Current Affairs Bulletin*, 70(7).
_____ (1994b), 'The Paradox of Ethnic-Based Self-Help Groups', in D. Da Cunha (ed.), *Debating Singapore*, Singapore: Institute of Southeast Asian Studies.
Rainwater, Lee (1970), *Behind Ghetto Walls: Black Life in a Federal Slum*, Chicago: Aldino.
Rajaratnam, S. (1989), 'Be Problem Solvers, Not Populists', *Petir*, January.
Ramesh, M. (1992), 'Social Security in Singapore: Redrawing the Public/Private Boundary', *Asian Survey*, 32(12).
Rawls, John (1971), *A Theory of Justice*, Cambridge: Harvard University Press.
Regnier, Philippe (1991), *Singapore: City State in Southeast Asia*, London: Hurst.
Reid, Ivan (1986), *The Sociology of School and Education*, London: Fontana.
Reid, Linda (1988), *The Politics of Education in Malaysia*, Monograph Series, Political Science Department, University of Tasmania, Hobart: University of Tasmania.
Rex, John and Mason, David (1986), *Theories of Race and Ethnic Relations*, Cambridge: Cambridge University Press.
Rex, John and Tomlinson, Sally (1979), *Colonial Immigrants in a British City: A Class Analysis*, London: Routledge & Kegan Paul.
Reynolds, Farley (1984), *Blacks and Whites: Narrowing the Gap*, Cambridge: Harvard University Press.
Rist, Ray (1970), 'Student Social Class and Teacher Expectations: The Self-Fulfilling Prophecy in Ghetto Schools', *Harvard Educational Review*, 40(3).
Robinson, R.; Higgott, R.; and Hewison, K. (1987), *Southeast Asia in the 1980s: The Politics of Economic Crisis*, Sydney: Allen & Unwin.
Rodan, Gary (1989), *Political Economy of Singapore's Industrialization*, London: Macmillan.
_____ (1990), 'Singapore: Continuity in Change as the New Guard's Agenda Becomes Clearer', in *Southeast Asian Affairs*, Singapore: Institute of Southeast Asain Studies.
_____ (1992), 'Singapore's Leadership Transition: Erosion or Refinement of Authoritarian Rule?', *Bulletin of Concerned Asian Scholars*, 24(1).
Rodkin, Philip (1993), 'The Psychological Reality of Social Construction', *Ethnic and Racial Studies*, 16(4).
Roff, William R. (1980), *The Origins of Malay Nationalism*, Kuala Lumpur: University of Malaya Press.
_____ (1985), 'Kaum Muda–Kaum Tua: Innovation and Reaction amongst the Malays, 1900–1941', in A. Ibrahim; S. Siddique; and Y. Hussain (eds.), *Readings on Islam in Southeast Asia*, Singapore: Institute of Southeast Asian Studies.
Rorty, Amelie (1992), 'Power and Powers: A Dialogue between Buff and Rebuff', in T. Wartenberg (ed.), *Rethinking Power*, New York: State University of New York Press.
Rosa, L. (1990), 'The Singapore State and Trade Union Incorporation', *Journal of Contemporary Asia*, 20(4).
Rose, H. and Rose, R. (1979), 'The I.Q. Myth', in D. Rubinstein (ed.), *Education and Equality*, Harmondsworth: Penguin.
Rothchild, Joseph (1981), *Ethnopolitics: A Conceptual Framework*, New York: Columbia University Press.

Roy, Denny (1994), 'Singapore, China and the Soft Authoritarian Challenge', *Asian Survey*, 34(3).
Runciman, W. G. (1966), *Relative Deprivation and Social Justice*, London: Routledge & Kegan Paul.
Rutter, M. et al. (eds.) (1979), *15,000 Hours: Secondary School and the Effects on Children*, London: Open Books.
Ryan, William (1971), *Blaming the Victim*, New York: Pantheon.
―――― (1976), 'Blaming the Victim: The Current Ideology of United States Racism', in W. Barclay; K. Kumar; and R. Sims (eds), *Racial Conflict, Discrimination and Power*, New York: AMS Press.
Said, Edward W. (1978) *Orientalism*, Harmondsworth: Penguin.
Salaff, Janet (1988), *State and Family in Singapore: Restructuring a Developing Society*, Ithaca: Cornell University Press.
Sanchirion, A. (1991), 'The Importance of Small Business Ownership in Chinese–American Educational Achievement', *Sociology of Education*, 64(8).
Sandhu, Kernial Singh and Wheatley, Paul (eds.) (1989), *Management of Success: The Moulding of Modern Singapore*, Singapore: Institute of Southeast Asian Studies.
Sarup, Madan (1983), *Marxism, Structuralism, Education: Theoretical Developments in the Sociology of Education*, London: Falmer Press.
Sasson, Anne (1982), *Approaches to Gramsci*, London: Writers and Readers Publishing Cooperative Society Limited.
Saw, Swee Hock (1969), 'Population Trends in Singapore', *Journal of Southeast Asian History*, 30(9).
―――― (1970), *Singapore Population in Transition*, Philadelphia: University of Pennsylvania Press.
Scarman, Lord (1984), 'Minority Rights in a Plural Society', in Ben Whittaker (ed.), *Minorities: A Question of Human Rights*, London: Pergamon Press.
Schaar, John (1981), *Legitimacy in the Modern State*, n.p.: Transaction Books.
Seah, Chee Meow (1973), *Community Centres in Singapore: The Political Involvement*, Singapore: Singapore University Press.
Seah, Chee Meow and Partoatmodjo, Soeratno (1974), *Higher Education in the Changing Environment: Case Studies: Singapore and Indonesia*. Singapore: Regional Institute of Higher Education and Development.
Sedlak, M. et al. (1986), *Selling Students Short*, New York: Teachers College Press.
Selvan, T. S. (1990), *Singapore: The Ultimate Island*, Sydney: Freeway Books.
Senu Abdullah (1971), *Revolusi Mental*, Kuala Lumpur.
Seow, Francis (1994), *To Catch A Tartar*, New Haven: Yale University Press.
Shaharuddin Ma'arof (1988), *Malay Ideas on Development*, Singapore: Times Books.
Sharom Ahmad and Wong, James (eds.) (1974), *Malay Participation in the National Development of Singapore*, Singapore: Eurasia Press.
Sharp, Rachel (ed.) (1986), *Capitalist Crisis and Schooling*, Sydney: Macmillan.
Siddique, Sharon and Suryadinata, Leo (1982), 'Bumiputra and Pribumi: Economic Nationalism (Indigenism) in Malaysia and Indonesia', *Pacific Affairs*, 54(4).
Sidek Saniff (1989), 'Upgrading the Educational Performance of Malay/Muslim Pupils', *Fajar Islam (Journal of Muslim Issues in Singapore)*, 2.
Silcock, T. H. (1959), *The Commonwealth Economy in Southeast Asia*, Durham: Duke University Press.
Simon, Roger (1982), *Gramsci's Political Thought*, London: Lawrence & Wisart.
Singapore Federation of Chinese Clan Associations (SFCCA) and Singapore

Chinese Chamber of Commerce and Industry (SCCI) (1991), *Lee Kuan Yew on the Chinese Community in Singapore*, Singapore.

Singh, Bilveer (1992a), *Whither PAP's Dominance*, Petaling Jaya: Pelanduk Publications.

_____ (1992b), 'A Small State's Quest for Security', in Ban Kah Choon et al. (eds.), *Imagining Singapore*, Singapore: Times Academic Press.

Sjoblom, Gunnar (1988), 'Some Democratic Regime Norms and Their Relations', in Dag Anckar; Hanna Nurmi; and Matti Wibergi (eds.), *Rationality and Legitimacy*, Helsinki: Finnish Political Science Association.

Slavin, R. and Madden, N. (1986), 'The Integration of Students with Mild Academic Handicaps in Regular Classrooms', *Prospects*, 16(4).

Smith, Anthony (1981), *The Ethnic Revival in the Modern World*, Cambridge: Cambridge University Press.

_____ (1988), 'The Myth of the Modern Nation', *Ethnic and Racial Studies*, 25(9).

Smith, H. and Kennedy, W. (1967), 'Effects of Three Educational Programs in Mentally Retarded Children', *Perceptual and Motor Skills*, 24(5).

Sniderman, Paul M. (1985), *Race and Inequality*, n.p.: Chatham House Publications.

Snow, C. E.; Dubber, C.; and De Blauw, A. (1982), 'Routines in Mother Child Interaction', in Lynne Feagans and Dale Farran (eds.), *The Language of Children Reared in Poverty*, New York: Academic Press.

Soffer, Arnon (1983), 'The Changing Situation of Majority and Minority and Its Spacial Expression—The Case of the Arab Minority in Israel', in Nurit Kliot and S. Waterman (eds.), *Pluralism and Political Geography*, New York: Croom Helm.

Solomos, John (1988), *Black Youth, Racialism and the State*, Cambridge: Cambridge University Press.

Soon, Teck Wee (1988), *The New Education Policy*, Singapore: Institute of Southeast Asian Studies.

Sopiee, Noordin (1974), *From Malayan Union to Singapore Separation: Political Unification in the Malaysian Region, 1945–1965*, Kuala Lumpur: University of Malaya Press.

Sorensen, A. and Hallinan, M. (1986), 'Effects of Ability Grouping on Growth in Academic Achievement', *American Educational Research Journal*, 23(8).

Sorokin, P. A. (1927), *Social Mobility*, New York: Harper & Brothers.

_____ (1959), *Social and Cultural Mobility*, New York: Free Press.

Southern, David (1988), *Gunnar Myrdal and Black–White Relations*, Baton Rouge: Louisiana State University Press.

Sowell, Thomas (1981), *Ethnic America: A History*, New York: Basic Books.

_____ (1983), *The Economics and Politics of Race*, New York: Basic Books.

_____ (1984), *Civil Rights: Rhetoric or Reality?*, New York: Morrow.

Stepan, A. (1988), *The State and Society: Peru in Comparative Perspective*, Princeton: Princeton University Press.

Stockwell, A. J. (1982), 'The White Man's Burden and Brown Humanity: Colonialism and Ethnicity in British Malaya', *Southeast Asian Journal of Social Science*, 10(1).

Suhrke, A. and Noble, N. (1977), *Ethnic Conflict in International Relations*, New York: Praeger Publications.

Sullivan, Gerard and Gunasekaran, Subbiah (1993), 'The Role of Ethnic Relations and Education Systems in Migration from Southeast Asia to Australia', *Sojourn*, 8(2).

Swettenham, Frank (1900), *The Real Malay*, London: John Lane.

_____ (1955), *British Malaya: An Account of the Origin and Process of British Influence in Malaya*, London: George Allen.
Syed Husin Ali (ed.) (1975), *Malay Peasant Society and Leadership*, Kuala Lumpur: Oxford University Press.
_____ (1984), *Ethnicity, Class and Development*, Kuala Lumpur: Persatuan Sains Social Malaysia.
Tajfel, Henri (1974), *Intergroup Behaviour, Social Comparison and Social Change*, Ann Arbor: University of Michigan.
_____ (1985), *The Social Psychology of Minorities*, Report No. 38, London: Minorities Rights Group.
Tajfel, Henri and Turner, J. C. (1979), *An Integrative Theory of Intergroup Conflict: The Social Psychology of Intergroup Relations*, Monterey: Brooks & Cole.
Tan, Bee Geok (1989), 'The Gifted Education Programme', *Commentary*, 8 (1 and 2).
Tan, Chee Beng, 'Nation-Building and Being Chinese in a Southeast Asian State: Malaysia', in Jennifer Cushman and Wang Gungwu (eds.), *Changing Identities of the Southeast Asian Chinese Since World War 2*, Hong Kong: Hong Kong University Press.
Tapper, Ted and Salter, Brian (1978), *Education and the Political Order*, London: Macmillam Press.
Tay, Eng Soon (1989), 'The Ends and Means of Education', *Commentary*, 8(1).
Taylor, William (1980), *Teacher Education in Singapore 1980: The Role of the Institute of Education*, Singapore: Institute of Education.
Terman, Lewis (1924), 'The Conservation of Talent', *School and Society*, 19(4).
Thomas, Murray (1983), 'The Symbol of Politics and Education', in Murray Thomas (ed.), *Politics and Education*, Oxford: Pergamon Press.
Thurow, Lester C. (1972), 'Education and Economic Equality', *Public Interest*, 12(6).
_____ (1981), *The Zero Sum Society*, New York: Penguin.
Tobias, Shiela (1978), *Overcoming Math Anxiety*, New York: W. W. Norton.
Tomlinson, S. (1982), *A Sociology of Special Education*, London: Routledge & Kegan Paul.
Townsend, H. and Brittain, E. (1972), *Organisation and Multiracial Schools*, Slough: NFER.
Trainer, F. E. (1985), *Abandon Affluence*, London: Zed Books.
Tremewan, Christopher (1994), *The Political Economy of Social Control in Singapore*, London: Macmillan.
Troyna, Barry (1978), 'Race and Streaming: A Case Study', *Educational Review*, 30(1).
_____ (1989), *Racial Inequality in Education*, London: Tavistock Publications.
Tumin, Melvin (1979), *Comparative Perspectives on Race Relations*, Boston: Little, Brown & Banfield.
Turnbull, C. M. (1977), *A History of Singapore 1819–1975*, Kuala Lumpur: Oxford University Press.
Turner, Bryan (1986), *Equality*, London: Ellis Harwood.
_____ (1990), 'Periodization and Politics in the Postmodern', in B. Turner (ed.), *Theories of Modernity and Post-Modernity*, London: Sage.
Ungku Abdul Aziz (1959), *Rencana-Rencana Ekonomi dan Kemiskinan*, Kuala Lumpur: Pustaka Antara.
_____ (1974), 'Footprints on the Sands of Time—The Malay Poverty Concept over Fifty Years from Zaaba to Aziz and the Second Malaysian Five-year

Plan', in *Malaysian Economic Development and Policies*, Kuala Lumpur: Malaysian Economic Association.

Urry, John (1982), *The Anatomy of Capitalist Societies*, London: Macmillan.

Useem, M. (1984), *The Inner Circle: Large Corporations and the Rise of Business Political Activity in the U.S. and U.K.*, New York: Oxford University Press.

Vallance, Elizabeth (1983), 'Hiding the Hidden Curriculum: An Interpretation of the Language of Justification in the Nineteenth Century Educational Reform', in Henry Giroux and D. Purpel, *The Hidden Curriculum and Moral Education*, Berkeley: McCutchan Publications.

Van den Berg, Pierre (1978), 'Race and Ethnicity: A Sociobiological Perspective', *Ethnic and Racial Studies*, 1(4).

Vasil, Raj (1971), *Politics in a Plural Society*, Oxford: Oxford University Press.

_____ (1992), *Governing Singapore*, Singapore: Times Books.

Vatikiotis, Michael (1993), *Indonesian Politics under Suharto*, London: Routledge.

Verba, Sidney and Pie, Norman (1972), *Participation in America: Political Democracy and Social Equality*, New York: Harper & Row.

Vlieland, C. A. (1932), *A Report on the 1931 Census and on Certain Problems of Vital Statistics*, London.

Walford, G. (1990), *Privatization and Privilege in Education*, London: Routledge.

Waltrous, Mary (1984), 'Excellence in Schools: A Matter of Who is Taught', *Education Digest*, 13(4).

Walzer, Michael (1979), 'Nervous Liberals', *The New York Review of Books*, 26(15).

Wang, M. (1982), *Effective Mainstreaming is Possible—Provided That ...*, Pittsburg: University of Pittsburg Press.

Wan Hashim (1983), *Race Relations in Malaysia*, Singapore: Heinemann Educational Books.

Wan Hussein Zoohri (1990), *The Singapore Malays: The Dilemma of Development*, Singapore: Singapore Malay Teachers Union.

Watson, Hugh Seton (1977), *Nations and States: An Enquiry into the Origins of Nations and the Politics of Nationalism*, London: Methuen.

Watson, Keith (ed.) (1984), *Dependence and Interdependence in Education*, London: Croom Helm.

Waxman, Chaim (ed.) (1968), *The End of Ideology Debate*, New York: Funk & Wagnalls.

Wee, Viviene (1976), 'Buddhism in Singapore', in Riaz Hassan (ed.), *Singapore: Society in Transition*, Kuala Lumpur: Oxford University Press.

Weeks, Richard (ed.) (1978), *Muslim Peoples: A World Ethnographic Survey*, Westport: Greenwood Press.

Weiner, R. R. (ed.) (1981), *Cultural Marxism and Political Sociology*, London: Sage.

Weis, Lois (1985), *Between Two Worlds: Black Students in an Urban Community College*, Boston: Routledge & Kegan Paul.

_____ (ed.) (1988), *Class, Race and Gender in American Education*, New York: State University of New York Press.

Welch, Anthony (1991), 'Knowledge and Legitimation in Comparative Education', *Comparative Education Review*, 12(7).

Wenger, Morton (1980), 'State Responses to Afro-American Rebellion: Internal Neo-Colonialism and the Rise of the New Black Petite Bourgeosie', *Insurgent Sociologist*, 10(2).

Werbner, Prina and Anwar, M. (eds.) (1991), *Black and Ethnic Leadership in Britain*, London: Routledge.

Wertheim, W. (1959), *Indonesian Society in Transition*, The Hague: E. J. Brill.

Westergaard, J. and Resler, H. (1975), *Class in a Capitalist Society: A Study of Contemporary Britain*, London: Heinemann.

Wetherell, M. and Potter, J. (1992), *Mapping the Language of Racism*, London: Harvester Wheatsheaf.

Wexler, P. and Grabiner, G. (1986), 'The Education Question: America during the Crisis', in R. Sharp (ed.), *Capitalist Crisis and Schooling*, Sydney: Macmillan.

Weyland, Petra (1991), 'International Muslim Networks and Islam in Singapore', *Sojourn*, 5(2).

Wilensky, Harold (1981), 'Democratic Corporatism, Consensus and Social Policy', in Harold Wilensky (ed.), *The Welfare State in Crisis*, Paris: Organisation for Economic Cooperation and Development.

Wilkinson, B. (1988), 'Social Engineering in Singapore', *Journal of Contemporary Asia*, 18(2).

Willard, Hanna (1970), *The Malays of Singapore*, Washington: American University Field Staff Reports Service.

Williams, Jenny (1985), 'Redefining Institutional Racism', *Ethnic and Racial Studies*, 8(3).

_____ (1986), 'Education and Race: The Racialization of Class Inequalities?', *British Journal of Sociology of Education*, 7(2).

_____ (1987), 'The Construction of Women and Black Students as Educational Problems: Re-evaluating Policy on Gender and Race', in M. Arnot and G. Weiner (eds.), *Gender and the Politics of Schooling*, London: Hutchinson.

Willis, Paul (1977), *Learning to Labour—How Working-Class Kids Get Working-Class Jobs*, London: Saxon House.

_____ (1983), 'Cultural Production and Theories of Reproduction', in Len Barton and and Stephen Walker (eds.), *Race, Class and Education*, London: Croom Helm.

Willmott, W. E. (1989), 'The Emergence of Nationalism', in Kernial Singh Sandhu and Paul Wheatley (eds.), *Management of Success: The Moulding of Modern Singapore*, Singapore: Institute of Southeast Asian Studies.

Wilson, Edward O. (1976), *Sociobiology—The New Synthesis*, Cambridge: Harvard University Press.

Wilson, James Q. (1966), *The Negro in American Politics: The Present in the American Negro Reference Book*, Englewood Cliffs: Prentice-Hall.

Wilson, William (1973), *Power, Racism and Privilege: Race Relations in Theoretical and Socio-Historical Perspectives*, New York: Macmillan.

_____ (1978), *The Declining Significance of Race*, Chicago: University of Chicago Press.

_____ (1989), *The Truly Disadvantaged*, Chicago: University of Chicago Press.

Winstedt, Richard (1929), 'More Notes on Malay Magic', *Journal of the Malayan Branch of the Royal Asiatic Society*, 7(4).

_____ (1938), *Malaya and Its History*, London: Anchor Press.

_____ (1981), *The Malays—A Cultural History*, Singapore: Graham Brash.

Wirth, Lois (1960), 'Preface', in Karl Mannhein, *Ideology and Utopia*, London: Routledge & Kegan Paul.

Wong, Evelyn (1983), 'Industrial Relations in Singapore: Challenges for the 1980s', in *Southeast Asian Affairs*, Singapore: Institute of Southeast Asian Studies.

Wong, Ruth (1974), *Educational Innovation in Singapore*, Paris: UNESCO Press.
Woodwiss, A. (1990), 'Re-Reading Japan: Capitalism, Possession and the Necessity of Hegemony', in Nicholas Abercrombie et al. (ed.), *Dominant Ideologies*, London: Unwin & Hyman.
Workie, Abaineh (1974), 'The Relative Productivity of Cooperation and Competition', *Journal of Social Psychology*, 92(8).
Worsley, Peter (1984), *The Three Worlds*, London: Weidenfeld & Nicolson.
Wu, David, Y. H. (1982), 'Ethnic Relations and Ethnicity in a City State', in David Y. H. Wu. (ed.), *Ethnicity and the Interpersonal Interaction—A Cross-Cultural Study*, Singapore: Maruzen Asia.
Wu, Yuan-li and Wu, Chun-hsi (1980), *Economic Development in Southeast Asia: The Chinese Dimension*, Stanford: Hoover Institution Press.
Yayasan Mendaki, *Aspire*, Singapore: Mendaki, various issues.
Yee, Albert H. (1992), *A People Misruled: The Chinese Stepping Stone Syndrome*, Singapore: Heinemann Asia.
Yeo, Kim Wah (1969), 'A Study of Three Early Political Parties in Singapore, 1945–1955', *Journal of Southeast Asian History*, 8(4).
Young, Loretta and Bagleg, Christopher (1982), 'Self-Esteem, Self-Concept, and the Development of Black Identity: A Theoretical Overview', in G. Verma and C. Bagley (eds.), *Self-Concept, Achievement, and Multicultural Education*, London: Macmillan Press.
Young, Michael (1973), 'Curricula and the Social Organisation of Knowledge', in R. Brown (ed), *Knowledge, Education and Cultural Change*, London: Tavistock.
_____ (ed.) (1978), *Knowledge and Control*, London: Collier & Macmillan.
Zainal Abidin bin Ahmad (1959), 'The Poverty of the Malays', translated in *Prosa Melayu Modern*, London: Longman, Green.
Zainal Abidin Wahid (ed.) (1970), *Glimpses of Malaysian History*, Kuala Lumpur: Dewan Bahasa dan Pustaka.
Zainal Kling (ed.) (1977), *Masyarakat Melayu Antara Tradisi dan Perubuhan*, Kuala Lumpur: Utusan Publications.
Zigler, E. (1970), 'Social Class and the Socialization Process', *Review of Educational Research*, 40(12).
Zuckerman, M. (1990), 'Some Dubious Promises in Research and Theory on Racial Differences', *American Psychologist*, 45(12).

## Unpublished Sources

Abdul Aziz bin Mohamed Yusuf (1990), 'Academic Motivation, Perception of Parental Pressure and the Academic Achievement of Malay Pupils', M.Edu. thesis, National University of Singapore.
Abu Bakar bin Alias (1969), 'Malay School Leavers in Singapore', BA thesis, University of Singapore.
Aljuneid, S. Zahra (1980), 'Ethnic Distribution of Employment in Singapore: The Malays', B.Econs thesis, National University of Singapore.
Asher, Mukul (1991), 'Planning for the Future: The Welfare System in a New Phase of Development', Paper presented at the Conference on Political and Economic Watersheds in Industrialising Singapore, Murdoch University, Perth.
Bambang Sugeng bin Kajairi (1989), 'The New Generation of Leaders in Singapore', BA (Hons.) thesis, National University of Singapore.
Bedlington, Stanley (1974), 'The Singapore Malay Community: The Politics of State Integration', Ph.D. thesis, Cornell University.

Betts, Russell (1975), 'Multiracialism, Meritocracy, and the Malays in Singapore', Ph.D. thesis, Massachusetts Institute of Technology.

Birch, David (1991), 'Singapore Media: Middle Class Citizenship and Crisis Discourse', Paper presented at the Conference on Political and Economic Watersheds in Industrialising Singapore, Murdoch University, Perth.

Birrel, R. and Seitz, A (1986), 'The Ethnic Problem in Education: The Emergence and Definition of an Issue', Paper presented at the Ethnicity and Multiculturalism Conference, Australian Institute of Multicultural Affairs, Melbourne.

Brown, David (1991), 'The Corporatist Management of Ethnicity in Contemporary Singapore', Paper presented at the Conference on Political and Economic Watersheds in Industrialising Singapore, Murdoch University, Perth.

Cheah, Hock Beng (1977), 'A Study of Poverty in Singapore', MA thesis, University of Singapore.

Chew, Joy Oon-Ai (1978), 'The Bataks in Singapore—A Study of Group Cohesion and Assimilation', M.Soc.Sc. thesis, University of Singapore.

―――― (1988), 'Moral Education in a Singapore Secondary School', Ph.D. thesis, Monash University.

Chiam, Tat Liang (1985), 'Ideology and Educational Change in Singapore', B.Soc.Sc. thesis, National University of Singapore.

Clammer, John (1991), 'Deconstructing Values: The Establishment of a National Ideology and Its Implications for Singapore's Political Future', Paper presented at the Conference on Political and Economic Watersheds in Industrialising Singapore, Murdoch University, Perth.

Clyne, Fiona and Woock, Roger (1993), 'Education for All—With Money to Pay', Proceedings of the 21st Annual International Conference of the Australian and New Zealand Comparative and International Education Society, University of Wollongong.

Figueroa, P. M. (1974), 'West Indian School-Leavers in London: A Sociological Study of Ten Schools in a London Borough, 1966–1967', Ph.D. thesis, University of London.

Ganapathy, A. (1988), 'Factors Outside the School Environment that Influence the Education of Indian Children', Paper presented at the Sixth Tamil Youth Seminar on the Educational Upliftment of Our Children, Singapore.

Gomez, James (1992), 'The Political Significance of Values Education in Singapore Schools', B.Soc.Sc. thesis, National University of Singapore.

Guskin, Judith (1971), 'The Social Perception of Language Variation: Black and White Teacher Attitudes towards Speakers from Different Racial and Social Class Backgrounds', Ph.D. thesis, University of Michigan.

Heng, Russell Hiang Khng (1990), 'Give Me Liberty or Give Me Wealth: An Essay on the Role of the Singapore Middle-Class in Political Development'.

Heng, Siew Hwee (1985), 'Educational Streaming in Primary School', B.Soc.Sc. thesis, National University of Singapore.

Jesudason, James (1993), 'Ethnicity and the Political Economy of Malaysia and Singapore', Paper presented at the Conference on Democracy, Ethnicity and Development in South and Southeast Asia, International Centre for Ethnic Studies, Colombo.

Johari, Hashima (1984), 'The Emerging Malay Social Structure in Singapore', MA thesis, National University of Singapore.

Kassim, Yang Razali (1979), 'Education and the Malays of Singapore, 1959–1979', B.Soc.Sc. thesis, National University of Singapore.

Kay, Swee Kee (1971), 'Life in School Survey', BA thesis, University of Singapore.
Khong, Cho Onn (1989), 'Values and Beliefs in the Singapore Polity', Paper presented at the Young Staff Lecture Series, Faculty of Arts and Social Sciences, National University of Singapore.
Khoo, Roland (1988), 'Management of Ethnic Relations in Singapore: Change in 1986', B.Soc.Sc. thesis, National University of Singapore.
Lim, Michael Teck Hau (1993), 'Forever Insecure: Race and Religion as Fundamental Determining Variables in Singapore's Foreign Relations with Malaysia, Indonesia, China and the United States', MA thesis, University of Sydney.
Lim, Puay Yin (1988), 'Independent Schools in Singapore and the Pursuit of Excellence in Education', B.Soc.Sc. thesis, National University of Singapore.
MacDougall, J. (1975), 'Technocrats as Modernizers: The Economic Development of Indonesia', Ph.D. thesis, University of Michigan.
MacDougall, John Arthur (1968), 'Shared Burdens: A Study of Communal Discrimination by the Political Parties of Malaysia and Singapore', Ph.D. thesis, Harvard University.
Mannarlingham, T. (1989), 'Access to Higher Education: A Case Study of the National University of Singapore', B.Soc.Sc. thesis, National University of Singapore.
Mariam Mohd. Ali (1985), 'Orang Baru and Orang Lama: Ways of Being Malay on Singapore's North Coast', B.Soc.Sc. thesis, National University of Singapore.
_____ (1990), 'Ways of Being Muslim in Singapore', MA thesis, National University of Singapore.
Myers, J. (1976), 'The Special Day School Placements for High I.Q. and Low I.Q. Educationally Mentally Retarded Pupils', Paper presented at the Annual Convention of the Council for Exceptional Children, Chicago.
National University of Singapore Students Union (NUSSU) (1984), 'Petition to Oppose the Graduate Mothers Scheme'.
Nurliza Yusuf (1986), 'Being Malay in Singapore: Perceptions and Articulations of Identity', B.Soc.Sc. thesis, National University of Singapore.
Pang, Keng Fong (1984), 'The Malay Royals of Singapore', B.Soc.Sc. thesis, National University of Singapore.
Pillay, Chandrasekaran (1974), 'Protection of the Malay Community: A Study of UMNO's Position and Opposition Attitudes', M.Soc.Sc. thesis, Universiti Sains Malaysia.
Quah, Marilyn Mayling, (1988), 'An Evaluation of the Implementation of a Curriculum for Slow Learning Primary School Children in Singapore', Ph.D. thesis, University of Queensland.
Rahim, Lily Z. (1991a), 'The Educational Marginality of the Indigenous Malay Community in Singapore', Proceedings of the 21st Annual International Conference of the Australian and New Zealand Comparative and International Education Society, University of Wollongong.
_____ (1991b), 'Political Representation of Malay Interests in Singapore', Paper presented at the Malaysia Society Colloqium, University of Melbourne.
_____ (1993), 'The Politicisation of the Education System in Singapore', Paper presented at the New Zealand Asian Studies Association Conference, Victoria University of Wellington.
_____ (1994), 'Containment of Malay Politics in Singapore', Paper presented at the Asia–Pacific Peace Research Association Conference, Penang.

_____ (1995a), 'The Politics of Cultural Engineering in Singapore', Paper presented at the Annual Conference of the Malaysia Social Science Association, Universiti Sains Malaysia.

_____ (1995b), 'The 1995 Elections and the Politics of Pragmatism', Paper presented at the Ninth Malaysia Society Colloquium, University of New England.

_____ (1996), 'In Search of the Asian Way: Cultural National and the Construction of Identity in Singapore and Malaysia', Paper presented at the International Conference on the Future of Nationalism and the State, University of Sydney.

_____ (1997), 'The Singapore Malay Identity', Paper presented at the Seminar on Islam, Identities and Politics in Southeast Asia, European Committee for Human Rights in Malaysia and Singapore, The Netherlands.

Ramakrishna, K. (1989), 'The Corporatist State: An Examination of the Concept and its Relevance to Singapore', BA thesis, National University of Singapore.

Ramesh, M. and Archaya, A. (1991), 'From Globalism to Regionalism: Implications for Security', Paper presented at the Conference on Political and Economic Watersheds in Industrialising Singapore, Murdoch University, Perth.

Rodan, Gary (1991), 'The Growth of Singapore's Middle Class and Its Political Significance', Paper presented at the Conference on Political and Economic Watersheds in Industrialising Singapore, Murdoch University, Perth.

Rosenau, James (1991), 'The New Global Order: Understanding and Outcomes', Paper presented at the 15th World Congress of the International Political Science Association, Buenos Aires.

Samsiah Sanip (1987), 'Educational Performance and Socialization in Malay Families: An Exploratory Study', B.Soc.Sc. thesis, National University of Singapore.

Saroja (1987), 'The Effect of Internal and External Factors on Student Academic Achievement in Singapore: A Research Proposal', Paper presented at the Sixth Seminar of the National University of Singapore Tamil Language Society on Tamil Language and Tamil Society in Singapore.

Saw, Swee Hock (1966), 'The Population of Singapore', MA thesis, University of Malaya.

Shaari bin Tadin (1987), 'A Sociological Study of Performance and Motivation of School Children in the Integrated Secondary School', M.Soc.Sc. thesis, National University of Singapore.

Soenarno, Raden (1959), 'The Political Attitudes of Malays before 1945', BA thesis, University of Malaya.

Suratman Markassan (1989), 'Pembangunan dan Masaalah Umat Islam Minoritas', Paper delivered at the Persidingan Antarabangsa Tamadun Melayu Ke-11th, Kuala Lumpur.

Suriani Suratman (1982), 'The Malay Problem: A Critical Overview', MA thesis, Monash University.

Tan, Rodney Kee Lian (1972), 'Impact of Relocation on HDB Tenants: A Case Study', M.Soc.Sc. thesis, University of Singapore.

Tan, Teng Lang (1983), 'The Evolving PAP Ideology: Beyond Democratic Socialism', B.Soc.Sc. thesis, National University of Singapore.

Tarrow, Sidney (1993), 'Collective Action and Social Movements', Paper presented at the University of Sydney Postgraduate Colloquium.

Useem, M. and Karabel, J. (1984), 'Educational Pathways through Top Corporate Management: Patterns of Stratification within Companies and

Differences among Companies', Paper presented at the American Sociological Association, San Antonio, Texas.

Yeo, Hock Quee (1982), 'Technocrats in Government: The Singapore Case', BA thesis, National University of Singapore.

Zahoor Ahmad bin Haji Fazal Hussein (1969), 'Policies and Politics in Malay Education in Singapore, 1951–1965, with Special Reference to the Development of the Secondary School System', M.Edu. thesis, University of Singapore.

# Index

ABBAS ABU AMIN, 95
Abdul Aziz Hussain, 245
Abdul Halim Kadir, 104
Abdullah, Datuk, 106
Abdullah Munshi, 50
Abdullah Tarmugi, 98–9, 111, 257–60;
  Israeli President's visit, 100; Mendaki
  chairperson, 32, 228, 229, 230; as
  minister, 98, 111, 187, 228, 229,
  230, 256
Abortion, 55
Accommodation politics, 93–5
ACIE, *see* Action Committee for Indian
  Education
Action Committee for Indian Education
  (ACIE), 172
*Adat*, 17
Adult Muslim Religious Students
  Association, *see* Perdaus
African–Americans, 52, 63, 68–9, 85, 93,
  158, 185, 243
Ahmad Boestemam, 14
Ahmad Halim, 90, 91
Ahmad Ibrahim, 88
Ahmad Mattar, 253–7; Israeli President's
  visit, 107, 112; Malay students, 166,
  187; Mendaki, 212, 228, 229, 230; as
  minister, 87, 88, 98, 101, 109, 110,
  212, 229
Alam Melayu, 13
Alatas, Syed Hussein, 60, 61
*Alat pemerentah*, 96, 99, 100
Al-Azhar University, 14
Alexander, K., 125
*Al-Imam*, 50
Ali Redha, 256
Aljuneid, S., 60
American Indians, 69, 245
American International Assurance, 144
Amir Jumabhoy, 245
Amnesty International, 45
AMP, *see* Association of Malay/Muslim
  Professionals

Anglo-Chinese School, 134, 141–2, 145,
  154, 155, 207, 210
Anson, 79, 89
Arabs, 18, 27, 50
ASEAN, 100, 106; students' programme,
  139, 155–6, 177–8
Asian values, 30, 32, 162–3, 179
*Asian Wall Street Journal*, 30, 44
*Asiaweek*, 30, 44, 88
Association for Muslim Welfare, *see*
  PITK
Association of Malay/Muslim Professionals
  (AMP), 85, 97; and Mendaki, 110, 216,
  225, 229; and PAP, 89, 108, 110, 230;
  and SAP, 130, 227; *see also* Mendaki;
  National Convention of Singapore
  Malay/Muslim Professionals
Association of Women for Action and
  Research (AWARE), 25
Australia: Aborigines, 69, 80, 245; White
  Australia Policy, 70
Autisitc children, 148
AWARE, *see* Association of Women for
  Action and Research
Aziz Nather, 219

BAHASA, 15
Baker, Donald, 69
*BAKTI*, 130
Barisan Socialis, 45, 75, 245
Barker-Lunn, J., 125
Bataks, 18, 27
Bedlington, Stanley, 15, 74
Bedok, 75, 76, 78, 91, 181
Bedok Town Secondary School, 222
*Berita Harian*, 102, 113
Betts, Russell, 62
Bhattacharya, S. K., 231
Bilingual policy, 119, 152
Bin, Dr, 35, 45
*Bintang Timor*, 62
Biological determinism, 24, 55, 184–5,
  187

# INDEX

Birth-rates, 3, 34, 72, 80–1; *see also* Population
Blake, Myrna, 41, 192, 204
Britain: colonial regime, 14; and Malays, 2, 27, 49–52, 61–2, 184–5; Nationality Act, 70; racial school quotas, 167; withdrawal of bases, 27, 46
Brown, Philip, 140, 204
Buang Omar Junid, 111
Bugis, 50
Bukit Timah Road, 76, 146, 157
*Bumiputra*, 2, 62, 71
Burhanuddin, 14
Bustanol Arifin Association, 111

CABINET APPOINTMENTS, 87–8
CATS, *see* Committee for Attracting Talent to Singapore
CCC, *see* Citizens' Consultative Committees
CDAC, *see* Chinese Development Assistance Council
CDC, *see* Community Development Council
Census: **1891**, 27; **1931**, 27; **1980**, 18, 96, 192, 211, 233; **1990**, 15–16, 192, 194
Central Provident Fund (CPF), 41, 47; Education Fund, 144–5; welfare funding, 228, 233, 236–7, 245
Chai Chee, 91
Chan Heng Chee, 81
Chandra Das, 131
Chao Yang Special School, 147, 148; *see also* Education system; Learning disabilities
Cheah Hock Beng, 41
Chee Soon Juan, 8, 35, 45; *see also* Singapore Democratic Party
Chen, John, 111, 136
Cheng, Vincent, 162
Cheung, Paul, 40, 188
Chew Sock Foon, 107
Chiam See Tong, 46, 81, 92, 100, 110, 158, 167, 183
Chia Thia Poh, 35, 45
Chiew Seen Kong, 107
Chinese: companies, 25; domination of society, 4, 55–6, 72; -educated, 103, 108, 170; electoral bias, 88, 91; housing, 21; immigrants, 3, 14, 55, 70, 72, 81; occupations, 19–20; perception of Malays, 57–8, 63; vulnerability, 5
Chinese Development Assistance Council (CDAC), 226, 227, 229, 233, 235, 236–9, 244
Chinese High School, 134, 135, 136, 142, 155

Chinese Language Review Committee (CLRC), 155, 171–3, 182
Chinese Press, 237
Chinese Teachers Association, 171
Chng Hee Kok, 110
Choo Wee Khiang, 153
Christian: missionaries, 162; priests, 34, 112
Christian Conference of Asia, 162
Citizens' Consultative Committees (CCC), 32, 46, 97
Civil: service, 25, 46–7, 59; society, 34, 35
Clan associations, 170, 237
CLRC, *see* Chinese Language Review Committee
Colonial society: structure, 50–1
Committee for Attracting Talent to Singapore (CATS), 72
Committee on Destitute Families, 41, 48, 203, 209
Communal voting, 85, 90–1, 103, 113
Community based organizations, 32, 232–9; financial assistance, 102–3, 111; Malay, 96–8, 229; politicization, 96–9
Community Centre Management Committees, 46
Community Chest, 48
Community Development Council (CDC), 35, 46
Confucianist values: and East Asia, 56, 63, 73; and education, 162–3, 168–9, 170; government policy, 3, 30, 32, 34, 44, 103, 112, 179
Constitutional position of Malays, 9, 13, 95
Consumer Price Index (CPI), 43, 47; *see also* Gross Domestic Product; Minimum Household Expenditure
Convent of the Holy Infant Jesus, 145
Corporatist state, 30–2
Corrupt Practices Investigation Bureau, 46
Cost Review Committee (CRC), 40
Council on Education of Muslim Children, *see* Mendaki
CPF, *see* Central Provident Fund
CPI, *see* Consumer Price Index
Crawfurd, John, 180, 185
CRC, *see* Cost Review Committee
Criticism of government: restrictions, 32–3
Cultural deficit thesis, 3–4, 24, 26; impact, 49–53, 58, 61, 62, 185–8, 206, 239–41, 248; 'lived reality', 3, 60; *see also* Marginality of Malays
Curriculum Development Institute, 152, 163, 181

# INDEX

Defence, 34, 106; expenditure, 44, 56, 113
Democracy, 1; PAP view, 30–1
Dhanabalan, S., 43, 81, 110
Dillingham, Gerald L., 85
Discrimination, 25, 26, 60
Divorce, 192, 209, 248
Domestic servants, 41
Drug addiction, 192, 209, 248
Dutch colonial regime, 14

East India Company, 185
Economic: growth, 34, 37; rationalism, 37
*Economist*, 30, 44
Educational: agenda, 117–20; marginality of Malays, 2–3, 19, 20–1, 26, 185–8, 191–202, 213–14, 249; policy-making, 120–3
Education system, 149–50; changes, 2, 119–23, 137–41; costs, 47, 118, 135, 141–5; early streaming, 8, 56, 119, 122, 123–8, 138, 140, 161, 198, 202; examination results, 200–2; expansion, 37; government control, 29, 35; hidden curriculum, 160, 179; and Malays, 3; moral education curriculum, 30, 162–3, 179; policy making, 120–3; politicization, 159–61; public discontent, 2; *see also* Free education; Gifted Education Programme; IQ tests; Junior colleges; Ministry of Education; Polytechnics; Universities
Edusave Scheme, 138, 142–3, 156, 157
Elected Presidency, 35; Bill, 42, 46; powers, 46
Elections: **1959**, 74; **1963**, 73–4; **1984**, 110, 158, 183; **1988**, 75–6, 103; **1991**, 79–80, 81, 103, 105, 108
Electoral clout: Malays, 4, 73–9, 86–7, 249
Élite programmes, 39; *see also* Education system
Embek Ali, 111
Emergency exercises, 34
Emigration, 2, 9, 27, 149
Employment: increase, 81; Malays, 25, 59, 190
Employment and Industrial Relations (Amendment) Act, 37, 46
English language: importance, 170–1, 173; and Malay students, 193–4; usage, 182, 190, 194, 221
Equal opportunity policy, 1, 2, 248; *see also* Meritocracy policy
Ethnic: -based welfare associations, 232–4, 247–8; bias, 132–3, 205–7, 248;
boundary maintenance, 25; minorities' political power, 68–70; minority leaders, 82–5; residential quotas, 75–7, 106, 248; school quotas, 166–8; stereotyping, 51
Eugenics beliefs, 55–6, 120, 132, 173–5, 184, 208, 218; *see also* Population
Eugenics Board, 55
Eunos, 76, 78, 105
Eurasian Association, 233
Eysenck, Hans, 63, 174

Families: Malay, 192, 204, 209; one-parent, 192, 209
*Far Eastern Economic Review*, 30, 44
FAS, *see* Financial Assistance Scheme
Fatalism, 60
Federation of Indian Muslims, 236
Federation of Malaya Agreement, 17
Feedback Unit, 134, 139
Financial Assistance Scheme (FAS), 141–2
Foreign: exchange turnover, 47; publications, 30, 32; workers, 55, 63, 72
Free education, 36; Malays, 18, 53, 62, 94–5, 112, 185, 190–1, 208, 215, 228, 229; *see also* Education system
Friedman, Milton, 38, 118
Fu, James, 74, 88

GDP, *see* Gross Domestic Product
Gender bias, 132–3
GEP, *see* Gifted Education Programme
Gerrymandering, 75
Geylang Serai, 73, 75, 86
Ghazali Shafie, 18–19
Gifted Education Programme (GEP), 8, 131–3, 154; *see also* Education system; IQ tests; Mendaki Enrichment Programme; Special Assistance Plan
GNP, *see* Gross National Product
Goh Chok Tong: Cabinet appointments, 87, 88; CDAC, 244; CDCs, 46; Confucianist values, 56; decision-making, 1–2; education system, 135, 143, 154, 170, 208–9; elections, 78, 81; ex-civil servant, 9; limits to criticism, 32; Malay MPs, 92–3, 105; and Malays, 101–2, 187; and Mendaki, 94, 102, 215, 226, 230, 231; political system changes, 36, 99, 108; social inequality, 38, 57; social welfare, 233, 235; *see also* Lee Kuan Yew
Goh Keng Swee, 37, 46, 56, 121, 183; *see also* Education system; Goh Report
Goh Kim Leong, 152
Goh Report, 121–2, 123, 124, 152; *see also*

Education system; Ministry of Education
Goods and Services Tax (GST), 43
Gopinathan, S., 160, 239
Graduate Mothers Policy, 56, 122, 158, 174–5; *see also* Education system; Eugenics beliefs; Population
GRC, *see* Group Representative Constituency
Gross Domestic Product (GDP), 1, 47; *see also* Consumer Price Index
Gross National Product (GNP), 34, 40, 47
Group Representative Constituency (GRC), 35, 45–6, 77–9, 81, 88, 91, 92, 103–4, 110, 113; *see also* Select Committee on the Group Representative Constituency
GST, *see* Goods and Services Tax
Guided democracy, 35

HARON YUSUFF, 111
Harun Ghani, 57, 99, 182
Hashimah Johari, 60
Hassan, Riaz, 54
HDB, *see* Housing Development Board
Health: charges, 47; expenditure, 43; privatization, 42–3; services, 37
Heng Chiang Meng, 110
Heng Siew Hwee, 140
Hertzog, Chaim, 100, 106, 113; *see also* Israel
High-rise living, 55; *see also* Housing
Hillgate Group, 118
Hinduism, 17, 62
History: study of, 163–6, 180
Hokkien Huay Kuan, 237
Home ownership, 1, 35
Hong Kong: source of immigrants, 55, 72, 81; *see also* Immigration
Hougang, 76, 81
Housing: private, 21, 76; public, 21, 31, 36, 74, 76, 81
Housing Development Board (HDB), 21, 31, 81
Hua, George, 245
Hua Wu Yin, 72
Hussein, Sultan, 80
Hussin Mutalib, 94
Huxley, Tim, 106, 169

IBRAHIM YAACOB, 14, 15
Immigration: Chinese, 3, 14, 55, 70, 72, 81; government policy, 55, 56, 72–3; Indians, 14, 70, 73, 81; Malays, 71, 73; *see also* Hong Kong; Macau; South Korea; Taiwan

Income: household, 20–1, 39, 41, 192; inequality, 19–22, 37, 40, 47; levels, 19–20, 22; per capita, 47; *see also* Minimum Household Expenditure
Indian Muslims, 18, 27, 50, 236
Indians: education, 197–8; housing, 21; immigration, 14, 70, 73, 80, 81; income, 19–20, 22, 27, 197; marginality, 62; students at NUS, 177; occupations, 20; *see also* Singapore Indian Development Association; Tamil language
Indonesia: Islamic resurgence, 18
Institute of Policy Studies, 58, 107
Insurance: education, 144
Internal Security Act (ISA), 35, 37, 44, 45, 46, 112, 162, 180
*International Herald Tribune*, 30, 44, 175
International Management Development Institute, 47
IQ tests, 126, 132–3; *see also* Education system; Gifted Education Programme
Iraq, 107, 114
ISA, *see* Internal Security Act
Ishak Haji Muhammad, 14
Islam, 13, 15, 17–19, 25, 27, 60, 101; foreign *ulama*, 162; resurgence, 18; *see also* Jamiyah
Israel: Immigration Act, 70; President's visit to Singapore, 100, 106, 112, 113; *see also* Hertzog, Chaim

JAMIYAH, 113, 182; *see also* Islam
Jayakumar, S., 110, 235
Jencks, Christopher, 139, 184
Jeyaratnam, J. B., 35, 45, 89, 110, 158, 175, 177, 255; *see also* Lee Kuan Yew; People's Action Party; Workers' Party
Johan Jaaffar, 105, 113
Johore, 105, 113
Juffrie Mahmood, 35, 45, 78, 79, 105, 113
Junior colleges, 119, 155, 209; *see also* Education system; Polytechnics; Universities

KAKI BUKIT, 75
Kampong Kembangan, 73–4, 78, 86
Kampongs: demolition, 74–5
Kassim Yang Razali, 3, 24
Katong Special School, 147; *see also* Education system; Learning disabilities
Kay Swee Kee, 171
Kemas Congress, 111
Ker Sin Tze, 244
Kesatuan Melayu Muda, 62
Kesatuan Melayu Singapura, 27
KGMS, *see* Singapore Malay Teachers Union

*Kiasu*, 35
Kindergartens, 182, 183; *see also* Education system
King, Martin Luther, 68–9; *see also* Malcolm X
Koh Lam Son, 110
Kok Lee Peng, 153
Kolam Ayer, 91
Kota Baru, 50

LATCHKEY CHILDREN, 192
Law Society, 32
Law Soon Beng, 155
Learning disabilities: diagnosis, 127; facilities, 147–9; *see also* Education system
Lee Hsien Loong, 9, 110, 111, 131; Edusave, 142–3; elections, 78; history, 165; and Malays, 100, 105; and Mendaki, 217; welfare, 235, 236
Lee Kuan Yew: birth-rate, 34, 72, 80, 182; Chinese-educated, 108, 170; communal voting, 90, 91, 103, 113; Confucianist values, 73, 168, 180; ethnic-based welfare, 234; eugenics beliefs, 55, 56, 120, 173–5, 240; government interference, 9; GRC, 113; as hero, 165; Indians, 63, 177, 183; Johore, 106; and Malays, 53, 55, 56, 62, 73, 100, 104, 166, 175, 183, 187, 196, 240, 246; Malaysia, 16–17, 33, 54, 165; Mandarin, 182; meritocracy, 25; PAP, 30; religious groups, 112; SAP, 128–9; social inequality, 37, 38, 42; and the West, 36, 151; *see also* Goh Chok Tong; People's Action Party
Legal Profession (Amendment) Bill, 32
Leong Choon Cheong, 57, 240
Libel suits, 45
Lien Ying Chow, 238
Lim, Linda, 160
Lim Boon Heng, 32, 45, 111, 113
Literacy rate, 15, 36; *see also* Education system; Free education
Low Thia Khiang, 81
Lower Primary Foundation Programme, 225; *see also* Association of Malay/Muslim Professionals; Education system; Free education; Mendaki;

MAAROF SALLEH, 172
MAB, *see* Malay Affairs Bureau
Macau: source of immigrants, 55, 72; *see also* Immigration
Mah Bow Tan, 110
Mahathir Mohamad, 9, 50; *see also* Malaysia; United Malays National Organization

Mahmud Awang, 111
Maintenance of Religious Harmony Bill (1990), 35, 101, 105, 112, 162
*Majlis*, 14
Majlis Pusat, 96, 109, 111, 216, 244
Majlis Ugama Islam Singapura (MUIS), 112, 255
Malacca Empire, 17, 80
Malay: definition of, 17–19, 25; identity, 13–15; Islamic identity, 17–19; migration, 14–16, 71; *see also* Islam; Malay language; Malaysian Malays; Marginality of Malays
Malay Affairs Bureau (MAB), 98, 99, 112
Malayan Communist Party (MCP), 62
Malayan People's Anti-Japanese Association (MPAJA), 62
Malay Archipelago, *see* Nusantara
Malay Education Advisory Committee, 189; *see also* Malay language
Malay land: restrictions, 49
Malay language: declining importance, 112, 172; National Language, 173, 188; promotion, 188–9; schools, 186, 188–91; use at home, 193–4; *see also* Malay
Malay loyalty debate, 100, 106–7, 248–9
Malay Nationalist Party (MNP), 15, 62
Malaysia: government economic policy, 2, 9, 246; inclusion of Singapore, 71–2, 85–6; Islamic resurgence, 18; Malay traders, 50; *see also* Singapore
Malaysian Chinese Association (MCA), 241, 246; *see also* United Malays National Organization
Malaysian Indian Congress (MIC), 241, 246; *see also* United Malays National Organization
Malaysian Malays, 9, 16–17, 26, 54, 72; Singapore work permits, 72
Malaysian Malaysia, 101, 241
Malaysian Solidarity Convention (MSC), 62, 71–2
Malay solidarity, 15
Malay World, 13, 71; *see also* Nusantara
Malcolm X, 52, 70; *see also* King, Martin Luther
Mandarin: campaign, 3, 34, 56, 103, 128, 130, 153, 168–9, 172, 182, 248; compulsory subject, 168; official language, 112; study by non-Chinese, 172; *see also* Education system; Singapore
Mannarlingham, T., 178
Mano Subrani, 61
Maoris, 69, 245
Margaret Drive Special School, 148; *see*

*also* Education system; Learning disabilities

Marginality of Malays: colonial and orientalist perception, 49–52; Malay perception, 59–61; non-Malay perception, 57–9; PAP leaders' perception, 53–7; socio-economic aspect, 2–3, 13, 15, 19, 21, 24, 26, 58, 191–8, 233, 248, 249; *see also* Cultural deficit thesis

Mariam Mohd. Ali, 27

Marshall, David, 88–9

Marxist conspiracies, 34, 44, 162, 180

MAS, *see* Mendaki Amanah Saham

Matchmaking, 56, 174; *see also* Social Development Section; Social Development Unit; Social Promotion Section

MCA, *see* Malaysian Chinese Association

MCP, *see* Malayan Communist Party

Media: government control, 29, 34, 35, 44; monopoly, 32; self-censorship, 29, 44

Melayu Raya, 14–15, 26

Members of Parliament, 75, 84–9; as Malay leaders, 92–109; as national leaders, 89–92

Mendaki: aims, 212–13, 241–3; and AMP, 110, 216, 225, 229; antagonism towards, 235–6; chairperson, 32, 212, 228, 229, 230; directors, 238, 245; establishment, 19, 51, 54, 101–2, 111, 211, 255–6; frustration with, 3, 24; funding, 111, 228, 233, 236–7, 245, 255; insurance, 242, 246; and PAP, 89, 97, 99, 102, 109, 241; *Papers*, 212–13; politicization, 215–16, 226–8; restructuring, 213–5; S1 Project, 222–6, 227; scholarships, 217, 230; tuition classes, 157, 213–14, 228; *see also* Association of Malay/Muslim Professionals; Mendaki 2

Mendaki Amanah Saham (MAS), 215, 242, 246

Mendaki Enrichment Programme (MEP), 210, 217–22; *see also* Education system; Gifted Education Programme; Special Assistance Plan

Mendaki Travels, 214–15, 229;

Mendaki 2, 94, 95, 111; *see also* Mendaki

MEP, *see* Mendaki Enrichment Programme

Meritocracy policy, 1, 2–3, 25, 39, 54, 58–9, 60, 92, 248; *see also* Equal opportunity policy

Methodist Girls School, 136, 142

MHE, *see* Minimum Household Expenditure

MIC, *see* Malaysian Indian Congress

Middle class, 40, 47, 59, 182, 196

Middle School Chinese Teachers Association, 171

Minangkabau, 50

Minimum Household Expenditure (MHE), 41; *see also* Consumer Price Index; Income

Ministry of Community Development, 41, 48, 203

Ministry of Defence, 152

Ministry of Education (MOE): agenda, 120, 138; donations to schools, 145; élitist attitude, 121; FAS, 141; GEP, 133; history syllabus, 163; independent schools, 134; language centres, 130; ministers, 152; surveys, 126, 127, 174, 191–2; *see also* Education system

MNP, *see* Malay Nationalist Party

MOE, *see* Ministry of Education

Mohd. Maidin Packer, 96, 104

Moral education curriculum, *see* Education system

Mosque Building Fund, 110; *see also* Islam

Mothers: and children's learning, 196–7

MPAJA, *see* Malayan People's Anti-Japanese Association

MSC, *see* Malaysian Solidarity Convention

MUIS, *see* Majlis Ugama Islam Singapura

Multinational companies: Malays, 24

Multiracialism policy, 1, 2–3, 54, 62, 72–3, 76, 130–1, 248; *see also* Racial Harmony Law

Muslim Missionary Society, *see* Jamiyah

Muslims: ASEAN, 26, Singapore, 27

Muzaffar, Chandra, 60, 240

NAIR, DEVAN, 46, 110

Najib Tun Razak, 18

Nanyang Girls School, 134, 154, 156

Nanyang Khek Community Guild, 237

Nanyang Technological Institute, 155, 198, 199, 202

Nanyang Technological University (NTU), 137, 155, 200

Nanyang University, 122, 169, 189, 209

National Association of Scholars, 118

National Convention of Singapore Malay/Muslim Professionals (NCSMMP), 25, 60; *see also* Association of Malay/Muslim Professionals

National Institute of Education (NIE), 126, 138

Nationalist movements, 14–15
National service, 34; Malays, 39, 90, 106
National Trade Union Congress (NTUC), 32, 45, 111, 212
National University of Singapore, 155–6, 176, 178, 198–9
National University of Singapore Society, 134, 176–5
Nazrifah Mohammad, 219
NCMP, see Non-Constituency Member of Parliament
NCSMMP, see National Convention of Singapore Malay/Muslim Professionals
NEP, see New Education Policy
NES, see New Education System
New Education Policy (NEP), 56, 121, 122, 123–4, 134, 161, 198–200, 247; see also Education system
New Education System (NES), 121, 122, 137–9; see also Education system
Newly Industrializing Country (NIC), 1, 47
Newspaper and Printing Presses Act 1986, 29–30, 32
Ngee Ann Kongsi, 237
Ngee Ann Polytechnic, 177
Ngee Ann Technical College, 189
Ng Pock Too, 110
NIC, see Newly Industrializing Country
NIE, see National Institute of Education
NMP, see Nominated Member of Parliament
Nominated Member of Parliament (NMP), 35, 45
Non-Constituency Member of Parliament (NCMP), 35, 45
NTU, see Nanyang Technological University
NTUC, see National Trade Union Congress
Nurliza Yusuf, 15, 60
Nusantara, 13–14, 16, 71; Islam, 17; see also Malay World

OCCUPATIONAL DISTRIBUTION, 19–20, 25, 41
OECD, see Organization for Economic Co-operation and Development
Official foreign reserves, 34
Ong, R., 154
Ong Beng Seng, 238
Ong Lay Khiam, 238
Ong Teng Cheong: CLRC, 171; education, 103, 131; and Malay MPs, 105; and NTUC, 45, 111; as President, 88, 97, 108, 110
Open University, 122, 152

Opposition politicians: elections, 110; GRC, 79, 81, 92; Malay concerns, 79; NCMP, 45; restrictions, 30, 45
Orang Gelam, 70
Orang Kallang, 70
Orang Laut, 70
Orang Seletar, 70
Organization for Economic Co-operation and Development (OECD), 1
Orientalists: perception of Malays, 49–52
Othman Haron Eusofe, 90
Othman Wok, 88, 96, 111
Overseas education, 147, 157; see also Education system
Ow Chin Hock, 108
Ow Chin Hock Report, 188, 194, 195, 210, 240

P1 PROGRAMME, see Lower Primary Foundation Programme
PA, see People's Association
PA, see Public Assistance
Pan-Malay identity, 13–17; see also Malay; Malay World; Nusantara
PAP, see People's Action Party
Parameswara, 80
Parentocracy, 140–1, 150
Party Raayat Malaya (PRM), 15
Pasir Panjang, 75
Pedra Blanca island, see Pulau Batu Putih
People's Action Party (PAP): electoral process, 79; hegemony, 29–36; leadership selection, 9; Malay MPs, 75, 85–109; Malays, 101–3; and Malaysia, 16–17, 33, 54, 71, 85; membership, 62; multiracialism, 62; perception of democracy, 30–1; perception of Malay marginality, 53–7; policies, 1–4; social inequality, 36–9; see also Goh Chok Tong; Lee Kuan Yew; Singapore Democratic Party; Workers Party
People's Association (PA), 32, 97
Per capita income, see Income
Perdaus, 111; see also Islam; Jamiyah
Pergas, 111; see also Islam; Jamiyah
Perkasa, 111; see also Islam
Pertubohan Kebangsaan Melayu Singapura (PKMS), 60, 74, 75, 77–9, 81, 100, 113
*Petir*, 30; see also People's Action Party
PITK, 111; see also Islam; Perkasa
PKMS, see Pertubohan Kebangsaan Melayu Singapura
Plantations, 70, 80; see also Rubber
Political: alienation, 107; marginality of Malays, 3, 4, 19, 67–80; resources and strategies, 67–70; system changes, 35

Polytechnics, 138, 198, 202; fees, 143, 155; *see also* Education system; Junior colleges; Universities
Poon Kit Foo, 244
Population: ethnic composition, 2, 9; policy, 70–3, 106, 173–6, 182, 248; *see also* Birth-rates; Eugenics beliefs; Rural–urban migration
Poverty, 40–1, 47, 191–2, 209
Pre-university centres, 155; *see also* Education system; Junior colleges
Presidents, 110
Private tuition, 144, 157
Privatization: health sector, 42–3; schools, 119; social security services, 42–3
Privy Council, 45
PRM, *see* Party Raayat Malaya
Professionals: employment, 25
Public Assistance (PA), 41, 48
Public transport charges, 47
Pulau Batu Putih, 165, 180

RACIAL HARMONY LAW, 46; *see also* Multiracialism policy
Racial riots, 75, 105
Raffles, Stamford, 164, 180
Raffles Girls Secondary, 134, 145, 154, 156
Raffles Institution, 126, 134, 135–6, 141–2, 154, 155, 157, 158, 207
Rahim Ishak, 96, 111, 253
Rahmat Kenap, 74, 111
Rajaratnam, S., 110, 180
RC, *see* Residents' Committees
Regnier, Philippe, 104
Religious bodies: government control, 35
Religious Harmony Bill, *see* Maintenance of Religious Harmony Bill (1990)
Religious Knowledge subject, 161–2, 179, 199–200, 209; *see also* Education system
Resettlement of Malays, 54, 74–5, 131; *see also* Housing
Residents' Committees (RC), 46, 97
*Rezeki*, 60, 63
Ridzwan Dzafir, 112, 245
Robertson, Geoffrey, 105, 113
Rohan Khamis, 245
Roslan Hassan, 111
Rubber: estates, 80; Malay restrictions, 49; *see also* Plantations
Rural–urban migration, 54; *see also* Population

SAF, *see* Singapore Armed Forces
Salaff, Janet, 188, 240
Salaries: civil servants, 46–7; politicians, 46–7
Salim Osman, 104
Sang Nila Utama, 14, 80, 163–4
Sang Nila Utama School, 189, 193
SAP, *see* Special Assistance Plan
Sathawalla, H. M., 245
Saw Swee Hock, 71
SBC, *see* Singapore Broadcasting Corporation
Scholarships, 39; *see also* Education system
School for the Deaf, 147; *see also* Education system; Learning disabilities
Schools: autonomous, 136, 155; Chinese clan, 170; Chinese language, 128–31; colonial era, 208; corporal punishment, 161; élite, 145–6, 179, 186; English-medium, 208; fees, 143, 148, 155, 156, 229; fund-raising, 145; independent, 120, 134–6, 141–2, 154, 155, 156, 157, 207, 210, 229; Malay-medium, 186, 188–91; Malay quotas, 166–8; monoethnic, 169–71; religious, 186, 209; special education, 147–9, 157; student responses, 202–4; *see also* Education system; Junior colleges; Polytechnics; Universities
SCSS, *see* Singapore Council of Social Services
SDP, *see* Singapore Democratic Party
SDS, *see* Social Development Section
SDU, *see* Social Development Unit
Seet Ai Mee, 109
Select Committee on the Group Representative Constituency, 18, 113; *see also* Group Representative Constituency
Self-help organizations, 32
Senu Abdullah, 50, 62
Seow, Francis, 35, 45, 46
Serumpun Chamber of Commerce, 16
Shaari Tadin, 90–1, 111
Shaharuddin Ma'arof, 62
Shared values, 30, 160
Shaw Vee Meng, 238
Sheares, Benjamin, 110
Sidek Saniff, 89, 91, 93, 94, 96, 105, 113, 199
Siege culture communities, 69
Siege mentality: Chinese, 104; PAP leaders, 106
SINDA, *see* Singapore Indian Development Association
Singapore: financial centre, 1; history, 14, 71, 80; as NIC, 1; population, 70–1
*Singapore: The Next Lap*, 160, 177

Singaporean Singapore, 72, 241; *see also* Malaysian Malaysia
Singapore Armed Forces (SAF): Malays, 39, , 93, 95, 100–1, 106, 110, 248
Singapore Broadcasting Corporation (SBC), 63
Singapore Chinese Chamber of Commerce and Industry, 237
Singapore Chinese Girls School, 134, 142, 207, 210; *see also* Chee Soon Juan
Singapore Council of Social Services (SCSS), 42
Singapore Democratic Party (SDP), 35, 45, 79, 81, 100, 110; *see also* Chee Soon Juan
Singapore Federation of Chinese Clan Associations, 237
Singapore Free School, 185
Singapore Indian Development Association (SINDA), 28, 157, 182, 227, 229, 235, 236, 244; *see also* Indians
Singapore International Foundation, 81
Singapore Kemunting Society, 16
Singapore Malays National Organization (SMNO), 74; *see also* United Malays National Organization
Singapore Malay Teachers Cooperative Society, 246
Singapore Malay Teachers Union (KGMS), 16, 130
Singapore Muslim Religious Teachers Association, *see* Pergas
Singapore Polytechnic, 177
Singapore Press Holdings, 44
Singapore Teachers Union, 128
Singapura, 80, 163; *see also* Singapore
SMNO, *see* Singapore Malays National Organization
Social engineering policies, 2; inequality, 36–9; mobility, 52–3; security services privatization, 42–3
Social Development Section (SDS), 56; *see also* Matchmaking
Social Development Unit (SDU), 56, 174; *see also* Matchmaking
Social Promotion Section (SPS), 56; *see also* Matchmaking
Socialism, 36–8
Socialist International, 37
Socio-economic marginality of Malays, *see* Marginality of Malays
South Africans, 69, 70
South Korea: source of immigrants, 55, 72; *see also* Immigration
Spanish colonial regime, 14
Special Assistance Plan (SAP), 103, 112–13, 122, 128–31, 167, 168, 169–71, 207, 248; *see also* Education system; Gifted Education Programme; Mendaki Enrichment Programme
SPS, *see* Social Promotion Section
Sri Vijayan empire, 80
State companies, 31
Status symbols, 35
*Straits Times*: articles by foreign scholars, 59; editorials, 102, 145, 157, 235, 240; letters to, 74, 127, 175; surveys, 107, 114, 144, 188, 196, 216, 217
St Joseph's Institution, 134, 136, 142, 145
Suicide rate: teenagers, 153
Sukarno, 15, 26
Sultan Idris Training College, 14
Suparman Adam, 218
Suratman Markassan, 111, 172
Syed Husin Ali, 60

TAIWAN: source of immigrants, 55; *see also* Immigration
Takaful, 242, 246
Taman Bacaan, 97, 111, 134
Tamil language, 172, 173, 182, 231; *see also* Indians
Tamil Teachers Union, 134
Tan, C. C., 88
Tan, Dixie, 41, 148
Tan, Nalla, 126
Tan, Rodney, 54
Tan, Tony, 110, 111, 119, 122, 134, 138, 152, 157; *see also* Ministry of Education
Tan Cheng Bok, 136, 156, 170
Tan Eng Joo, 238
Tan Guan Seng, 244
Tan Kong Yam, 47
Tan Malaka, 27
Tan Tam How, 203
Tan Wah Piow, 180
Tang Liang Hong, 35, 45
Tang See Chim, 110
Taxation, 43, 48; *see also* Income
Tay Eng Soon, 112, 154, 174, 177
Teachers: alienation, 2; low morale, 206–7; resignations, 127; training, 119; *see also* Education system; Ministry of Education
Technical Institute (TI), 137, 139
Technocrats, 33, 44
Temasek: history, 14, 71, 80
Teo Chee Hean, 150
Thailand: Muslims, 26
Tham, June, 149
TI, *see* Technical Institute
*Time*, 30, 44

Tin mines, 70, 80
Toh Chin Chye, 175
Trade unions, 97; government control, 35, 46
Tsoi Wing Foo, 153
Tun Seri Lanang Secondary School, 192
Tunku Abdul Rahman, 71; see also Malaysia; Singapore
Turnbull, C. M., 70, 178

*Ubah sikap*, 60
UMNO, see United Malays National Organization
Unemployment policy, 37, 46
Ungku Aziz, 60
Uniformed school groups, 160-1
United Malays National Organization (UMNO), 19, 54, 62, 241-2, 246; see also Singapore Malays National Organization
United States military bases, 106
Universities, 138-9; fees, 143-4; enrolments, 20-1, 23; 198-9; see also Education system; Junior colleges; Polytechnics
University of Singapore, 122, 169, 189
Urban resettlement programmes, 73-5, 86; see also Housing; Resettlement of Malays
*Utusan Melayu*, 14

Vasoo, Dr, 62

Wan Hussein Zoohri, 50, 96
Wee Cho Yaw, 237, 238
Wee Kim Wee, 88, 110
Welfare assistance, 41-2, 232
Women's organizations, 25, 48
Wong Kan Seng, 105, 108
Workers Party, 35, 45, 78, 91, 105, 110, 180; see also Jeyaratnam, J. B.
World Competitiveness Report, 47
World Economic Forum, 47

Ya'acob Mohammad, 74, 96, 99, 104, 111, 229
Yatiman Yusof, 93, 94, 96, 99, 187, 199
Yayasan Mendaki, see Mendaki
Yeo, George, 9, 31, 33, 38, 54, 109, 111, 112, 230, 250
Yeo Hock Quee, 140
Young Muslim Women's Association, 244
Yu Foo Yee Shoon, 111
Yusoff Ishak, 110

Za'aba, 50, 59
Zainal Abidin bin Ahmad, 50
Zainul Abidin Rasheed, 96, 110, 112, 113, 229, 231, 245
Zulkifli Mohammed, 93, 96, 111, 230, 256